SURVEYS OF ECONOMIC THEORY
Volume II

In the same series

✻

SURVEYS OF ECONOMIC THEORY

Growth and Development

PREPARED FOR
THE AMERICAN ECONOMIC ASSOCIATION
AND
THE ROYAL ECONOMIC SOCIETY

VOLUME II

SURVEYS V–VIII

PALGRAVE MACMILLAN

First edition 1965
Reprinted 1966, 1967, 1968, 1969, 1972

Published by
THE MACMILLAN PRESS LTD
London and Basingstoke
Associated companies in New York Toronto
Dublin Melbourne Johannesburg and Madras

Library of Congress catalog card no. 65–26933

SBN 333 06785 1

ISBN 978-1-349-00462-1   ISBN 978-1-349-00460-7 (eBook)
DOI 10.1007/978-1-349-00460-7

CONTENTS

FOREWORD

THE surveys printed in this volume and the two accompanying volumes in the series have been produced by the American Economic Association and the Royal Economic Society with the encouragement and financial support of the Rockefeller Foundation, and were first published in the *American Economic Review* and the *Economic Journal* respectively. The initiative in their planning and preparation was taken by the late Professor Norman Buchanan when he was Director for the Social Sciences at the Foundation. The purpose of the surveys cannot be better described than in the memorandum which he prepared for submission to the councils of the two bodies which is printed below.

The American Economic Association and the Royal Economic Society have collaborated throughout in the planning of the surveys in order that the two series should so far as possible be complementary to each other. They have also been fully informed of the similar series of surveys being published by *Econometrica* and have taken account of those also in making their plans.

The problems of publication were already in Professor Buchanan's mind when he wrote his memorandum. The two bodies both reached the same conclusion—that, to reach the widest audience, initial publication within the covers of the *American Economic Review* and the *Economic Journal* was most effective. But at the same time the two bodies have agreed that the surveys should also be made more readily available to students and research-workers and teachers in volumes of convenient size, planned in a single series on the basis of subject matter rather than of national origin. It was agreed that they should be printed for the two societies by the printers of the *Economic Journal*, using the type already set up for those surveys in the *Economic Journal* series. In order to make the whole series available as cheaply as possible to all students, the two societies have contributed to the cost of printing the American series in the style of the *Economic Journal*. They have received also very valuable help and advice from Messrs. Macmillan, publishers for the joint venture.

It is the belief of the two societies that this series of surveys, admirably prepared for them by the authors whom they have chosen, will fulfil in great degree the objectives set out by Professor Buchanan and enthusiastically accepted by all concerned. Since Professor Buchanan wrote his memorandum the flow of economic literature has continued to increase and the need for such reviews has grown even greater.

As development of economics continues, new surveys will unquestionably be needed. When the time comes for this the two societies will again consider together the need to carry such surveys further.

PREFACE

THE PURPOSE OF THESE SURVEYS

MEMORANDUM BY

NORMAN S. BUCHANAN
of the Rockefeller Foundation

I

INCREASING concern has been expressed in many quarters over the swelling volume of published products of research in the social sciences.   Books pile up at an alarming rate.   Scientific journals and monographs have increased at an even greater rate.   With many more social scientists and more abundant research funds from public and private sources, these trends are likely to be accelerated.

Unlike some other sciences and the law, the social sciences have so far not evolved any effective way of meeting the problem of keeping track of what is being published, where, on what topics, with what significance. Consequently, important contributions often go long unnoticed;   there is duplication of effort, while at the same time important topics in research are neglected.   Perhaps the most serious consequence, however, is that social scientists are increasingly becoming narrow specialists in some small segment of a particular subdivision of anthropology, economics, political science or sociology.

Scarcely less serious than the narrowing areas of competence of the best social scientists are two other problems.   First, the task of training the on-coming generations of social scientists with any semblance of breadth and depth is becoming more and more difficult in all the social science disciplines. Those teaching the graduate courses acknowledge that increasingly their offerings fall far short of what they would wish because, on the one hand, they themselves find it impossible to be intimately acquainted with all the work in their aspect of the discipline to make a wise selection of subject-matter and emphasis for the graduate course and because, on the other hand, the time allotted to them within the whole graduate programme is far too short. In economics, for example, a poll of those individuals offering graduate work for the Ph.D. at any large university as to how much work *should* be required to provide a " reasonably adequate " Ph.D. programme would, if summed, raise the duration of the Ph.D. programme by at least a factor of two.   In other words, eight to ten years instead of the present four to five.

The second problem arises in those many countries where the social sciences heretofore have been neglected or only slightly recognized as fields of serious study.   Nowadays, however, the leaders in these countries realize

their need for skilled economists, statisticians, sociologists, etc., that such
persons cannot be imported from the more developed countries in adequate
numbers, and that therefore they must train their own people in the social
sciences. Moreover, once trained they must be able to keep *au courant* in
their specialities. Yet both the training and the keeping up present enor-
mous problems in these countries because there are no effective means
available for doing so. To try to stock the libraries and to subscribe to the
important scientific journals would be far too costly and usually wholly
impractical on other grounds.

Thus, the cascade of published research in the social sciences in books and
journals would appear to raise important problems in three directions, viz.,
for the established and promising social scientists, for graduate training in
the social sciences, for the development of social sciences in the underdeveloped countries.

II

Other sciences have encountered and partially overcome the problem
just described for the social sciences. Two approaches have been used: first,
a systematic abstracting programme for the journal literature, and secondly,
a carefully planned sequence of analytical review-articles authored by the
best specialists. The quality of the persons doing the abstracting and
writing the review-articles determines the worth of these ventures.

For the social sciences at the present juncture it seems unwise to attempt
the abstracting approach. This is inevitably a large, costly and uncertain
undertaking, which is not made more appealing by the experience of the ill-
fated *Social Science Abstracts*. The analytical-review approach, however,
seems to hold certain promise. What is here proposed is set forth in terms
of economics, though presumably the comments made below would apply
equally to the other social sciences.

III

The bulk of the most important work in economics is in English, and the
American Economic Association and the Royal Economic Society are large
and effective professional societies. Their journals, the *American Economic
Review* and the *Economic Journal*, have a circulation of approximately 11,000
and 8,000. These two associations, with their excellent journals with a
world-wide circulation, seem the logical bodies to undertake the systematic
review-article programme. Such articles could be included in the journals
or made *separate* to be distributed to their subscribers.

How could such a programme be organized? Several points seem to
be relevant here. First, the present editors should not be asked to undertake
this task as an added burden. They need an advisory committee—which
perhaps need meet *in camera* only rarely, if at all—to designate what branches
of the science are ripe for a review-article and who would be the best person

to do it. Second, once the topic and author are selected, the chairman of the committee, perhaps most suitably the editor of the journal, should be able to offer a proper honorarium to the prospective author. Such an honorarium, along with the scientific recognition in being solicited to do a difficult but important task, should assure that the best-qualified persons would accept the assignments. Third, since both the *A.E.R.* and the *E.J.* are already declining perhaps three-quarters of the manuscripts submitted to them, the pressure on space is severe. Hence the review-articles would mean adding to the total pages published and so to the total costs, perhaps about as much as the honorarium. Fourth, if the two professional associations were to undertake this proposal the two topic–author advisory committees should keep in close touch to avoid duplication. This could be easily arranged.

If the above proposal has merit, a grant-in-aid to each of the associations would allow the plan to be tried out. At the outset, perhaps, no more than two review-articles should be tried annually. As experience accumulated, this could be increased.

V

THE THEORY OF ECONOMIC GROWTH: A SURVEY [1]

By

F. H. HAHN AND R. C. O. MATTHEWS

ἆρ᾽ οὖν πάντα τὰ τοιαῦτα ἀκριβῶς μὲν διορίσαι οὐ ῥᾴδιον;
πολλὰς γὰρ καὶ παντοίας ἔχει διαφορὰς καὶ μεγέθει καὶ
μικρότητι . . . . ὅτι δ᾽οὐ πάντα τῷ αὐτῷ ἀποδοτέον, οὐκ
ἄδηλον.

Aristotle, Eth. Nic., IX ii.

OUR purpose is to survey the contributions that have been made to the theory of economic growth in the last twenty-five years and endeavour to place them in relation to one another. It will be clear that the survey cannot hope to cover all of growth economics. We have accordingly restricted ourselves in the following ways: (1) We take up the story with Harrod's famous article of 1939 and make no attempt to cover writings before this date. The seriousness of this omission is evident when one recalls that this decision not only excludes the classical economists but also Wicksell, Marshall, Robertson and Cassel. (2) We restrict ourselves (except for occasional references) to the theoretical literature. Our central concern is with models of economic growth. The authors of these models have naturally had in mind as a rule that their work should contribute to an understanding of the way economies actually grow over time; but this approach to growth theory is none the less different from that which would be used if the *immediate* purpose was to provide the best available explanation of the variety of historical growth experience.[2] (3) While it has been found appropriate to give some summary of results in the theory of efficient accumulation, the problems of optimum saving and the development of backward countries have not

---

[1] The authors are Fellows of Churchill College, Cambridge, and St. John's College, Cambridge, respectively. They are indebted for fruitful discussions and helpful criticisms to economists in Cambridge and elsewhere too numerous to name. They accept joint responsibility for its contents. They have practised division of labour in which one author (Matthews) has been mainly responsible for Section II and the other (Hahn) for Section III; the remaining sections have been written jointly.

[2] Our coverage is thus different from that of the survey of growth theory by Abramovitz published twelve years ago in the *Survey of Contemporary Economics* (Abramovitz (1952)). Abramovitz there addressed himself directly to the forces determining growth in reality, and actually excluded from his survey models of the Harrod–Domar type on the grounds that they made no assertion about the likely development of the economy over time (*ibid.*, p. 170, n. 78). The scope that has been chosen for the present survey reflects the increasingly formal character that has been manifested, for better or worse, in much of the literature in the period since Abramovitz's survey was written.

been considered. (4) No discussion is presented of growth theory as applied to international trade.

A fully articulated model of growth requires to be made up of a number of building blocks. It requires to specify functions relating to the supply of labour, saving, investment, production, technical progress and the distribution of income, to name only the most important. For each of these there are numbers of possibilities that are entirely plausible and have been seriously proposed by one writer or another. Combination of them produces thousands of possible distinct models, none of which can be dismissed as unreasonable. It would be out of the question to try to consider them all. We shall for the most part seek to indicate the strategic significance of the possible formulations of each function separately, rather than to consider each in conjunction with the other assumptions that happen to have been made by the authors who have chiefly used it. Exceptions are made where the various assumptions are related in some especially significant way.

What follows is arranged in three main sections. We have found it convenient to bring together in Section I those parts of the theory of growth that can be dealt with in abstraction from technical progress. Section II deals with technical progress and includes treatment of the problems raised by " non-malleability " of capital. Section III, on Linear Models, deals with the formal development of the type of treatment of growth that stems from the work of Neumann, Mrs. Robinson and Morishima, on the one hand, and Leontief, on the other.

The detailed arrangement of contents is as follows.

I. GROWTH WITHOUT TECHNICAL PROGRESS
I.1. *Equilibrium Methodology*

Before embarking on the main part of our story there are certain methodological points which it will be useful to get out of the way.

Hicks (1963) recently wrote: " What used to be called the theory of long-period equilibrium has turned, in modern economics, into the theory of growth." The concept in growth theory that is the counterpart of long-period equilibrium in static theory is *steady-state growth*.[1] In steady-state growth (steady state for short) the rate of growth of all the relevant variables remains constant over time (here and generally, unless otherwise stated, the rate of growth should be taken to mean the proportional rate of growth). A good deal of the work on which we report is concerned with characterising an economy in steady-state growth and with analysing its properties. It is necessary to bear firmly in mind the distinction between the following questions that may be asked about the steady-state properties of any given model:

(1) Is a steady-state solution possible? In other words, given that the structure of the model, its parameters, etc., do not change, is there any set of economically meaningful values of the relevant variables that will permit the system to grow along a steady-state path without any tendency to diverge from it? This is the question of *existence*.

(2) Assuming that a steady-state solution does exist, what are its properties? What must the value of the variables be if steady-state equilibrium is to be achieved, and how are these values affected by the values of the parameters? (For example, how is the level of the capital–output ratio required for steady-state growth affected by the rate of population growth?) These are questions of *comparative dynamics*, similar to the questions of comparative statics in static equilibrium theory. Answering these questions typically means solving a number of simultaneous equations. In certain

---

[1] In Mrs. Robinson's terminology, conditions of steady-state growth are described as a Golden Age " thus indicating that it represents a mythical state of affairs not likely to obtain in any actual economy." Robinson (1956, p. 99).

cases the system may " decompose " so that one variable may be determined by a particular equation, or subset of equations, independently of the other equations in the system, but the general case is of simultaneous determination rather than uni-directional causation. A good deal of confusion and unnecessary controversy can be avoided if this is borne in mind.

(3) Does the system tend towards the steady state path if it is initially off it? This is the question of *stability*. This question subdivides into two aspects:

(i) Many of the models we shall examine are capable of generating paths that are not steady-state paths, in that growth is not proceeding at a constant rate, but that are none the less equilibrium paths in the sense that all markets are cleared and any mistakes are instantly corrected, so that there is no divergence between planned and realised expenditures and receipts. One sense in which a steady-state growth path may be said to be stable is that, when the system is initially off it, the ensuing equilibrium path tends to return to it. We describe as *equilibrium dynamics* the study of the behaviour of all equilibrium paths of any given model, whether they converge to the steady-state path or not. It is possible for a model to have no steady-state solution, and yet to result, from any given starting-point, in continuous growth of some other kind (*e.g.*, acceleration through time).

(ii) A given equilibrium path may itself be said to be stable if, when the system is initially off it, the pattern of people's reactions to the disequilibrium is such as to tend to bring the system back to the equilibrium path. (Clearly if this requirement is not satisfied, stability of the steady-state path in sense (i) is not complete stability.) In order to investigate in this way the behaviour of models in which mistakes are made or markets are not always cleared, it is necessary to introduce further assumptions, describing how people behave in these circumstances. We shall call this class of problems *disequilibrium dynamics*. The definition of equilibrium used in this distinction between equilibrium dynamics and disequilibrium dynamics is to some extent arbitrary (Samuelson (1947)). None the less, as we shall see, the distinction is important in understanding the literature.

The questions of existence and comparative dynamics of steady-state growth have been much more fully investigated in the literature than questions of equilibrium dynamics or disequilibrium dynamics. This will be reflected in the relative amounts of space we shall give to each. Concentration on the steady-state solution and its properties can be defended on the same kind of grounds as equilibrium analysis in general in economics can be defended, but it does, of course, impose limitations on the extent to which much of the theory is applicable to reality. Some examples of these limitations will be encountered as we proceed.

I.2. *Point of Departure: the Harrod–Domar Model*

Our procedure will now be to take as our point of departure one well-known model, the Harrod–Domar model, from which much subsequent work has stemmed (Harrod (1939), (1948), Domar (1946), (1947)). We shall then consider in turn the consequences of altering the various assumptions on which it is based. In considering the Harrod–Domar model, and throughout Section I of this Survey except where otherwise indicated, we shall make the far-reaching simplifying assumption that there is only one good. This good can be used either for consumption or else as an input in production. A unit of the good when consumed disappears from the scene; when used in production it is infinitely durable and is called capital. " Capital " is thus used at this stage to mean the quantity of the (single) good currently being used in production. Labour is the only other input in production. There are constant returns to scale, and no technical progress.

These assumptions are made not because Harrod or Domar used them, nor because we regard them as sensible " as if " hypotheses, but because we want to postpone to a later stage problems associated with measurement and definition of capital and technical change. Important as these problems are, quite a number of the issues in growth theory can be discussed in abstraction from them, and these are the issues we want to consider first. In a one-good economy output and capital can, of course, be measured unambiguously in units of the good. Labour is measured in its own natural units (assumed homogeneous).

The distinctive assumptions of the Harrod–Domar model, in the schematic form in which we shall now present it, are as follows: (1) A constant proportion (s) of income (Y) is devoted to savings. (2) The amounts of capital and of labour needed to produce a unit of output are both uniquely given; for the moment this may be thought of as the result of technological considerations—fixed coefficients in production (though as we shall see presently this is not the way Harrod himself thought of it). (3) The labour force grows over time at a constant rate n, fixed by non-economic, demographic, forces.

The requirements for steady growth in Y may be looked at from the side of the two inputs, labour and capital, in turn. They are not on a par, because capital is a produced means of production, and labour is not.

Labour. Since labour requirements per unit of output are given, it is impossible for Y permanently to grow at a constant rate greater than n, the rate of growth of the labour supply. Hence if there is to be steady growth in Y we must have $g \leqslant n$, where g is the rate of growth of Y. If $g < n$ there will be increasing unemployment over time. If we make the further assumption that the labour market works in such a way that increasing unemployment would be incompatible with equilibrium, the necessary condition for steady

assumptions referred to will be discussed in Sections I.3–6, and their out-of-steady-state behaviour in Section I.7.

I.3. *Unemployment Equilibrium Models*

This is the class of models closest to static Keynesian theory. It depends on the assumption that the presence of unemployment, even of continuously increasing amounts of unemployment, is not incompatible with equilibrium. This assumption has commonly been made in models of the cycle and also in econometric models. There is, however, an asymmetry: it may be possible for employment to grow less fast than the labour force, but employment cannot permanently grow faster than the labour force because a ceiling will be met. So what we are doing is dropping as a condition of equilibrium the equation that the rate of growth of employment is equal to n, the rate of growth of the labour force, and replacing it by an inequality requiring that the rate of growth of employment should not be greater than n. Growth at the warranted rate s/v is therefore compatible with equilibrium if $s/v \leqslant n$, but not if $s/v > n$. It may still happen, therefore, that no equilibrium rate of growth exists, but there is now a range of values for the parameters s, v and n compatible with equilibrium, and it is no longer necessary to have the special case where $s/v = n$. Provided the above inequality is satisfied, it is possible to regard Harrod's warranted rate of growth s/v as an equilibrium steady-state growth rate. (It is what Kahn (1959) called a Bastard Golden Age, as opposed to a true Golden Age in which $s/v = n$.)[1]

We then have a system in which the equilibrium growth rate is determined, in truly Keynesian spirit, by what are essentially demand-side considerations—savings and investment—rather than by the underlying supply-side limitation reflected in the natural rate of growth. A high level of s means that the equilibrium rate of growth (s/v) is high, because only with a high rate of growth will there be enough investment to absorb the available savings; a low v will likewise call for a high rate of growth, because capital requirements per unit of output are small and a high rate of growth is again needed to absorb the available savings. (Whether a high s or low v will tend to *bring about* a high rate of growth is another matter—this is the stability question to be discussed in Section I.7. For the present we are concerned only with the properties of the equilibrium path, supposing it were to be achieved.)

Numbers of other authors have developed similar models, more explicit mathematically than Harrod's, where the equilibrium growth rate is likewise determined from the demand side (Alexander (1949), Smithies (1957), Duesenberry (1958)). The equilibrium rate of growth in such models is determined by the parameters of the system—the saving ratio, the capital-

---

[1] In Kahn's usage a Bastard Golden Age is also said to exist if growth is taking place at a steady rate *greater* than the natural rate, this being made possible, for a limited period, by the existence of unemployed labour in the initial position.

output ratio or whatever other parameters may be involved in more complicated formulations of the underlying functions. Mrs. Robinson's model (see especially Robinson (1956), (1962a), (1963)), in which the rate of growth of the capital stock, and hence of income in equilibrium, is wholly determined by entrepreneurs' " animal spirits " (themselves possibly a function of the profit rate), also belongs in this general class.[1]

Such demand-dominated models have much in common with cycle models, and indeed, as is well known, identical models may in some cases lead to either growth or cycles according to the values of the parameters in the investment function, the saving function and so on. Further elements, such as ratchet effects, may also be introduced, together with other refinements to bring the models closer to reality and closer to the type of macro-model used by econometricians. When the structure and parameters of the model are such that the equilibrium solution is one of steady growth there is no particular reason why the rate of growth should tend to equality with an externally given natural rate.[2] Viewed as equilibrium systems, these models either need to drop the assumption of a constant level of unemployment from the list of equilibrium requirements, as suggested above, or else need to treat the natural rate of growth as a variable rather than a constant as discussed in Sections I.6 and II.5 below. Viewed as approximations to reality, such models have therefore usually been proposed by authors who are either unimpressed by the degree of success of the capitalist system in attaining full employment (or even a constant level of unemployment) or else believe that the rate of population growth and/or the rate of technical progress respond sensitively to economic pressures so that the adjustment takes place on the side of the natural rate.

I.4. The Neo-classical Model: Flexibility in Capital–Output Ratio

We now consider what has been called the neo-classical approach. Typical representatives of it are Meade (1961), Solow (1956), Swan (1956), Samuelson (1962).

Let us revert to Harrod–Domar as our starting-point. We restore the assumption dropped in the preceding section that employment must grow at the same rate as the labour supply in order for there to be equilibrium. What we drop is the assumption that the amount of labour and capital required to produce a unit of output are fixed. Instead we postulate a continuous function linking output to the inputs of capital and labour. We continue to assume that there are constant returns to scale and no technical

---

[1] If animal spirits are a non-linear function of the profit rate multiple equilibrium is a possibility, with one equilibrium showing the profit rate and the rate of accumulation both high and another equilibrium showing them both low: see Robinson (1962a), p. 48. For further development of this line of thought see also Rose (1963).

[2] Indeed it is possible for absurdly large growth rates to be generated that are bound to infringe the requirement that the equilibrium rate should not exceed the natural rate (Alexander (1949).)

progress. The capital–output ratio is now a variable. (This raises certain conceptual difficulties when only a single good is assumed to exist. For the moment we suppose that the good can be given any desired " shape " which makes it suitable for co-operation with the varying amounts of labour. This is not a realistic assumption and it is dropped later.)

However, the maximum permanently maintainable rate of growth is still n. Output can for a while be made to increase at a faster rate than this, even if there is initially full employment, by increasing the ratio of capital to labour; but given constant returns to scale (and hence diminishing returns to capital) the maintenance of such a faster rate would require a permanently rising capital–output ratio, v, and this is incompatible with a constant level of s/v, since s is subject to an upper limit of unity.

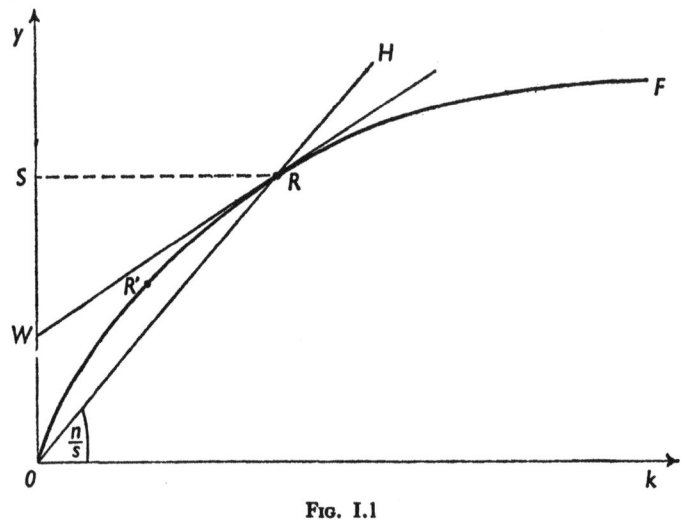

Fig. I.1

If full-employment equilibrium is to be possible, therefore, we must still have $n = s/v$, which may alternatively be written $v = s/n$. This, in turn, provided the production function is " well behaved," [1] and provided that factors are paid the value of their marginal products, implies a particular value of real wages (w) and the rate of profit (p). *That is, we can determine what these must be in order that* v *should take the desired value.* The diagram illustrates. We write y for output per man and k for capital per man. In Fig. I.1 we have plotted OF to represent the production function relation between output per man (y) and capital per man (k). OH is a straight line with slope n/s. The slope of the straight line connecting any point on OF with O measures the reciprocal of the capital–output ratio v. Warranted

[1] Suppose $y = F(k)$ in the notation of the text. Then F is " well behaved " if $F'(k) > 0$, $F''(k) < 0$ and $F'(0) = \infty$, $F'(\infty) = 0$. These assumptions are by no means innocuous. The last two imply that isoquants are asymptotic to the axis. These assumptions can be weakened if we know that the rate of growth lies within a given range of values. The Cobb–Douglas production function $y = Ak^\beta$, $0 < \beta < 1$ is " well behaved " (Inada, 1963).

and natural growth rates are equal at R, where $v = s/n$. The slope of the tangent $WR \left(i.e., \dfrac{WS}{SR} \right)$ measures the marginal product of capital, $\left(\dfrac{\partial y}{\partial k} \right)$ and hence the rate of profit at R. Output is divided between profit (WS) and wages (OW). R therefore represents a constellation of all our unknowns such as to ensure full employment. The existence of such a point arises from the presence of a smooth production function.[1] It contrasts with the case of fixed proportions, where there is a single point instead of the curve OF, and there is no presumption that this point lies on OH. What the neo-classical argument thus amounts to is that any tendency for the capital stock to grow more or less rapidly than population can be avoided by choosing a method of production of the appropriate capital intensity.

This neo-classical model occupies a central place in much of the recent literature. In contrast to the demand-dominated models considered in the previous section, it is a model where the rate of growth is determined by supply-side considerations. The steady-state equilibrium rate of growth is the natural rate, and the Harrod problem of divergence between warranted and natural rates is avoided by making the warranted rate s/v a variable, because of the flexibility of v, instead of a constant. Whereas in the Harrod model a high level of s means a high rate of growth in steady-state equilibrium, in the neo-classical model the steady-state rate of growth is independent of s. Comparing two economies with the same rate of population growth but different levels of s, both in steady-state equilibrium, the economy with the higher s will have the higher v, and hence the higher absolute level of income per man. But there will be no difference between the rates of growth of the two economies.

The above is all on the assumption that there is only one good, and hence that capital is " malleable "—that is to say, the capital stock can be adapted without difficulty to more or less capital-intensive techniques of production. It is convenient to postpone till later (Section II.3) full discussion of the case of non-malleability, where capital built for use with a given amount of labour cannot subsequently be adapted for use with a different amount of labour. However, it may usefully be noted at this point that the properties of *the steady-state solution* cannot be affected by non-malleability, because in the steady state the profit rate is constant over time and therefore all machines, whatever their date of construction, must have been designed for use with the same amount of labour. There is therefore no question of complications arising due to the existence at the same time of machines adapted for different techniques of production.

It would be wrong to suppose that Harrod was unaware of the arguments on which the neo-classical model is based. His grounds for rejecting them

---

[1] Essentially the same model can, however, be constructed on the basis of a linear-programming type of production function, where there are only a finite number of alternative techniques. Discussion of this is postponed to Section I.5.

were not that he maintained that the capital–output ratio was unalterable for technological reasons. Harrod considered and rejected the neo-classical approach on orthodox Keynesian grounds of a kind which must now be examined.

In its basic form the neo-classical model depends on the assumption that it is always possible and consistent with equilibrium that investment should be undertaken of an amount equal to full-employment savings. The mechanism that ensures this is as a rule not specified. Most neo-classical writers have, however, had in mind some financial mechanism. In the ideal neo-classical world one may think of there being a certain level of the rate of interest (r) that will lead entrepreneurs, weighing interest cost against expected profits, to carry out investment equal to full-employment savings. In the absence of risk, etc., the equilibrium rate of interest would equal the rate of profit on investment; otherwise the rate of profit will be higher by the requisite risk premium. As we are at this stage concerned only with the possibility and characteristics of steady growth we may assume that initially the capital stock is that appropriate to steady growth, so that the rate of interest that makes investment equal to full-employment saving in the short period is also the rate of interest required in steady growth. The rate of interest may adjust to this level either (a) in a non-monetary economy (or one where the demand for money is not interest-elastic) by the operation of Say's Law; or (b) because the price level can always be made to adjust in such a way as to produce the appropriate interest rate through its effect on the level of real money balances (Eisner (1958), Kahn (1959)); or (c) by the actions of the monetary authorities (Meade (1961)). The familiar Keynesian difficulties therefore arise: (1) that r may be prevented from adjusting to this level; (2) that the investment function may be such that there is no level of r that will bring investment to the required level.

(1) If r is monetarily determined the neo-classical reconciliation of the warranted and natural rate through the capital–output ratio v may fail. Suppose that in equilibrium the expected profit rate is required to be equal to the rate of interest. Suppose that monetary forces fix r at the level indicated by the slope of the tangent at R' in Fig. I.1. Then the economy is stuck at R'. The monetarily determined r causes entrepreneurs to choose a capital–output ratio that is other than the one required for steady growth with full employment. This was Harrod's argument. An alternative possibility is that monetary forces establish a *minimum* r so that full-employment equilibrium is prevented if the required r is below it, but not if it is above it.

It must be admitted that it is not clear how liquidity preference, particularly the speculative motive for holding money and the notion of a lower limit to the rate of interest, survives transplantation from the Keynesian short period to the Harrodian long period. Certainly the authors who have made use of it have not adduced much in the way of justification. But it must also be admitted that no clear reasons have been put forward on the other side to explain why and how these monetary troubles disappear in the long period.

Even given a monetarily determined rate of interest, it has been argued by Tobin (1955), Kaldor (1959) and Solow (1956) that there is a way out. In equilibrium we require the own rate of interest on capital, ρ, to be equal to the money rate of interest in terms of the good. If P is the money price of the good, then by using one unit in production I finish the year with £P ($\rho + P'/P$) where P' is the expected price. If I lend £P at the going interest rate r, I finish the year with £P $(1 + r)$. These two outcomes must, in equilibrium, be the same, and so we have

$$\rho = r - \frac{P' - P}{P}$$

All assets then yield the same rate of return (including expected appreciation). Hence, even if r is fixed there exists some expectation of a rate of rise in money prices which will allow ρ to be as small as we like. The logical cogency of this argument is beyond reproach, provided the appropriate expectations can be generated and maintained. It is not clear that in the absence of government action in one form or another this way out of the Keynesian difficulty is feasible. This is well discussed by Eisner (1958), who also considers the alternative escape route via the " Pigou effect." The underlying problem is, of course, essentially the same as the familiar static one whether full employment is assured notwithstanding a highly interest-elastic demand for money.

Finally, the profit rate required to give steady-state equilibrium may be un-attainable because it calls for a real wage below the subsistence level. The introduction of the notion of a subsistence wage really involves a departure from the assumption of an externally given rate of population growth.

It should also be noted that the role of a positive lower limit to the money rate of interest can also be taken by a minimum rate of profit necessary to induce investment. Accumulation may be associated with trouble and effort, and also with risk if uncertainty is introduced into the model. The required rate of profit is then equal to the pure rate of interest plus the premium for the trouble and effort and risk. A *zero* lower limit to the rate of interest will then be sufficient to establish a *positive* lower limit to the accept-able profit rate, and this may preclude equilibrium.

(2) This last point leads on to the question of the investment function. Most neo-classical models do not specify an investment function, just as they do not include the interest rate, as opposed to the profit rate, as an explicit variable; the financial mechanism referred to above for equating saving and investment is left implicit. Supposing that such a mechanism exists, neo-classical type models can accommodate a wide range of investment functions, so long as investment is sufficiently interest-elastic to allow the financial mechanism to work. (The range is less wide when we depart from

earners' propensity to save is higher than that of wage-earners, so that the overall saving–income ratio depends on the *distribution of income*. (Boulding (1950), Hahn (1951), Kaldor (1956), Kalecki (1939), Robinson (1956), Schneider (1958), Weintraub (1958).) A special case is where the propensity to save out of wages is zero and the propensity to save out of profits is positive and constant: the overall propensity to save (s) is then equal to profit earners' propensity to save (s_π) multiplied by the ratio of profit (π) to national income (Y). We shall refer to this as the " classical " saving function, in reference to its Ricardian antecedents: it has also been variously referred to as Kaldorian, Robinsonian, Cambridge, Marxian, " new," etc. A special case of the classical saving function—the " extreme classical saving function "—is where $s_\pi = 1$ and hence $s = \pi/Y$.

With fixed coefficients in production, and hence fixed v, it is obvious that adjustability in the overall saving–income ratio through the distribution of income will suffice to make steady-state growth possible, so long as the value of s required to satisfy the equation $s/v = n$ is not less than the wage-earners' propensity to save nor greater than the profit-earners'. With fixed coefficients in production relative factor rewards are not constrained by any marginal productivity conditions, and the distribution of income can therefore be whatever is needed to give the required overall s.

However, most of the authors who have used the classical saving function have not adopted the assumption of a rigidly fixed v. We shall therefore not pursue this case further, but shall consider instead the case where there is both scope for variation in v and scope for variation in s because of the classical saving function. Adjustment of the warranted rate of growth can then in principle take place on the side of both s and v. The results can then be compared with those of the model considered in Section I.4, where all the adjustment was through v.

(b) *The Classical Saving Function, Capital-Output Ratio Variable*

With a classical saving function, simple substitution shows that Harrod's equation $\dfrac{\Delta Y}{Y} = \dfrac{s}{v}$ becomes

$$\frac{\Delta Y}{Y} = \frac{s_\pi \pi}{Y} \cdot \frac{Y}{K} = s_\pi \rho$$

where ρ is the rate of profit on capital, π/K. The rate of growth of income must be equal to the rate of growth of capital; the increase in capital is equal to savings, which is equal to profits multiplied by s_π; hence, dividing by K, the rate of increase of capital is equal to the profit *rate* multiplied by s_π. The requirement for equality of natural and warranted rates of growth therefore becomes $n = s_\pi \rho$. In the special case where $s_\pi = 1$ this reduces to $n = \rho$; this conclusion—the profit rate equals the growth rate—plays an important part in Neumann-type models, and will be further discussed below (pp. 86–90).

Given a smooth production function, there is a unique relationship between the distribution of income and the amount of capital per man (and hence v). The result may be seen in Fig. I.2, which adapts Fig. I.1 to the case of the classical saving function. Equilibrium occurs at the point when the slope of OF equals n/s_π, since the slope of OF measures the profit rate, ρ. As in Fig. I.1, the wage is OW. The line WR, which expresses the requirement of warranted growth, has a different slope from the line (OH) which expresses this requirement in Fig. I.1 (n/s_π instead of n/s) because s_π differs from s; but it starts from W instead of from the origin, because saving takes place only out of non-wage incomes (WS).

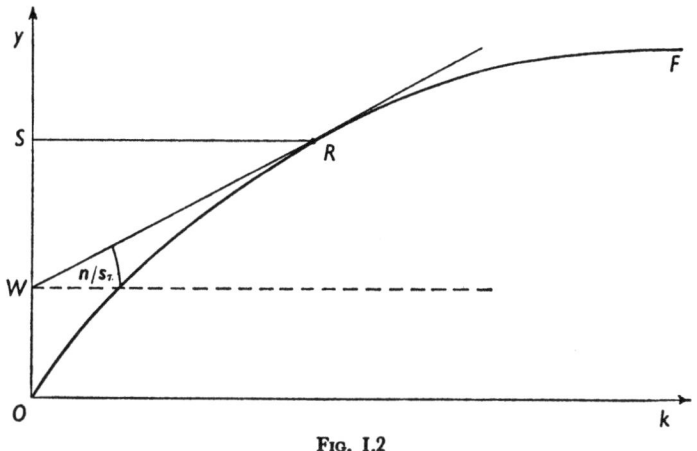

FIG. I.2

In Fig. I.2 a steady-state solution exists at R and factors receive their marginal products. In this sense the introduction of the classical saving function does not alter the model qualitatively. But it does make the model "decompose" differently. *With a proportional saving function, K/Y in steady growth is independent of the shape of the production function OF, but the rate of profit is not; with a classical saving function the rate of profit is independent of the shape of the production function, but K/Y is not.* In both cases, however, the share of the national income going to capital $\left(\dfrac{\pi}{Y} = \dfrac{\rho K}{Y}\right)$ will depend on the shape of the production function.

We may now contrast the effects of the two types of saving assumption in the case where instead of having a smooth production function we have a production function of the linear programming type, with only a finite possible number of possible techniques, as used in much of Mrs. Robinson's work.[1] Such a function is shown by $RR'R''$ in Fig. I.3. R, R' and R'' show

[1] An interesting special form of such a non-continuous production function is Bensusan Butt's model (1960). Here there are many commodities, each of which can be produced in either of two ways, a non-mechanised way and a mechanised way. The process of capital accumulation leads to the successive mechanisation of different industries. A similar model is worked out mathematically by Champernowne (1961).

three alternative capital–output ratios, corresponding to three alternative techniques.   Because there is not a continuum of technique, the technique represented by R' will be chosen if the rate of profit is anywhere between the slope of the segment RR' and that of $R'R''$.   The slope of RR' represents a profit rate such as to make the choice between the two techniques corresponding to R and R' a matter of indifference.   Along the flat stretch RR' of the production function some plants are operating with one technique and some with the other.

Consider first the proportional saving function.   If the ray through the origin derived from the angle n/s passes through a corner of the production function the profit rate, and hence the real wages, are not uniquely determined.   But in most cases the ray from the origin will intersect OF on one

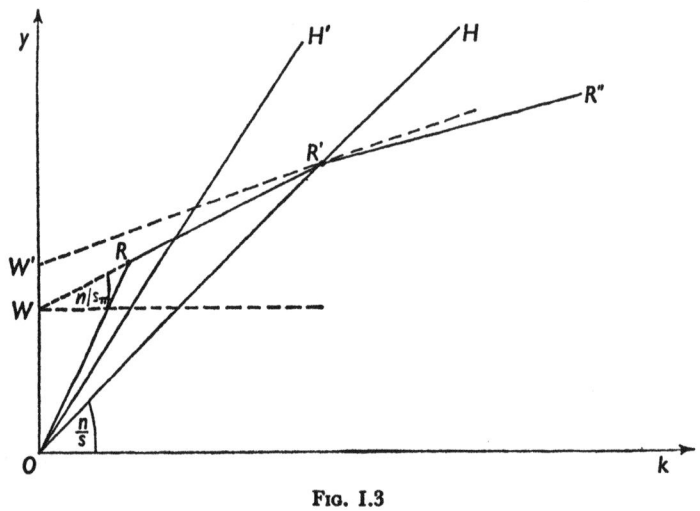

Fig. I.3

of the flat stretches, like OH', and there will then be no indeterminacy.   In any event K/Y is determined.

Now consider the classical saving function.   If the slope of the WR' curve, as determined by n/s_π, happens to be the same as that of RR', equilibrium can be anywhere between R and R'. K/Y will be indeterminate.   But in most cases this will not be so, and the curve will be like $W'R'$, leading to a determinate K/Y.   In any event the rate of profit is determined.

The proportional-saving function will thus cause the economy normally to find equilibrium on the flat, and ρ will be indeterminate within a certain range in the special cases where the equilibrium is at a corner; the classical saving function will cause the economy normally to find equilibrium at a corner, and K/Y will be indeterminate within a certain range in the special cases where the equilibrium is on the flat.   Indeterminacy in either ρ or K/Y will, of course, involve indeterminacy in capital's share in national income ($\rho K/Y$).

In the limiting case where there is only one possible technique of production so that $RR'R''$ reduces to a single point, the classical saving function will permit the existence of steady-rate equilibrium, so long as $s_\pi \geq nK/Y$ (if this condition is not satisfied negative wages would be needed). With a proportional-saving function no such equilibrium will exist, unless it happens that $s = nK/Y$, this being, of course, the basic Harrod–Domar problem.[1]

(c) The Kaldor Model

The models just considered differed from the basic neo-classical model only by having a classical saving function and/or by having a linear-programming-type production function. The Kaldor model, which is also based on the classical saving function, contains in addition certain other distinctive features. An additional equation is added (an investment function), but one of the equations in the neo-classical model (factor rewards equal to marginal products) is dropped.

Kaldor's views have undergone a number of changes, and there is reason to believe that they have not yet attained their steady state. What follows is based mainly on the latest published version (Kaldor and Mirrlees (1962)).

The main elements in the Kaldor model are as follows: (1) A classical saving function. (2) Rejection of an orthodox production function in favour of a " technical progress function." This is further discussed later (p. 69); but for the present purpose it is sufficient to note that some sort of short-run production function does survive in most of Kaldor's formulations, and a marginal product of labour in the short-run sense can therefore be identified. (3) An investment function in which the desired capital–output ratio is an increasing function of the excess of the profit rate over a monetarily determined interest rate (1957); or, in the Kaldor–Mirrlees version (1962), one that depends on a fixed pay-off period for investment per worker. (4) Rejection of perfect competition, as a result of which the profit margin per unit of output at a given capital–labour ratio becomes a variable. The introduction of this extra variable liberates the distribution of income from the shackles of marginal productivity. It thereby permits the existence of steady-state equilibrium at full employment, notwithstanding element (3), which adds an equation to the standard neo-classical set and would therefore otherwise make the system overdetermined.

The variability of the profit margin comes about in two ways, both of which involve departure from the rigid form of full-employment assumption. (i) The elasticity of supply of labour to an individual firm is held to be a diminishing function of labour scarcity. Variations are possible in the intensity of demand for labour within the general range describable as full employment, and these lead to variations in the degree of monopsony in the

---

[1] The combination of fixed K/Y and classical savings function is the situation where Kalecki's aphorism holds, that workers spend what they earn and capitalists earn what they spend: the higher capitalists' consumption, the higher, by an equal amount, must be their profits in steady-state equilibrium.

labour market, and hence to variations in the ratio of real wage to the marginal product of labour. (ii) The short-run production function is held to exhibit increasing returns,[1] as witnessed by the empirically observed tendency for output and output per man to fluctuate together (Neild (1963)). An increase in the intensity of demand thus raises profit per unit of output. This mechanism is held to operate in the consumer-goods industries and mechanism (i) in the capital–goods industries. (For discussion of other aspects of Kaldor's model, see below pp. 33–4, 69–72.)

(d) *Other Saving Functions*

We now consider briefly certain other formulations of the saving function relevant to growth theory, without examining their consequences at length.

(1) The classical saving function can be refined to allow for the possibility that workers do some saving. Suppose they save a proportion s_w of their income. Then we have

$$s = \frac{\pi}{Y}(s_\pi - s_w) + s_w$$

Substituting in the equation $n = s/v$ gives

$$n = \rho(s_\pi - s_w) + \frac{s_w}{v}$$

We may grant $s_\pi > s_w$, but, even so, that simplicity of the earlier arguments has gone, now that we no longer have $n = s_\pi \rho$.

If workers save ($s_w > 0$) they must come to own some of the capital stock, and to that extent become capitalists. The foregoing treatment of s_π and s_w as independently given constants implies that s is independent of the distribution of profits between persons. The essential distinction drawn is between the saving propensities out of different classes of income, not of different classes of person; one may think, for example, of a situation in which everyone has the same propensity to save out of personal disposable income, but a proportion of profits is saved by corporations before distribution to persons. This is the approach that has been adopted by Kaldor and most other exponents of the classical saving function. Thus Kaldor (1960) emphasised the fundamental nature of the distinction between wages and profits as two classes of *income* in his reply to Tobin (1960). Tobin, in a satirical article, had suggested that the Kaldorian model should be generalised by postulating n classes of *income-receivers* instead of two and n outlets for income ($n-1$ different consumer goods, and saving) instead of two, so that the relative output of the different goods, together with the investment–income ratio, would determine the amount of income going to each of the n classes of income-receivers.

Pasinetti (1962) has examined the consequences of the different assumption, that differences in saving propensities are differences between classes of persons. On the assumption that they are infinitely long-lived (or that

[1] Kaldor has now abandoned that part of the version of his model published in 1959, which depends on the assumption of constant prime costs (private communication from Mr. Kaldor).

children behave like their parents), he shows that in the very long run the equation $s_\pi \rho = n$ may hold, even though there are two (or more) classes, each with differing positive saving propensities.   It is assumed that there exists a class of persons called " capitalists " whose distinguishing feature is that profits comprise their sole source of income; the average propensity to save of these persons is s_π.   " Workers " receive wages and may receive some profits as well; they save a proportion s_w of their *total* income, irrespective of what proportions of it come from wages or profits.   Pasinetti uses the following argument to show that these assumptions and some others enable the rate of profit to be determined independently of s_w.   Assume that " workers " and " capitalists " earn the same rate of profit on their capital.   Then

$$\pi_w / K_w = \pi_c / K_c$$

where π_w and π_c refer to the profits received by " workers " and " capitalists " respectively, and K_w and K_c to the capital they own.   Now in steady growth the ratio of saving to capital is constant over time and equals the rate of growth, for the economy as a whole; and as the distribution of income will also be constant in steady growth, the same is true for the saving–capital ratios of workers and capitalists separately.   Hence (writing S_c, S_w for the savings of " capitalists " and " workers ")

$$\frac{S_c}{K_c} = \frac{S_w}{K_w}$$

Combining this with the previous equation, we have

$$\frac{S_w}{\pi_w} = \frac{S_c}{\pi_c} = s_c$$

Hence

$$S = S_c + S_w = s_c(\pi_c + \pi_w) = s_c \pi$$

and

$$n = s_c \rho$$

which is the result reached before for the case where there is no workers' saving.   The rate of profit is thus determined by the propensity to save of those with no earned income.[1]

(2) The saving–income ratio may be an increasing function of the rate of growth of income.   This could be so because of the life-cycle element in savings: the rate of growth affects the relative magnitudes at any one time of the saving done by those of working age and the dissaving of the retired. The same result also follows from the hypothesis that consumption is a function of past income (or past consumption) as well as of current income. These hypotheses have found good support in the empirical literature on the consumption function, but they have not featured prominently in growth

---

[1] Other long-run outcomes are possible: thus it is possible that the assets of wage-earners, while not growing at the same rate as those of capitalists, have become a negligible fraction of the latter. Alternatively, the assets of pure capitalists may become a negligibly small fraction of all assets. In the latter case the long-run equilibrium of the system will display a proportional saving function (Meade (1964)).

models.   Introduction of direct dependence of s on the growth rate in the neo-classical type of model will evidently lessen the extent to which v needs to adjust to accommodate a given change in the natural rate.

(3) The proportion of income saved may be a function of the *profit rate*, typically an increasing function.   This is in sympathy with the approach of the classical economists. s will then vary in the opposite direction from v.   An exogenously high natural growth rate n will be associated in steady growth with high s as well as a low v, and the extent to which the steady-growth value of v varies with n is therefore reduced.   Moreover, the variability of s means that even with fixed coefficients a range of values of n is compatible with steady growth, instead of just a unique value as in Harrod–Domar.

(4) A slight modification of (3) occurs when s is a function of the *interest rate* r rather than the profit rate ρ.   Sensitivity of s to r might then permit continuous full employment.   Other modifications where s depends on wealth, real balances, etc., can also produce this result.

(5) At the opposite pole from the neo-classical doctrine (that investment somehow adjusts to the level of full-employment saving) is the assumption that apparently underlay Schumpeter's view of growth (Schumpeter (1939)).   All saving is done by businesses, and (at least in the long run) *they save whatever is needed to finance the investment* that they have decided on other grounds to do.   The saving function then disappears from the model, and an investment function takes its place.   The upshot will depend on the form of this investment function.   If it states that I/K is fixed a steady-state full-employment solution will exist only in a special case where this rate coincides with the rate of population growth.   If, on the other hand, I/K is a function of ρ, a steady-state full employment will exist if ρ can adjust to the point required to make $I/K = n$.

(6) If growth takes place with oscillations around the steady-state path, effects may be felt on s similar to those which oscillations may cause in v (above, p. 15).   Thus the average degree of underutilisation of capital may affect the distribution of income and s; or the distribution of income may be affected by the average degree of unemployment of labour over the cycle through its effect on labour's bargaining power or the degree of monopoly (this is analogous to the Kaldor theory mentioned above); or the average degree of unemployment may affect saving because of differences between the savings propensities of the employed and the unemployed (Matthews (1955)).

It is plain that a wide variety of treatments of saving are possible.   The empirical literature is vast, and research is continuing.   With regard to the main issue that has divided writers on growth theory—the issue between the proportional and the classical saving functions—it would be difficult to deny that the proportion of profits saved is greater than the proportion of wages saved, since the propensity to save out of corporate profits is so high.   It is tempting therefore to base support of the classical savings function on the institutional characteristics of corporate enterprise without invoking any difference in attitudes between the households that receive profits and households that receive wages.   However, it is necessary in this connection to look beyond the mere proportions of corporate and personal income saved.   For the addition to the real assets of corporations made possible by corporate savings must affect share values, and in the long run it is difficult to see how share values can diverge widely from the value of real assets.   Change in share values is likely to have an influence on the saving behaviour of the owners of the shares.   In the extreme case where shareholders regard an increase in share values brought about by corporate saving as fully equivalent to the increase in their wealth that would have been brought about by personal saving of an equal amount, a given act of corporate saving will lead to a fully equivalent reduction in personal saving below what it would otherwise have been.   The retention policies of corporate management will then have no influence on the overall propensity to save of the economy.   In that event saving functions of the classical type would have to be based on the supposition of different attitudes on the part of shareholders and wage-earners as persons.   This is not the place to pursue these matters.

I.6. *Induced Changes in the Rate of Population Growth*

We now consider the possibility that the rate of population growth n is a variable, so that the adjustment needed to ensure the possibility of equality between natural and warranted rates can take place on the side of the natural rate instead of or as well as on the side of the warranted rate.[1]

Let us first suppose, in the Malthusian spirit, that the supply of labour is perfectly elastic at a certain real wage corresponding to subsistence.   The population grows at whatever rate will keep the wage at this level.   In terms of Fig. I.1, this means that OW is externally determined and n is a variable. The profit rate is equal to the slope of the tangent from W to the production function, and since OW is given it is independent of the saving function. This applies whether the saving function is proportional or classical, and whether the production function is smooth or is of the linear-programming type or reduces to a single point because there are fixed proportions.   (The result thus resembles that reached for the case of given n and classical saving function in that ρ is uniquely determined, even if production is at a corner.) The propensity to save (s or s_π as the case may be) determines the rate of growth of population, and hence of total output.[2]   This result is, of course,

---

[1] The analogous possibility of induced changes in the rate of technical progress will be discussed in Section II.5.

[2] With a proportional saving function, a linear programming production function, and the rate of profit happening to equal the slope of a flat section of the production function, equilibrium is possible anywhere along the flat and n is indeterminate within a range.   Within a classical saving function the rate of growth is always uniquely determined, since $n = s_\pi \rho$, although the capital-output ratio may be indeterminate.

different from that which holds when the rate of growth of population is
externally given and the propensity to save affects the absolute level of
income but not its steady growth rate.

An extreme classical saving function ($s_\pi = 1$) and fixed real wages comprise part of the assumptions of the Neumann model, which is concerned with
the *maximum* rate of balanced growth. This is discussed fully below (III.1
and III.2); here we refer to it in parentheses, illustrating the simplest case.
Given the real wage at which the labour supply is perfectly elastic, we wish to
find that capital–labour ratio k which maximises the steady-state rate of
growth. Evidently this is equivalent to finding that k which maximises the
rate of growth of the capital stock. If the real wage is OW (Fig. I.1 or Fig.
I.3) the slope of the line from W to any point on F measures the rate of growth
of the capital stock. This follows from the extreme classical savings assumptions, since n is then equal to ρ. Thus the rate of growth is maximised when
the line from W to F is tangent to F. But the slope of this line also measures
the rate of profit. Suppose we had asked the following different question:
what is the minimum rental per unit of capital we could charge capitalists
such that whatever k they chose there was nothing left over after paying the
rental and wages? Inspection of the diagram shows that the required
rental is given by the slope of the line from W tangent to F. Thus the
minimum rental per unit of capital (rate of profit) is equal to the maximum
rate of growth. The two problems are said to be " duals " of each other.
Of course, in Fig. I.3 we may get various values of k for our first question.
But once the real wage is given the rate of profit and rate of growth are fully
determined.

Induced changes in population may be admitted to the model without
going to the Malthusian extreme of treating population as in perfectly elastic
supply at a given real wage. Authors who have introduced more complex
population functions into their models include Haavelmo (1954), Solow
(1956), Leibenstein (1957), Jorgenson (1961), Kaldor (1957) and Niehans
(1963).

The central hypothesis is that the rate of growth of the labour force, n,
is an increasing function of the real wage, w. The relationship may, for
example, be of the form $n = a(w - \bar{w})$, where $\bar{w}$ is the " subsistence " level
of income at which population is stationary. n may be subject to an upper
limit $\bar{n}$, the " biological maximum." Other possible refinements are to
make the function non-linear, approaching $\bar{n}$ asymptotically; to make it
reverse its direction above a certain level of w; or to make n depend on income
per head rather than the wage. All of these have been suggested.

The general way in which this type of model works out can be seen if
we take as an example the case where there is a proportional saving function
and a smooth production function. (As yet no technical progress, it will be
remembered, and also no diminishing returns from land.) There will then
exist a steady-state solution with n and w simultaneously determined, as in

Fig. I.4. The population function $n = a(w - \bar{w})$ establishes a direct relationship between n and w; and the production and saving functions between them establish an inverse relationship (in steady growth, the higher n the lower is K/Y, hence the lower are K/L and w). As in the Malthusian model, the rate of growth depends on the propensity to save; but in contrast to the Malthusian model a high s also makes for a high real wage, this indeed being what induces the high rate of population growth. In the Malthusian model the population function $n = a(w - \bar{w})$ in the diagram is replaced by a vertical line at the subsistence level of w.

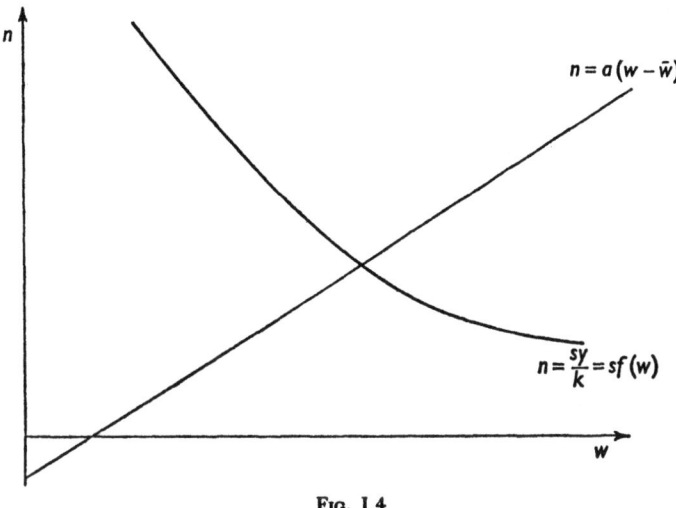

$$n = a(w - \bar{w})$$

$$n = \frac{sy}{k} = sf(w)$$

FIG. I.4

If there is a fixed factor, land, it is clearly impossible that there should be a constant rate of growth of income with income per head constant. If the scope for substitution between land and other factors is small, the growth of *total* income may ultimately be halted, even if the rate of population growth is fixed and unchanging. In some cases where there is sufficient substitutability between factors (*e.g.*, Cobb–Douglas) steady growth may be possible in the limited sense of growth of total income at a constant rate which is less than the rate of population growth and which therefore leads to a constant rate of decline of real income per head. This is ruled out if the rate of population increase is a function of the real wage. To make steady growth compatible with a fixed supply of land technical progress has to be introduced. Induced changes in population growth in a world with technical progress are discussed below (p. 56).

Models of the above type, where the rate of growth of the labour force is a variable, have a twofold significance.

In the first place, they can show the working of economic influences on mortality and fertility, as in the original Malthusian theory. The population functions used in the more recent literature provide a more sophisticated treatment of this, though they are still for the most part too simplified to bear any very close resemblance to reality; the main value of the models in this respect is thus illustrative.

In the second place, and perhaps more important, they provide a link between the theory of growth in the sense used in this survey and the theory of development, through the notion of " unlimited supplies of labour " (in Lewis's phrase) available from a backward sector. Although there is not general agreement about what constitutes an underdeveloped country (or indeed whether the concept means anything more than " poor "), a very general feature of countries classed as underdeveloped is the existence of " dualism." An advanced and a backward sector coexist, and in the course of development labour flows into the advanced sector, until in a fully advanced economy the backward sector becomes vestigial. Growth theory of the type dealt with in this survey can be thought of as limited in its application to the advanced sector, but with allowance for the possibility that growth in the advanced sector is influenced by the availability of labour from the backward sector (regarding the world as a whole as a semi-developed economy, this includes the possibility of migration from backward countries to advanced ones). It does not concern itself with defining the exact institutional or other respects in which the backward sector fails to conform to the norm of the advanced sector, nor does it concern itself with the effect of the growth process on the state of affairs within the backward sector, these being regarded as part of the theory of development rather than the theory of growth.[1]

I.7. *Non-steady-state Behaviour*

Given that there exists a possible steady-state equilibrium path, there remains the question of its stability. This problem will be discussed first in connection with Harrod's model, and then for the neo-classical model and for other models.

It will be recalled that in the introduction we distinguish two types of stability problem: (i) whether the equilibrium path converges to a steady state—a question in equilibrium dynamics; (ii) whether the system converges to an equilibrium growth path from a disequilibrium position—a question in disequilibrium dynamics. Two further distinctions may be noted: (*a*) between local and global stability; (*b*) between stability and relative stability. (*a*) A path is *locally* stable if any path starting in its vicinity tends to return to it. It is *globally* stable if the system tends to return to it whatever the starting-point. (*b*) In growth models an equilibrium is often fully defined by the relative magnitudes of certain variables, *e.g.*, the capital–labour

---

[1] In the models just discussed the rate of growth of the labour supply (to the economy as a whole or to the advanced sector) is represented as a function of the real wage. In underemployment equilibrium models of the type discussed above in Section I.2 it may be more appropriate to treat it as a function of the availability of employment, and this is what has often been assumed in theories of development.

ratios or the capital–output ratios.   A path is said to be *relatively stable* if the difference between any actual *ratio* of two variables and the ratio in the given path approaches zero as time approaches infinity.[1]

The Harrod Model

In the case of the Harrod warranted growth path the equilibrium dynamics question is trivial, since the equilibrium path is itself a steady-state path. The disequilibrium dynamics question, the so-called knife-edge problem, is much more complex.[2]

The Harrod model does not presuppose automatic equality of savings and investment.   Harrod's argument was that a chance rise in investment above the level required to maintain growth along the warranted path will raise incomes through the multiplier by a larger proportion than it will raise the capital stock.   There will therefore be a fall in the capital–output ratio.   This will make investment more profitable.   Investment, instead of reverting to the warranted path, will therefore diverge from it further. Hence the warranted growth path is unstable.

The validity of this conclusion has been much debated in the literature. Harrod did not furnish a precise model of the out-of-equilibrium behaviour of his model, and the verbal argument outlined above does not clinch the matter.   As Jorgenson (1960) has pointed out, the fact that disequilibrium may lead to action that increases that disequilibrium, even if it is admitted, does not yet prove that the system is *relatively* unstable.

Many attempts have been made to formalise Harrod's model.   The conclusion that emerges from this work is that the instability or otherwise of the system depends on the exact error-adjustment assumptions made.   Some formalisations of the model support Harrod's main conclusion, while others do not, and yet others conclude that it depends on the exact values taken by the parameters.   This is not surprising when we consider how sensitive dynamic models are to the precise assumptions made.   It is also possible for the model to yield oscillations;   the assumptions are indeed very close to

---

[1] To illustrate let v^* be the steady state, and v_t, the actual capital–output ratio.   If the steady state is relatively stable $v_t \rightarrow v^*$ as $t \rightarrow \infty$.   If we write K_t^* as what the capital stock would have to be in order that $\dfrac{K_t^*}{Y_t} = v^*$ along any actual path we may write

$$(v^* - v_t) = \frac{K_t^* - K_t}{Y}$$

This expression must approach zero by the assumption of relative stability.   But this will occur if the difference $(K_t^* - K_t)$ grows less rapidly than Y_t.   It is by no means necessary therefore for relative stability that $(K_t^* - K_t) \rightarrow 0$.   Samuelson and Solow (1953) have given a good account of relative stability.

[2] It is important to distinguish clearly between the two quite separate obstacles to steady growth that were considered by Harrod in his pioneering contribution.   (1) The warranted rate may be unequal to the natural rate.   (2) The warranted rate may itself be unstable, even without reference to the natural rate.   The second of these problems is the " knife-edge " properly so-called, though the term is sometimes used confusingly to refer to the first problem as well.

those used by Hicks and others [1] as the basis of cycle models, as was mentioned above (p. 793).

Space permits consideration of only three of the many proposed formalisations of the Harrod problem. We restrict ourselves to models in which the desired capital–output ratio and the propensity to save are both constant. As the results depend crucially on the details, some mathematics in the treatment cannot be avoided.

We write K_t for the capital stock at t, Y_t as output at t and a dot over a symbol for the operation $\partial/\partial t$. The warranted rate of growth is written as $g_w = s/v$ and the actual rate of growth at t as g_t. Suppose now that actual investment at t is given by

$$\dot{K}_t = h_t \dot{Y}_t; \quad h_t > 0 \quad . \quad . \quad . \quad . \quad . \quad (1)$$

The coefficient h_t differs from v because past mistakes have made the current capital stock deviate from the desired one. We suppose that [2]

$$\text{sign } (h_t - v) = \text{sign } \left(v - \frac{K_t}{Y_t} \right) \quad . \quad . \quad . \quad . \quad (2)$$

and

$$\dot{h}_t = b \left(v - \frac{K_t}{Y_t} \right); b > 0 \quad . \quad . \quad . \quad . \quad (3)$$

That is, for instance, h_t exceeds v if the desired capital–output ratio exceeds the actual (and vice versa), and h_t is increasing if the desired capital–output ratio exceeds the actual (and vice versa). The spirit of Harrod's assumption may certainly be put in this way. Since savings equal investment we have

$$g_t = \frac{s}{h_t} \quad . \quad . \quad . \quad . \quad . \quad . \quad . \quad (4)$$

Now measure the deviation of g_t from g_w by

$$M_t = (g_t - g_w)^2 \quad . \quad . \quad . \quad . \quad . \quad (5)$$

Clearly $M_t \geqq 0$ and $M_t = 0$ if, and only if, $g_t = g_w$. How does M_t behave through time? To find out we differentiate it with respect to t to get

$$\dot{M}_t = 2(g_t - g_w)\dot{g}_t = \text{by (4)} = -2(g_t - g_w)g_t \frac{\dot{h}_t}{h_t} =$$

$$\text{by (3)} = 2(g_t - g_w) \frac{g_t}{h_t} b \left(\frac{K_t}{Y} - v \right) \quad (6)$$

But if $g_t > g_w$, then $\frac{s}{h_t} > \frac{s}{v}$ and so $h_t < v$, and so by (2), $\frac{K_t}{Y_t} > v$ and b is

positive. If $g_t < g_w$ then $h_t < v$ and by (2) $\frac{K_t}{Y_t} < v$ and again (6) is positive.

---

[1] Harrod's own cycle model in his earlier 1936 book, *The Trade Cycle*, was essentially a model of periodically interrupted growth, and it was therefore natural that in the further development of his thoughts similar assumptions should have been used to yield a growth model.

[2] One must make sure that (2) and (3) are consistent. Thus $(h_t - v)$ must be of the same sign as $\left(v - \frac{K_t}{Y_t} \right)$. Since, as we shall show, $\left(v - \frac{K_t}{Y} \right)$ does not change sign no further problem arises.

It is now easily verified that since these results hold for $\dot{M}_0$ they will hold for all $t \geq 0$. Hence M_t is increasing through time and the two growth rates diverge—the system is relatively unstable, and that is so however small the initial deviation of g_t from g_w. Clearly there is a possibility of formalising Harrod's " knife edge ", which is quite independent of the size of coefficients such as b.

The question now is whether this is a good theory. In our formalisation we have not made h_t at all precise and simply required it to have certain general properties; it is a rather loose investment theory. A formalisation of Harrod which gives exactly the opposite result is that of Rose (1959). We interpret and formulate this model in a slightly different way than he does to bring out his implicit assumptions. (A similar approach to Rose is found in Jorgenson (1960a).)

Let us write ξ_t as $\dot{K}_t/K_t$, and $K_t{}^*$ as the desired capital stock at t. Suppose that producers find themselves short of capital (or the reverse) at date t. Suppose further that: (a) they want to catch up in T periods from now; (b) they expect output to grow at the warranted rate. Then ξ_t is determined by the following equation:

$$K_t e^{\xi T} = K_t{}^*{}_{+T} = K^*{}_t e^{g_w T} \quad . \quad . \quad . \quad . \quad (7)$$

or

$$\xi_t = \frac{1}{T}(\log K_t{}^* - \log K_t) + g_w \quad . \quad . \quad . \quad . \quad (7a)$$

Hence the rate of accumulation depends on the current discrepancy between desired and actual capital stock and on the expected rate of growth of output. Since (7a) may also be written as

$$\frac{\partial}{\partial t}(\log K_t - \log K_t{}^*) = \frac{1}{T}(\log K_t{}^* - \log K_t) \quad . \quad . \quad (8)$$

it follows from elementary differential equation theory that $K_t \rightarrow K_t{}^*$ as $t \rightarrow \infty$, and this must evidently mean that $g_t \rightarrow g_w$ as $t \rightarrow \infty$. We have reached the reverse conclusion for the knife edge. Two things are clear: Rose reaches this conclusion only because: (a) producers expect output to grow at the warranted rate through time, and (b) because desired investment always becomes actual. His treatment of the latter problem by means of stock accumulation and the reverse on the market for goods is somewhat unconvincing, because no attention is paid to the difficulty that " stocks may run out." There is also the further difficulty that we are not told what it is that is expected to grow at g_w—is it current output, *whatever* it happens to be, or is it some " normal " output?

But, quite apart from all this, Harrod's " knife edge " reappears pretty smartly if the spirit of Rose's construction is preserved but its form slightly altered. This can be seen from Phillips's model (1961), (1962). He distinguishes between the desired and actual rate of capital accumulation. These may differ because of decision and implementative delays. If $\xi_t{}^*$ is the desired rate of accumulation, Phillips writes this (ignoring his interest rate component, not here appropriate) as:

$$\xi_t^* = \alpha g_w + h\left(\frac{K_t^* - K_t}{K_t}\right); h > 0 \quad . \quad . \quad . \quad (9)$$

Taking $\alpha = 1$, this is in the same spirit as Rose's formulation. The rate at which accumulation changes depends on the discrepancy between the desired and actual accumulation rates:

$$\dot{\xi}_t = c(\xi_t^* - \xi_t); \quad c > 0 \quad . \quad . \quad . \quad . \quad (10)$$

But we have $\frac{sY_t}{K_t} = \xi_t$ and multiplying both sides of this by $v = \frac{K_t^*}{Y_t}$ gives

$$\frac{K_t^*}{K_t} - 1 = \frac{\xi_t v}{s} - 1 \quad . \quad . \quad . \quad . \quad . \quad (11)$$

Substituting (11) into (9) and thence into (10) allows us to solve for ξ_t:

$$\xi_t = \frac{s}{v} + \left(\xi_0 - \frac{s}{v}\right) e^{c\left(\frac{hv}{s} - 1\right)t}$$

Evidently $\xi_t \to \frac{s}{v}$ as $t \to \infty$ if, and only if, $h < \frac{s}{v}$. Taking the year as the unit of time and say $\frac{s}{v} = 0.025$, we would need to suppose that producers are willing to take 40 years in adjusting the capital stock discrepancy if we are to avoid the knife edge. Since this is pretty silly for most sensible values of $\frac{s}{v}$ and h, we are back with Harrod's conclusion. We note that in this case $\left[\frac{K_t^*}{K_t} - 1\right]$ diverges with t so that we have a case of relative instability.

The stability problems raised by other demand-dominated growth models are closely similar to the Harrod knife-edge. Duesenberry's model, for example, reduces to a second-order difference equation (in contrast to the first-order equation that results from the most simple formalisation of Harrod). The parameters therefore need to fall within a certain range to produce growth rather than fluctuations or constant output; but so long as the system keeps within this range, its growth path turns out to be stable. In Mrs. Robinson's model, where the investment function is governed by animal spirits, the stability of growth depends on the exact nature of entrepreneurial expectation patterns and other details of the model.

The fact that a growth path is unstable (or relatively unstable) does not necessarily mean that deviations from it are unbounded. The admission of floors and/or ceilings permits the knife-edge to lead to a theory of the cycle. Moreover, as is well known, cycles can also arise in another way: in models like those of Rose or Duesenberry, which (at least for certain neighbourhoods of the equilibrium path) yield stability of one sort or another, a suitable choice of functions and parameters can bring it about that the return to equilibrium is oscillatory. Given such damped oscillations, the persistence of cycles has to be explained by recurrent shocks. Since fluctuations rather than either complete stability or instability are observed in practice, this would appear to be the realistic context within which to view the stability problem.

When dealing with highly aggregated models many modes of behaviour may be lost. Thus, suppose that the rate of change of some variable at a given point of time depends on the state of n other variables at that time. We may then have a system of n differential equations of the first order, but the solution for any one variable involves n roots. It is perfectly possible that some paths lead to the equilibrium path while others have fairly regular oscillations around it (Allen (1960), Caff (1961)). It is unlikely that an economic model based on second-order differential or difference equations will provide an adequate approximation to reality. Builders of econometric models have taken this to heart. In a sense, therefore, so far from there being a difficulty in devising models that reconcile growth and fluctuations, there is an *embarras de richesse*.

The Neo-classical Model

It can readily be shown that, if the production function is " well behaved," the equilibrium path of a neo-classical model converges towards a steady-state path, and that the steady-state solution is therefore stable as far as equilibrium dynamics are concerned. This was shown by Solow (1956), whose argument may be summarised as follows.

Assume a proportional saving function, an exogenous rate of population growth and a smooth production function. Assume that there is always full employment of labour and capital, and that investment is equal to full employment saving: the system is thus always on an equilibrium path. Suppose that initially the capital stock is such as to cause the capital–output ratio, v, to be below the level required to give steady-state equilibrium, then the warranted rate, s/v, is above the natural rate. This means that full-employment saving is more than sufficient to cause the capital stock to grow at the same pace as the labour force. There is consequently a rise in the capital–labour ratio (when the production function is well behaved), and hence in the capital–output ratio, v. This deepening of the capital structure lowers the warranted rate, s/v. So long as the warranted rate continues to exceed the natural rate, the deepening process will continue, and the warranted rate will therefore go on falling until it becomes equal to the natural rate. Thereafter no further deepening takes place, and growth proceeds along the steady-state path. What has happened is that the rise in the amount of capital per man brought about by deepening has increased the amount of widening investment that is required in each period to keep pace with the increase in population, until the point is reached where the widening investment absorbs the whole of full-employment savings. The reverse process operates when we start from a situation where the capital stock is too high and the warranted rate is therefore less than the natural rate.

The foregoing all relates to a one-commodity world in which capital is perfectly malleable. In a many-commodity world stability is no longer assured unless further restrictions are introduced, since differences between the capital-intensity of different goods are capable of bringing about perverse movements in the overall capital–output ratio. This is further discussed below (I.8).

The stability of the steady-state solution means that the system will *in the long run* tend to approach the steady-state path and to revert to it after any disturbance. Sato (1963), however, has shown that the time taken to return to within a reasonable vicinity of the steady-state path may be very long indeed—of the order of a hundred years!

This conclusion will have to be tested for a wider variety of models before its significance can be properly judged. In so far as it is generally valid, however, it means that steady-state solutions are likely to be of very limited value as an approximation to reality. Such conclusions as that the propensity to save does not affect the rate of growth have to be understood with this in mind. Some authors (for example, Meade) have on this account relegated the steady-state solution to a relatively subordinate place in their exposition. In order to ascertain the real-life implications of any given model, it is necessary to investigate its equilibrium dynamics in full. This is naturally much more difficult than investigating the properties of the steady-state solution.

We turn now from the equilibrium dynamics of the neo-classical model to its disequilibrium dynamics. In the first part of this section we have seen that the model's introduction of flexible coefficients resolves one of Harrod's problems (non-equality of warranted and natural rates). But, contrary to what has sometimes been supposed, it does not as such contribute towards solving the other Harrod problem, the knife-edge, because it does not specify the adjustment mechanism that is supposed to bring the system back to the equilibrium path once it is disturbed. A central feature of the Solow type of model is that equilibrium requires investment to be equal to full-employment savings. In order to establish the stability of the growth path, it would be necessary to investigate the stability of the factor-price mechanism or whatever other mechanism is supposed to ensure this equality, in conjunction with an investment function appropriate to the growth context (Hahn (1960), Sargent (1963)). Even without introducing complications from the side of the investment function, it is clear that in some circumstances the system is unlikely to be stable. Suppose the mechanism involved is that changes in the real rate of interest require to be brought about by expectations of price change, the nominal rate of interest being sticky (above, p. 13).

Suppose from an initial equilibrium position there is an increase in the propensity to save. For investment to be stimulated, what is needed is the expectation of rising prices, so as to bring about a fall in the real rate of interest. But an increase in saving will in itself be deflationary, and will therefore tend to bring about a fall in prices rather than a rise. So the expectations created are likely to be in the wrong direction; and if they are the system will be unstable.

Some Solowesque models have been constructed in which producers are allowed to make mistakes and investment is not necessarily equal to full-employment savings (Hahn (1960), Phillips (1961), (1962)). These models using implicitly or explicitly neo-classical production functions once again show that the knife-edge remains a problem even when production coefficients are flexible. In particular is this true when an initial situation is chosen that is not in the immediate vicinity of the equilibrium path.

Classical Savings Function

The stability of the steady-state solution, as far as equilibrium dynamics are concerned, is not impaired by the substitution of a classical saving function for a proportional one. If the elasticity of substitution between labour and capital σ is not equal to unity the change in v will be associated with a change in the distribution of income, and hence now in s. This may go in either direction. If $\sigma < 1$, profits' share and hence s fall as v rises, and both s and v contribute to bringing the warranted rate into equality with the natural rate. If $\sigma > 1$, s rises as v rises, so a given change in v does not bring about so large a change in the warranted rate; but this cannot upset the stability of the steady-state solution, since the rate of profit (π/K) must move in the opposite direction to v, and therefore the movement in profits' share $(v\pi/K)$, and hence in s, must be smaller than the movement in v.

As noted above, the disequilibrium dynamics of the neo-classical model with a proportional saving function have not been thoroughly explored, and the same holds of models with a classical saving function.

Kaldor Model

In the Kaldor model unemployment equilibrium is assumed to be unstable. Any chance disturbance of such an equilibrium will unleash forces of the multiplier–accelerator type driving the system towards the ceiling. However, unlike, for instance, the Hicksian model, the economy does not " bounce back " again. The mechanism of redistribution, in addition to providing the extra variable which permits the existence of steady-state equilibrium, also, in Kaldor's view, secures its stability. The argument is that excess demand raises profits' share of national income; this raises the proportion of income saved because of the assumed classical saving function; and this is deflationary, and so ensures the correction of the excess real demand.

As with the Harrod model, the validity of this argument depends on the exact way in which the model is formalised, and space does not permit us to go into the details here.   The chief threat to stability in the Kaldor model is that increased profit margins may encourage investment (by increasing the chosen K/Y) by as much as or more than they encourage savings.   In all forms of the Kaldor model a rising rate of profit does induce some increase in investment.   This increase may be limited by a higher profit margin being required as compensation for risk when the capital–output ratio rises (1957); or by the pay-off period stopping the capital–output ratio from " running away " (1962).   Such considerations as these, and/or judicious choice of lags, may be sufficient to ensure stability.   It is clear, however, that while the redistribution mechanism, assuming it to be valid, does work in a stabilising direction, the danger of instability has by no means been banished, as Kaldor and Mirrlees themselves emphasised.

I.8. *Two-sector Models*

We shall now consider an economy in which two different goods are produced: a consumption good and a capital good.   When the coefficients of production are fixed in both sectors one gets a Leontief dynamic model, when the production possibilities are of the linear programming variety, a Neumann model.   Both of these are best considered in the general framework of linear economic models (Section III).   Accordingly, we shall here concentrate on the neo-classical version of two-sector models (Meade (1961), Uzawa (1961, 1963), Inada (1963), Takayama (1963), Kurz (1963), Solow (1961), Drandanakis (1963)).   We shall deal first with questions concerning the existence and characteristics of steady-state equilibrium, then with the question of stability.

Steady-state Equilibrium

With two goods there are further variables to be considered in addition to those present in a one-sector model: relative prices, sectoral capital–labour ratios and the relative amounts of labour allotted to the two sectors.   As well as complicating the picture, these can in certain circumstances introduce qualitatively different results, in the form of multiple and/or unstable equilibrium.

The capital good is supposed to be perfectly malleable, so that it can be combined with varying amounts of labour to produce either itself or the consumption good; both goods can be produced by the aid of labour and capital, the consumption good not being used as an input in the productive process (models where the last assumption is relaxed are dealt with in Section III).   There are constant returns to scale, no technical progress and infinitely long-lived capital, and the production functions in the two sectors are " well-behaved."

Most of the work that has been done on two-sector models is based on the classical saving function. This simplifies matters, because it enables the steady-state rate of profit to be immediately deduced from the rate of growth n and capitalists' saving propensity s_π. The analogous decomposition with a proportional saving function, whereby the capital–output ratio in value terms can be directly deduced from n and s, is not so helpful in a two-sector model, because the relative prices of capital goods and consumption goods remain to be determined; the whole system has therefore to be solved simultaneously.

Fig. I.5 illustrates steady-state equilibrium on the extreme classical saving assumption that workers do not save and capitalists do not consume ($s_\pi = 1$). Sector 1 is the capital good, sector 2 the consumption good.

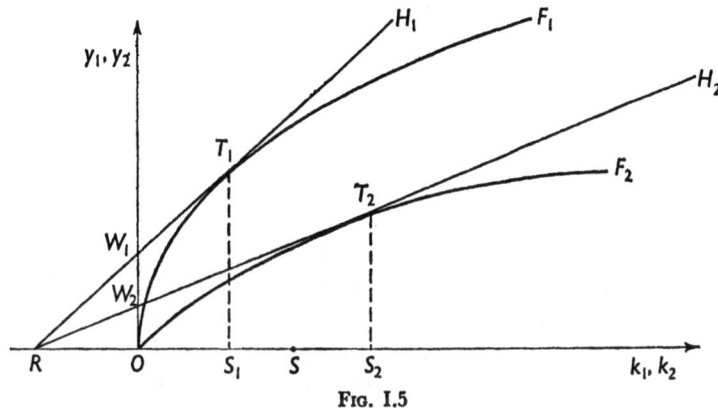

FIG. I.5

The horizontal axis measures capital per man in the two sectors, k_1 and k_2, measured in physical units of the capital good. The vertical axis measures output per man in the two sectors, y_1 and y_2, measured in physical units of the two goods respectively. We write k for the overall capital–labour ratio, L_1/L for the proportion of the labour force employed in sector 1 and L_2/L for the proportion of the labour force employed in sector 2.

The slope of OF_1 measures the marginal product of capital in the capital-good industry. Since both the numerator and the denominator involved in the measure of this marginal product are in terms of the capital good, no question of relative prices arises, and the slope therefore measures the rate of profit ρ. This must be equal to n, the rate of population growth, in steady-state equilibrium, since we are assuming $s_\pi = 1$. OW_1 is the wage in the capital-good industry, measured in the capital good. OR is the wage-rental ratio, OW_1/ρ; this ratio we denote by z.

The slope of OF_2 measures the marginal product of capital in the consumption-good industry, measured in terms of the consumption good. The rate of profit must be equal in the two sectors; therefore this consumption good–marginal product must equal the capital good–marginal product

(the slope of OF_1) multiplied by the ratio of the price of the consumption good
to the price of the capital good. In addition, the money wage must be
equal in the two sectors; so this price ratio must be equal to the wage
measured in terms of the capital good divided by the wage measured in
terms of the consumption good. The latter is evidently OW_2. The price
ratio is therefore OW_1/OW_2. It follows that the condition of equality in
profit rates between the sectors requires that OR (the wage–rental ratio)
should be the same in both sectors. The line tangent to OF_2 must therefore
originate at R, as shown.

We now have to determine the allocation of labour between the sectors,
and the overall capital–labour ratio k. Since we are assuming no consumption by capitalists, consumption per head is equal to the wage in terms of
consumption goods, OW_2. The output of consumption goods per head in
the whole economy is the output per head in the consumption-good industry,
T_2S_2, multiplied by the proportion of the total labour force that is engaged
in the consumption-good industry, L_2/L. Hence $OW_2 = \dfrac{L_2}{L} \cdot T_2S_2$ and
$\dfrac{L_2}{L} = \dfrac{OW_2}{T_2S_2}$, the real wage divided by output per man in the consumption-
good industry.

Having determined L_2/L (and hence L_1/L, since the sum of the two is
unity), it is possible to determine the overall capital–labour ratio k. This is
a weighted average of the capital–labour ratios in the two sectors, k_1 and k_2,
the weights being the proportions of the labour force allotted to the two
sectors. A little manipulation shows that the overall capital–output ratio
k, measured by OS in Fig. I.5, is equal to $OS_2 \cdot \dfrac{RS_1}{RS_2}$.[1] This is equivalent
to $\dfrac{z + k_1}{z + k_2} \cdot k_2$. Since the steady-state values of z, k_1 and k_2 are all uniquely
determined by ρ (given the two production functions), and since $\rho = n$ in
steady-state equilibrium, it follows that k is uniquely determined.[2] This
completes the steady-state solution of the system.

A similar two-sector model can be worked out on the assumption of a

---

[1] $\dfrac{L_2}{L} = \dfrac{OW_2}{T_2S_2} = \dfrac{OR}{RS_2}$, by similar triangles.

$\dfrac{L_1}{L} = 1 - \dfrac{L_2}{L} = \dfrac{RS_2 - OR}{RS_2} = \dfrac{OS_2}{RS_2}$

$k = k_1\dfrac{L_1}{L} + k_2\dfrac{L_2}{L}$

$\quad = \dfrac{OS_1 \cdot OS_2}{RS_2} + \dfrac{OS_2 \cdot OR}{RS_2} = \dfrac{OS_2(OS_1 + OR)}{RS_2} = OS_2 \cdot \dfrac{RS_1}{RS_2}$

[2] It should be noted that although k is thus a unique function of ρ, it does not follow, unless further
conditions are imposed, that k is a continuously diminishing function of ρ. It follows that there may
be more than one equilibrium value of ρ corresponding to any given value of k. This is important
for the question of stability, discussed later (pp. 39–42).

proportional saving function, *e.g.*, Uzawa (1963), Inada (1963). It is more complicated than the model just considered, but, as would be expected, equilibrium steady-state values of the variables can be shown to exist. The change in the saving function does bring about a difference, however, in one respect. With a proportional saving function it is possible that the equilibrium may not be unique. The equilibrium capital–output ratio in value terms, K/Y, is uniquely determined by s and n. But there may be more than one level of z, and hence of k, that gives the required K/Y. This is because of the possible effects of changes in the relative prices of the capital good and the consumption good (Mrs. Robinson's "Wicksell effect"). An intuitive account may be given as follows.

The effect of the wage–rental ratio z on the value capital–output ratio K/Y may be divided into: (i) a price effect, and (ii) a quantity effect. Let us suppose that the capital good happens to be more capital intensive in production than the consumption good $(k_1 > k_2)$; this is the case where trouble arises.

(i) *Price Effect.* A rise in z will lower p_1, the price of the capital good relatively to the price of the consumption good.[1] This taken by itself will tend to lower K/Y.

(ii) *Quantity Effect.* A rise in z will raise k_1 and k_2. This will raise the capital–output ratio in volume terms within each sector. In addition, since p_1 is reduced, and since the *value* of capital-goods output is a constant proportion s of the *value* of total output, the volume of capital-goods output will be raised relatively to the volume of consumer-goods output. As the capital-good industry is assumed to be the more capital-intensive, there is a shift in relative weights in favour of the more capital-intensive industry. This reinforces the effect of the rise in k_1 and k_2 in increasing the overall capital-output ratio in volume terms.

On these assumptions, therefore, the price effect and the quantity effect go in opposite directions. Hence it is possible that they may offset each other in such a way that two or more values of z, and hence of k,[2] lead to the same K/Y.[3] Further assumptions have to be introduced if this possibility of

[1] This is quite easy to see. Let p be the price of a good x in terms of a good y. Let y be more capital intensive. If z rises, then evidently p must rise if there are no factor-substitution possibilities in either sector. For labour costs are more important in the unit cost of x than in that of y and there is perfect competition. Now allow factor substitution. This may reduce p again but cannot restore it to its former level. For if it did x and y would have to become of equal capital intensity, an eventuality ruled out by assumption.

[2] On present assumptions k is a single-valued function of z. This is proved below.

[3] Multiple equilibrium could not come about in this way with a classical saving function, because the two different values of k, being associated with different values of ρ, would lead to different values of $\rho K/Y$ (profits' share) if K/Y were the same, and hence would lead to different proportions of the national income being saved. Multiple equilibrium with a classical saving function would require more than one value of k to be associated with a given ρ, and that, as we have seen from Fig. I.5, is impossible. The same complication about relative prices is, however, what is responsible for the possibility referred to in the last footnote but two, that the unique equilibrium position with the classical saving function may be *unstable*.

multiple equilibrium is to be excluded.   One assumption that will achieve
this is plainly that the consumption good is more capital intensive in production than the capital good.   This assumption is often made in the literature,
but it has generally been felt to be an artificial one.   A perhaps more natural
way of achieving the same result is to impose more stringent restrictions than
usual about the shape of the production functions; this has been studied
by Takayama (1963).

There are two further propositions that the two-sector model helps us to
establish.

It is evident from Fig. I.5 that once we know the rate of profit, which need
not be equal to n if we drop the extreme classical savings assumption, relative
prices are also determined.   Since there are constant returns to scale, the
composition of output between consumption and investment goods cannot
affect the relative prices so determined.   Thus, once the rate of profit is
fixed, the savings assumption, whatever it may be, will affect only the
composition of output and the steady-state equilibrium value of k; it leaves
relative prices unchanged.   Exactly the same conclusion can be reached
if we imagine wages to be fixed in terms of either consumption good or investment good or both.   The result (that, given either the rate of profit or the
wage in terms of one of the goods, equilibrium relative prices are fully
determined independent of demand) can be extended to an economy of many
goods (Sraffa (1960), Morishima (1959), Arrow (1951), Samuelson (1951),
etc.), provided we postulate constant returns to scale, the absence of joint
production and " sufficient " productive interdependence between the goods.
It is not hard to see that the same result holds if the production functions have
the form we gave them in Fig. I.3.   We return to this later in section
III.2.

The second proposition we can get from the model is that the position
shown in Fig. I.5, where the rate of profit is equal to the rate of growth, is
the steady-state growth path that maximises consumption per head.   This
result (the " neo-neo-classical theorem " or " golden rule ") has recently
received a great deal of attention (Swan (1963), Robinson (1962), Meade
(1961), Pearce (1962), Allais (1962), Champernowne (1962), Black (1962),
Phelps (1961), Desrousseaux (1961), Solow (1961), Weizsäcker (1962)).   It
is easily proved.

In any steady-state growth path the overall capital–labour ratio (k)
remains constant through time.   Hence, whatever savings assumptions we
care to make, the output of capital goods per head in each period is equal to
nk, the growth rate times capital per head.   We wish to find the value of k
which maximises consumption per head.   Now if (in Fig. I.5) we had a
slightly higher k and had allocated this entire increase to the capital goods
sector (keeping consumption constant), the output of the capital good
would increase by n, since this is the marginal product of capital in its own
production.   But this is precisely the extra output of capital we now require

to maintain steady growth (*i.e.*, keep *k* constant). Hence the output of consumption goods will remain unchanged and there is no gain. If, however, the rate of profit, *i.e.*, the marginal product of capital in its own production, had exceeded *n*, then some of the extra capital could have been allocated to the production of consumption goods and the latter would therefore have increased. In the reverse case, where the rate of profit is less than *n*, we would have gained by reducing *k* by a small amount, since that would still have economised in the production of capital sufficiently to allow some capital to be transferred to consumption without disrupting the steady-state growth. The proposition that under steady growth consumption per head is maximised when the rate of growth in output is equal to the rate of profit can be shown to hold irrespective of the number of commodities (see Section III). It is important to note that it has only limited optimality implications, since the consumption stream which maximises welfare need not be a steady-state stream at all.[1]   (Phelps (1961), Pearce (1962).)

An inherent feature of the two-sector models just considered is that in steady growth relative prices remain constant over time and the outputs of the different goods grow at the same rate. This is also true of the more elaborate two-sector (or *n*-sector) models discussed in Section III. Inasmuch as economic growth in practice is observed to be intimately associated with changes in the structure of production, this of course reduces the real-life applicability of the steady growth concept. Two-sector models of the type we have been considering do not represent any great advance in realism over one-sector models. As far as conclusions are concerned, while those two-sector models do point to certain complications absent from one-sector models, the modifications that need to be made to the broad results found in one-sector models are not very fundamental.

Stability

(a) *Classical Savings Function.*   Let us write $k(t)$ as the arbitrarily given overall capital–labour ratio. To each such ratio there will correspond a wage–rental ratio $z(OR$ of Fig. I.5), which will allow the economy to find a momentary equilibrium at *t*. We investigate whether a sequence of momentary equilibria will lead to a steady-state equilibrium. To do this we first establish the following: If the consumption sector is the more capital intensive, then $k(t)$ and *z* will vary together. (Uzawa (1961), Solow (1961), Inada (1963).)

Suppose the proposition false: $k(t)$ and *z* are inversely related (or not

---

[1] The consumption stream society regards as optimal depends on the social valuation of consumption at various moments of time. Clearly, maximising the social value of consumption over time need not be identical with choosing the maximum steady rate of growth of consumption, that is to say the maximum *constant level* of consumption per head (given no technical progress). For instance, a society might well wish to have a decrease in consumption now in order to enjoy higher levels later. However in a Ramsey-type problem of finding the optimum rate of accumulation, the best asymptotic path may on certain assumptions be the golden rule path.

related at all). Then when z is higher and $k(t)$ lower (or unchanged) total wage payments must rise relatively to total profits. By the savings assump- this must mean a rise in the amount spent on consumption goods relatively to investment goods. But since the consumption sector is the more capital- intensive sector, the price of consumption goods must decline relatively to the price of investment goods (see p. 37). Hence in the new situation the output of consumption goods must have risen relatively to that of investment goods. But since the former is the more capital intensive of the two sectors, and since the capital intensity of neither sector can decline with a rise in z (production function " well behaved "), it follows that $k(t)$ must have risen. We have thus forced a contradiction, and the proposition must be true.

The rest of the story is now easy and is illustrated in Fig. I. 6. In the left- hand quadrant we have drawn the curve relating the (short period) equili- brium value of the wage–rental ratio to the overall capital–labour ratio. In

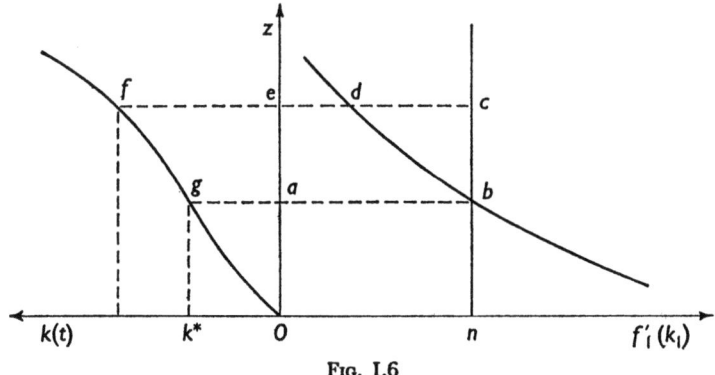

Fig. I.6

the right-hand quadrant we have drawn the marginal product of capital in producing capital as a function of z. The reader can satisfy himself that this is the " right " shape for this curve for " well-behaved " production functions. In a steady state one has $f'_1(k_1) = n$ (see p. 35), and so the steady-state value of $z = Oa$ and k^* is the steady-state capital–labour ratio. Suppose the story to start with $z > Oa$. Evidently, then, for momentary equilibrium $k(t) > k^*$, as Fig. I.6 shows. Also $f'_1(k_1) < n$. But $f'_1(k_1)$ is equal to the rate of growth of the capital stock, which is thus less than the rate of growth of the labour force. Hence $k(t)$ must be falling. But this must mean that z is falling, and so the distance dc is being reduced. Proceeding in this way, it is easily seen that the steady state will be approached.[1]

[1] It is not hard to see what happens when the propensity of capitalists to save is greater than that of workers. Suppose the consumption sector to be more capital intensive. If a rise in z fails to raise k the share of profits must fall. This raises the ratio of the value of consumption goods to that of investment goods produced. But the price of consumption goods falls relatively to that of investment goods, and so the value of consumption output must rise relatively to that of investment- good output. But since the consumption-good sector is the more capital intensive, this contradicts the assumption that k falls with rising z. Hence k and z are directly related. If the capital intensity hypothesis is not made, this result can no longer be deduced (Inada (1963)).

If the capital-intensity assumption is not made, then it may happen that as $k(t)$ falls, z rises and so $k(t)$ will fall even farther, and so on indefinitely (Inada (1963)). This is because the direct relationship between $k(t)$ and z can no longer be established. It is possible that even when the capital-intensity condition is dropped, convergence to the steady state can be proved if some more specific restrictions are placed on the forms of the production functions (Takayama (1963), Guha (1963), Drandanakis (1963)). We do not pursue this farther here.

(b) *Proportional Savings Function.* We first establish the proposition that with this assumption z and k move in the same direction, whatever the capital-intensity conditions.

A rise in z will raise k_1 and k_2. It can therefore fail to raise k only if there is a shift in weight to the less capital-intensive industry. Since the value of capital-goods output is a constant fraction s of the value of total output, there will be a shift in weight in volume terms to that commodity whose relative price has fallen. When z rises, there will be a fall in the relative price of the more capital-intensive industry. There will therefore be a shift towards the more capital-intensive industry, not towards the less capital-intensive one. The rise in z must therefore raise k.

We also know that at every moment of time momentary equilibrium requires that the rate of growth of capital equals sy/k. We can now show that every equilibrium path must approach a steady-state path, as follows:

Suppose $sy/k > n$. Then k must be rising. Hence z is rising. But $sy/k = \frac{L_1}{L} \cdot \frac{y_1}{k} \leqslant \frac{y_1}{k}$, where y_1 is the output per man in the capital-good industry. As $z \to \infty$ the capital–labour ratio in each sector must rise and $k \to \infty$. Because of the concavity of the production function, y_1 will rise less rapidly than k, and so $y_1/k \to 0$, and thus $y/k \to 0$ also. When z is falling we have the following picture: the rental of capital in terms of capital ρ is equal to the marginal product of capital in its own production. ρ goes to infinity as $z \to 0$, since $k_1 \to 0$. But $y = \rho (k + z)$ and so $y/k \to \infty$ as $z \to 0$. These results can now be used to show that every warranted path approaches the steady-state path.

In Fig. I.7 we have drawn an irregular curve, but have ensured that $y/k \to \infty$ as $z \to 0$, and $y/k \to 0$ as $z \to \infty$. Possible steady states are at a, b and c. Suppose we start at a point to the left of E, say at h. Then k is falling. If this means that y/k is falling we must be at a point such as b'. But since the curve *must* bend back on itself, it can easily be verified that y/k must approach a.

If the capital-intensity condition is reintroduced, then we already know the steady state to be unique, and instead of the squiggly line of Fig. I.7 we get a curve monotonically falling from left to right. The system will thus always approach a unique equilibrium monotonically.

It should be noted that the above argument is not much affected if smooth production functions are replaced by production functions of the linear-programming type.

Two-sector models: summary.   The chief results can be summed up as follows, on the assumption that production functions are " well-behaved ":

(*a*) With a classical saving function the steady-state k and z are uniquely determined.   But, given any arbitrary initial k, a number of different values of z may be compatible with momentary equilibrium, unless we assume that

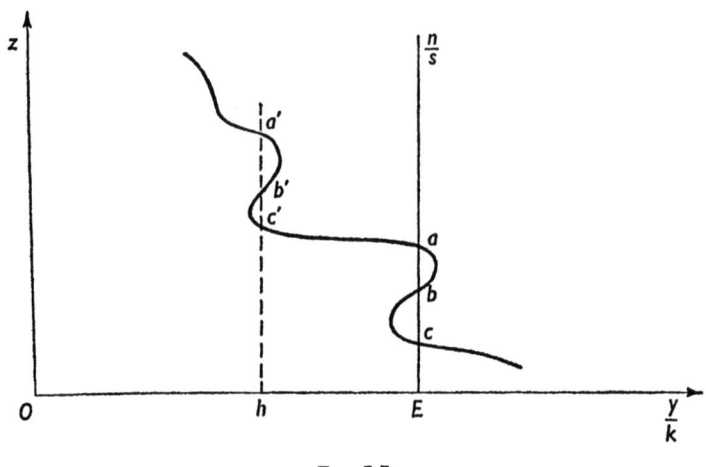

Fig. I.7

the consumption-good industry is more capital-intensive than the capital-good industry.   If the latter assumption is made, the path of momentary equilibria approaches the steady-state.

(*b*) With a proportional saving function the steady-state values of k and z are not necessarily uniquely determined, unless the assumption is made that the consumption-good industry is the more capital-intensive.   On the other hand, given any arbitrary initial k, the momentary equilibrium value of z is uniquely determined, and moreover the sequence of momentary equilibria approaches some steady-state path.

The reader will notice that the assumptions that ensure a unique momentary equilibrium for an arbitrarily given k are also sufficient to ensure the convergence of every equilibrium path to the steady-state path. This is no accident.   Conditions giving a unique momentary equilibrium are required, since a multiplicity of such equilibria would make it impossible to predict the equilibrium path of the system from an arbitrary initial position. We know that for uniqueness we require the equilibrium wage-rental ratio to be a monotone function of the initial capital-labour ratio.   For good economic sense we chose assumptions which give an increasing function. But this in turn then turns out to give convergence to the steady state. It is as if we required a demand and supply curve to intersect only once, and postulated that the supply curve cuts the demand curve from below. The analogy of course is not exact, but it is a similar state of affairs.[1]

I.9. *Depreciation*

So far we have supposed capital equipment to be infinitely long-lived. We now drop this assumption. Excellent, simplified, accounts of some of the main problems exist (Robinson (1960), Meade (1961)). We therefore feel brevity to be justified. However, the reader is warned that we are still abstracting from technical progress, so that physical and economic life of equipment coincide.

(a) "*Sudden Death*"

Although we are still supposing a one-good economy, it will be convenient to call a unit of the good when used in production a "machine." Suppose that a machine yields a constant quasi-rent q for T periods and then dies. How is depreciation calculated? We distinguish three cases: (i) the producer has a balanced but stationary outfit of equipment; (ii) the producer has a balanced but growing outfit; and (iii) he has an unbalanced outfit.

(i) If the producer has a machine of every age, then one machine will wear out each period and will have to be replaced. Now, if the economy is in equilibrium, then the present value of a brand-new machine calculated at the going rate of profit (interest) must equal the price of the machine. Hence if in each period $\frac{1}{T}$th of the original cost (= value) of each machine is put by for depreciation this will just be enough to buy one new machine in each time period.

Moreover, the value of the balanced outfit is made up of the value of a new machine plus the value of a machine one period old, etc. Evidently the value will be less than T times the value of a new machine. Or put differently: the average value of a machine over its lifetime will be less than its value when new. It can, however, be shown (Champernowne and Kahn (1954)) that the average value is greater than $\frac{1}{2}$ times the value of the machine when new. The depreciation procedure method in the previous

---

[1] Most work on two-sector models stipulates that the production functions be " well-behaved ". It will not be difficult for readers to appreciate the reason for postulating diminishing marginal productivity in stability and uniqueness problems. The assumption concerning the asymptotic values of the marginal products, however, is less transparent. It is made in order to ensure the existence of a steady-state solution in which factor prices are strictly positive. It is thus not essential to the analysis, since we all know that we can describe equilibria in which certain prices are zero. On the other hand, the assumption lends some realism to the analysis in this instance.

paragraph keeps the average value of machines " intact," and it is on this value that the producer earns the prevailing rate of profit.[1]

(ii) Suppose the producer increases his gross investment at the rate q. Then evidently the proportion of new to old machines will be greater than in the previous case. If he then pursues a policy of straight-line depreciation appropriate to (i) he will be accumulating depreciation funds faster than he needs them for replacement. This has been investigated in detail by Domar (1957). The footnote makes it precise.[2]

(iii) Suppose the producer has equipment all of the same age—say brand new. Then he will not need to replace it for T years. If he depreciates at the rate d per period he can earn interest—supposed equal to the prevailing rate of profit on his depreciation fund. Hence he can earn the same rate of return on the value of his investment still " locked up " in machines as he can on the value of his depreciation fund. This makes it obvious that he can for ever earn the prevailing rate of profit on the total amount he invested in the machines when new. The rate at which he sets aside funds for depreciation must be such that at the end of T years, when the

---

[1] Let V_{T-t} be the value of a machine t years old $(T - t$ years to go). Let r be the profit rate, q the quasi-rent, C the average value of machine over its lifetime or equivalently the average value of total equipment per plant. One has:

$$V_{T-t} = q \int_0^{T-t} e^{-rv} dv \quad \cdots \cdots \cdots \quad \text{(i)}$$

$$C = \frac{1}{T} \int_0^T V_{T-t} dt \quad \cdots \cdots \cdots \quad \text{(ii)}$$

One easily finds:

$$\frac{\partial C}{\partial t} = \frac{-V_T}{T} \quad \cdots \cdots \cdots \quad \text{(iii)}$$

So since depreciation is to keep C "intact," $\frac{V_T}{T}$ is the appropriate depreciation per machine. Differentiating (i) with respect to t gives

$$\frac{\partial V_{T-t}}{\partial t} = r V_{T-t} - q \quad \cdots \cdots \cdots \quad \text{(iv)}$$

Integrating (iv) over $(0, T)$ and dividing by T gives

$$\frac{-V_T'}{T} = rC - q \quad \cdots \cdots \cdots \quad \text{(v)}$$

Hence net profit per machine is rC.

[2] If V is the value of the total outfit and C' the average value of equipment per plant one has:

$$V = \int_0^T e^{g(T-t)} V_{T-t} \, dt = C' \int_0^T e^{g(T-t)} \, dt$$

Whence

$$C' = \frac{g}{e^{gT} - 1} \int_0^T e^{g(T-t)} V_{T-t} \, dt$$

and

$$\frac{\partial C'}{\partial t} = \frac{-g}{e^{gT} - 1}$$

Since $\frac{g}{e^{gT} - 1} < \frac{1}{T}$, the rate of depreciation which will which will keep C' intact is less than in the previous case. Straight-line depreciation would therefore be depreciating at " too fast " a rate and would certainly exceed replacement.

value locked up in machines has become zero, his depreciation fund including accumulated interest allows him to exactly replace the equipment which has died.[1]

For the economy as a whole this procedure may lead to replacement cycles (Kaldor (1954)).

(b) Radioactive Decay

One now supposes that the quasi-rents to be earned on a machine fall at a proportionate rate $- \delta$. That is a proportion of the value of the machine " evaporates " at every moment of time. The proportionate fall in the value of equipment of any age is independent of its age. Replacement and depreciation must hence be a constant fraction of the value of machines. One notes that in this world machines do not die in finite time.[2]

(c) Implications for Growth Models

(i) One obvious implication concerns the valuation of the capital stock in the economy. Even if there is only one physical good, its valuation will not in general be independent of the age distribution of the equipment which in turn will reflect past history. Many difficulties which might arise here, disappear if we can suppose that accumulation has been proceeding at a given constant rate for a very long time. The age distribution can then be taken as given, and there is then a definite relationship between the existing capital stock and its value when new.

In a one-good economy of the abstract " malleable " kind the capital-output ratio is still well defined in physical terms. If there is a perfect market in machines of all kinds the price of second-hand machines must be such that no one can make a profit by buying, say, a balanced outfit rather than a brand-new one, or vice versa. In steady-state growth, therefore, there

---

[1] If D_t is the depreciation fund at t (including accumulated interest) and $A_t = D_t + V_{T-t}$ we: (i) wish to keep A_t " intact," and (ii) have enough for replacement when the machines die. But

$$A_t = q \int_0^{T-t} e^{-rv}\, dv + d \int_0^t e^{r(t-v)}\, dv \quad . \quad . \quad . \quad . \quad . \quad (i)$$

So if $\dfrac{\partial A_t}{\partial t} = 0$ we must have, on differentiating (i) with respect to t and setting equal to zero,

$$r(A_t) + d - q = 0 \quad . \quad . \quad . \quad . \quad . \quad . \quad (ii)$$

Since one has A_t constant, $A_t = A_0 = V_T$, and so from (ii)

$$q = rV_t + d \quad . \quad . \quad . \quad . \quad . \quad . \quad . \quad (iii)$$

Evaluating V_T from (i) footnote, p. 44 (with $t = 0$) gives

$$d = qe^{-rT} \quad . \quad . \quad . \quad . \quad . \quad . \quad . \quad (iv)$$

It is easily verified that d accumulated at r for T years gives V_T, i.e., just enough for replacement.

[2] $V =$ machine t years old $= qe^{-\delta t} \int_0^\infty e^{-(r+\delta)v}\, dv$

$$\frac{\partial V_t}{\partial t} = -\delta V_t$$

will be a well-defined relative relationship between the physical and value capital–output ratio. Once we leave the steady state all is chaos and confusion.

(ii) Depreciation introduces a fuzziness into the savings hypotheses and may lead us to agree a variety of fundamental growth equations. To see this suppose " radioactive decay." Let K be the value of the capital stock at a moment of time in steady growth and let $G = $ *gross saving*. In equilibrium gross savings equal gross investment. The latter is given by $\frac{\partial K}{\partial t} + \delta K$. If there is full employment $\frac{\partial K}{\partial t} \frac{1}{K} = n$, the rate of population growth. Now consider the following hypothesis:

(1) Net saving $= s(Y - \delta K)$. Producers withhold δK, their depreciation allowance, but distribute the rest of their receipts to households who save s of their receipts. One then has

$$G/K = \frac{s(Y - \delta K)}{K} + \delta = n + \delta: \frac{sY}{K} = n + s\delta$$

(2) Net saving is proportional to gross income, *i.e.*, equal to sY. One has

$$G/K = \frac{sY + \delta K}{K} = n + \delta: \frac{sY}{K} = n$$

(3) Gross saving is a constant fraction s of gross income. One has

$$\frac{G}{K} = \frac{sY}{K} = n + \delta: \frac{sY}{K} = n + \delta$$

In each of these cases gross output grows at the rate n. But the ratio of capital to gross output may be entirely different. The latter ratio is simply the ratio of the value of capital to total output. Some authors (Uzawa (1961)) use (3) others (2) (Harrod (1947)). No final agreement has been reached on this matter, and it can be settled only by an appeal to the facts.

Exactly the same variety of cases can be obtained from a classical savings function, except that now the rate of profit (net) may be ambiguous. If we suppose capital and net savings to be proportional to net profits we get the usual result, already discussed. If capitalists' net savings are proportional to gross profits, then the equilibrium ratio of gross profit to the value of capital will be proportional to the rate of growth, n. If gross savings are proportional to gross profits, then the equilibrium ratio of gross profits to capital will be $n + \delta$.

If one replaces the assumption of " radioactive decay " by that of " sudden death " care must be taken in the valuation of the capital stock. Replacement is not now a fixed proportion of the value, but rather depends on the rate of growth, the rate of profit and on T. No new problems of principle arise, but some of the simplicity of our earlier discussions disappears.

II. Technical Progress

In the models so far considered, growth has been the result solely of population increase and/or capital accumulation. We now introduce technical progress.[1]

II.1. *The Simplest Case.   Neutrality and Non-neutrality*

In the simplest treatment technical progress is regarded as something that goes on at an externally given rate and serves to bring about an increase over time in the output that can be produced by any combination of factors of production. Its effects can then be separated conceptually from those of capital accumulation, even when the two are going on at the same time. It will be shown that if technical progress is of this kind and is " Harrod-neutral " its effects are closely analogous to those of population growth.

The purpose of a definition of neutral technical progress is to indicate characteristics of technical progress which will in some sense leave unchanged the balance between labour and capital, and so will permit steady growth.

Technical progress shifts the entire production function, and an index-number type of problem therefore arises in deciding which point on the old production function to compare with which point on the new one. This problem has led to the formulation of a number of alternative definitions of neutral technical progress. The question was originally raised in the 1930's (Hicks (1932), Robinson (1938)), and there has been a revival of interest in it more recently (Harrod (1947), Salter (1960), Uzawa (1961), Kennedy (1961), (1962), Asimakopulos (1963)).

Consider first a one-commodity world. Compare production functions at two different dates, between which technical progress has occurred. Assume constant returns to scale. The definition of neutral technical progress given by Hicks (1932) is based on comparing points on the two functions where the labour–capital ratio L/K is constant, L being measured in number of men and K is physical units (in the one-commodity case, with infinitely long-lived capital, this is equivalent to units of final output). Neutral technical progress is defined as taking place if the ratio of the marginal product of labour to the marginal product of capital is unchanged when K/L is unchanged. (Likewise technical progress is capital-saving if the marginal product of labour is raised by more than that of capital, given K/L, and it is labour-saving in the opposite case.) Technical progress may be neutral in this sense for one value of K/L but not for others, in which case there is the usual index-number problem of whether to take as the criterion the old K/L or the new one or some third one. But the definition is usually taken in the stricter sense to require that the ratios of marginal products should be unaffected by technical progress at *any* (constant) value of K/L.

In our usual diagram (Fig. II.1) we have shown the production function

[1] Reference may be made here to three recent survey articles which cover parts of this and adjacent fields in more detail: Walters (1963); Blaug (1963); Nelson (1959).

before and *after* Hicks-neutral technical change. We already know (*e.g.*, p. 35) that *OR* measures the wage–rental ratio, *i.e.*, the ratio of the marginal products. The distinctive feature of Hicks-neutral technical progress is that for any given value of the capital–labour ratio k, this remains unchanged by the technical change. It can be shown that in this case the curve F' can be derived from F by raising output per head for all values of k in the new proportion.[1]

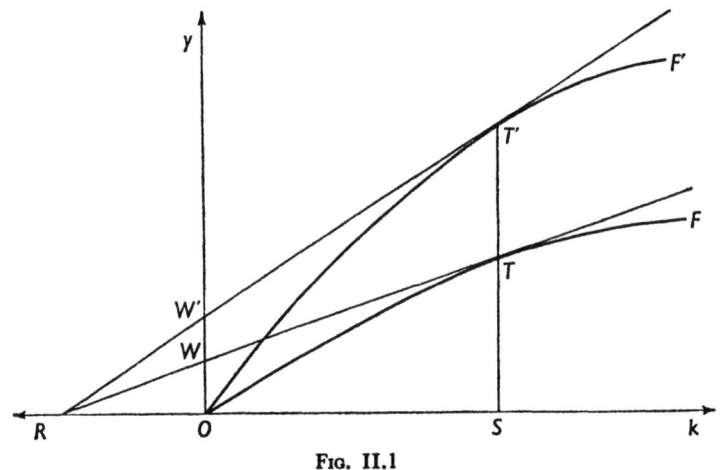

FIG. II.1

Restating the above in algebraic form, the treatment of technical progress as an exogenous function of time (t) implies that the production function can be written

$$Y = f(K, L, t)$$

In order for technical progress to be Hicks-neutral, the production function must be of the more specific form

$$Y = A(t) f(K, L)$$

where $A(t)$ is any (increasing) function of t.

Hicks-neutrality takes as its standard of reference what would happen if K/L remained constant. In most growth models, and in reality, K/L does

---

[1] Let $f(K, L, t)$ be the production function with constant returns to scale. Let f_i, ($i = K, L, t$), be the partial derivative of f with respect of its *i*th argument. (t = the technological shift parameter.)

(*a*) Since f_i ($i = K, L$) is the marginal product of i, Hicks-neutrality implies $\partial \log f_k = \partial \log f_L = c$, say.

(*b*) Consider $\alpha \equiv \dfrac{f_i}{f}$. By constant returns to scale α is homogeneous of degree zero in K and L.

But $\dfrac{\partial \alpha}{\partial K} = \dfrac{\frac{\partial f_i}{\partial K}}{f} - \dfrac{f_i f_K}{f^2} = \dfrac{f_K}{f}\left(c - \dfrac{f_i}{f}\right)$. So $K\dfrac{\partial \alpha}{\partial K} + L\dfrac{\partial \alpha}{\partial L} = \dfrac{(f_K K + f_L L)}{f}\left(c - \dfrac{f_i}{f}\right) = c - \dfrac{f_i}{f}$ (1)

Since α is homogeneous of degree zero in K and L, (1) $= c - \dfrac{f_i}{f} = 0$, and so $\dfrac{\partial \alpha}{\partial K} = 0$. Hence the production function may be written as $A(t)F(K, L)$, where $\dfrac{A'(t)}{A} = \alpha$. (Uzawa and Watanabe (1960) for the n inputs case.)

not remain constant. The Harrod definition is based instead on the comparison of points on the production function at different times where the marginal product of capital, assumed equal to the rate of profit ρ, is constant. With K/L unchanged, technical progress will normally raise the marginal product of capital. For the marginal product of capital to remain constant in face of technical progress, K/L must normally rise.[1] Technical progress is neutral in the Harrod sense if the level of K/L which causes ρ to remain constant after a technical improvement is such as to cause the capital–output ratio to remain constant. Likewise technical progress is labour-saving (= capital-using) or capital-saving (= labour-using) if a constant ρ is associated with a higher or lower capital–output ratio respectively. This has the corollary that if ρ remains constant neutral technical progress leaves

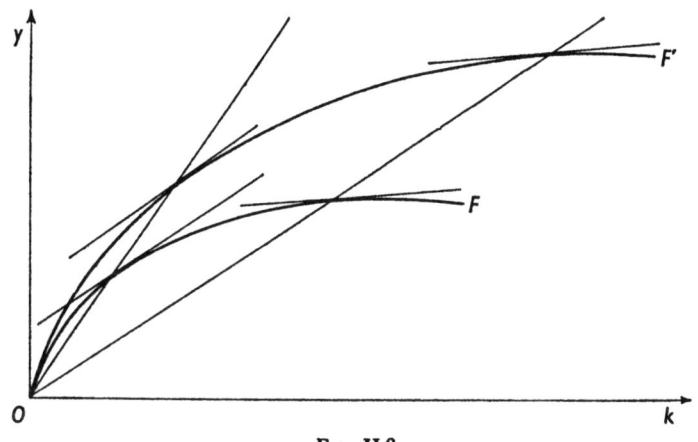

FIG. II.2

the distribution of income between capital and labour unchanged, assuming perfect competition. (As with the Hicks definition, the Harrod definition is usually understood to require that this should hold at all possible (constant) values of the relevant ratio, here K/Y.) Using the usual diagram, we depict Harrod-neutral technical progress in Fig. II.2. Here OF' is derived from OF by " radial projection," that is to say, on any ray through the origin the slope of OF' is the same as the slope of OF. This is so because the slope of the line through the origin is the ratio of output to capital, and technical progress is such that if this ratio is constant, then so is the rate of profit (the slope of the tangent).

The general form of Harrod-neutral technical progress with two factors of production can be shown to be

$$Y = f(K, A(t)L)$$

[1] The movement along the production function that causes the marginal product of capital to remain constant is comparable to the substitution of capital for labour that would be undertaken by a single firm, to which finance was available at a fixed rate of interest, in response to a fall in the price of capital goods relatively to labour brought about by technical progress in the production of capital goods (Salter (1960), pp. 39–44).

The t term is thus prefixed to L instead of to $f(K, L)$, as in the Hicks-neutral case.[1]   With such a production function, assuming constant returns to scale, it is apparent that an equal proportional rise in K and $A(t)L$ must lead to an equal proportional rise in Y. The whole economy rises in scale, and ρ remains constant.   The requirement of neutrality by the Harrod definition is thus satisfied. (For a proof that it is a necessary and sufficient condition of Harrod-neutrality that the production function should have this form, see Uzawa (1961).)

This formulation shows why Harrod-neutral technical progress is closely akin to population growth.   Population growth increases the labour force, L; Harrod-neutral technical progress increases the labour force *measured in efficiency units*, $A(t)L$.   Population growth causes there to be two men where there was previously one; Harrod-neutral technical progress causes one man to be able to do twice what he could have done previously.   The analogy is complete.   It is therefore unnecessary for us to go over again for the case of Harrod-neutral technical progress the models worked out in Section I for population growth.   All that is necessary is to substitute efficiency units of labour for heads.   This means, of course, that there will be a rise over time in real wages per head (real wages per efficiency unit of labour remain constant).   This affects the formal structure of the model only if the absolute level of the real wage per head is itself a strategic factor, for example if it affects the rate of population growth (see below, pp. 56–58).

The analogy to population growth makes it clear that under Harrod-neutral technical progress output will grow at the same rate, whatever the level at which K/Y is held constant (Robinson (1938), Uzawa (1961)). This rate provides a measure of technical progress.   In the case of technical progress that is both Hicks- and Harrod-neutral (see below) this measure will be a higher one than that offered in conjunction with the Hicks definition (the rate at which output rises if K/L is constant), since it incorporates the effects of increasing K *pari passu* with Y.   It is the rate at which income per head will grow if there is no deepening in the sense of a rise in K/Y, although there *is* a rise in K/L.   It corresponds to Harrod's natural rate of increase of Y per head.[2]

---

[1] If there are factors of production other than capital and labour, such as land, the t term must be prefixed to all factors other than capital, not just to labour.

[2] In our usual notation the Cobb–Douglas production function with neutral technical progress is $y = e^{mt}k^\beta$, $0 < \beta < 1$, or $\log y = mt + \beta \log k$. Hence

$$\text{Hicks measure of technical progress} = \frac{\partial y}{\partial t}\Big/ y = m$$
$$k = \text{constant}$$

$$\text{Harrod measure of technical progress} = \frac{\partial y}{\partial t}\Big/ y = \frac{m}{1 - \beta}$$
$$\frac{k}{y} = \text{constant}$$

(In the Harrod case one has on differentiation $\frac{\partial y}{\partial t}\Big/y = m + \beta\frac{\partial k}{\partial t}\Big/k$.   Since $\frac{\partial k}{\partial t}\Big/k = \frac{\partial y}{\partial t}\Big/y$ by assumption, the above result is obtained.)

If technical progress is non-neutral in the Harrod sense it is impossible for the economy to stay on a path of steady growth in which Y and K are both growing at the same, constant, rate. If K and Y *were* growing at the same rate the distribution of income would then be altering. The rate of growth of output per head is equal to the exogenous time term plus capital's share multiplied by the rate of growth of capital per head. If the exogenous time term is constant, and capital's share is changing, then evidently the overall rate of increase of output and capital cannot both remain constant, and steady growth is not maintainable. This is true even if technical progress is Hicks-neutral. Nor is it even possible in these circumstances for there to be a constant rate of growth of Y alone. For if the rate of growth of Y and the propensity to save are both constant the rate of growth of K *must* tend asymptotically to equal the rate of growth of Y. Hence if a constant rate of growth of Y is not compatible with constant K/Y it is not maintainable at all. This is also true with a classical saving function.

If technical progress is not Harrod-neutral it is thus plain that there cannot normally be steady growth. Not a great deal of work has been done in inquiring into the equilibrium dynamics of what *will* then happen, though a number of writers have considered the question on the assumptions of their own models (Robinson (1956), Robinson (1962), Champernowne (1958), Meade (1961)). Labour-saving bias in technical progress serves to increase the importance of capital relative to labour in production; since capital is growing over time relatively to labour, such a bias therefore tends on most assumptions to cause the rate of increase of output to grow over time. Likewise capital-saving bias tends to lead to deceleration; in the limiting case where capital's share approaches zero as time advances, the rate of growth slows down until in the limit increase in capital per head ceases to make any contribution to growth. A constant growth rate or constant shares (but not both) can be derived on more complicated assumptions, such as a non-constant rate of technical progress.

It is possible for technical progress to be both Hicks-neutral and Harrod-neutral. For this the elasticity of substitution between labour and capital must be unity, as can be shown as follows: Assume given labour force. Hicks-neutral progress retains the same distribution of income in the event that K remains unchanged. Harrod-neutral technical progress retains the same distribution in the event that K rises in the same proportion as Y. For both requirements to be satisfied, the distribution of income must therefore be the same as between two situations that differ only in the level of K. This implies unit elasticity of substitution between L and K. The only production function with this property is the Cobb–Douglas production function (see footnote, p. 50). This is the production function used by Solow and Swan in their neo-classical models. Its unequivocal neutrality, together with its ease of manipulation, has caused it to be used in innumerable

other growth models. However, steady growth is compatible with other
production functions as well, so long as they are Harrod-neutral.[1]

Because its effect is similar to that of population increase, Harrod-neutral
technical progress can be described as " labour-augmenting." A third type
of neutral technical progress has recently been discussed (Solow (1963)),
" capital-augmenting " technical progress, where the production function is

$$Y = f(A(t)K, L)$$

This is the mirror-image of Harrod-neutral technical progress, and it has
similar properties, with K and L reversed in every case: thus at constant
L/Y the wage and, hence, the distribution of income, are constant. The
Cobb–Douglas production function, as might be expected, is the only one
that conforms both to this definition and to the definition of Harrod-
neutrality. The concept of capital-augmenting technical progress is useful
in the study of vintage-capital models (below, Section II.3). But it does
not take the place of Harrod-neutrality as the concept of neutrality relevant
for the feasibility of steady growth; since constant K/Y, the Harrod bench-
mark for constant distribution, is something that is necessarily present in
steady growth as a result of the saving function, whereas constant L/Y, the
analogous bench-mark with capital-augmenting technical progress, is clearly
not a feature of steady growth.[2]

The concept of neutral technical progress is a good deal more complicated
in a world where there is more than one good (Kennedy (1961), Kennedy
(1962), Meade (1961), Asimakopulos (1963), Asimakopulos and Weldon
(1963)).[3] The overall neutrality will now depend not only on the character
of technical progress in each industry but also on the relative rates of technical progress in each, and the relative weights of each in the whole. Obviously technical progress is neutral overall if it is neutral in each industry
and equally rapid in each, and if the relative weight of each remains constant.

---

[1] Recently attention has been given to a more general class of production function, constant-
elasticity-of-substitution (CES) production functions. Cobb–Douglas is the special case of this
class, where the elasticity of substitution (σ) is unity. The general form without technical progress
is

$$Y = (aK^{-\beta} + bL^{-\beta})^{-\frac{1}{\beta}},$$

where $\beta = \frac{1 - \sigma}{\sigma}$, Harrod-neutral technical progress may be introduced by multiplying L in the
above by a time term. See Arrow, Chenery, Minhas and Solow (1961), Minhas (1963), Pitchford
(1960), Uzawa (1962), McFadden (1963). For further general discussion, including a survey of
econometric applications of the Cobb–Douglas and CES functions, see Walters (1963).

[2] The three concepts of neutral technical progress can be shown in terms of the Factor-price
Frontier (below p. 93). Hicks-neutral technical progress causes the function to move outward in a
constant proportion along rays through the origin; Harrod-neutral (= labour-augmenting) causes
it to shift upwards in a constant proportion along the w-axis; capital-augmenting causes it to shift
outwards in a constant proportion along the r-axis.

[3] Reference may also be made to the related literature on biased technical progress in the theory
of international trade, surveyed by Bhagwati (1964).

But it could also be neutral overall because of offsetting influences. For example, if technical progress is faster in the capital-goods industries than in consumer-goods industries, this by itself tends to produce an overall capital-using bias; but it could be offset if within each industry technical progress were capital-saving. Moreover, because a change in the relative importance of more and less capital-intensive industries will influence the overall result, the nature of technical progress in the economy as a whole ceases to be a wholly technological matter and becomes influenced by demand (Fellner (1961)).

Removing the one-good assumption introduces the possibility of variations in relative prices. The Harrod-definition of neutral technical progress (constant rate of profit at constant K/Y) must then be understood to refer to constant K/Y in value terms.[1] This needs to be emphasised because statistical data on capital–output ratios are usually given in volume terms.[2] If K/Y is not constant in value terms at a constant profit rate the distribution of income will not be constant. In any case, K/Y in volume terms ceases to have an unambiguous meaning when prices are changing; an index-number problem is involved. For the same reason the Hicks-definition of neutrality ceases to have an unambiguous meaning when there are different kinds of capital good. Various writers have studied the consequences in a two-sector model of changes in relative prices (Meade (1961), Gordon (1961)).

Our argument so far contains no *a priori* reason why technical progress should be exactly Harrod-neutral. It is just one special case (comparison suggests itself with the other Harrodian special case: that where warranted and natural growth rates are equal). This is a further limitation on the value of steady-state growth models as representations of reality. In order to defend their usefulness in this role, one must either maintain that technical progress just happens to have been neutral or else suggest reasons why a tendency to Harrod-neutrality should exist. It is difficult to advance convincing reasons for this without making assumptions that amount more or less to assuming the answer. In the early days of the discussion it was argued that there would exist an inherent tendency to neutrality, because greater efforts would be made by entrepreneurs to devise ways of reducing the input of whichever factor was becoming more expensive. Against this it has been pointed out that, while *substitution* will be practised in the light of relative factor prices, entrepreneurs will be equally anxious to reduce *all* costs by means of technical improvements, so that no inherent tendency to neutrality in technical progress can necessarily be inferred (Fellner (1961)). More recently the matter has been discussed in connection with Kaldor's technical progress function; see below, p. 71.

---

[1] Mrs. Robinson's definition ((1956), p. 133; (1962), p. 112) is equivalent to this: the ratio of capital, measured in cost in labour-hours, to labour is constant when ρ is constant.

[2] Divergent movements in value-K/Y and volume-K/Y, as conventionally measured, have been noted in the empirical literature (Gordon (1961), Anderson (1961)).

Much empirical work in the 1950's was inspired by the simple type of
approach to technical progress we have been discussing, in which the effects
of technical progress (as represented by a time term) and capital accumulation are separated conceptually (Kendrick (1961), Abramovitz (1956),
Solow (1957), Reddaway and Smith (1960), etc.). The basic procedure is
to estimate the contributions made to the growth in output by increases in
inputs of labour and capital over a period by multiplying the observed
increases in inputs by observed factor prices (taken as a measure of marginal
products) and deducting the result from the overall growth in output; the
" residual " is attributed to technical progress.[1] The result is almost always
to show that technical progress contributes much more to growth than
capital accumulation does. (That this result is likely is obvious from the
crude calculation that, with normal orders of magnitude, ρs, the profit rate
multiplied by the saving–income ratio, which is a measure of capital's
contribution to increased output, is considerably less than the rate of increase
in productivity per man, instead of exceeding it as it would do if there were
population growth and no technical progress (Cairncross (1953)).[2] Policy
conclusions were drawn to the effect that national policies of belt-tightening
are unlikely to be worthwhile.

More recently, a good deal of scepticism has come to be felt about this
approach. First, by attributing the residual to " technical progress " other
influences are implicitly excluded, such as improvement in the quality of
labour due to education, etc. However those who used the " residual "
approach were well aware that the residual, as its name implies, is a catch-all
and that in practice the task of research would be to break it up into its
constitutent components;[3] so this is hardly a criticism of the method as
properly applied. Secondly, the method depends on the assumption that
factors receive the value of their marginal products, and it will therefore lead
to misleading results unless there is (or the system behaves " as if " there is)
perfect competition. This may have a serious effect on the statistical conclusions drawn from the method in practice, though it does not necessarily
involve any fundamental challenge to the view of technical progress underlying the approach. Thirdly, the approach can be criticised for its basic
assumptions. In the remainder of this section we shall consider the consequences of departing from these assumptions.

---

[1] This is a measure of technical progress in the Hicks sense not the Harrod sense; in the symbols
of footnote (2), p. 50, it is a measure of m, not of $m/(1 - \beta)$.

[2] Taking the Cobb–Douglas production function, one has, without technical progress,

$$\frac{dy}{dt}\Big/ y = \beta \frac{dk}{dt}\Big/ k = \beta\left(\frac{dK}{dt}\Big/ K - \frac{dL}{dt}\Big/ L\right) = \beta\left(\frac{dK}{dt}\Big/ K - n\right).$$

Remembering that β = profits' share in income, and assuming $dK/dt = sY$, one has

$$\frac{dy}{dt}\Big/ y = \frac{\rho K}{Y} \cdot \frac{sY}{K} - \beta n = \rho s - \beta n.$$

[3] A well-known bold attempt along these lines is Denison (1962); see also Griliches (1963).

II.2. *Non-constant Returns to Scale*

The first departure to be considered from the assumptions of the simple approach is the least fundamental conceptually.

Considering the prominent part played by *increasing returns* in past discussions of growth since Adam Smith, the mainstream of recent neo-classical theory has neglected it to a surprising extent, and has been criticised on these grounds (Hicks (1960)). The reason for the neglect is no doubt the difficulty of fitting increasing returns into the prevailing framework of perfect competition and marginal productivity factor pricing. Recently the subject has come to attract more attention. On the empirical side some sort of increasing returns have been inferred from the very well-attested correlation between the rate of growth of productivity and the rate of growth of production, between industries as well as between countries (Salter (1960), Verdoorn (1947)). On the theoretical side learning theory has suggested a way of formalising the relation between increasing returns and technical progress, and so providing the basis of a non-static treatment of increasing returns, as pleaded for by Marshall in the famous Appendix H of the *Principles*; this will be further discussed below.

Waiving for the moment the question of the *causes* of increasing returns, it is not difficult in principle to incorporate increasing returns into a steady-state growth model, subject to certain conditions. Suppose, for example, that the whole economy is subject to external economies, and that the production function is Cobb–Douglas raised to a power higher than one; and suppose that the distribution of income remains as it would be if the power *were* one (the benefits of the external economies are divided between the factors in proportion to the incomes they would have earned if there had been no external economies). So long as the tendency to increasing returns to scale is not so powerful as to cause increasing social returns to capital by itself, steady growth is possible, with Y growing at the same rate as K, and ρ constant. Even in the absence of technical progress, the economies of scale will bring about steady growth in income per head so long as population is growing (though with neither population growth nor technical progress there can, of course, be no steady growth). In contrast to the ordinary kind of model, the rate of growth of total income will then be a *multiple* of the rate of growth of population.[1] Rapid growth of population conduces to rapid growth of income per head, because of the economies of scale that it makes possible. On the other hand, growth at a constant rate is obviously impossible if there are increasing returns to capital taken by itself. *Growth* is then possible, even without population growth or technical progress, but

---

[1] Thus if the production function is $Y = A(e^{mt}K^{\alpha}L^{1-\alpha})^{\mu}$, where $\mu > 1$, then if g, the rate of growth of Y, equals the rate of growth of K we have ($n =$ rate of population growth)

$$g = \frac{m\mu}{1 - \alpha\mu} + n\left(1 + \frac{\mu - 1}{1 - \alpha\mu}\right)$$

not steady growth. And, of course, other increasing returns production functions can be devised where the effect of increasing returns either damps out over time or else progressively strengthens, instead of continuing at an even pace, as in the case cited.

The classic reason for a tendency to *diminishing returns* is the existence of a third factor, land, which is in fixed supply. (The consequences of introducing land into growth models has been particularly studied by Meade (1961).) It is obvious that if there is no technical progress a tendency to diminishing returns to labour and capital taken together will make steady growth impossible. If there is technical progress the tendency to diminishing returns will act as a drag on the rate of growth of income, but it will not necessarily make steady growth impossible. The extent of the downward pressure on income per head exerted by diminishing returns depends on the importance of land in the production process and on the rate of population growth, n. Given the rate of technical progress and the shape of the production function, there is a certain value of n such that the effects of diminishing returns exactly offset technical progress, and income per head is constant. With a Cobb–Douglas production function this value of n will remain constant as population rises, and a steady growth state can exist in which Y and L are growing at the same rate.[1] If n is lower than this, income per head will be rising at a steady pace.

In the history of thought discussion of diminishing returns from land has been closely associated with the Malthusian theory of population. We may therefore conveniently resume at this point our discussion of the possibility of induced changes in the rate of population growth (above I.6), only now on the assumption that technical progress does take place. Assume first that there are no diminishing returns from land. If the function relating the rate of growth of population to real income per head does not have an upper limit we reach the absurd result of an ever-increasing rate of population growth. If an upper limit exists, it will ultimately be reached, since technical progress guarantees an increase in income per head over time. Induced changes in the rate of population growth then appear as only one phase in the course of growth. Presently n reaches its maximum, and thereafter it can be treated as exogenous, as in the standard kind of model. In this final stage income per head will tend to grow at the rate set by technical progress. In the earlier phases income per head will grow less rapidly than this, because the progressive increase in n will lead to a progressive reduction in K/Y, which will act as a drag on the rate of growth. In the early stages of economic advance, in other words, the rate of growth of income per head will

---

[1] Say $Y = e^{mt}K^{\alpha}L^{\beta}E^{\gamma}$ ($E =$ land; $\alpha + \beta + \gamma = 1$), then the rate of growth of income per head is given by

$$g - n = m + \alpha(\dot{K}/K - n) - \gamma n$$

If $S = sY$, then $\dot{K}/K$ must equal g when g is constant. There will be steady growth of population with constant income per head ($g = n$) if $m = \gamma n$.

be limited because such rise in it as does occur will stimulate more rapid population growth, and this will make for a shortage of capital.

Now allow for the existence of diminishing returns from land. If n has no upper limit, then the rise in income per head must presently bring n to the level at which the pressure of diminishing returns exactly offsets technical progress, leaving income per head constant; n will then cease to rise further. A high rate of technical progress therefore leads to a high level of income and a high rate of population growth, but it does not lead to permanently rising income per head. Things are different if n has an upper limit. If technical progress is rapid enough to offset diminishing returns from land when n is at its maximum value the position is similar to the case where there are no diminishing returns and permanent growth is possible. The interesting conclusion follows that differences in the rate of technical progress below the critical point that allows n to reach its maximum will affect the *level* of income per head, whereas differences in the rate of technical progress above this critical point will affect the *rate of growth* of income per head. If the rate of technical progress exceeds the critical level and income per head starts at a low level, the growth process will consist of two phases: in the first phase population rises at an increasing rate with only a slow rise in income per head; in the second phase population increases at a high but constant rate and income per head rises more rapidly than before (Kaldor (1957), Jorgenson (1961)). Something in the nature of a " take-off " in income per head can therefore be identified.[1] But it is not a take-off in the sense used by development theorists of a situation of which a certain minimum effort is needed by the economy to get past a threshold.

Several writers have, however, developed this general line of argument in ways that might justify a take-off theory in this " big push " sense (Solow (1956), Leibenstein (1957), Buttrick (1958), Niehans (1963)).

Theoretically what is involved is a multiple equilibrium solution, with a low-level equilibrium that is stable to small disturbances but not to large ones. Such models can be based on the economies of scale or non-linearity in the n function or non-linearity in the inducement to invest or innovate because of threshold effects. The multiple equilibrium kind of case may be illustrated by Fig. II.3, which formalises another often-cited possibility. Suppose the income-elasticity of demand for land-intensive products (food) is less than one. Then as income per head rises, land becomes less important and there is a fall in the extent of the reduction in productivity due to diminishing returns from land associated with any given rate of increase of population. In Fig. II.3 the curve labelled d.r. measures the proportional reduction in productivity due to the effect of diminishing returns at different levels of income per head.[2] At first this rises because n is rising, then it falls,

---

[1] In Jorgenson's model it is further assumed that a shift in demand to manufactures away from food begins when income per head has reached the level at which n is at its maximum.

[2] Corresponding to γn in the footnote on p. 56.

because the effect of further increases in *n* is more than offset by the diminishing importance of land as income per head rises.   The dotted line measures
the difference between technical progress and the effect of diminishing returns, and so measures the rate of change of productivity.   This shows an
inverse pattern to the curve d.r.   *A* is a point of stable equilibrium—a " low-
level equilibrium trap."   Income per head is low, but not low enough to
stop population from increasing, and technical progress is offset by diminishing returns from land so that income per head is constant.   But if the
economy could somehow get past point *B* there would be continuous growth
in income per head.   *B* is a point of unstable equilibrium, because if income
per head rises the result is positive growth of productivity, and progress is
self-reinforcing.   The take-off into self-sustaining growth to the right of
point *B* might come about from large effort induced by government policy.
It could also come about as a result of an upward drift over time of the
dotted line until it became tangential to the horizontal axis.

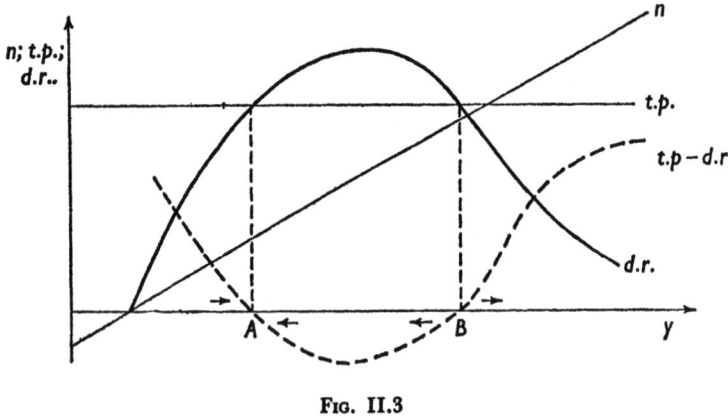

FIG. II.3

II.3. *Non-malleable Capital.   The Vintage Approach*

The simple approach to technical progress described in Section II.1
represents technical knowledge (in an often-used phrase) as falling like
manna from heaven.   If the rate of fall of manna is a function of socio-
cultural forces it is perhaps fair to treat it as exogenous, but not if it is a function of investment or the rate of profit or some such economic variable.   In
particular, it has been contended that capital accumulation and technical
progress influence each other in such a way as to make separation of the two
impossible or useless.

Consider first the effect of capital accumulation on technical knowledge.
" The use of more capital per worker . . . inevitably entails the introduction
of superior techniques which require ' inventiveness ' of some kind " (Kaldor
(1957), p. 595).   The suggestion is that it is artificial to try to separate this

kind of inventiveness from the inventiveness that shifts the whole function. The production-function approach, taken literally, implies that at any moment entrepreneurs have blueprints for techniques appropriate to any value of K/L. This is plainly absurd. Suppose the opposite extreme: that entrepreneurs at any time know *only* the technique of production suitable to existing factor supplies. If more K becomes available they think out ways of using it. This in itself does not necessarily upset the theory. It means that the production function " in any state of technical knowledge " is something which will be discovered as occasion arises (like one interpretation of the demand curve facing a firm). At the same time manna is falling which causes the technique used, with any given supply of factors, to be superior to what would have been used earlier.

A more substantial amendment is required if the new knowledge gained as a result of seeking ways of using the additional capital reveals methods of production that would have been better than the old ones, even with the old K/L. A yet more substantial amendment is made if it is asserted that there is *no* manna and that all advance in technical knowledge accrues from the stimulus of capital accumulation. Arrow's model makes use of this hypothesis in a special form (see below).

In addition to the influence of capital accumulation on technical progress, there is also the inverse relationship. To quote Kaldor again: " Most, though not all, technical innovations which are capable of raising the productivity of labour require the use of more capital per man " (*ibid.*). If this is taken to refer merely to the *quantity* of capital of a homogeneous kind it is not necessarily at odds with the orthodox approach. If true, it is likely to mean that technical progress is Hicks-labour-saving, but it does not necessarily mean that it is not Harrod-neutral. But if technical progress cannot be implemented without introducing new *kinds* of machine—whether more or less expensive than those previously used—it is not possible to speak of " capital " as a homogeneous entity. An extensive literature exists on the implications of this; and we proceed to consider it now.

In this approach new capital accumulation is regarded as the vehicle of technical progress. Technical progress increases the productivity of machines built in any period compared with machines built in the previous period, but it does not increase the productivity of machines already in existence. Technical progress is " embodied " in new machines. Machines unalterably embody the technology of their date of construction. Machines built at different dates (machines of different " vintages ") are therefore qualitatively dissimilar, and cannot in the general case be aggregated into a single measure of capital. A separate production function is needed for each vintage. Total output is the sum of output from all the vintages in use.

The vintage approach does not as such involve necessarily any departure from the assumption that technical progress takes place at an externally given rate. The difference from the orthodox approach is merely that now the manna of technical progress falls only on the latest machines. This is not such a fundamental difference, so it is not surprising that vintage models can be made to yield results quite like orthodox ones. (The vintage approach can, however, be used in conjunction with other more far-reaching changes in assumption about technical progress, and these will be considered in the next section.)

The notion of embodied technical progress represents one departure from the assumption of complete homogeneity (malleability) of the capital stock. Another, but in principle distinct, departure from it is the following. On the orthodox approach, variation in the amount of labour per unit of capital is possible at all times, along some production function, such as the Cobb–Douglas. It may be, however, that while an entrepreneur is able to choose between techniques with varying capital–labour ratios at the time when he is installing a new machine he loses his freedom of action once the machine has been bought: each machine is designed to be worked with a given crew of men, and the size of the crew cannot thereafter be changed. In the terminology of Johansen (1959) there is then " *ex ante* substitutability " between labour and capital, but no " *ex post* substitutability "; or in that of Phelps (1963), capital is " putty-clay " (putty *ex ante*, clay *ex post*), instead of being pure putty. Intermediate cases are, of course, possible: there may be *some* scope for variation in labour requirements *ex post*, but not as much as *ex ante*. Likewise technical progress may be partly embodied and partly disembodied. In addition, technical progress in all these cases may be Harrod-neutral or not; we shall confine ourselves to the cases where it is. As machines of different vintages are not homogeneous, a difficulty arises in the choice of unit in defining " a " machine; the most convenient unit is that amount of capital equipment which, when new, has a cost of production, and hence a value, equal to that of a unit of final output.

We will consider first the case of thorough-going non-malleability, where capital once built is both incapable of benefiting from later technical progress and has fixed labour requirements (embodied technical progress, putty-clay). This has been treated by Johansen (1959), Kaldor and Mirrlees (1962), Phelps (1963), Robinson (1952), Salter (1960), Solow (1962) and others. There is much overlap between these writings, and we shall summarise the main conclusions arising from them without seeking to attribute each finding to its first author.

The complete solution of models involving the kind of assumptions described can present considerable mathematical difficulty. But if the appropriate assumptions are made about savings, etc., it is possible to derive models that resemble in general character those considered earlier in this survey and admit the possibility of growth at a steady rate. The steady-state characteristics of such models are not too difficult to analyse; it is their out-of-steady-state behaviour that tends to be intractable.

Let us assume for simplicity that there is no physical limit to the life of machines, so that their economic life is limited solely by obsolescence. Rises in running costs due to physical deterioration are assumed to be zero, or, alternatively, are assumed to be exactly balanced by elements in technical progress that *are* disembodied. (Models incorporating a mixture of embodied and disembodied technical progress have been investigated by Phelps (1962).)

The capital stock in use comprises machines of different vintages. The more recent vintages will have lower labour costs per unit of output, because they embody technical progress.[1] They therefore earn higher quasi-rents at any given time. The real wage rises over time, and the quasi-rents earned by any given old machine correspondingly fall. At the date when quasi-rents fall to zero the machines are scrapped. Machines thus have finite lives for economic reasons, not because of physical collapse.[2] The length of life of machines (written T) is a variable that adds a new dimension to the model as compared with non-vintage models. A condition of steady-state growth is plainly that T should be constant over time. The forces determining T will be considered shortly.

A further respect in which the conditions of steady growth on present assumptions differ from those in models considered earlier is that expectations are much more important. Because capital is non-malleable, an act of investment commits a hostage to fortune. The amount of investment and the technique chosen therefore depend not only on present circumstances but also on expectations about the future. This obvious-sounding conclusion does not apply in an extreme neo-classical world in which the rate of discount is always equal to the rate of profit, and there is only one commodity, disembodied technical progress, and completely malleable capital. In such a world any future developments that may reduce quasi-rents earned by a machine will also lower the quasi-rents earned by all other machines, since they are perfectly alike, and so will lower the general rate of profit, and hence the rate of discount; the present value of discounted future quasi-rents

[1] This is in conformity with the assumption of Harrod-neutrality, which, as noted above, permits the effects of technical progress to be shown as the multiplication of the labour term in the production function by a time term. Writing K_τ for the number of machines of vintage τ, Q_τ for the output from machines of vintage τ and L_τ for the labour employed on machines of vintage τ, we have as the *ex ante* production function for machines of each vintage

$$Q_\tau = f(K_\tau, A(\tau)L)$$

Ex post there are (in the present putty–clay case) fixed proportions, and the production function for each vintage becomes instead

$$Q_\tau = \min \begin{cases} aK_\tau \\ bA(\tau)L_\tau \end{cases}$$

[2] A differing treatment of depreciation is that of Johanssen (1959), who assumes that a proportion of machines of each vintage disappear from use in each period and then treats this proportion as a variable, so as to reflect decisions about obsolescence. This procedure does not seem entirely appropriate, because in the absence of *ex post* substitutability obsolescence will take place for all machines of a given vintage at the same moment of time.

will thus be unaffected. With embodied technical progress, however, there is no presumption that a fall in quasi-rents on existing machines will be matched by a fall in the general rate of profit. (This is true even if there is *ex post* substitutability between capital and labour.) Expectations thus determine the choice of technique at a given wage and the valuation of the capital stock. They therefore determine the path followed by the economy from any starting-point. Most vintage models assume that income is expected to grow at the steady-growth rate. Some models have been stated (Salter (1962), Svennilson (1963)) in which entrepreneurs are represented as expecting the wage-rate to stay constant, even though it is actually rising; for this to be compatible with steady growth it is, of course, necessary that entrepreneurs should be willing to persist in erroneous expectations.

What, then, can be said about the characteristics of steady growth on assumptions such as those described? The existence of the length of life of equipment, T, as an economic variable adds an " extensive " margin to whatever intensive margin there may be in the substitution of labour and capital.[1] Productivity per man depends on: (*a*) the capital intensity of the machines in use; (*b*) their average age. Equilibrium conditions must be satisfied at both margins. There is an obvious affinity to the Ricardian theory of rent. Different vintage machines are comparable to Ricardo's acres of differing fertility. The machine on the margin of being scrapped earns no quasi-rent and corresponds to Ricardo's no-rent land. Wage-costs on the marginal machine absorb the whole value of the product. The wage of labour is therefore equal to the average product of labour on the oldest machine in use. This can be regarded as the marginal product of labour, since, if the supply of labour were slightly reduced, competition for labour would drive up wages and make the marginal plant unprofitable; this plant would be scrapped, and the output that it formerly produced would constitute the net reduction in output in the economy as a whole due to the reduction in the supply of labour.

The condition of steady-state equilibrium with respect to the life of machines is thus that when the economy is growing at the steady-state rate quasi-rents become and are expected to become zero at the end of T units of time. T depends: (1) on the rate of increase of wage-rates, which in the steady state must be equal to the rate of increase of income per head; (2) on the proportion of wage-costs to total output on the machines when new; this will depend (except under Cobb–Douglas) on the capital intensity chosen for new machines, and the steady-state levels of capital intensity and of T

---

[1] Because of the extra dimension offered by variations in the scrapping date, steady growth may be possible in conditions where it would not be with disembodied technical progress—for example, with a proportional saving function, fixed coefficients and an exogenous rate of population growth. In this case there is still a limit in one direction, since scrapping is a way of absorbing saving rather than a way of economising on it. The Harrod–Domar problem of divergence of natural and warranted rates will thus arise if the natural rate of growth still exceeds the warranted rate even when no scrapping on account of obsolescence occurs at all and machines are kept for ever.

are thus variables that are simultaneously determined.[1] With constant population, the labour needed to man the machines that are currently being built in each period is made available by the scrapping of machines T years old. (Machines of intermediate age do not surrender any of their labour force, despite the rise in wages, because of the absence of *ex post* substitution.) A consequence of this is that under steady growth, with constant population, the labour-force must be divided equally between the different vintages. The more modern machines have lower labour requirements, because they embody technical progress, but they are more numerous, because they are the fruit of saving out of a higher income.

The capital intensity chosen will depend on the level of the wage, the expected rate of increase of wages and the profit rate (discount rate). The condition of equilibrium is that the discounted stream of the extra revenue to be had over the life of the machine from choosing a machine requiring one more man to operate it should be equal to the discounted sum of the stream of his wages.[2] The level of the wage is determined in the manner stated above (given the capital stock and the level of employment) by the average product of labour on the oldest machine. The rate of increase of wages is determined by the steady-state rate of growth. The rate of profit, if there is a classical saving function, can be determined directly from the rate of growth and the profit-earners' propensity to save; with a proportional saving function it is determined in a more complicated way by the simultaneous working of the whole system (including the requirement that the growth rate must be equal to the saving propensity divided by the value–capital–output ratio).

It may be noted that on present assumptions the wage will *not* normally be equal to the marginal product at the intensive margin, as obtained by differentiating the *ex ante* production function, that is to say the extra output to be had from employing one additional man on the new machines currently being built and designing these machines accordingly. Because of

---

[1] Using the same notation as in the footnote on p. 61, $w(t) =$ wage prevailing at time t, $T =$ the age of machines on the margin of scrapping, we have

$$Q_\tau - L_\tau w(\tau + T) = 0$$

Under steady growth the wage rises at an exponential rate:

$$w(\tau + T) = w(\tau)e^{gT}$$

and solving for T we have

$$T = \frac{1}{g} \log \left(\frac{Q_\tau}{w(\tau)L_\tau} \right)$$

The expression inside the bracket is the reciprocal of the ratio of wage-costs to total output at the time when the machine is new, and the equation therefore expresses T as a function of this ratio and of the rate of growth, g.

[2] In the Kaldor model this condition is replaced by the requirement that the undiscounted sum of quasi-rents per man over a specific pay-off period (h) should equal the cost of investment per man. This does not affect the steady-state structure of the model, but it may affect its comparative dynamics.

the absence of *ex post* substitution, a decision to do this creates a commitment to go on employing the additional man throughout the life of the machine. If wages are expected to rise, the current wage will therefore be less than the marginal product at the intensive margin. How much less depends on the expected rate of increase of wages and also on the rate of interest.

We may now consider the comparative dynamics of the model. In steady growth the level of the propensity to save does not affect the rate of growth but does affect the absolute level of income and wages, exactly as in non-vintage neo-classical models.[1] It can now do this by affecting the average age of machines in use as well as or instead of by affecting their capital intensity. In the steady state it will not necessarily work in *both* of these ways (though an *increase* in *s* will necessarily both lower the average age and increase the capital intensity of machines during the transition from one steady state to another). It may perfectly well happen, for example, that the higher wage and lower profit rate associated with a higher *s* causes the capital intensity of machines to be higher by just such an amount as to leave unchanged the ratio of wage costs to output on new machines. Since this ratio, together with the rate of increase of wages, is what determines *T*, *T* will then be independent of *s*, and a high *s* will conduce to a high level of income only by its effect on the intensive margin. It is even possible in some cases that *T* will vary in the *same* direction as *s*.[2] The less scope there is for substitution at the intensive margin, the more tendency is there for *T* to vary inversely with *s* under steady growth. In the extreme case of fixed coefficients *ex ante* as well as *ex post* ("clay-clay"), *T* and *s* must obviously vary inversely: the higher *s*, the more investment there is in each period, so more labour must be released to man the new machines, and the vintage being scrapped must therefore be larger, and hence more recent in date (Phelps (1963), Matthews (1964)).

Similarly complicated are the effects of variations in other parameters, such as the rate of population growth. In special cases the effects may be obvious: for example, with fixed coefficients a high rate of population growth must mean a high *T*. But in general the effects of the rates of population growth and technical progress on *T* cannot be ascertained without specifying the details of the model. Moreover, the average age of equipment, and hence the average output per worker, depends on the rate of growth as well as on *T*. Thus if two countries have the same *T* but differing rates of growth, the one with the faster growth rate will have the newer equipment

[1] The proposition that in steady growth the level of consumption is highest when the profit rate is equal to the growth rate has also been demonstrated for vintage models (Robinson (1962), Black (1962)).

[2] This will happen if the *ex ante* production function is Cobb–Douglas. Instead of getting, for a given difference in wage between two steady states, an exactly proportional difference in capital intensity, leaving labour's share on new machines constant, as would happen in a non-vintage model, what happens is that there is a somewhat *greater* than proportional difference in capital intensity, because the higher wage is associated with a lower discount rate, and hence more weight is given to the future, when labour will be dearer.

on the average, because the new generations of machines will be more numerous relatively to the old ones.

The behaviour of these models when off the path of steady growth is much more complicated than in the standard neo-classical case, since the initial conditions to be specified include the number of machines built at each past date. Echo-effects and oscillations are therefore likely. The marginal product of investment can likewise not be defined without full specification of these conditions. Lack of *ex post* substitutability causes problems to arise in this connection, even in the absence of technical progress (Solow (1962), Robinson (1962)).

We turn now to the case nearer to neo-classical orthodoxy, where technical progress is embodied but there is the same scope for substitution between labour and capital *ex post* as there is *ex ante*. This has been studied by Solow (1960), (1962a), (1963) and Phelps (1962) on the further assumption of Cobb–Douglas. Output from the machines of each vintage is then given by the function

$$Q_\tau = Ae^{g\tau} K_\tau^\alpha L_\tau^{1-\alpha}$$

The Cobb–Douglas assumption permits certain notable simplifications. Old machines are never scrapped entirely (except because of physical deterioration), but the labour attached to them dwindles asymptotically to zero as wages rise over time. In each period some labour is withdrawn from *all* existing machines in order to man the new ones. The marginal product of labour is kept equal on machines of all vintages. Technical progress can be regarded as consisting of a progressive reduction in the cost of producing machines, or, alternatively, as a progressive improvement of the quality of machines. A machine of vintage t is equivalent to $(1 + g)$ machines of vintage $t - 1$. Technical progress is " capital-augmenting " (above, p. 52) in the vintage sense. It is then possible to derive a measure of " equivalent capital," J, by adding up the number of machines of different vintage, weighted according to their vintage.[1] A production function $Y = J^\alpha L^{1-\alpha}$ can then be written with no explicit term representing technical progress. J rises relatively to Y over time, and a steady growth solution is possible with a constant rate of growth of Y, constant distribution of income, and constant rate of interest. The average age of the capital stock under steady growth turns out to be independent of the propensity to save (Phelps (1962)), and the increase in the absolute level of income made possible in steady growth conditions by a rise in s is therefore the same as it would be if technical progress were disembodied.

These conclusions, including the last one, depend a good deal on the Cobb–Douglas assumption, which is a special case of the assumption that technical progress is of the capital-augmenting type. Not much work

[1] Under the steady growth J can be shown to be equal to the market valuation of the capital stock that will result from perfect foresight (Solow (1960), p. 100).

has yet been done on the properties of models of this kind with different production functions. If technical progress is not capital-augmenting, embodied technical progress cannot be represented as exclusively an improvement in the quality of machines, and the machines of different vintage cannot be aggregated into a single measure of equivalent capital.

Some econometric calculations have been made on the assumption of embodied technical progress, *ex post* substitutability and Cobb–Douglas. If the economy had actually been in a state of steady growth the rate of technical progress to be inferred from the record would be the same whether technical progress were embodied or disembodied. However, the statistics for the United States do not exactly correspond to the steady-growth pattern, and it appears that the best fit in the embodied model shows a somewhat lower rate of technical progress, and hence a higher contribution of capital accumulation to growth than has usually been found with disembodied models (above, p. 54). It is also found that the benefit from an increase in *s* is felt more *quickly* than in embodied models. However, the assumption of *ex post* substitutability along a Cobb–Douglas function seems to be too restrictive for these results to be useful for purposes other than illustration.

It is to be noted that throughout this discussion of vintage models we have been assuming perfect competition. Without perfect competition the basic principle that machines are not scrapped until they yield zero quasi-rents is no longer valid. The criteria often laid down in other contexts in discussions of scrapping policy, such as " scrap if total costs with the new machine are less than variable costs with the old," are, by contrast, based on the assumption that the total output of the firm is limited. An area in which there appears to be both need and scope for further development is the development of vintage models in which more explicit attention is paid to the factors limiting the size of firms in an imperfect competition context.

One important consequence of the vintage approach is that emphasis is shifted from net saving and investment to gross saving and investment. Replacement of one machine by another does not leave the *status quo* unaffected. Most of the models referred to assume a constant ratio of gross saving to gross income (or gross profit). This assumption is made largely for the sake of convenience, since the level of net investment, in the sense of the net addition to the capital stock in value terms, that results from any level of gross investment is something that cannot be calculated without solving the whole system. The same applies to the measurement of net income. But the difference between this assumption and the more usual assumption of a constant net saving ratio (whether out of income or out of profit) is, of course, a difference of substance, susceptible in principle to empirical testing.

II.4. *Learning*

Technical progress is an increase in one particular kind of knowledge or skill. Light on its causes may therefore be looked for in the findings of other social sciences concerned with the causes of increases in knowledge of other kinds, or in knowledge generally.   One such area of study, which has not yet had much systematic attention from economists, is the theory and history of scientific discovery.   Another which has recently attracted attention and seems likely to attract more in the future, is the theory of learning in psychology.

The view of technical progress as a learning process is part of the general move away from the crude notion of economic decision-making as a process in which the entrepreneur instantly perceives and adopts the best line of action in any given situation.   Instead he is seen as perpetually groping in a mist of uncertainty, gradually and imperfectly learning his way on the basis of experience accruing to him.   There are differences of opinion among psychologists about the exact way in which experience conduces to learning and as to the importance of experience relative to other factors, such as motivation and insight.   Moreover, learning theorists have mainly been concerned with the learning process in an individual (human or animal), whereas technical progress is eminently a social phenomenon.   But it is common ground that experience is important.   This provides a link with economies of scale.   It supplies a possible cause of economies of scale quite different from the indivisibilities, etc., of traditional economic theory.

The hypothesis is that improvements in technique do not become available from the passage of time as such but by familiarity with the problems involved.   Learning is the product of experience.   If experience in this context can be measured by the amount of a commodity produced, then the higher is production, the greater will be the opportunities for learning and the faster the rate of technical progress.

The consequences are analogous to increasing returns in the usual sense rather than identical.   In the first place the knowledge gained from working on a large scale is not forgotten if the scale is later reduced.   The economies are therefore irreversible, as envisaged by Marshall and by Shove (1942).   In the second place, it is not productivity that is a function of scale but the rate of increase of productivity.   In the third place, scale or experience is more naturally measured by the sum of all past output than by the level of current output.   If the economy settles down to a steady state of exponential growth these two measures come to the same thing, but they imply different behaviour when the economy is off the steady-state path.

Much the most fully worked-out growth model along these lines is that of Arrow (1962); an earlier model was that of Haavelmo (1954).   Arrow uses a vintage approach, with fixed coefficients.   Labour requirements per unit of output on new machines fall over time as experience permits a better design of machines.   Consistently with the emphasis on new machines as the vehicle of progress, Arrow takes " experience " to be measured by the integral of past gross investment in the economy rather than by the integral of past output.   Following a formula that has been found to measure the benefits of experience in the production of airframes, he writes the function expressing the labour requirements of the latest machine in a specific form, $G^{-\mu}$, where G is the total number of machines ever produced, and μ is a parameter, $0 < \mu < 1$. No technical progress takes place other than that embodied in new machines and shown by this function. An act of investment does not raise the productivity of labour working on existing machines, but it raises the productivity of labour working on any machines that are built subsequently, since it raises G. The private benefit of investment is therefore less than the social benefit.

Arrow shows that, given the appropriate pattern of expectations, output in his model is capable of steady growth at the rate $\dfrac{n}{1-\mu}$, where n is the rate of population growth. As in the straightforward increasing-returns case (p. 55), the steady-state rate of growth is thus a *multiple* of the rate of population growth and is zero if that is zero. The reason is plain: steady growth calls for an equal rate of increase of G and output, but, since the rise in productivity is smaller in proportion than the rise in G that causes it (μ being less than one), this would not be maintainable if there were no other source of growth, and the economy would progressively slow down. (The case of $\mu > 1$ resembles the case of increasing returns to capital alone mentioned on p. 55.) Population growth provides a source of increase in output and experience additional to that built into the investment learning process itself. Growth could alternatively be maintained at a steady rate if there were some strictly exogenous technical progress going on as well as learning.

The concept of learning from experience is perhaps more naturally applied to an individual industry or industrial process rather than to the economy as a whole, as is done in Arrow's model. The airframe case itself is of this nature: the fall observed in costs is a function of experience in producing one particular kind of airframe, not airframes in general, far less industrial output in general. So also is the much-quoted Horndal case described by Lundberg (1961). Where a single process or product is concerned, a slowing-down over time in the benefits from learning is to be expected, as improvements become more difficult to find. This is most obvious where the learning in question is not the discovery of totally new methods but the diffusion of a particular improvement through an industry. The diffusion has an upper limit of 100%. Research on the rate of diffusion of new ideas has, as expected, revealed a logistic pattern, with the number of firms adopting the improvement first increasing then diminishing as the limit is approached [1] (Mansfield (1961)). The logistic curve can be regarded as exponential growth modified by the existence of a ceiling. It has been suggested (Svennilson (1963)) that the pattern of increase in output over

---

[1] Investment in a new process by an imitator contributes to the advancement of knowledge not by revealing an original idea but by publicising an existing idea and hastening its adoption by others.

time from a given machine resulting from learning may follow a similar pattern: accelerating increase at first, as teething troubles are overcome, followed by tailing off (this, of course, is different from Arrow's strict vintage model, in which output from a machine is fixed once it has been produced). Schumpeter's picture of the invention–innovation–imitation sequence is similar. In Schumpeter there are limits to the scope for improvement in any one area, but the steady growth of the system is maintained by the exogenous infusion of totally new ideas. In the same spirit numbers of authors have noted a tendency for output in individual industries to follow a logistic path over time, without there necessarily being any similar tendency in the economy as a whole. If this is interpreted as the result of a learning process subject to diminishing returns within each industry, learning is responsible for part of the increase in production over time, but an essential part is also played by the exogenous infusion of new ideas and the development of new industries. (On this reckoning new products may play a crucial part in growth, with consequent difficulties for aggregative measures and models.)

A notion of this sort underlies Kaldor and Mirrlees' treatment of technical progress, which is, in addition, based on the vintage approach. They suggest that the basic functional relationship (at least in the long period) is not a production function, expressing output per man as an increasing function of capital per man, but a technical progress function, expressing the rate of increase of output per man on the latest machine as an increasing function of the rate of increase of investment per man. (The hypothesis thus relates to the increase in productivity on machines of latest vintage.) Investment benefits productivity largely because it provides opportunities for learning new methods. (Learning is thus made a function of the rate of increase of gross investment $(\dot{I}/I)$, rather than of the integral of gross investment as in Arrow.) Kaldor and Mirrlees draw the function as in Fig. II.4 ($\dot{P}/P$ = rate of increase in productivity per worker on latest machine). In steady growth the two rates of growth must be the same, so equilibrium is reached at the point of intersection of the technical progress function and the 45° line.

The technical progress function in Kaldor's treatment is non-linear, showing a diminishing rate of response of productivity increase to investment increase. This is not the same as diminishing returns to capital in the ordinary sense. The underlying notion is that technical progress has two elements: an exogenous increase in ideas, and the extension and exploitation of these ideas by learning. More investment permits the stock of ideas currently available to be more thoroughly explored and developed, but there are limits to their potentialities; hence the tendency to diminishing returns. An increase in the stock of capital at a steady rate permits a greater increase in productivity than an equal increase in capital carried out at an uneven pace, because in the latter event too many resources relatively would be

devoted to the exploration of the ideas available in one period and not enough
to the ideas available in the next.[1] It is not now possible to derive a production function from the technical progress function, because productivity at
any time depends not only on the stock of capital but also on the rate at
which it was installed. The technical progress function is not integrable
(Black (1962)). The implications of these ideas remain to be studied, because

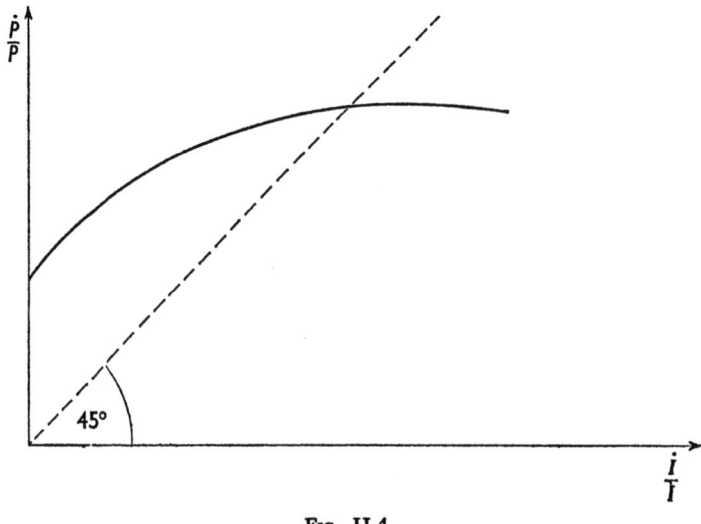

Fig. II.4

in the algebraic statement of his model Kaldor uses as an approximation a
linear technical progress function which *can* be integrated into a production
function, and the production function turns out to be identical to Cobb–
Douglas save for one respect.[2] The special properties of his technical progress function therefore play no part in the final working of his model. As far
as the steady-state properties of the system are concerned, it is plain that the
curvature of the technical progress function cannot be significant, since if the
curve is smooth it can be approximated by a straight line in the neighbourhood of its intersection with the 45° line.

Kaldor (1961) first expressed this technical progress function in non-
vintage terms: $\dot{Y}/Y = F(\dot{K}/K)$ (population constant). It has been shown
by Kennedy (1964) that the Kaldor technical progress function in this version
can also be derived from assumptions in which the learning process plays no
explicit part. Kennedy postulates that the improvement in technical

---

[1] Kaldor also speaks (1962) of the limited capacity of the human mind to take in new ideas
over a given period of time. This seems to be a rather different point.

[2] The difference is that in integrating the technical progress function to obtain a production
function the constant of integration remains undetermined, and is therefore fixed by the initial
conditions. This means that two countries differing only in their starting-points will have permanently different income per head. Countries that start backward have to learn by experience and
cannot take a short cut.

knowledge between two periods offers the producer a range of alternatives between reducing capital input and reducing labour input and that he chooses between these alternatives by maximising profits in the light of relative factor prices.   On the assumption that the function describing these alternatives is uniquely given and of a particular form, he reaches a result identical with the Kaldor technical progress function.

From the formal point of view the Kaldor technical progress function can be regarded as an extension of Cobb–Douglas in a particular direction: Cobb–Douglas implies that the slope of the technical progress function $(\partial(\dot{Y}/Y)/\partial(\dot{K}/K))$ is constant in all circumstances, Kaldor has it varying with $\dot{K}/K$.   Both have in common the assumption that this slope is independent of K/Y.   Without this assumption a unique technical progress function relating $\dot{Y}/Y$ and $\dot{K}/K$ cannot be drawn.[1]   Production functions of the orthodox kind that have Harrod-neutral technical progress but are not Cobb–Douglas imply that $\partial(\dot{Y}/Y)/\partial(\dot{K}/K)$ varies with K/Y but is independent of $\dot{K}/K$.   They can therefore not be differentiated into a unique technical progress function, and the equivalent to the technical progress function is a family of straight lines with different slopes, each corresponding to a different K/Y.   Non-Cobb–Douglas Harrod-neutral production functions, on the one hand, and the Kaldor technical progress function, on the other, can thus both be regarded as extensions of Cobb–Douglas, but in different directions, making $\partial(\dot{Y}/Y)/\partial(\dot{K}/K)$ dependent on K/Y and $\dot{K}/K$ respectively.   The underlying visions of the nature of technical progress are, of course, entirely different, but both permit steady growth with constant shares, because in steady growth both K/Y and $\dot{K}/K$ are constant.   Kennedy, indeed, regarded his derivation of the Kaldor technical progress function as amounting to a demonstration of how there might exist a systematic tendency to neutral technical progress.

An important feature of models like Kaldor's and Arrow's is the divergence of private and social marginal net product.   Investment has external benefits, because the extra knowledge it leads to cannot be fully appropriated by the investor, and he therefore receives less than the value of his social marginal net product.   If reality corresponds to these models econometric calculations of capital's contribution to growth based on actual factor shares will therefore lead to an underestimate.   A further consequence is that investment in a competitive economy will tend to fall below the socially optimum level.[2]

In manna-type neo-classical models of technical progress those responsible for technical progress not merely get less than their marginal products: they do not get any reward at all.   Either technical progress occurs completely effortlessly or else those who have undertaken the effort find their rewards

---

[1] In Kennedy's formulation this assumption takes the form that the shape of the function relating $-\frac{1}{L} \cdot \frac{dL}{dt}$ and $-\frac{1}{K} \cdot \frac{dK}{dt}$ is independent of K/L.

[2] If learning is a function of output or its integral rather than investment the labour supply (participation rate) may also be below the social optimum.

immediately and fully bid away as a result of competitors imitating their ideas. If the latter were really the case the amount of resources devoted to the advancement of knowledge would certainly fall gravely below the socially desirable level. The unrealism of such extreme assumptions has been generally recognised in connection with the problem of expenditure on research. In the neo-classical model this is unlike expenditure on physical capital, because the benefits cannot be wholly appropriated by the investor; but it is unlike manna in that the rate at which the extra knowledge accrues depends on decisions about how much to spend seeking it. The implication of the learning by experience approach is that *all* investment has to some extent the characteristics of investment in research, because it contributes to the advancement of knowledge. This assumes, of course, that the additions to knowledge that result from the activities of one firm become available to other firms. If this is not so, and if in addition firms are aware of their own learning functions, the conclusions that follow are much more orthodox. (This is well discussed by Weizsäcker (1964).)

Before leaving the question of learning, reference may be made to a hypothesis which points in the opposite direction. The hypothesis of the " disadvantage of an early start " suggests that old capital embodying old methods hinders the adoption of new methods and is worse than no capital at all (Frankel (1955), Gordon (1956), Kindleberger (1961)).[1] The arguments for and against this paradoxical view will not be recited here; they depend largely on the extent and nature of market imperfections. However, one case where the hypothesis is unobjectionable in principle is if old capital has to be demolished to make room for the new and demolition has a cost. What is interesting in the present context is the analogy to this in the sphere of know-how. Managers and workers who are very experienced in old methods of production may find it more difficult to learn improved methods than they would if they had no experience at all: there is a cost of demolishing their obsolete intellectual equipment. This tendency is likely to be more important relatively to its opposite, learning by experience, if technical progress is of a revolutionary rather than an evolutionary nature. Not much has been done towards incorporating this idea in formal models. (Some suggestions towards this end are contained in Ames and Rosenberg (1963).)

II.5. *Factor Scarcities and Technical Progress*

We make no attempt to survey the large and rapidly growing literature of the forces affecting the rate of technical progress more generally; this would be a subject for a survey on its own (see Carter and Williams (1957),

---

[1] Similar but not identical is the hypothesis that forcible destruction of old capital (*e.g.*, by enemy action in war) may be ultimately to a country's advantage. This hypothesis asserts that it is advantageous to lose capital; the early-start hypothesis that it is advantageous never to have had it. The war hypothesis can be reconciled more easily with the learning approach, in so far as the knowledge gained in the acquisition of the old capital is not lost when it is destroyed, and its destruction encourages a high level of investment, which then leads to new learning.

(1958), (1959), Nelson (1959), NBER (1962)). Much of this literature is concerned with micro-aspects, such as the effects of monopoly on technical progress and the optimum allocation of research funds; it therefore does not bear directly on theories of growth in the economy as a whole, though it may have important indirect bearing.

But one group of hypotheses in this area, in addition to the learning hypothesis, does have a direct bearing and has been drawn on by growth theorists: hypotheses based on the idea that technical progress is stimulated by shortage of labour (or other factors). If true, this has consequences like those of induced changes in labour supply (above, p. 56). It means that the natural and warranted rates of growth may be brought into equality by flexibility in the natural rate as well as, or instead of, by flexibility in the warranted rate.

This is a group of hypotheses rather than a single hypothesis, because "scarcity of labour " does not specify scarcity relative to what. Vagueness on this point is the source of some confusion in the literature. Three chief variants may be distinguished.

(i) Technical progress may be stimulated by *a scarcity of all factors, including labour, relatively to demand*. The full-employment assumption rules out this possibility in a large proportion of formal growth models. Where this assumption is not made, the hypothesis can play a part, as it does in Mrs. Robinson's model.[1] It has also been much canvassed in empirical discussion of post-war growth performance, especially with reference to the allegedly unfavourable effects of deflation on the rate of growth in the United Kingdom and in the United States (Eckstein (1959), Beckerman (1962)). In its extreme form it amounts to the assertion that production can always be increased if the pressure to do so is sufficient: " We managed to do the impossible in war-time, so why not in peace-time too? " This leads to a demand-dominated theory of growth. Supply can look after itself, at least within the limits relevant in practice.[2] The Harrod–Domar knot is cut in drastic fashion. This view of induced technical progress can be based on a number of considerations. One possible basis lies in the existence, even

[1] " . . . when the urge to accumulate . . . is high relative to the growth of the labour force, technical progress has a tendency to raise the ' natural ' rate of growth to make room for it, so that near-enough steady growth, with near-enough full employment, may be realised " (Robinson (1963), p. 410). She adds: " In the converse case, the existence of a growing surplus of labour, though it may slow down technical progress, cannot be relied upon to bring the ' natural ' rate of growth down to the sluggish rate of accumulation."

[2] It has been maintained, however, within the context of this general approach, that supply conditions *are* important because of their effect on demand in an open economy. Slow growth of productivity relative to other countries causes an adverse balance of payments, and this leads to demand deflation because of government policy. On this reckoning rapid productivity increase is important, not because it removes a physical ceiling on output but because it enables a country to get an adequate share of total world demand. An implication is that different government policy towards demand would justify itself by speeding up growth and thereby raising productivity and curing the balance-of-payments trouble (so long as the benefits of rising productivity are not neutralised by wage increase) (Lamfalussy (1963), especially Chap. IX).

in advanced economies, of certain low-productivity sectors, such as agriculture and domestic service. A more general argument is that if there are unemployed resources production can be increased by existing methods without a rise in costs, so entrepreneurs are half-hearted in looking for improvements. (This implies that the urge to expand output is stronger than the urge to reduce costs.) Likewise strong demand for labour will help to overcome the tendency of labour to resist innovations for fear of redundancy. It is also argued that high demand promotes growth by encouraging capital formation through its effects on the distribution of income; but this, of course, on normal assumptions will not affect the steady-state growth rate.

(ii) Another variant of the labour-scarcity thesis is that a high rate of technical progress is induced by *scarcity of labour relative to capital*. In so far as this means that capital accumulation stimulates technical progress, it has already been discussed. Another possibility is that for technological reasons there is more scope for technical progress in the economy as a whole at high than at low values of K/Y (just as technical progress is generally believed to be faster in capital-intensive *industries* such as manufacturing than it is, for example, in services).[1]

A rather different basis for the hypothesis is that scarcity of labour relative to capital influences the *motivation* of entrepreneurs. This idea is implicit in many statements of the labour-scarcity thesis. The reason may be that labour scarcity depresses the rate of profit on capital and so makes cost-reducing innovation a matter of urgent necessity to entrepreneurs. In an ultra-neo-classical world, where entrepreneurs are merely co-ordinating agents who hire labour and capital, there is no obvious reason why their motivation should be affected one way or the other by the relative scarcity of the hired factors. The assumption is, of course, that the owners of capital are the entrepreneurs and have the responsibility for making technical advances; hence the asymmetry. Some sort of backward-rising supply curve of entrepreneurial effort is also assumed; otherwise the scarcity of labour might have the opposite effect and make the entrepreneurs throw in the sponge, an ambivalence familiar in a different context in discussions of the effects on efficiency of the severity of competition. If this argument is correct it implies an external unappropriated benefit from capital accumulation separate from the various other such benefits already mentioned: it puts entrepreneurs on their mettle.

(iii) The hypothesis that technical progress is stimulated by *scarcity of labour relatively to land* has a long history as a suggested explanation of high productivity in the United States and other countries of recent European settlement. A famous statement of it is that of Rothbarth (1946); recently Habakkuk (1962) has provided a very thorough though mainly non-

---

[1] This will mean that technical progress is not Harrod-neutral over the entire length of the production function; but it does not rule out the possibility that technical progress is Harrod-neutral *locally* and hence compatible with steady growth.

statistical survey and analysis of the evidence relating to it and kindred hypotheses.   Rothbarth argued that the open frontier in nineteenth-century America made wages high and provided an inducement for the adoption of more efficient labour-saving techniques in manufacturing.   This idea does not appear to have been incorporated in any formal growth model, and indeed its logic in theory is not entirely clear, as Habakkuk shows.   Abundance of land does not automatically make labour scarce relative to capital, which is presumably what is needed to induce labour-saving in manufacturing: a further postulate is needed that land is more substitutable for capital than it is for labour (farms drain off labour, but do not need much capital). Supposing this is correct, it still does not lead to a fast rate of technical *progress* unless one of the arguments under (ii) above is valid.   It might, perhaps, be better to think of the open frontier as having made labour scarce relative to entrepreneurship rather than relative to capital, so that entrepreneurs were forced to exert themselves to keep going.

III. LINEAR ECONOMIC MODELS

Introduction

In much of the foregoing it has been supposed that only a single good was used in production.   Hence problems of the measurement of capital can be avoided.   In this part of the survey we shall always suppose that at least two different goods are used in production.   But everything that holds for such a case can also be shown to be true when the number of different goods is *n*.   We restrict ourselves to the case of two goods for expositional purposes only.

We first examine Neumann's model (Neumann (1938)) without consumption.   Here labour is paid a predetermined subsistence wage and is in perfectly elastic supply at that wage.   Neumann was concerned with the existence and properties of balanced growth paths expanding at the highest possible rate.   As such this appears like an optimisation problem.   But Neumann showed that associated with such a path there are prices and an interest rate which, if they ruled, would lead a competitive economy to expand along this path.   It thus turns out that the Neumann model may be of descriptive interest also.   The problem of measuring " capital " never arises. For production possibilities are specified in terms of concrete objects and alternative activities.   However, on the equilibrium path a relationship can be established between the rate of return of spending £1 on capital goods at the Neumann prices and the Neumann rate of interest.   All these matters are fully discussed in Section III.1.

In the simple Neumann model all " surpluses " are reinvested, and it is thus similar to an extreme classical savings assumption.   If one drops the hypothesis of a given subsistence wage the real wage becomes an unknown, and we gain one degree of freedom.   However, we may continue to postulate

that only capitalists save. This kind of model has been investigated by
Robinson (1956), (1960) and Morishima (1960). It proceeds as follows:
We know that the balanced growth rate of the system must equal the rate
of profit times the capitalists' saving propensity. Suppose we wish the
balanced growth rate to be equal to the exogenously given rate of population
growth. Then we know what the rate of profit must be. One of the unknowns has now been fixed, and we can now find what the relative prices
(including that of labour) and the composition of output and machines must
be in order for the system to grow at the predetermined rate. For most
normal cases a solution exists. One could, however, proceed in another
and symmetrical way. For any arbitrarily fixed wage we can find the
Neumann growth rate and so the rate of interest. The growth rate thus
found will be a continuous function of the wage fixed over a certain range.
Now vary the wage until the associated growth rate is the full-employment
rate. As a mathematical procedure of timeless solving of equations, the
two procedures come to the same thing. Viewed as an actual dynamic process in time they do not. All these matters are fully discussed in Section III.2
and again in the Leontief model, Section III.3, which is a special case of the
construction here considered. If the classical savings assumption is replaced
by the proportional one we may again proceed by specifying either the rate
of interest or the wage, finding the associated growth rate, and continue this
iteration until a full-employment solution is found. The latter will exist
for a certain range of growth values. However, this and the actual dynamics
(as opposed to equation solving) have not yet been rigorously investigated.

We next turn to an examination of the stability of such systems (Section
III.5). We confine ourselves here to the Leontief system and to a model
proposed by Samuelson and Solow (1953).

The last two sections are concerned with efficient accumulation. The
first part surveys Malinvaud's work (Malinvaud (1953)), on efficient paths of
infinite duration. The second concerns itself with optimum paths of finite
duration (turnpikes). The " neo-classical theorem " is re-examined in the
light of these efficiency propositions. It is shown that a social rate of return
on investment, calculated at the efficiency prices, can be found, and that it
can be brought into proper relation with the efficiency rate of interest.

The models to be considered now differ from the foregoing in making
somewhat special assumptions about the " book of blueprints." As the
heading indicates, it is supposed not only that there are constant returns to
scale but also that productive processes are additive. On the other hand,
we no longer suppose that the production functions are smooth and differentiable.

III.1. *The Neumann Model*

We suppose that there are only two goods, which we label " 1 " and
" 2." To produce anything at all requires labour, and the unit of labour

has to be paid amounts of the two goods in fixed proportion if it is to be available at all.   On the other hand, any amount of labour can be had.   It follows that if, say, q units of labour are required to produce output by some technique we can convert this into equivalent amounts of commodities 1 or 2 needed to " produce " q units of labour.

There are a (finite) number of productive processes available.   A process, L_i, is characterised as follows: one unit of L_i requires an input a_{i_1} of good 1 and a_{i_2} of good 2 to produce b_{i_1} unit of good 1 and b_{i_2} units of good 2 *one period later*.   If we use λ_i units of process L_i our input requirement is multiplied by λ_i, as is the output of each of the goods.   Where two processes are used in conjunction, the total input requirement is the sum of the input requirements of each of them, and similarly for the output.   In the earliest version of the Neumann model (1938) it was assumed that all $a_{ij} + b_{ij}$ are strictly positive.   However, due to the work of Kemeny, Morgenstern and Thompson (1956) this unattractive assumption can be relaxed.   We now only require that the economy has the following properties:

1. Every process uses some input, *i.e.*, in our simple case one of a_{i_1} and a_{i_2} at least is non-zero for each i.

2. It is possible to produce each good by one process, *i.e.*, b_{i_1} and b_{i_2} are non-zero for some i.

3. It is possible to dispose of unwanted goods costlessly.   Let us now state the first part of the problem posed by Von Neumann.

Let $\lambda_i(t)$ be the level at which the ith activity is used at t and $\lambda_i(t + 1)$ the level at $t + 1$.   In the nature of things $\lambda_i(t)$, $\lambda_i(t + 1) \geq 0$ all i.

Then abstracting from stocks and gifts the total supply of good 1 available at $(t + 1)$ is $\sum b_{i_1}\lambda_i(t)$ and of good 2, $\sum b_{i_2}\lambda_i(t)$.   The total demand for each of the goods is $\sum a_{i_1}\lambda_i(t + 1)$ and $\sum a_{i_2}\lambda_i(t + 1)$.   Now if we could find some number α such that

$$\lambda_i(t + 1) = \alpha\lambda_i(t) \text{ all } i \text{ and } t$$

the output of all goods would change at the same rate $(\alpha - 1)$, and the ratio in which goods are produced would remain constant.   To see this let x_i be the amount of the ith good available at t and y_i the amount available at $t + 1$.   Then the condition gives:

$$x_j = \sum b_{ij}\lambda_i(t) = \frac{1}{\alpha}\sum b_{ij}\lambda_i(t + 1) = \frac{1}{\alpha}y_j \qquad j = 1, 2 \text{ and so } y_j = \alpha x_j \atop \alpha \neq 0$$

Our problem is to find the largest α such that

Demand for good 1 at $t + 1 = \alpha\sum a_{i_1}\lambda(t) \leq \sum b_{i_1}\lambda_i(t) = $ availability of 1 at $t + 1$

Demand for good 2 at $t + 1 = \alpha\sum a_{i_2}\lambda_i(t) \leq \sum b_{i_2}\lambda_i(t) = $ availability of 2 at $t + 1$

where $\lambda_i(t) \geq 0$.   We note that solving this problem will yield not only maximum α but also the ratios in which the activities are to be used. For we note that if for any α, $\lambda = (\lambda_1, \ldots \lambda_m)$ satisfies the constraints so will $k\lambda$, $k > 0$ and so only the ratios of the λ_i's will be determined.

It is not hard to show that our problem has a solution. Because of what has been said above we may restrict ourselves to the set of non-negatives λ_i's which add up to one. We call this set S. Looking at the constraints, we see that setting $\alpha = 0$ and each $\lambda_i = 1/m$, we have a feasible solution, since by assumption for some i, $b_{i_1} > 0$ and some j, $b_{j_2} > 0$. Moreover, the λ so constructed belongs to S. Therefore F, the set of feasible α and λ belonging to S, is not empty. By a simple but technical argument, best discussed by Howe (1960), it can be shown that F must contain a maximum α say a^* and an associated λ belonging to S. The reader can proceed as Gale (1960) suggests: we already know that a possible solution exists for $\lambda = 0$. Since for each i either a_{i_1} or $a_{i_2} > 0$, it is obvious that for some α large enough no solution exists. By the argument referred to we can show that as α increases from zero the limiting values of α^* and λ^* belong to the set F, and so a maximum can be attained in this set.

Let us briefly investigate the structure of the solution by means of some elementary geometry.

Take any arbitrary two processes, say the rth and the sth. In the negative quadrant of Fig. III.1 we have shown the inputs each of the processes requires if $\alpha = 1$ and they are each used at unit level. We label the two vectors $a^r(\alpha = 1)$ and $a^s(\alpha = 1)$. Their components give the inputs required (*e.g.*, the components of $a^r(\alpha = 1)$ are $-a_{r_1}$ and $-a_{r_2}$). In the positive quadrant we show the output vectors of each of the activities where each is used at unit level. We label these b^r and b^s. Their components are the outputs of r and s (*e.g.*, the components of b^r are b_{r_1} and b_{r_2}). The vector $Z^r(\alpha = 1)$ is the sum of the vector $a^r(\alpha = 1)$ and b^r. Its components are $b_{r_1} - \alpha a_{r_1}$ and $b_{r_2} - \alpha a_{r_2}(\alpha = 1)$, and are thus the excess supplies of goods 1 and 2 of process r at unit level. The vector Z^s ($\alpha = 1$) is derived in a similar way. If we now take $0 \leqslant \lambda_r < 1$ units of process r and $\lambda_s = 1 - \lambda_r$ units of process s and form the sum $\lambda_r Z^r$ ($\alpha = 1$) $+ (1 - I_r)Z^s(\alpha = 1)$ we obtain a vector $Z^{rs}(\alpha = 1)$ which must lie somewhere on the segment $Z^r Z^s$. Indeed, this segment gives the locus of all such sums for all λ_r, λ_s belonging to S. The components of $Z^{rs}(\alpha = 1)$ measure the total excess supply for each of the goods. We now note that part of the segment $Z^r Z^s$ ($\alpha = 1$) lies entirely in the positive quadrant. This means that we could chose some λr, λs belonging to S such that at $\alpha = 1$ both goods would be in excess supply. But this must mean that we could increase α without running out of supplies. Now as we increase α in any proportion we increase both inputs into any process in the same proportion. Thus, *e.g.*, the point $a^r(\alpha^*)$ for $\alpha^* > \alpha = 1$ must lie to the south-west of $a^r(\alpha = 1)$, on the straight line through the origin passing through $a^r(\alpha = 1)$. Similarly for $a^s(\alpha^*)$. We now form $Z^r(\alpha^*)$ and $Z^s(\alpha^*)$ as before. In the example we have chosen we find the two vectors to be mirror images of each other. Hence for some $k > 0$ we have $-kZ^s(\alpha^*) = Z^r(\alpha^*)$ or setting $k = \dfrac{\lambda^*_s}{1 - \lambda^*_s}$, $\lambda^*_s Z^s(\alpha^*) + (1 - \lambda^*_s)Z^r(\alpha^*) = 0$. Hence where the two activities are used at the levels λ^*_s and λ^*_r $(= 1 - \lambda^*_s)$, and $\alpha = \alpha^*$, the demand for each good is just equal to its supply. If we now tried to increase

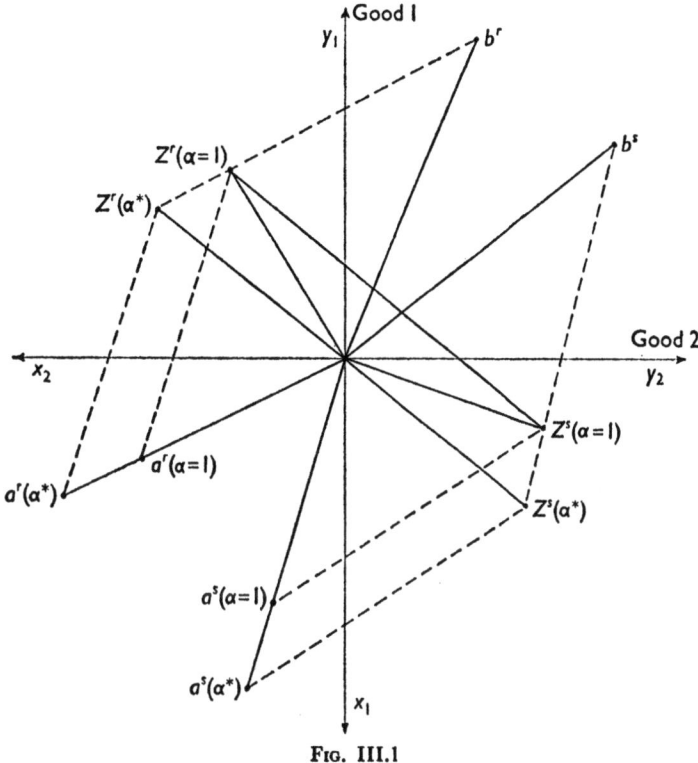

Fig. III.1

α above α^*, $Z^r(\alpha^*)$ would move towards the negative axis of good 2 and $Z^s(\alpha^*)$ to that of good 1, and if we look at the segment joining these two points it would everywhere have a negative component, *i.e.*, the good would always be in short supply for any λ_r and λ_s non-negative and adding to one. Hence α^* is the highest α we can attain for the activity pair r and s, and λ^*_r and λ^*_s are the levels at which these activities must be used. The ratio in which the two goods would be produced is

$$\frac{y^*_1}{y^*_2} = \frac{x^*_1}{x^*_2} = \frac{a_{r_1}\lambda^*_r + a_{s_1}\lambda^*_s}{a_{r_2}\lambda^*_r + a_{s_2}\lambda^*_s} = \frac{b_{r_1}\lambda^*_r + b_{s_2}\lambda^*_s}{b_{r_2}\lambda^*_r + b_{s_2}\lambda^*_s}$$

We now note that our assumptions guarantee only that some b vector has a positive first and some b vector a positive second component and that the vector a lies in the non-positive quadrant. Thus the picture we have drawn is not the only possible one, and we briefly consider some special cases.

(a) Suppose $Z^t(\alpha^*)$, $Z^r(\alpha^*)$, $Z^s(\alpha^*)$ all lie on the segment $Z^r(\alpha^*)$, $Z^s(\alpha^*)$. Then if $Z^t(\alpha^*)$ and $Z^s(\alpha^*)$ are both in the south-eastern quadrant and $Z^r(\alpha^*)$ in the north-western, we may use a mixture of L_r and L_s or L_r and L_t without violating our constraints. Hence there is an indeterminacy

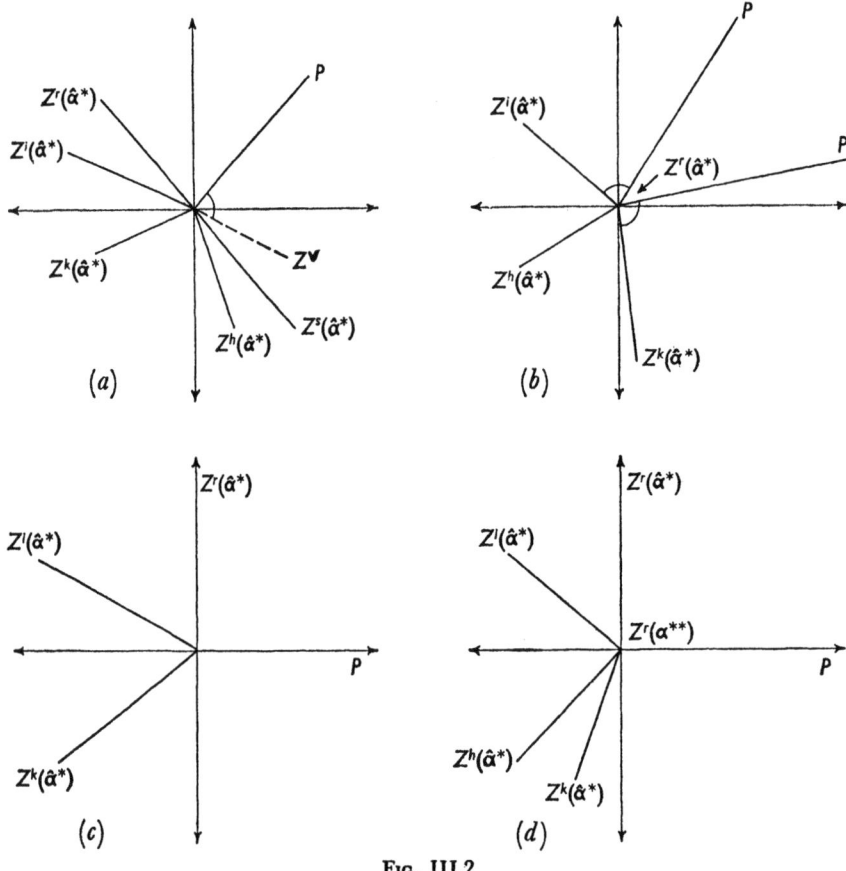

Fig. III.2

in the sense that we can get the same growth rate for goods produced in different proportions. Suppose that $x(rs)$ is the vector of outputs which can be produced by Lr and Ls at α^* (such that $\lambda^*_r + \lambda^*_s = 1$) and $x(rt)$ the vector of outputs which can be produced by Lr and Lt at α^* ($\lambda^*_r + \lambda^*_t = 1$). Then evidently any mixture:

$$x(1) = kx(rt) + (1 - k)x(st)\quad 1 > k > 0$$

is also a possible for α^*. If we were to plot the vectors $x(rs)$ or $x(rt)$ in the plane x_1x_2, then all vectors such as $x(1)$ would lie on the straight-line segment joining them. This segment gives us all output ratios consistent with the maximum rate of growth if only activities L_r, L_s and L_t were available. If there are other possible activities α^* may not be the largest expansion factor (see below, p. 82).

(*b*) Suppose b^r lies on the y_1 axis and a^r on the $-x_1$ axis. Then L_r produces only what it uses as input. Evidently for some α^* large enough the corresponding vector $Z^r(\alpha^*)$ will coincide with the origin, and so there exists a balanced growth path (maximal for L_r), such that only good 1 is produced. A system containing activities such as this (here there are only two goods) is called reducible.

(*c*) It is possible that for some α^* a process L_r using both inputs and producing both outputs has $Z^r(\alpha^*)$ on one of the positive axes. In that case the corresponding good would always be in excess supply at the growth rate α^* using only process L_r. Since there is free disposal, this does not matter.

The reader can construct other examples. It should be noted that the highest growth rate possible for any single activity L_r or any pair L_r, L_s need not be positive. For instance, if L_r uses good 1 as input and produces only good 2 the maximum α possible for this activity alone is zero.

We may proceed in this way and for any activity and any possible activity pair L_r and L_s calculate the maximum α^*. We shall want to choose that process or combination of processes which have the largest α^*. We have already argued that such a maximum exists. Let us call it $\hat{\alpha}^*$. If we now draw all possible vectors $Z(\hat{\alpha}^*)$ we will get one of the following typical pictures:

Consider first Figs. III.2 (*a*) to III.2 (*c*) only. In each we have drawn the vectors $Z^i(\hat{\alpha}^*)$ for the maximum possible growth rate. It is clear in Fig. III.2 (*a*) that there can be no $Z^i(\hat{\alpha}^*)$ above (north-east) of the segment, $Z^r(\hat{\alpha}^*)Z^s(\hat{\alpha}^*)$. For if there were (as indicated by the dotted vector Z^v) there would exist a combination (of L_r and L_v) at $\hat{\alpha}^*$, which would produce more of each good than is used up, and we could evidently increase $\hat{\alpha}^*$ contrary to assumption. The same reasoning explains the positions of the vectors $Z^i(\hat{\alpha}^*)$ in Fig. III.2 (*b*) and Fig. III.2 (*c*).

In Fig. III.2 (*a*) a combination of L_r or L_s gives us the maximum α the system is capable of. Draw a vector P at right angles to the segment $Z^r(\hat{\alpha}^*)Z^s(\hat{\alpha}^*)$. Elementary algebra tells us that the product of two vectors at right angles to each other is zero. If two vectors form an obtuse angle their product is negative. Let P_1 and P_2 be the components of P (only their ratios matter). Then

$$PZ^j = P_1(b_{j1} - \hat{\alpha}^* a_{j1}) + P_2(b_{j2} - \hat{\alpha}^* a_{j2}) \begin{array}{l} = 0 \text{ for } j = r, s \\ < 0 \text{ for all other } j \text{ and all com-} \\ \text{binations of } j \end{array}$$

Suppose we interpret P_1 and P_2 as the prices of the two goods, and $\hat{\alpha}^*$ as $1 + r$, where r is the rate of interest (see p. 86). Then since production takes time, so that inputs have to bear an interest charge, the above relation tells us that there exists a set of prices and an interest rate such that if it ruled only L_r and L_s could be used without loss (or profit), while all other activities would make a loss. If we established this set of prices and that interest rate (evidently equal to $\hat{\alpha}^* - 1$), then a perfectly competitive economy (in case III.2 (a)) would be able to choose those activities which gave the maximum rate of growth.

In III.2 (b), where $Z^r(\hat{\alpha}^*)$ coincides with the origin (only Z_r is used), the reader can verify that for $r = \hat{\alpha}^* - 1$ and any set of prices which can be represented by vectors P or P', or any combination of these, will lead to the choice of L_r and no activity makes a loss. In III.2 (c) $Z^r(\alpha^*)$ coincides with the vertical positive axis. Hence at $\hat{\alpha}^*$ more of good 2 is produced than is needed as input—it is in permanent excess supply. We see that the appropriate price vector, which gives zero surpluses on L_r and negative surplus on all other activities, coincides with the horizontal axis—the over-produced good is " free."

We may summarise our result so far in the following way. Let us write $\beta = (1 + r)$ as the " interest rate factor." We started out with the problem of finding the maximum α such that at the given technology no less of any good is produced than is required for further production. Our Fig. III.2 (a)–III.2 (c) shows at what levels activity must be used at the maximum $\hat{\alpha}^*$ subject to these constraints (we know that this level may not be unique). Thus, for instance, in III.2 (b) we set $\lambda^*_r = 1$ and all other $\lambda_i = 0$ and satisfy the constraint. But we may now reverse the question and ask what is the lowest value of β which ensures that no possible combination of activities makes a positive profit at some $P \geqslant 0$. In our simple examples the answer is that the smallest β satisfying this constraint $= \hat{\alpha}^*$. Take, for instance, Fig. III.2 (a). If we took $\beta < \hat{\alpha}^*$ and constructed the vectors $Z^r(\beta)$, $Z^s(\beta)$ which are the vectors $Z^r(\hat{\alpha}^*)$, $Z^s(\hat{\alpha}^*)$ with β replacing $\hat{\alpha}^*$ in the components, these vectors would, as we know, be bent towards the positive axis. But then, as the reader can verify, there would exist no $P > 0$ such that both activities gave zero profit. Hence the two problems seem to be duals of each other and min β = max α subject to the constraints as stated.

But this conclusion is too hasty, as is shown in Fig. III.2 (d), which illustrates the reducible case. In Fig. III.2 (d) $\hat{\alpha}^{**} > \hat{\alpha}^*$. At $\hat{\alpha}^{**}$, L_r is just self-sustaining (uses as much of good 1 as it produces), while all other activities, such as L_s, are impossible at this expansion rate. Hence $\hat{\alpha}^{**}$ is the largest α subject to the usual constraints. On the other hand, at $\beta = \hat{\alpha}^*$, $Z^r(\hat{\alpha}^*)$, $Z^s(\hat{\alpha}^*)$ take the positions shown. If we choose P to coincide with the horizontal axis clearly no process makes a surplus. If we reduced β further this would no longer be true, as is easily verified ($Z^s(\hat{\alpha}^*)$ moves into the south-east quadrant as $\hat{\alpha}^* = \beta$ is reduced, $Z^r(\hat{\alpha}^*)$ slides up the vertical axis and at no P will both be profitless). Hence min β < max α. The reducible case is thus an exception to the rule we have formulated in the previous paragraph (Gale (1960)).

It is easy to put this a little more generally. In Fig. III.2 (d) the vector b^r lies somewhere on the positive vertical axis, since L_r produces only good 1. Hence at the Neumann prices shown $Pb^r = 0$ (the two vectors are at right angles), and the growth path produces nothing of value. This gives us our clue. For suppose we formulate our problem as follows: Find α max, β min, $P \geqslant 0$, $\lambda \geqslant 0$, $a_{ij} > 0$ some j each i, $b_{ij} > 0$ each j some i and

$$\sum (b_{ij} - \alpha a_{ij})\lambda_i \geqslant 0 \qquad j = 1, 2 \quad . \quad . \quad . \quad . \quad (a)$$

$$\sum_{ij} p_j (b_{ij} - \alpha a_{ij})\lambda_i = 0 \quad . \quad . \quad . \quad . \quad . \quad . \quad . \quad (b)$$

$$\sum (b_{ij} - \beta a_{ij}) P_j \leqslant 0 \qquad i = 1 \dots m \ . \quad . \quad . \quad . \quad (c)$$

$$\sum p_j (b_{ij} - \beta a_{ij})\lambda_i = 0 \quad . \quad . \quad . \quad . \quad . \quad . \quad . \quad (d)$$

$$\sum p_j b_{ij} \lambda_i > 0 \quad . \quad . \quad . \quad . \quad . \quad . \quad . \quad (e)$$

Conditions (a) or (c) are as usual—we must not use more inputs than we produce and we must not make a surplus on any activity. Condition (b) states that the price of a good in excess supply should be zero, condition (d) that an activity with negative surplus is not used. Condition (e) states that something of value is produced. If α^*, β^* are the solutions to this problem, it follows from (e) and the other constraints that $\sum a_{ij}\lambda_i P_j > 0$, and so $\alpha^* = \beta^*$. (For more detail see Gale, Howe.) It is clear that in the reducible case (Fig. III.2 (d)), $\hat{\alpha}^{**}$ is not a solution to this problem, since (e) would be violated. Hence, provided we use (e) in stating the problem, there exists a solution with the rate of growth always equal to the minimum interest rate compatible with the constraints.

We shall see presently that many of these beautiful results carry over in a modified form to models where the rather drastic assumptions concerning the labour supply are not made. As it stands, the model is perhaps not of great economic interest—there is no consumption and only a dreary process of reproduction of each good. But, as often happens, once the simpler case is understood, the stage is set for useful modifications. Before pursuing these matters we shall make a number of observations.

(a) If we imagine an economy in which each activity produces only a single good but with the aid of durable (capital) inputs, then it is convenient to regard each activity as having joint products: the actual output of the good it produces and the amounts of durable equipment transferred from one period to the next (Morishima (1958), McKenzie (1963)).

(b) We may formulate the Neumann model rather more generally than we have done so far (Radner (1961), Karlin (1959)). Let the technology be defined by a set T, the set of all possible input and output pairs x and y. As before, $x = (x_1 x_2)$, $y = (y_1 y_2)$. If we invent a disposal activity for each of the two goods, e.g., L_1 is the activity which uses one unit of good 1 to throw away and produces no output, T of the Neumann model is defined as: the set of all $x \geqslant 0$, $y \geqslant 0$ such that for some $\lambda = (\lambda_1 \ldots \lambda_m) \geqslant 0$, $x_j = \Sigma a_{ij} \lambda_i$, $y_j = \Sigma b_{ij} \lambda_i$ $(j = 1, 2)$.

More generally all we need to assume about T are the following: (i) There are constant returns to scale. (ii) If both (x, y) and $(x'y')$ belong to T, then $x(k)$, $y(k)$ also belong to $T(y)$, where $x(k) = kx + (1 - k)x'$,

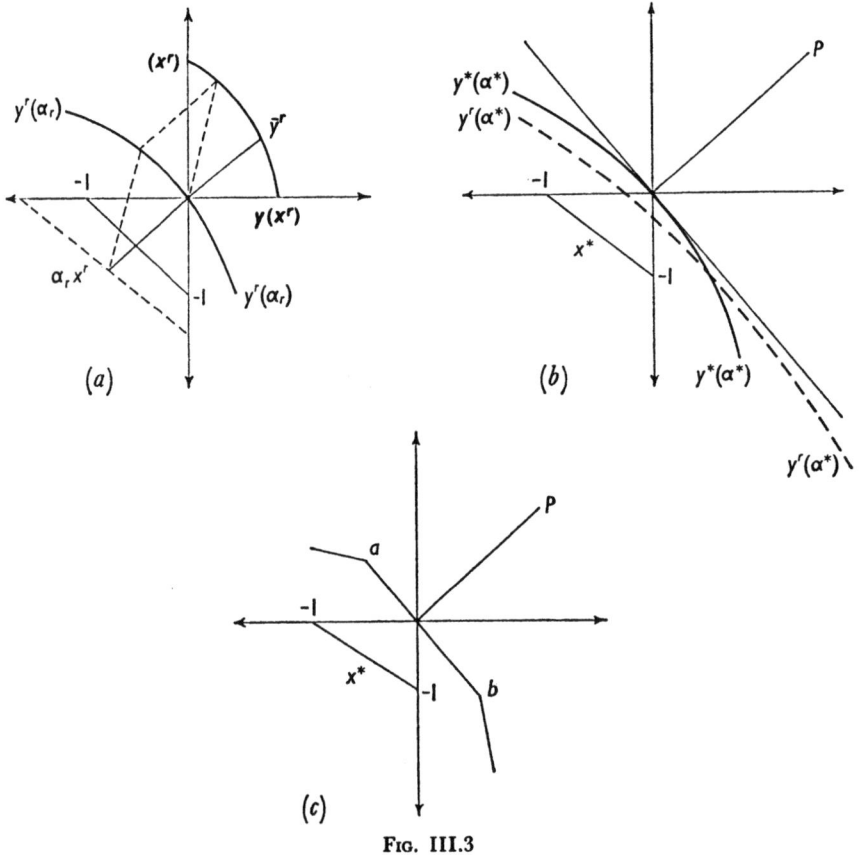

Fɪɢ. III.3

$y(k) = yk + y'(1 - k)$ and $1 \geqslant k \geqslant 0$. This means that there are non-increasing marginal productivities. (iii) Free disposal is possible. (iv) Nothing can be produced without inputs (*i.e.*, $x = 0$ implies $y = 0$ if x, y in T). (v) It is possible to produce any good. It should be noted that (iv) together with (i) implies that $\max \frac{y_i}{x_i}$ is bounded from above (Radner (1961)).

Our problem is now as follows: We seek the max $\alpha = \alpha^*$ and x^* for which $(x^*, \alpha^* x^*)$ belong to T. We also seek β and p^* such that $p^*(y - \beta x) \leqslant 0$ all (x, y) belonging to T.

We illustrate this formulation in Fig. III.3. Consider Fig. III.3 (a). In the negative quadrant we again measure inputs. Since there are constant returns to scale, and since nothing can be produced without inputs, we concentrate on those which add up to minus one, *i.e.*, all those combinations lying on the line with intercepts $(-1, -1)$. Choose any x^1 on this line. To it corresponds a curve $y(x^r)\, y(x^r)$ bounding all the outputs we could have from that input combination. We have drawn this curve such that any arc joining two points on the boundary lies wholly inside the boundary. That is, we assume the production set *strictly convex*. From the diagram we see that $\bar{y}^r$ is the maximum balanced output from x^r, and so we can find the maximum growth rate α_r by taking $\dfrac{\bar{y}_i{}^r}{x_i{}^r} = \alpha_r$. Now transfer $y^r = \alpha_r x^r$ into the negative quadrant in an obvious way. Take any other point y^r on the boundary $y(x^r)\, y(x^r)$. Form $y^r - \alpha_r x^r$ in the usual way by adding the vectors y^r and $-\alpha_r x^r$. Forming all possible vectors sums of this kind gives us a curve such as $y^r(\alpha_r), y^r(\alpha_r)$, *i.e.*, the vector from the origin to any point on this curve is $y^r - \alpha_r x^r$ for some y^r on the boundary of the production possibility curve.

Now take Fig. III.3 (*b*). We imagine we have found α_r for every x^r lying on the line $(-1, -1)$ as in Fig. III.3(*a*). We can be sure (by an argument already used) that for some x^* we get $\alpha^* \geqslant \alpha_r$ all r. In Fig. III.3 (*b*) we have plotted the curve $y^*(\alpha^*)y^*(\alpha^*)$ just as we plotted $y^r(\alpha_r)y^r(\alpha_r)$ before. If we were now to plot $y^r(\alpha^*)y^r(\alpha^*)$, *i.e.*, the curve we would have obtained in Fig. III.3 (*a*) had we taken α^* rather than α_r, it cannot pass through the origin if $\alpha^* > \alpha_r$. Indeed, it is easy to prove that all such curves other than $y^*(\alpha^*)\, y^*(\alpha^*)$ must pass below the origin.

Drawing the tangent to $y^*(\alpha^*)y^*(\alpha^*)$ at the origin and taking P normal to it, we may again interpret the components of P as prices and α^* as $(1 + r) = \beta^*$. We see that β^* is certainly the smallest β such that $P(y - \beta^*x) \leqslant 0$ all possible y and x and that $P^*(y^* - \beta^*x^*) = 0$. We have thus solved our problem.

Provided the envelope frontier we have derived is strictly convex, x^* is unique and that for all other possible input combinations (adding to -1), we have $P(y - \beta^*x) < 0$. For, suppose that y^*, x^* and y, x both gave zero profits. Interpret $x(h)$ as $hx^* + (1 - h)x$ and $y(h)$ similarly where $1 > h > 0$. Then certainly $P(y(h) - \beta^*x(h)) = 0$. But $y(h)$ lies on the chord joining y^* and y and so inside the production frontier. Hence, with $x(h)$ we could produce some $y > y(h)$. But then there exists y and $x(h)$ such that $P(y - \beta^*x(h)) > 0$, which is impossible if we have maximised α^*.

This result, however, does not hold in Fig. III.3 (*c*), where we have drawn the same picture as in Fig. III.3 (*b*) but for a Neumann technology. The production frontier and the locus of vectors $y - \alpha_r x^r$ is now a series of straight-line segments and corners. It is now clear that not only the Neumann combination x^*, y^* earns zero profit at the Neumann prices and interest rates but all x, y associated with the segment (*ab*). Therefore, it may well happen that there are pairs x, y other than x^*, y^* (which are

Neumann pairs). The set of all (x, y) which earn a zero profit at the Neumann prices and interest rates Mackenzie calls a Neumann Facet, and we return to it later (p. 107).

The reader can easily supply variations of the possibilities illustrated in III.3 for himself.

Let us return to our Neumann prices and interest rate. Suppose that the sth activity makes no surplus at the maximum expansion rate. Let us now write this as follows

$$P_1(t + 1)b_{s1} + P_2(t + 1)b_{s2} = a_{s1}P_1(t) + a_{s2}P_2(t) \qquad (1)$$

where $P_i(t)$ is the ith price at t. We know that only relative prices are determined. Hence (since we have nothing to say about the role of money), choose an arbitrary normalisation as follows:

$$P_i(t) = P'_i(t), i = 1, 2$$
$$P_i(t + 1) = P'_i(t + 1), i = 1, 2 \qquad v > 0$$

For instance, P' may be chosen so that $P'_1(t) + P'_2(t) = 1$. Suppose first that we choose to make $P'_i(t + 1) = P'_i(t)$ $(i = 1, 2)$. Then substituting in (1) we find that $\frac{1}{v} = \beta$ the interest factor as before. If, however, we do not choose to have the level of prices the same in both periods we get

$$P'_1(t + 1)b_{s1} + P'_2(t + 1)b_{s2} = \frac{1}{v}[a_{s1}P'_1(t) + a_{s2}P'_2(t)]$$

But we also know that for the Neumann β we have

$$P'_1(t)b_{s1} + P'_2(t)b_{s2} = \beta[a_{s1}P'_1(t) + a_{s2}P'_2(t)]$$

and so
$$\beta = \frac{1}{v} - \frac{P'_i(t + 1) - P'_i(t)}{P'_i(t)}$$

(The choice of i does not matter, since relative prices remain unchanged.) Thus the Neumann interest factor is the real interest-rate factor. The nominal interest-rate factor $\left(\frac{1}{v}\right)$ is only determined once we have said something about the level of prices in subsequent periods (Malinvaud (1953), Koopmans (1959), Solow (1959), Jorgenson (1960)).

III.2. *The Neumann Model with Consumption*

Let us now see whether some of the rather strong assumptions of the Neumann model can be relaxed. Our main guide here will be Morishima (1960). His results, cast in a mathematical form, are closely related to the work of Robinson and Kaldor.

We first inquire how in the Neumann model the choice of arbitrary real wage-rate is related to the maximum growth rate. If we return to

Fig. III.1 and imagine the real wage-rate [1] higher than there assumed, then the vectors $a^r(\beta = 1)$ and $a^s(\beta = 1)$ will be lower. It is not hard to see that the maximum growth rate for the pair of processes r and s will thus be smaller. The same is true for every pair, and so the maximum growth rate for the system, α^*, will also be smaller. This result, that the maximum growth rate is a declining function of the real wage, can be rigorously established (Morishima (1960)). If we are now given, independently, the maximum rate of growth of the labour supply (n), then, provided it is not " too large, " there will exist a positive real wage low enough to make the maximum rate of growth of the system equal to n. Thus we can use the condition of " continued full employment " to close the system, *i.e.*, to determine the real wage-rate. It should be explained that this procedure says nothing about how real wages are actually determined. It simply gives us what, in this world, the real wage-rate would have to be to give full-employment balanced growth. Of course this real wage may be less than is required for subsistence, etc., and so all the difficulties already observed in the one-sector world arise here.

We may now wish to relax the assumption that capitalists save all their income. Let us, then, imagine a world in which wages are paid at the *end* of the productive period, as are profits, and that profit recipients save a proportion of their income. We continue to suppose that wage-earners consume all of their income. For *convenience only* we suppose that they and the capitalists always consume all goods in fixed proportion independently of prices. We shall now write a_{ij} as the input coefficient of the ith process for the jth good when the amount of the jth good paid to labour is included. We write $\hat{a}_{ij}$ as the coefficient net of wage payments. Our equilibrium may now be written as follows: [2]

(*a*) Total demand $\leqslant$ total supply for each good, *i.e.*,

$$\alpha\sum_i \hat{a}_{ij}x_i(t) + \sum_i (a_{ij} - \hat{a}_{ij})x_i(t) + (\beta - 1)c_j(\sum_{ij} x_i \hat{a}_{ij}P_j) \leqslant \sum_i b_{ij}x_i \quad (1)$$

In the above expression $\beta = 1 + r$ so $(\beta - 1)$ is the rate of interest. The last bracketed term on the left-hand side evidently gives total money cost excluding wages, so $(\beta - 1)$ times that gives us total money profits. The c_j is the proportion of income spent on the jth good divided by the price of the jth good, and the whole expression gives us the capitalist's demand for the jth good. Note that $\sum c_j P_j = 1 - s$.

(*b*) Total cost of any process $\geqslant$ Total receipts, *i.e.*,

$$\beta\sum \hat{a}_{ij}P_j + \sum(a_{ij} - \hat{a}_{ij})P_j \geqslant \sum b_{ij}P_j i = 1, \ldots m$$

This expression is obvious, and we need only note that there are no interest charges on wage payments.

---

[1] The real wage is defined in terms of some price-index with non-negative weights.

[2] Morishima (1960) has also investigated a " Marxian " system where wages are advanced and must therefore earn profit.

(c) Something of value can be produced in the economy, *i.e.*,

$$\sum_{ij} b_{ij} x_i P_j > 0$$

If we now multiply each of the expressions in (a) by P_j and sum over j, and each of the expressions in (b) by x_i and sum over i, then recalling that goods in excess supply have a zero price and unprofitable processes are not used, they must be the same. Subtracting the (b) sum from the (a) sum yields.

$$(\alpha - \beta) = r(s - 1)$$

or

$$(\alpha - 1) = rs$$

which is an expression already fully discussed in the one-sector case: the rate of growth of the system must equal the capitalist's propensity to save

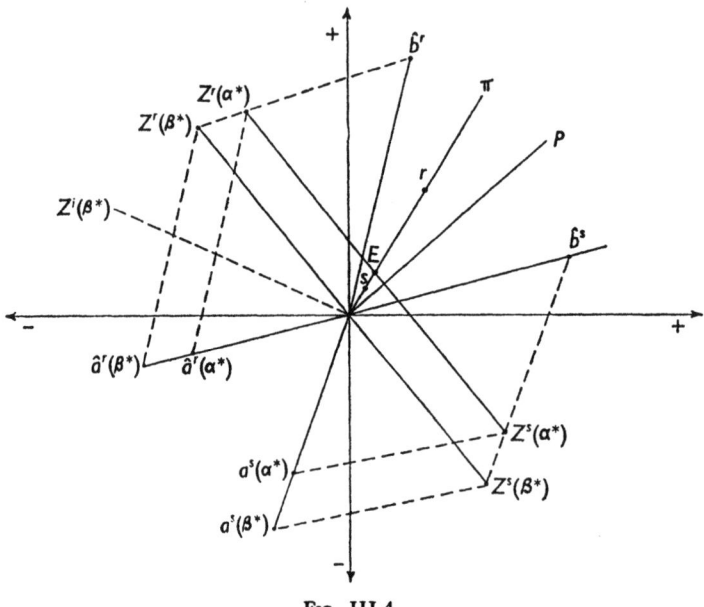

FIG. III.4

times the rate of profit, if an equilibrium exists. It is Morishima's considerable achievement to have shown that an equilibrium will indeed exist, although the equilibrium shown above implies that the system is capable of growth which need not be true. It may be helpful to illustrate the equilibrium geometrically.

Fig. III.4 shows the system in equilibrium. Consider equilibrium condition (b) first. We have defined the vector b^r as having the components $b_{r_1} - (a_{r_1} - \hat{a}_{r_1})$; $b_{r_2} - (a_{r_2} - \hat{a}_{r_2})$, *i.e.*, the output of each good by one unit of the rth process after labour has taken its share. b^s is defined similarly. The vector a^r has components $\hat{a}_{r_1}$, $\hat{a}_{r_2}$, *i.e.*, non-labour input of each good. The vector $\hat{a}^s$ is defined similarly. We multiply $\hat{a}^r$ and $\hat{a}^s$ by β^*, the equilibrium interest factor, to get $\hat{a}^r(\beta^*)$ and $\hat{a}^s(\beta^*)$. Adding $\hat{a}^r(\beta^*)$ to $\hat{b}^r$ gives the vector $Z^r(\beta^*)$ with components:

$$(b_{r_1} - (a_{r_1} - \hat{a}_{r_1}) - \beta^* a_{r_1}), \ (b_{r_2} - (a_{r_2} - \hat{a}_{r_2}) - \beta^* \hat{a}_{r_2})$$

The vector $Z^s(\beta^*)$ is defined similarly. We have drawn this in such a way as to be mirror images of each other. For all other activities the corresponding vector $Z^t(\beta^*)$, etc., indicated by the dotted vector starting at the origin, lie below the segment $Z^r(\beta^*)Z^s(\beta^*)$. The vector P is at right angles to the segment and its components are prices. As before, we see that only activities r and s make a zero surplus and all others a negative surplus.

In the positive quadrant we have drawn the vector π, the slope of which measures the ratio in which capitalists consume the goods 1 and 2. The point r shows what their consumption of each good would be if activity r were used at unit level, and if the prices were as given and $\beta = \beta^*$. Point s is similarly defined for process s. Now take $\alpha^* < \beta^*$ and multiply each of the vectors $\hat{a}^r$ and $\hat{a}^s$ by α^* to give $a^r(\alpha^*)$, $a^s(\alpha^*)$. The scalar α^* is such that forming the vector sums $a^r(\alpha^*)$ and b^r and $a^s(\alpha^*) + b^s$ yields vectors $Z^r(\alpha^*)$ and $Z^s(\alpha^*)$, the segment between which (i.e., $Z^s(\alpha^*)Z^s(\alpha^*)$) cuts π somewhere between the points r and s. Moreover, the intersection (E) is such that for some $1 \geqslant x^*_r \geqslant 0$, $x^*_r Z^s(\alpha^*) + (1 - x^*_r)Z^s(\alpha^*)$ gives a point equal to x^*_r times π at r and $(1 - x^*_r)$ π at s. The reader can verify that all equilibrium conditions are fulfilled, and that the relation $r(\alpha^* - 1)$ $= (\beta^* - 1)s$ does indeed hold.

Thus for the chosen arbitrary real wage we have found the maximum rate of growth and the prices and interest rate which would induce a perfectly competitive economy to choose it. If now the rate of growth of labour supply is given we must choose a real wage which will make the maximum rate of growth of the system equal to the " natural rate." We have already indicated how this is done.

It is now extremely important to understand what the logic of the model implies. We may start with a given rate of increase in population n. We know that if equilibrium is to be possible we must have $n = sr$, and so we know what the interest rate will have to be. But this is not enough. For we must also ensure that the supply side is in equilibrium, i.e., that conditions (a) are met. This means finding a real wage-rate and a set of prices such that at the interest rate already determined no process which is not used makes a positive profit. That is, we must be able to find a set of prices such that for the chosen processes the interest rate also measures the marginal return of finance: $(\sum a_{rj}P_j)r$ must not be greater or less than the return to be

made from using a sum of money to buy a_{r_1} units of good 1 and a_{r_2} units of good 2 at the going prices and selling one more unit of output. Moreover, while it is true that from the relation $n = sr$ we can read off what the equilibrium r must be, it tells us nothing about how it is actually determined.

Lastly, it is self-evident that the equilibrium distribution of income between profits and wages depends on technology as well as on n and on s. (See Robinson (1960), Morishima (1960).)

As already noted, the "generalised Neumann model," as Morishima calls it, is extremely similar to the work of Robinson and Kaldor. These authors have been greatly impressed by the fact that the value of the full-employment equilibrium r can be determined, with suitable savings assumptions, without reference to technology. This is certainly correct, but we have seen that in equilibrium technology and prices must so have adapted themselves that the equilibrium rate of interest also measures the equilibrium rate of return over cost, which is a conclusion not dissimilar from that of other writers. No doubt the Neumann model can also be adapted to deal with the case where the proportion of total income saved is constant.

III.3. *The Closed Leontief Model*

This model (Leontief (1951)) can be looked at as a special case of the Neumann model. Recent work by Samuelson (1951), Arrow (1951), Solow (1959), Morishima (1958, 1959, 1961) and Mackenzie (1957) has greatly increased our understanding of its features. In the outline which follows, the notation is different from what is usual in order to allow us to bring out more clearly the relation of this model to what has gone before.

It is assumed that each process produces only one good. On the other hand, each process uses stocks of goods in production, which it transfers from one period to the next. There is thus joint production in this sense, but only in this sense.

Consider the ith process. If used at unit level it provides one unit of output of the first good but uses up c_{i_1} units of the good in production and c_{i_2} of the second good. On the other hand, it transfers a_{i_1} units of good 1 from one period to the next and a_{i_2} units of good 2. Hence if we write b_{i_1} and b_{i_2} as the net assets of goods 1 and 2 available next period from using the ith process at unit level we have

$$b_{i_1} = 1 - c_{i_1} + a_{i_1}, \; b_{i_2} = a_{i_2} - c_{i_2} \quad . \quad . \quad . \quad . \quad (1)$$

To produce these amounts we know already the process requires (taking inputs as negative) $-a_{i_1}$ units of good 1 and $-a_{i_2}$ units of good 2 in the form of stocks (capital). Hence a process, as before, is specified by an output vector and input vector.

Suppose that there is free disposal and that x_1 and x_2 of goods 1 and 2 are available now and it is desired to produce y_1 and y_2 of goods 1 and 2 in the next period. Then if process i produces good 1 and process j produces good 2, and if using the processes at intensities λ_i and λ_j makes the programme possible we must have

$$\left. \begin{array}{ll} b_{ik}\lambda_i + b_{jk}\lambda_j \geqslant y_k & k = 1, 2 \\ -a_{ik}\lambda_i - a_{jk}\lambda_j \geqslant -x_k & k = 1, 2 \end{array} \right\} \quad . \quad . \quad . \quad . \quad (2)$$

The set of all couples (x, y) which satisfy (2) for some combination of processes at non-negative level fully describes the Leontief technology.

We may now proceed exactly as before. We seek to find a possible pair (x, y) such that $y = \alpha x$ and α is as large as it can be made. Suppose the picture looks like in III.2 (a). Then we know that the Neumann programme would use only two processes, one for each good, and it would produce both goods in positive amounts. How can we make sure that the picture looks like that? One answer is immediate—we must suppose that the Leontief technology is irreducible, else we may get a picture like III.2 (d). But there are further assumptions we shall need. To understand these it is best to construct a new diagram.

Suppose that, as in Fig. III.2 (a), the rth process and the sth process are used when α is at its maximum, the co-ordinates (elements) of the vector $Z_r(\hat{\alpha}^*)$ in this case are:

$$b_{r_1} - \hat{\alpha}^* a_{r_1}, \; b_{r_2} - \hat{\alpha}^* a_{r_2}$$

Substituting again for b_{r_1} and b_{r_2} from (1), we easily find that the components of $Z_r(\hat{\alpha}^*)$ can be written

$$((1 - c_{r_1}) + (1 - \hat{\alpha}^*)a_{r_1}), \; (-c_{r_2} + (1 - \hat{\alpha}^*)a_{r_2})$$

and similarly for s. In Fig. III.5 we have plotted the vectors $c_r = (1 - c_{r_1}, -c_{r_2})$ for r and s and the vectors $a_r = (a_{r_1}, - a_{r_2})$ for r and s. If we add c^r

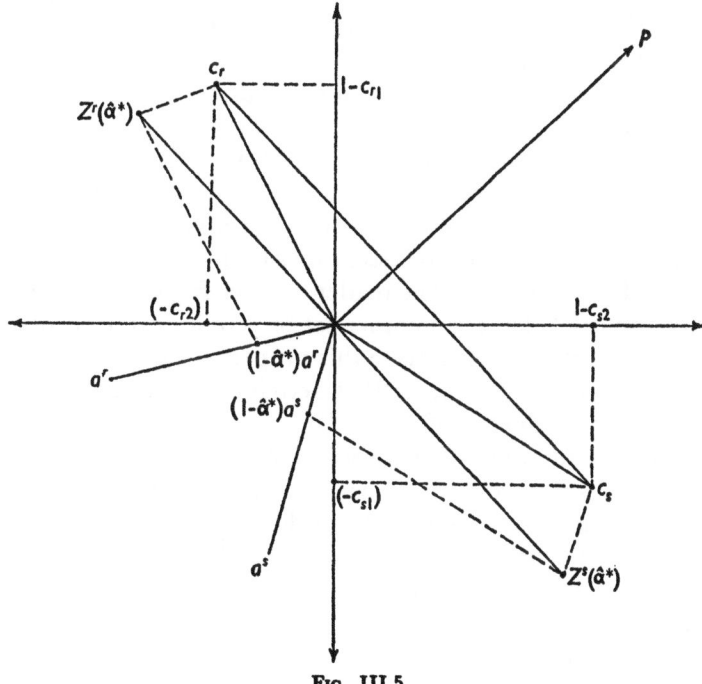

Fig. III.5

and $(\alpha^* - 1)a^r$ and similarly for s we again get the vectors $Z^r(\alpha^*)$ and $Z^s(\alpha^*)$. But if we are to have $\alpha^* > 1$ it is obvious from the diagram that the segment joining c^r to c^s must pass through the positive quadrant. For, if growth is to be possible, then at zero growth ($\alpha^* = 1$) it must be possible to use the two processes in some combination which will allow more of each good to be produced than is used up in production, so that if we did have some growth goods would be available to augment the stocks needed.

If c^r and c^s are to look as in Fig. III.5, then evidently $1 - c_{r1}$ and $1 - c_{s2}$ must be both positive, else c^r and c^s would both be in the negative quadrant. If c^r and c^s had the same slope, then $\alpha^* = 1$ (*i.e.*, zero growth) would be the only possible solution, since no possible combination of processes would give us more of any good than is used up in production. Hence, for more to be produced than is used up the slope of c^r, $\left(\dfrac{(1 - c_{r1})}{-c_{r2}}\right)$, must be larger than that of c^s, $\left(\dfrac{(-c_{s1})}{(1 - c_{s2})}\right)$, or

$$\frac{1 - c_{r1}}{c_{s1}} > \frac{c_{r2}}{1 - c_{s2}} \quad . \quad . \quad . \quad . \quad . \quad (3)$$

Condition (3) is called the Hawkins–Simon (1949) condition, which simply says that goods must use up less of themselves—directly or indirectly—in production than is produced of them. This criterion, together with irreducibility (*e.g.*, we must not have c^r on the positive vertical axis and $-a^r$ on the vertical negative axis), is enough to ensure that for a pair of activities r and s, $Z^r(\alpha^*)$ and $Z^s(\alpha^*)$ look as drawn for $\alpha^* > 1$, so that both goods are produced in positive quantities.

Just as before we note that there is a set of prices (strictly positive) such that if the interest rate is $(\alpha^* - 1)$ no process can make a positive profit. If that were not true, then as before, we could have found a higher growth rate (see above). If we now strengthen our assumptions to say that the possible processes for each good form a strictly convex production set, then it is not hard to prove that all processes other than r and s make a negative profit at the indicated prices. The reader can verify (as we did once before in the Neumann case) that for no other set of activities is it possible to find prices and an interest rate which have this property. Later we shall discuss the proposition that this must mean that activities r and s are the only ones which enable us to produce " efficiently."

The significance of this result is considerable. It shows that Samuelson's (1960) famous substitution theorem can be extended to the case of intertemporal production. For what has been shown is that under our assumptions a perfectly competitive economy would choose to produce each good by one process only, and that the competitive prices are quite independent of the composition of output. That this is so follows from (*a*), the fact that we have shown that there is only one set of prices and interest rate at which no profit can be made on any process, *i.e.*, a competitive equilibrium (*b*) that

processes r and s can, of course, be used to produce and to use other combinations of output and input than the balanced one (see p. 78). This being so, we may treat the Leontief model as if its coefficients were fixed.[1]

It is of importance to understand this result correctly, and the reader is referred to Morishima's excellent (1959) article for further detail. In the above we have taken the wage-good input into each process as fixed, $i.e.$, we have made the Neumann assumption that labour is " produced." If we regard the real wage as a parameter, then for different values we give it we will get different processes used and different Leontief prices. Alternatively, we could start by taking the rate of interest as fixed and treat labour as a direct input. We would now need three axes, but it is again possible to show that at that interest rate there will be a unique set of prices (for goods and labour) which ensure the unprofitability of all processes but two. In all this we have supposed that perfect competition ensures zero profitability on all unit processes. If we take a weaker proposition that the profitability over all used processes should be the same (they should have the same profit margins), then we have yet another unknown—the uniform profit margin. Here we must fix two unknowns from " outside," $e.g.$, the real wage and the rate of interest, to determine our Leontief processes and prices.[2]

All we need do now is to assemble the pieces. If there is perfect competition only processes r and s are used. Both goods are produced in positive amounts, and $\alpha^* > 1$ is possible. For r and s we may satisfy (2) with equality signs. Let us write y_i as $x_i\,(t+1)$ and x_i as $x_i(t)$ $i = 1, 2$. Using (2) and substituting from the definition for b_{rk}, etc., we have

$$\left.\begin{aligned}(1 - c_{r1} + a_{r1})\lambda_r + (a_{s1} - c_{s1})\lambda_s &= x_1(t+1)\\(a_{r2} - c_{r2})\lambda_r + (1 - c_{s2} + a_{s2})\lambda_s &= x_2(t+1)\end{aligned}\right\}\quad\cdot\quad\cdot\quad(4a)$$

$$\left.\begin{aligned}a_{r1}\lambda_r + a_{s1}\lambda_s &= x_1(t)\\a_{r2}\lambda_r + a_{s2}\lambda_s &= x_2(t)\end{aligned}\right\}\quad\cdot\quad\cdot\quad\cdot\quad(4b)$$

We may now solve for λ_r and λ_s in terms of $x_1(t)$, $x_2(t)$ from (4b), if we assume that a^r and a^s are linearly independent ($i.e.$, in this simple case that the two vectors do not coincide in Fig. III.5.) Substituting the solution in (4a), we obtain a set of two difference equations in x_1 and x_2. This is best shown by a little matrix algebra. Rewrite (4a) and (4b) as

$$[I - C + A]\lambda = x(t+1)\quad\cdot\quad\cdot\quad\cdot\quad\cdot\quad(4a')$$

$$A\lambda = x(t)\quad\cdot\quad\cdot\quad\cdot\quad\cdot\quad\cdot\quad(4b')$$

[1] McKenzie has pointed out to us that these results depend on the restriction that input and output prices must be proportionate.

[2] We have seen that with a given real wage we can associate an equilibrium rate of interest (profit). Similarly, for any given rate of profit we can put the corresponding real wage. The pairs of equilibrium values of these two variables have been called the factor-price frontier (Samuelson (1962)). In certain special cases, but only in those, it is possible to derive the frontier we get from the disaggregated activity model of the text, from an " as if " (" surrogate ") aggregate production function of the text-book kind.

where $\lambda = (\lambda r, \lambda s)$, C is the matrix of the c_{rj} and A that of the a_{rj}. A is non-singular, and so $\lambda = A^{-1}x(t)$. Substituting in (4a) gives

$$[I - C + A]A^{-1}x(t) = x(t + 1) \quad . \quad . \quad . \quad . \quad . \quad (5)$$

or

$$[I + G]x(t) = x(t + 1) \quad . \quad . \quad . \quad . \quad . \quad (6)$$

where $G = (I - C)A^{-1}$. All couples $(-x_t, x_{t+1})$ satisfying (6') will give zero profit at the Leontief prices and interest rate. We also know that there exists $\alpha^* > 1$ such that $(-x_t, \alpha^* x_t)$ satisfy (6') for all t and $x > 0$. The behaviour of the system will be further investigated below.

III.4. *Sausage Machine Model*

There remains only one further type of model to consider which was first put forward by Samuelson and Solow (1953) and which is best called the " sausage machine " model. It is assumed that the process of allocating goods between uses has been solved in such a manner that we may write the output of any one good as a function of the total supply of each of the goods of the previous period:

$$x_i(t + 1) = h_i(x_1(t), x_2(t)) \quad i = 1, 2$$

The functions h_i have the following properties: (*a*) they are homogeneous of degree 1 in their arguments, and (*b*) they have strictly positive partial derivatives for all $x_2 x_2 \geqslant 0$. The latter assumption is pretty strong and it can be slightly relaxed (Morishima (1959)). It means not only that every

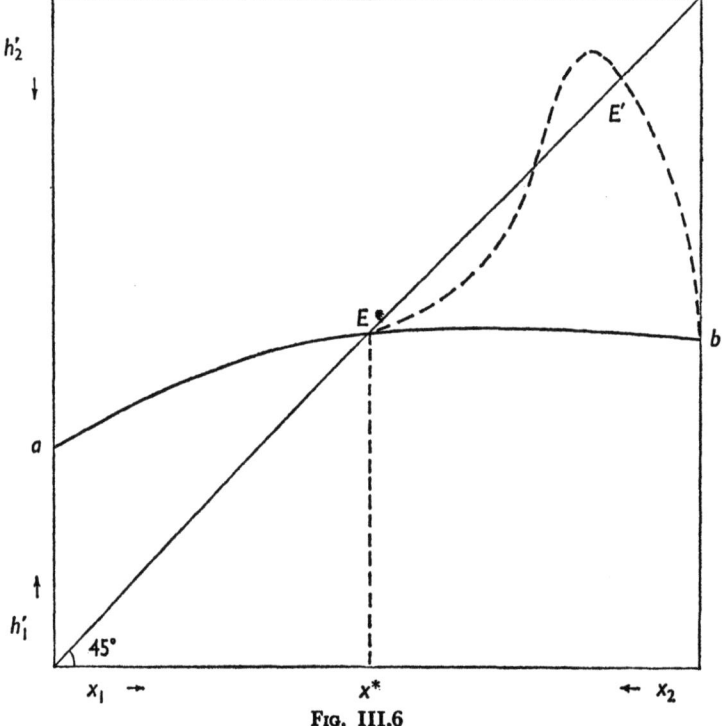

FIG. III.6

good is useful in the production of any other but that if we have only one good we can produce both goods. (This sort of system is often called " primitive.")

Since there are constant returns to scale, we confine ourselves to those x such that $x_1 + x_2 = 1$ and $1 \geqslant x_i \geqslant 0$ $i = 1, 2$. If we now define $h'_i = \dfrac{h_1(\ )}{h_1(\ ) + h_2(\ )}$ $i = 1, 2$ the $h'_1 + h'_2 = 1$ also. The diagram on p. 872 will be used to show the existence of a balanced growth equilibrium.

In Fig. III.6 we have drawn a square with sides of unit length. We measure x_1 along the horizontal from left to right and x_2 along the same axis from right to left. Hence any point in the axis represents a combination of outputs adding up to one. On the vertical axis we measure h'_1 upwards and h'_2 downwards. Any point thus represents a combination of h'_1 and h'_2 adding up to one. We have drawn the diagonal which evidently has unit slope.

Now if $x_1 = 0$, $x_2 = 1$, then by assumption (b), h_1 and h_2 and so h'_1 and h'_2 both positive and so the combination of h'_1 and h'_2 must be at a above the diagonal. Similarly, if $x_2 = 0$ $x_1 = 1$, $h'_1 > 0$, $h'_2 > 0$, and so the combination must be below the diagonal. As x_1 goes from 0 to 1 (x_2 from 1 to 0) we trace out the combinations h'_1 and h'_2 which result. The curve is continuous by assumption. It must therefore intersect the diagonal at least once, say at E. But let x^*_1 and x^*_2 be the coordinates at E. Then at E

$$x^*_1 = h'_1(x^*_1, x^*_1) = \frac{1}{h_1 + h_2} h_1(x^*_1 x^*_2)$$

$$x^*_2 = h'_2(x^*_1, x^*_2) = \frac{1}{h_1 + h_2} h_2(x^*_1 x^*_2)$$

Multiplying both sides by $h_1 + h_2$ gives

$$(h_1 + h_2)x^*_i = h_i(x^*_1, x^*_2) \quad i = 1, 2$$

If we now let $(h_1 + h_2) = \alpha$ and $x^*_i(t + 1) = \alpha x^*_i(t)$ we have

$$x^*_i(t + 1) = \alpha x^*_i(t) = h_i(x^*_1(t), x^*_2(t)), i = 1, 2$$

and we have found a balanced growth path where clearly x^*_1 and x^*_2 are both strictly positive. It can be shown that the growth equilibrium is unique.

III.5. *Stability*

We shall now briefly discuss the stability of the Leontief and Sausage Machine Models.

(a) *Leontief*

We have already discussed the closed Leontief dynamic model. We know that the output system can be characterised by a set of simultaneous difference equations (eq. 6) which we here repeat:

$$x_{t+1} = \bar{G}x_t \qquad (\bar{G} = I + G) \quad . \quad . \quad . \quad . \quad (1)$$

We also know that for any x_0 proportional to a vector x^* which is strictly positive we obtain $x_{t+1} = \bar{\alpha} x_t$ all t, *i.e.*, a steady state. We also know that (1) represents an " equilibrium dynamic " system, *i.e.*, demand is everywhere equal to supply at all times, and the coefficients of G are those which maximise the profits of all producers. The question asked is this: if x_0 is not proportional to the balanced growth vector x^*, will the absolute difference between the actual and equilibrium output ratios become indefinitely small as $t \to \infty$, *i.e.*, is the steady state relatively stable? The following answers can be given:

(i) The steady state is relatively stable for any initial x_0 if, and only if, for some finite m, $\bar{G}^m > 0$ (Tsukui (1961)). This is a purely mathematical condition and there is nothing in the economics to ensure that it will hold. Even when the system is relatively stable, it is possible that for some meaningful initial conditions the path would have some negative components, and cease to make economic sense.[1]

(ii) If the system is relatively unstable, then for some $x_0 \geqslant 0$ strict adherence to (1) will eventually lead to some output(s) becoming negative (Jorgenson (1960)). Thus for some meaningful initial conditions the system ceases to make economic sense. The reason is the insistence that all markets be exactly cleared and all stock requirements exactly met at all times. With fixed coefficients this may be possible only if the output(s) of some good(s) decline(s) continually. Two ways have been taken out of this difficulty. One of these is to replace the assumption that stocks of goods are exactly equal to production requirement by the postulate that they are no smaller (Dosso (1958)). Free transfer between sectors is assumed. This means that we no longer have a determinate system like (1). To make it so, intertemporal optimisation criteria (*e.g.*, the turnpike) have been introduced. The second way out is to suppose that the rate of decumulation of stocks is limited (as, *e.g.*, in Hicks (1950)), so that there are two modes of behaviour for each sector. These (non-linear) " switching " models have been investigated by Leontief (1951), Macmanus (1959), Jorgenson (1960). They appear somewhat artificial.

(iii) It is possible, by adding another term for exogenous demand in (1), to consider an " open model." The conclusions as so far stated are unaffected if the exogenous term is taken as independent of time. This is done by Morishima (1959) and Solow (1959). It evidently does not make good economic sense if the exogenous demand is household demand. No analysis seems to be available of the case (analogous to the " generalised Neumann " model (p. 87)), where household demands are generated with the aid of the price equations of the system, giving household incomes.[2] Certain mathe-

---

[1] Morishima (1964) also introduces the notion of " regular stability." The system is regularly stable if for $x(0) \geqslant x'(0)$ there is some $T > 0$ such that $x(t) \geqslant x'(t)$, all $t > T$.

[2] Morishima (1964) also considers such a system but on the assumption that prices are constant at their long-run equilibrium level.

matical results for the case of an exogenous term which is a function of time are available (Nikaido (1962)), but no proper economic application appears to have been tried.

(iv) We know that, unless we assume it, there is no reason why equilibrium prices should be constant from period to period (p. 86). We may set up price equations for the Leontief model analogous to equation (1) p. 86. Given an arbitrary rate of interest not exceeding a certain maximum, we know that there is some real wage and a set of relative prices which are consistent with a steady state (Solow (1959)). If we fix the money wage, then the steady-state level of prices is fixed. But it can now be shown that if the output system is relatively stable, then the Leontief prices will not approach the steady-state value, and vice versa (Jorgenson 1960b). That means, of course, that we shall have difficulties in ensuring that both all prices *and* all outputs remain non-negative at all times.

It is seen that the equilibrium dynamics of a Leontief model are somewhat unsatisfactory. This, of course, does not mean that it may not be useful in planning. Indeed, considerable use has been made of it for this purpose by Stone and his associates.

As long as we stick to equilibrium dynamics all paths generated by (1) which make economic sense are " warranted " paths in the sense of Harrod. To investigate the " knife edge " therefore requires the construction of a disequilibrium model. The first person to realise this was Sargan (1958). He argues that the equilibrium model of Leontief may be taken as an approximation to the disequilibrium model of reality if the " knife edge " were not true. For then the paths of the disequilibrium model would converge on to the warranted paths of the equilibrium model. He, however, finds that the reverse is true. Allowing producers to react to errors with some delay instead of taking this reaction as instantaneous, as is done in (1), he shows that for his models either (*a*) the behaviour of the disequilibrium system is quite different from that of the equilibrium one or (*b*) as the " error reaction delay " gets indefinitely small the disequilibrium system generates paths which increasingly diverge from the warranted paths. He therefore confirms Harrod's " knife edge " and argues that therefore the Leontief equilibrium system cannot be held as a true approximation to the underlying disequilibrium system.

Sargan's result is probably somewhat more dependent on the particular disequilibrium models he investigates than he is prepared to admit. He pays no attention to prices and expectations. Leontief (1961) has suggested some models, somewhat implausible, in which Sargan's results do not hold. Somewhat more plausible models have been investigated by Rose (1959), Jorgenson (1961) and Hahn (1963). Jorgenson finds relative stability for a rather wide class of initial conditions. Jorgenson's model, however, is open to a number of objections (Macmanus (1963)). He supposes producers to hold speculative stocks. He makes the rate of stock accumulation a function, among other things, of the difference between desired and actual stocks. However, the rate at which this discrepancy is reduced if output were constant is made identically equal to what is available for this purpose. There seems to be no good reason why this should be so in a disequilibrium model.

The main conclusion to be drawn from this seems to be two-fold: It is extremely unlikely that a generally acceptable disequilibrium model can be produced in an " armchair." In particular, the delay structure is extremely relevant to the kind of conclusions we can draw, and *a priori* speculations are unlikely to be helpful here. Secondly, there is no general presumption that we may take equilibrium dynamics models as idealisations of some disequilibrium model—Sargan's work has shown that, for a wide variety of cases at least, this is not so.

(c) *Sausage Machines*

Lastly we return to the Samuelson–Solow " sausage-machine " model. The answer here is unambiguous and clear: the system described is always relatively stable. The reader can verify this for the case of two goods with the aid of Fig. III.7. We already know that the curve must intersect the 45° line in the manner shown. Since we are concerned with relative stability, we may restrict our attention to the " normalised " production process where outputs add up to unity. Starting, say, to the left of the intersection, we get a process as illustrated below.

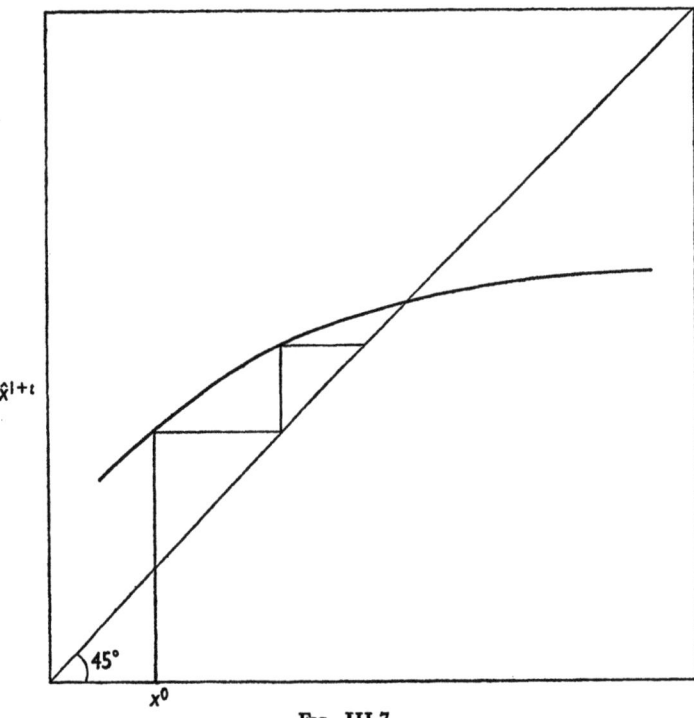

FIG. III.7

This result can be generalised to any number of goods.   It is not clear what comfort can be drawn from this.

III.6. *Efficient Accumulation*

As noted in the introduction, it is not possible to give an exhaustive account of developments in this field here, and only the most immediately relevant results will be discussed.   One of the most important (and beautiful) propositions of atemporal welfare economics is the following: In an economy with convex technology and preferences in which individuals are not satiated it is possible to assign a set of non-negative prices to the goods in any efficient allocation such that the prices are equilibrium prices for a competitive economy.   Conversely, in this economy every competitive equilibrium is efficient (Debreu (1961), Koopmans (1951), Dosso (1958)).   Let us refer to this as the " efficiency " and " competition " results respectively.   Efficiency is here Pareto–optimality: no individual can be made better off without another being made worse off.   Given the preference assumptions, this also means that it must be impossible to have more of one good without having less of another.   It is well known that at the efficiency prices the value of final output is maximised over all possible final outputs.

As far as this survey is concerned, the most important contribution is Malinvaud's 1953 paper, which is a landmark in the theory of capital (see also Malinvaud (1962)).   Malinvaud examines the problem of extending the " efficiency " and " competition " results to allocation problems over infinite horizons.   This is of considerable interest, because all finite horizon formulations either lead us to plan to consume everything by the terminal date or introduce rather arbitrary requirements on the stock of terminal goods it is required to have.   On the other hand, of course, infinite programmes not only imply that we take account of generations yet unborn but also that, in practice, uncertainty would play a large role.   As for unborn generations, most people would probably agree that some account should be taken of them.

Rather difficult mathematical problems are encountered in dealing with efficient infinite intertemporal allocations, and Malinvaud has circumvented one of them by an ingenious device.   Consider first a finite horizon problem. Since we may treat goods which are physically identical as different goods if they are delivered at different dates, we shall expect the efficiency and competition result to hold, since all that has happened is that we have more goods.   Moreover, if we really consider the world to end after the periods there will be no terminal stocks.

Let us take a world where the technological possibilities are given by T as already described (83 ff.).   (We again call x and y vectors of inputs and outputs, the former preceding the latter by one period.)   Let P_t be the vector of present prices of goods to be delivered at t.   Then for an efficient allocation the present value of consumption is maximised at one set of non-negative price vectors. $P_1, \ldots P_n$. Since consumption is the difference between output at t and what is put back into further production, we have for all possible sequences $x_t, y_t (t = 1, \ldots n)$

$$P_1 y_1 + \sum_{t=1}^{n-1} (P_{t+1} y_{t+1} - P_t x_t) - P_n x_n . \quad . \quad . \quad . \quad (1)$$

is at a maximum. Of course, here $x_n = 0$. If (1) is to be at a maximum, since there are constant returns to scale, it can easily be shown[1] that we must have

$$P_{t+1} y_{t+1} - P_t x_t = 0 \qquad t + 1, \ldots n - 1 \quad . \quad . \quad (2)$$

which is the expression we have met before (p. 85). In particular, once we have decided on a normalisation of prices, (1) defines an interest rate associated with an efficient programme (see p. 86).

If we now split the economy into firms and give a subscript k to each of the sectors in (1) to denote that they refer to the kth firm, it can be shown that if the resulting expressions are at their maximum for each firm the allocation is efficient. Each firm supposes the world to end at n, so $x_{nk} = 0$ all k. That is, if at a set of strictly positive prices all firms have maximised the present value of profit the allocation will be efficient. We note that for this to be true the marginal rate of substitution between any two commodities must be the same whether considered as outputs of one period or as inputs of the next period. This is shown by the fact that P_t occurs in $P_t y_t - P_{t-1} x_{t-1}$ and $P_{t+1} y_{t+1} - P_t x_t$, the present value of profits in $t - 1$ and t. It can also be easily shown that at these prices (and our preference assumptions), the present cost of a consumption stream which would make someone better off without worsening the position of any other consumer would be higher than that of the actual consumption stream.

Thus, as long as we stick to finite horizons, everything is fine. But now suppose we are considering an infinite problem. Then x_n in (1) cannot be put equal to zero as a matter of course for any finite n. Malinvaud proves the following two results: (*a*) for any efficient infinite allocation, for the technology and preferences postulated, there exists an infinite sequence of non-negative price sectors $P_1, P_2, \ldots$ such that for any n (1) is greater than for any other feasible programme identical with the given one for $t > n$. If there exists an infinite sequence of positive price vectors such that (1) with subscripts k (see above) is greater for every n than any other feasible sequence with subscript k identical to the given one for $t > n$ *and* if $P_n \sum_k x_{nk} \to 0$ as $n \to \infty$, then the programme is efficient.

It is seen that (*b*) is not quite the same as the " competition result " for the atemporal case. The intuitive reason is as follows. Take any finite n, but suppose the world to continue for ever thereafter. Then whether or not

[1] Malinvaud (1953), p. 247

the allocation x_{nk} between firms is efficient can be discovered only by considering outputs resulting from it after n.   But this is true for every finite n, so that an inefficient allocation of terminal production goods can never be discovered in finite time.   Put slightly differently, there is nothing in perfect competition equilibrium to ensure that at the end of any time period the distribution of capital and its volume will be such as to make the remainder of an infinite production programme efficient.   If, however, the conditions of (b) hold, then it can be shown that the " competition result " follows.   An interesting example of an inefficient perfect competition equilibrium over infinite time is given by Samuelson's (1958) article on pure consumption loans.   Another example is given by Koopmans (1959).   If the only activity of firms is storage, and if the interest rate is zero, firms may store certain quantities indefinitely without violating (1) at some set of prices, yet consumption could evidently be increased.

A good deal of further work remains to be done in this field—especially on uncertainty.   But it should not be thought that a study of the infinite efficiency problem is of no practical importance.   Even if in practice we must limit ourselves to finite horizons, the infinite case will almost certainly help us to formulate reasonable rules concerning terminal stocks.   In any case, even if we can look ahead for only five years, the future shifts forward from year to year so that, for instance, in planning, considerable practical difficulties may arise if we take the five-year period literally.   It is now interesting to consider proportional growth problems in the light of the foregoing results.

Suppose we consider a Neumann path of finite duration such that the associated prices are strictly positive.   Then a rather straightforward application of Malinvaud's theorems assures us that this path is efficient. If $\bar{x}_t \bar{y}_{t+1}$ is the Neumann input–output pair and $x_t y_{t+1}$ any other possible pair we know (see p. 863)

$$-P_t \bar{x}_t + P_{t+1} \bar{y}_{t+1} = 0 \qquad t = 0 \ldots T-1 \quad . \quad . \quad \text{(i)}$$

$$-P_t x_t + P_{t+1} y_{t+1} \leqq 0 \qquad t = 0 \ldots T-1 \quad . \quad . \quad \text{(ii)}$$

If the Neumann path from $\bar{x}_0$ to $\bar{y}_T$ is not efficient, then there is some other path from $\bar{x}_0$ to some y_T such that $y_T \geqslant \bar{y}_T$.[1]   But now add (i) over t and (ii) over t to obtain

$$-P_0 \bar{x}_0 + P_T \bar{y}_T = 0 \quad . \quad . \quad . \quad . \quad . \quad \text{(i')}$$

$$-P_0 \bar{x}_0 + P_T y_T \leqq 0 \quad . \quad . \quad . \quad . \quad . \quad \text{(ii')}$$

---

[1] We are here defining efficiency with respect to terminal quantities only.   This is not identical with Malinvaud's definition for finite T.   But on the Neumann path there is no consumption before the " end " of the story at T.

Since $P_t > 0$ and $y_T \geqslant \bar{y}_T$, substituting $P_T y_T$ for $P_T \bar{y}_T$ in (i) gives us

$$-P_o \bar{x}_o + P_T y_T > 0$$

which contradicts (ii′). Hence $y_T \geqslant \bar{y}_T$ is impossible (Mackenzie (1963), Furoya and Inada (1962)).

But, of course, the above conclusion does not tell us anything about efficient paths starting from an arbitrary point $x_o \neq \bar{x}_o$. There is, however, an interesting result for infinite efficient paths starting at an arbitrary x_o. Finite efficient growth will be further considered in the next section.

Furoya and Inada have proved (see also Fisher (1963)) that, if in addition to the property of T given on p. 84, the following assumptions also hold, every infinite efficient path starting from any point must converge on to the (unique) Neumann path. The additional assumptions are quite strong, they are:

(a) If (x, y) and (x', y') are in T, the $(x + x', \bar{y})$ is also in T with $\bar{y} \geqslant y' + y$. This is called *strong super additivity* and is (with constant returns to scale) similar to the strong convexity assumption we have met before.

(b) For $x_o \geqslant 0$ there is some finite t such that $y_t > 0$ is technically possible. That is if initial stocks include some goods in positive amounts, then in finite time it is possible to produce all goods in positive amounts. The production set is said to be *primitive*. If this is not so it is *inprimitive*.

Both (a) and (b) are quite strong. Thus, while it is not unreasonable to suppose that the sum of two processes gives us just the sum of their separate outputs, it is not easy to see why there should always be " external economies " present. The primitivity assumption is also pretty drastic. On the other hand, one need not be too worried by the fact that the assumption, among other things, excludes a technology where goods can be grouped into disjoint batches $x(i)$, $(i = 1, \ldots m)$ such that goods for batch i can only produce goods in batch $(i + 1)$. (Sometimes also called the cyclic case.) It is clear here that if we start with only batch $x(i)$, then after every multiple of m periods we can only have goods in batch $x(i)$, and so assumption (b) will not be fulfilled. But if into such an economy we introduce storage processes for each good it will cease to be cyclic. Since storage is not unheard of in the world, the fact that (b) excludes the cyclic case should not worry us unduly. Still (a) and (b) are strong—but, then, so is the theorem, and we cannot get something for nothing.

So far we have considered only proportional growth paths in which there is no final consumption (labour is " produced "). Suppose consumption is present. The first thing we can do is to prove the neo-neo-classical theorem for this more general case (p. 38). It will be seen to be an almost trivial consequence of the efficiency theorem. (This proof is based on Malinvaud (1961).)

Let C_t be the vector of net consumption. A positive component means the good is consumed by households, a negative that it is supplied by them for production.   With free disposal we have

$$y_t = x_t + C_t \quad . \quad . \quad . \quad . \quad . \quad (3)$$

We suppose that we have found a growth rate g and a path such that if $\bar{C}_t$ is the net consumption vector for the path, then for no other possible path growing at g can one have $C_t \geqslant \bar{C}_t$. Now $\bar{y}_t = (1 + g)^{t-1}y_1$, $x^t = (1 + g)^t x_0$, $\bar{C}_t = (1 + g)^t C_0$. Hence, omitting the t subscript, we have from (3)

$$\frac{y}{1 + g} - x = C \quad . \quad . \quad . \quad . \quad . \quad (4)$$

If the production set is convex, then the set of possible C defined by (4) is convex.   Hence if $\bar{C}$ in this set $\geqslant$ all other C in this set we must have some price vector such that $P(\bar{C} - C) \leqslant 0$.   The argument is just as in, say, Fig. III.9.   But then from (4) we have

$$\frac{P}{1 + g}(\bar{y} - y) \leqslant P(\bar{x} - x) \leqslant 0 \quad . \quad . \quad . \quad (5)$$

all possible (x, y).   Hence there exists an interest rate $r = g$ which makes all processes yield a non-positive surplus and satisfies (1) when prices have been so normalised as to keep them constant from period to period.   It can be shown that such, constant, prices can be found (Malinvaud (1953), (1959)).   It is also interesting to consider the question in a different light. Let $(\bar{x}_t, \bar{y}_{t+1})$ be an efficient proportional growth path and P the vector of efficiency prices associated with it.   Let (x_t, y_{t+1}) be another efficient proportional growth programme.   Both programmes have the growth rate g. Assuming the production surface differentiable, consider

$$\lim_{x_t \to \bar{x}_t} \frac{P[(y_{t+1} - x_t) - (\bar{y}_{t+1} - \bar{x}_t)]}{P(x_t - \bar{x}_t)} = \lim_{x_t \to \bar{x}} \frac{(1 + g)}{g} \cdot \frac{P(C - \bar{C})}{P(x - \bar{x})} + g \ (6)$$

(Use has been made of (3) in obtaining the second part of (6).)

There are no great objections in calling (6) the marginal social return on investment for an efficient proportional growth programme.   Of course, there are many other social returns which might be calculated, depending on the consumption plans contemplated.   Moreover, we must decide on the prices to be used in the calculation.   Here we follow the natural line of using the efficiency prices of the path, (small) virtual displacement for which are being considered.   Certainly if the path (y_{t+1}, x_t) is far away " from our given path " its own efficiency prices will be different from the ones here used.   In any event, once one has decided on a definition the only question of concern is whether it is either interesting or useful.

It is easily seen that the definition adopted is at least interesting. For from (6) if $(\bar{x}_t, \bar{y}_{t+1})$ maximises permanent maintainable consumption it follows that the first term on the right-hand side of (6) is zero, so that the marginal social return on investment is g. This we already know must be equal to the "efficiency" interest rate for such a programme. This is comforting.

We may also easily see that for all proportional growth programmes which do not maximise the permanently maintainable consumption stream the efficiency rate of interest is still equal to the marginal social return for investment. For we know that for all (x_t, y_{t+1}) not proportional to $(\bar{x}_t, \bar{y}_{t+1})$ one has

$$\frac{P(1+g)v}{1+r} - Px \leqslant 0 \quad . \quad . \quad . \quad . \quad . \quad (7)$$

Using (3), this becomes

$$\frac{P(r-g)x}{1+g} \geqslant PC \quad . \quad . \quad . \quad . \quad . \quad (7')$$

But

$$\frac{P(r-g)\bar{x}}{1+g} = P\bar{C} \quad . \quad . \quad . \quad . \quad . \quad (8)$$

Subtracting (8) from (7) and taking $P(x_t - \bar{x}) > 0$, one has

$$r \geqslant g + (1+g)\frac{P(C - \bar{C})}{P(x - \bar{x})} \quad . \quad . \quad . \quad . \quad (9)$$

Letting $x \to \bar{x}$ gives equality in (9).

All that these results say is that there exist consistent ways of calculation and definition which allow us to find a relationship between what we call the efficiency rate of interest and what we choose to call the marginal social return on investment (Malinvaud (1953), (1962), Solow (1963)).

III.7. *Turnpike Theorems*

While it is instructive to examine the case of infinite horizons, we know that for most practical purposes, so far, one seeks programmes which are optimal over a finite horizon. In particular, the following may be a practical problem: goods are required in certain proportions T periods hence; find that accumulation path which will maximise the scale at which these goods will be available. Alternatively, we may be asked to find that programme which will reach a given specified output level of goods in the shortest time. It is true that usually one would expect to find certain consumption preferences given for the planning period as well. We do not pursue this but suppose that during the planning period the only consumption allowed is that necessary (in the Neumann sense) to " produce " household services. This may not be altogether unrealistic in certain cases.

The solution to this problem was first discussed by Dosso (1958) (although it was faulty), and has since given rise to an extensive literature.   No more can be done here than to provide a brief outline.   The main proposition sought is this: supposing there to be a unique Neumann growth ray (see p. 85), then, whatever the initial endowments, any efficient programme for the above problem will stay within a certain neighbourhood of the Neumann ray for " most of the time."   The time spent in the neighbourhood may be independent of the horizon T.   This will depend on the precise assumptions made.   The intuition leading to the theorem is simply that we know that on the Neumann ray we attain the fastest balanced growth.   This, of course, is not enough to confirm the " Turnpike conjecture."

The most elegant, simple and satisfactory turnpike theorem is undeniably Radner's (1961), and it will be the only one to be discussed in any detail here.

Consider a technological possibility of set T as defined on p. 84.   Supposing it to be strictly convex, we know that there is a unique x^* associated with the maximum balanced growth rate α^* such that $y^* = \alpha^* x^*$.   We also know that associated with this " ray " there is a price vector P^* and interest factor $\beta^* = \alpha^*$ such that $P^*(y - \beta^* x) < 0$ for all y and x not proportional to x^* and y^*.

Let us suppose that the initial endowment is x_o and that we wish to maximise the utility $u(x_T)$ of goods available at T.   Radner takes this utility function as linear and homogeneous, so that the case where goods are desired in fixed proportions is a special instance of this function.   Suppose it is feasible to reach the Neumann proportions x^* in one step, i.e., for some $h > 0$, (x_o, hx^*), belong to T.   Note that this may involve disposing of some goods.   Once on the Neumann ray if we stick to it we have $x^*_{t+1} = \alpha^* x^*_t$, and since the utility function is linear and homogeneous we would obtain

$$u(x^*_t) = h(\alpha^*)^{T-1} u(x^*_T) \quad . \quad . \quad . \quad . \quad . \quad (1)$$

at T.   Evidently every other feasible path if it is to be chosen must do at least as well as this.

We now introduce a further, rather innocuous assumption: there exists a $k > 0$ such that for all x, $u(x) \leqslant kP^* x$.   If, for instance, $P^* > 0$ the reader can easily verify that this will be so given the other postulates.   The rest is now easy.

Suppose we introduce a measure of distance between any two vectors. Radner uses one which is equivalent to taking the angle between them.   Let us write $d(x, x^*)$ as this distance between any vector x and the Neumann vector.   (Note that this distance is defined independently of scale—only the ratios of the goods in x and to those in x^* are compared.)   It is easy to show (using the strict convexity of T and its boundedness) [1] that for all x such that $d(x, x^*) \geqslant \epsilon > 0$ there exists some $\delta > 0$ such that

$$P^*y - \alpha^*P^*x \leqslant -\delta P^*x \quad . \quad . \quad . \quad . \quad . \quad (2)$$

This simply says that the " value loss " of being away from the Neumann ray cannot be less than a given fraction of the value of inputs.

The stage is now set and we illustrate the rest of the argument by a simple diagram applicable to the case where there are only two goods. In Fig. III.8 we have given x_0 the initial endowment of the two goods. The curve

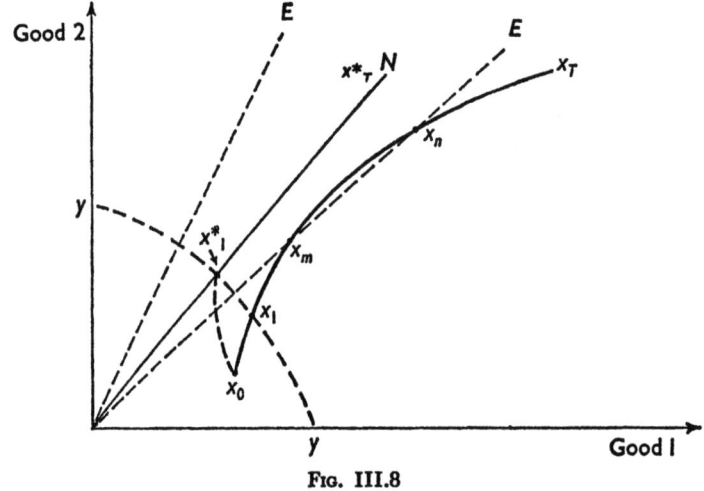

Fig. III.8

yy shows the possible outputs we can reach from x_0 in the next period. The line N gives the Neumann proportions. It is seen that we may move to x^*_1 on this ray. Continuing thereafter on this may for the remaining $(T - 1)$ periods brings us to x^*_T. The two vectors E, on either side of N, define the area within which all vectors with $d(x, x^*) \leqslant \epsilon$ must lie. The path $x_0x_1x_T$ is some feasible path other than the Neumann path. We see that it lies within the ϵ-neighbourhood of N between the mth and nth stage of the programme.

We may now perform some simple calculations. From the application of (2) and the fact that for all points inside the ϵ neighbourhood $P^*y \leqslant \alpha^*P^*x$ we have

$$\begin{aligned} P^*x_m &\leqslant (\alpha^* - \delta)^m P^*x_0 \\ P^*x_n &\leqslant (\alpha^*)^{n-m}P^*x_m \quad \text{so } P^*x_T \leqslant (\alpha^*)^{n-m}(\alpha^* - \delta)^{T-(n-m)}P^*x_0 \quad (3) \\ P^*x_T &\leqslant (\alpha^* - \delta)^{T-n}P^*x_n \end{aligned}$$

Now $T - (n - m)$ is the total number of periods spent outside the ϵ neigh-

---

[1] Let x^q be a sequence of input vectors such that $\|x^q\| = 1$. Suppose that for this sequence $\|y^q\| \to \infty$. Since $(x^q y^q)\epsilon T$ it follows from constant returns to scale that $\left(\dfrac{x^q}{\|y^q\|}, \dfrac{y^q}{\|y^q\|}\right)\epsilon T$. But as $q \to \infty$, we then have $(0, \bar{y})\epsilon T$ where $\|\bar{y}\| = 1$, since the sequence is bounded and $\|y^q\| \to \infty$. This, however, contradicts the assumption that we cannot get something for nothing.

bourhood and let us now call this S. Using the assumption $U(x_T) \leqslant kP^*x_T$ we have

$$U(x_T) \leqslant k(\alpha)^{T-S}(\alpha^* - \delta)^S P^* x_o \quad . \quad . \quad . \quad . \quad (4)$$

Clearly if the path $x_0, x_1, \ldots x_T$ is at least as good as $x_0, x^*_1, \ldots x^*_T$ we must have $U(x_T) \geqslant U(x^*_T)$. Using (7) we thus have $h(\alpha^*)^{T-1}U(x^*) \leqslant$ the right-hand side of (4) or

$$\frac{k}{h} \frac{\alpha^* P^* x \delta}{U(x^*)} \left(\frac{\alpha^* - \delta}{\alpha^*}\right)^S \geqslant 1 \quad . \quad . \quad . \quad . \quad (5)$$

Writing C for the expression outside the bracket, we get that for the actual path to be no worse than the Neumann path

$$S \leqslant \max\left(1, \frac{\log C}{\log\left(\dfrac{\alpha^*}{\alpha^* - \delta}\right)}\right) \quad . \quad . \quad . \quad . \quad (6)$$

which gives us the largest number of periods any efficient path can stay outside the ϵ-neighbourhood. It does not follow that an optimum path will not stay outside their neighbourhood for a shorter period still. It is clear that S does not depend on T.

One drawback in Radner's proof has been quickly remedied by Nikaido (1964). As it stands, the proof does not exclude the possibility that the periods spent by the path in the ϵ-neighbourhood are not consecutive. There may be repeated entry and re-entry. Nikaido shows that if we can suppose all goods to be strictly positive along the Neumann ray, and if something can be produced whatever the initial endowment and if utility is increased by having more of every good then the optimum growth path will stay continuously in a given neighbourhood for " most of the time." Since these assumptions are pretty harmless, this is a noticeable strengthening of Radner's result.

It is also fairly clear that Radner's result depends rather crucially on the assumption that all activities other than Neumann activity make a loss at the Neumann prices (strict convexity of T). We already know (see above) that in the polyhedral case this need not be so and that there may be many pairs (x, y) besides the Neumann pair which make zero loss.[1] We recall that the set of all such pairs has been called the Neumann facet (p. 86). Since many production models are of the polyhedral type, considerable effort and ingenuity has gone to provide a " turnpike theorem " for these cases also. The main contributors are Morishima (1961) and Mackenzie (1963).

Before briefly describing their work we may give an intuitive account of

---

[1] In any case strict convexity of T implies the existence of external economies. If these are absent, then even " neo-classical " production functions, one for each sector, will in general give rise to Neumann facets.

the problem.   Consider some technological set T which gives rise to a Neumann facet.   In the first instance we may suppose the Neumann prices to be unique so that there is only one Neumann facet.   Let us call it F.   We may now define a distance $d(z, F)$ of any vector z from the facet as the smallest angle we can find between z and any vector in the facet.   One may now apply the Radner procedure to show that at the Neumann prices: (a) any (x, y) not in the facet (by definition) makes a non-positive profit, and (b) that any (x, y) with distance greater or equal to $\epsilon > 0$ makes a loss not less than a fraction $\delta > 0$ of the value of its inputs.   It is then fairly easy to use the rest of Radner's procedure to show that any optimum path must spend most of its time in the vicinity of the facet.

But this is not yet the turnpike, since the facet contains many non-Neumann pairs (x, y).   Suppose, however, we could show: (a) that there is a path of pairs (x, y) in the facet which spends " most of its time " near the Neumann ray; (b) that the optimum path which we already know is most of its time near to the facet is also " most of its time " near the path given in (a), then we would be home and a turnpike theorem results.

It is not surprising that to get results like these requires some further precise assumptions.   The most useful are those which ensure that the Neumann ray is unique, that on it all goods are produced in positive amounts and that associated with it is a unique, strictly positive set of prices.   But even if that is not so it is possible that turnpike theorems can be proved, although so far they have only been sketched (Mackenzie).   Evidently as a minimum we will require that the value of output on a Neumann ray be positive, else the comparison with the efficient path will break down.   But if, say, the system is reducible, so that there may be a number of paths of balanced growth at different rates and so a number of associated facets (see p. 81), we may still be all right—at least as far as convergence to a facet is concerned.   For we know from Malinvaud that every efficient path has associated with it a set of efficiency prices as defined above (p. 100).   If now there is a Neumann ray which can be reached from a given initial endowment and if on this ray the Neumann price of any good is positive if its efficiency price is positive and if the good in question is produced in positive amounts, then the comparison between the two paths can go on as before.   The particular efficient path must spend most of its time near that particular facet.   These are possibilities not yet thoroughly investigated, and we do not pursue them here.

Mackenzie considers an economy in which each process produces only one good, although it transfers also capital stocks from one period to the next (see p. 90).   For each good there are many possible processes.   By suitable assumption on the set of possible processes he ensures that the system can be represented as is done by Morishima (1959) in another context, and which we have discussed on pp. 92–94.   That is: there is a unique set of positive efficiency prices such that each good is produced by one process and there is no process which would make a positive profit at these prices. Recall that in the Neumann model real wages are fixed [1] and we know that those prices are uniquely determined. By imposing strict convexity he ensures that in fact for each good all processes other than the one chosen would make a loss at these prices. We have thus a Leontief model as already discussed where the " efficient " coefficients can be treated as fixed. Assumptions are introduced to ensure that the efficient processes are capable of a unique balanced growth path with all outputs positive. On the other hand, there are many combinations (x, y) attainable with these processes which make zero profits but are not Neumann combinations, and we thus have a Neumann facet. Indeed, it is easy to show that the set (x, y) in the facet can be represented as a simple set of first-order difference equations given above (p. 94).

Mackenzie proves convergence to the facet of the optimum path in a manner already sketched. He then shows that starting with any vector $Z_o \geqslant 0$ in the facet we can trace out, by help of the difference equation structure, all subsequent Z_t. It can be shown that for a proportion of the horizon time T this path must lie in the ϵ-neighbourhood of the Neumann ray. This can be shown to be so, because if this were not so the Leontief system would force negative output of some goods. He then shows that the optimum path must lie near to one of these paths in the facet. This then allows him to show that an optimum path must stay near the Neumann ray for a period not less than a certain minimum. It should be explained again that to say that the optimum path is near the Neumann ray means roughly that the ratios in which goods are produced are close to those in the Neumann ray.

Morishima's (1961) Turnpike theorem—although proved somewhat differently from this, differs only in using a generalised Leontief model where there is no transfer of capital stock. He also shows that this result will not hold for the cyclic case (see p. 102 for description). Lastly we should return to where the story started. Dosso initially considered a neo-classical smooth convex transformation set $T(x, y)$ and examined the behaviour of paths with starting and end points in the vicinity of the Neumann ray. They did not then succeed in establishing a turnpike theorem, but Samuelson (1960) and Mackenzie (1963) have since clinched the matter. Since global results are now available, this seems of less importance than it was.

It is evident that more progress can be expected in this field. It is not easy to judge its practical significance at the moment. The theorems are typical of economic theory, *i.e.*, they are qualitatively descriptive of a pro-perty of optimum paths—but it is not clear that they will help in planning. The most important gap is the neglect of utility considerations along the planning period. It should also be noted that there may be other measures of " distance " which are more relevant than the ones so far employed. Thus

---

[1] *I.e.*, the input coefficients for " the production " of the unit of labour are fixed.

it may be possible to get useful results by comparing the Neumann growth rate in the value of output with the growth rate of any other path.

IV. RETROSPECT

IV.1. *Theoretical Controversies*

The variety of growth models is very great and with ingenuity can evidently be almost indefinitely enlarged. This is very largely due to the rather extreme level of abstraction employed and the very artificial nature of the problems considered. It is not easy to bring facts to bear on " steady states " and " equilibrium dynamics." This lack of empirical discipline is best exemplified in the rather unfortunate dichotomisation between " Keynesian " and " Neo-Classical " growth models.

As we have seen, it is perfectly possible to have coherent growth models which employ a classical savings function but postulate a neo-classical production function with perfect competition. Conversely it is easy to analyse a model where there is " learning by doing " and an absence of perfect competition and yet savings are proportional to income. The question, which kind of savings hypothesis is appropriate, is not one of belief and dogma but of fact.

Again the recognition that there is a great variety of machines (as of course there is a great variety of men and of consumer goods), while serving the purpose of leading to a sharpening of theoretical tools, can hardly on its own be of decisive importance. For it seems fairly clear that any confrontation or theory with fact will have to proceed by the use of some agigregative methods. Moreover there can be few economists who do not understand the index number problem. The real problem here is to find theoretical constructs which, without being downright misleading, are crude enough to bear the weight of the crude evidence. To say that this or that theory rests on an abstract idealisation, (*e.g.* homogeneous flexible capital), is not enough to condemn it if the alternative offered has no hope of empirical applications or verification. We want theories that can be used as plumbers use a spanner—not simply abstract systems.

As far as pure theory is concerned the " measurement of capital " is no problem at all because we never have to face it if we do not choose to. With our armchair omniscience we can take account of each machine separately. Moreover the measurement business has nothing whatsoever to do with the question of whether imputation theory is or is not valid. In an equilibrium of the whole system, provided there is perfect competition, no learning by doing and no uncertainty, the neo-classical imputation results hold. This should now be beyond dispute. It is also of little comfort to the empirically inclined.

Where recent discussions have made a decisive contribution is in the recognition that investing and technical progress may be Siamese twins. Once the possibility is admitted, very fascinating problems of formulating and specifying production possibilities arise. For instance, we have seen that it has led Kaldor to the technical progress function and Arrow to his formalisation of the process, both of which are ripe for empirical testing. Moreover, if the " learning process " is not internalised (see page 72) by the firm a real dent is made to imputation theory. Happily this does not appear to be a matter of controversy—most growth theorists regard it as a peculiarly appealing nut to try to crack.

Indeed the division between formal models which do and those which do not take account of learning by doing, seems to us to be perhaps the most important dichotomisation which could be made.

Returning once more to the question of the validity or otherwise of imputation theory, there is a further, purely theoretical, point of some importance to be made. When an economy with many goods is considered, we must also find the relative equilibrium prices of these goods. Whether these are determined à la Leontief-Samuelson-Sraffa or à la Walras, imputation is at once involved. If we abandon imputation entirely then the whole question of relative prices must be reconsidered afresh. Perhaps it ought to be, but recognition that this problem exists seems desirable.

IV.2. *Theory and Reality*

Different contributors to the theory of growth have differed a good deal in their views about the aims of the exercise. This makes for difficulty in drawing conclusions about how far the aims have been realised.

Some authors have tried to construct models which, though simplified as any model must be, do correspond to the most important features of reality (the " stylised facts," in Kaldor's terminology), and they have proceeded to draw inferences about the explanation of observed events and about policy. Others have been less ambitious and have viewed their models as illustrations of how an economy *would* move on certain assumptions, in the hope that understanding of the laws of motion of their imaginary world might cast light, even if only by analogy, on the laws of motion of the infinitely more complex world of reality. Yet others have been more interested in an individual element (the learning process, for example) than in the model as a whole, and have constructed overall models mainly to illustrate how this element is capable of working out, without setting any particular store by the other assumption chosen to complete the model.

It is not difficult to devise a multiplicity of models to fit the " stylised facts," if these are defined narrowly enough. But for a model to be *directly* useful for the understanding of reality it should be able to do more than this: it should be able to yield testable, non-trivial " predictions." Thus it is well established that there have been substantial differences between countries and between periods in rates of growth. It would be difficult to claim that any of the models we have discussed goes far towards explaining these differences or predicting what will happen to them in the future.

Given the assumptions common to the models (no government, no international trade and so on), this is not surprising, and it may reasonably be argued that most model-builders have not been trying to do this, anyway. However, the general preoccupation with the case of steady-state growth and also, perhaps, an unduly restricted and over-simplified background concept of the phenomenon to be explained (" growth of the U.S. economy since 1865 at a constant rate with constant capital–output ratio and distribution of income ") have drawn the theory into directions which severely limit its direct empirical applications or usefulness. The historical patterns of economic growth, as summarised, for example, by Kuznets (1959) and Paige (1961), are too complex to be describable in terms of steady growth.

This does not detract from the value of the conclusions that have been reached in the pursuit of the less ambitious, illustrative purposes stated above. Many of these conclusions are important and by no means obvious or trivial. And it does not detract from the value of the work done in evolving the individual building blocks out of which the models have been constructed. Some of the ideas that have come out in the course of this work—the vintage approach to capital theory, for example—may turn out to be of more enduring value than the comprehensive growth models in which they are enshrined.

IV.3. *Future Prospects*

When we take a broad view of the work we have surveyed it becomes clear that a large part of it is concerned with different aspects of one particular topic: how to analyse the working of a system in which one of the inputs in the productive process is capital, which is itself a produced good and is durable. Great progress has been made in understanding the intellectual problems involved, particularly as regards the properties of steady-state growth. Great progress has also been made in understanding the problems of efficient allocation that arise when there is more than one sector—though this work is perhaps more directly useful for planning purposes than for explaining history.

While not disparaging the insights that have been gained, we feel that in these areas the point of diminishing returns may have been reached. Nothing is easier than to ring the changes on more and more complicated models, without bringing in any really new ideas and without bringing the theory any nearer to casting light on the causes of the wealth of nations. The problems posed may well have intellectual fascination. But it is essentially a frivolous occupation to take a chain with links of very uneven strength and devote one's energies to strengthening and polishing the links that are already relatively strong.

Two aspects may be singled out as requiring more attention in future work (without implying that there are not others). The motivation of economic agents needs analysis in a way that avoids the twin dangers of empty formalism and inconclusive anecdote. And more thought should be given to the concept of the world as a whole as an underdeveloped economy, in which even the evolution of the advanced sectors may be impossible to understand properly in isolation from the sectors that are less developed.[1]

BIBLIOGRAPHY[2]

Abbreviations:

AER	*American Economic Review*
EJ	*Economic Journal*
ER	*Economic Record*
Ec	*Economica*, New Series
Em	*Econometrica*
IER	*International Economic Review*
JB	*Journal of Business*
JPE	*Journal of Political Economy*
Kyk	*Kyklos*
Met	*Metroeconomica*
OEP	*Oxford Economic Papers*
OIS	*Oxford University Institute of Statistics Bulletin*
QJE	*Quarterly Journal of Economics*
REStat	*Review of Economics and Statistics*
REStud	*Review of Economic Studies*
YB	*Yorkshire Bulletin of Economic and Social Research*

Abramovitz, M. (1952) " Economics of Growth," in *A Survey of Contemporary Economics*, Vol. II, edited by B. F. Haley (Homewood, Illinois: Irwin, for *American Economic Association, 1952*).

Abramovitz, M. (1956) " Resource and Output Trends in the United States since 1870," *AER Papers and Proceedings*, Vol. XLVI, May 1956.

Abramovitz, M. (1962) " Economic Growth in the United States." *AER*, Vol. LII, September 1962.

Adelman, I. (1962) *Theories of Economic Growth and Development* (Stanford, 1962).

Alexander, S. S. (1949) " The Accelerator as a Generator of Steady Growth," *QJE*, Vol. LXIII, May 1949.

Alexander, S. S. (1950) " Mr Harrod's Dynamic Model," *EJ*, Vol. LX, December 1950.

Allais, M. (1962). "The Influence of the Capital–Output Ratio on Real National Income," Em, Vol. XXX, October 1962.

Allen, R. G. D. (1960) " The Structure of Macroeconomic Models," *EJ*, Vol. LXX, March 1960.

Ames, E., and Rosenberg, N. (1963) " Changing Technological Leadership and Industrial Growth," *EJ*, Vol. LXXIII, March 1963.

Anderson, P. A. (1961) " The Apparent Decline in Capital–Output Ratios," *QJE*, Vol. LXXV, November 1961.

---

[1] For discussion of this last point see Hart, Kaldor and Tinbergen (1964).

[2] We are indebted to Mr. A. G. Armstrong and to Miss A. Ewing for assistance in preparing this bibliography. Reference to papers published in collected volume form is generally to the latter and not to the original place of publication.

Ando, A., and Simon, H. A. (1961) "Aggregation of Variables in Dynamic Systems," *Em*, Vol. 29, April 1961.

Ando, A., and Fisher, F. M. (1963) "Near-decomposability, Partition and Aggregation, and the Relevance of Stability Discussions," *IER*, Vol. IV, January 1963.

Ando, A., Fisher, F. M., and Simon, H. A. (1963) *Essays on The Structure of Social Science Models* (Cambridge, Mass.: M.I.T. Press, 1963).

Arrow, K. J. (1951) "Alternative Proof of the Substitution Theorem for Leontief Models in the General Case," in *Activity Analysis of Production and Allocation*, ed. T. C. Koopmans (New York: Wiley, 1951).

Arrow, K. J. (1962) "The Economic Implications of Learning by Doing," *REStud*, Vol. XXIX, June 1962.

Arrow, K. J., Chenery, H. B., Minhas, B., and Solow, R. M. (1961) "Capital–Labour Substitution and Economic Efficiency," *REStat*, Vol. XLIII, August 1961.

Asimakopulos, A. (1963) "The Definition of Neutral Inventions," *EJ*, Vol. LXXIII, December 1963.

Asimakopulos, A., and Weldon, J. C. (1963) "The Classification of Technical Progress in Models of Economic Growth," *Ec*, Vol. XXX, November 1963.

Beckerman, W. (1962) "Projecting Europe's Growth," *EJ*, Vol LXXII, December 1962.

Bhagwati, J. N. (1964) "The Pure Theory of International Trade," *EJ*, Vol. LXXIV, March 1964, reprinted in this volume, pp. 156–239.

Black, J. (1962a) "The Technical Progress Function and the Production Function," *Ec*, Vol. XXIX, May 1962.

Black, J. (1962b) "Technical Progress and Optimum Savings," *REStud*, Vol. XXIX, June 1962.

Blaug, M. (1963) "A Survey of the Theory of Process Innovations," *Ec*, Vol. XXX, February 1963.

Boulding, K. (1950) *A Reconstruction of Economics* (New York: Wiley, 1950).

Brown, J. A. C., and Stone, J. R. N. (1962) "Output and Investment for Exponential Growth in Consumption," *REStud*, Vol XXIX, June 1962.

Butt, D. M. Bensusan (1960) *On Economic Growth: An Essay in Pure Theory* (London: Oxford University Press, 1960).

Buttrick, J. (1958) "A Note on Professor Solow's Growth Model," *QJE*, Vol. LXXII, November 1958.

Caff, J. T. (1961) "A Generalisation of the Multiplier–Accelerator Model," *EJ*, Vol. LXXI, March 1961.

Cairncross, A. K. (1953) "The Place of Capital in Economic Progress," in *Economic Progress*, Proceedings of International Economic Association Conference, edited by L. H. Dupriez (Louvain: Institut de Recherches Economiques et Sociales, 1955).

Carter, C. F., and Williams, B. R. (1957) *Industry and Technical Progress* (London: Oxford University Press, 1957).

Carter, C. F., and Williams, B. R. (1958) *Investment in Innovation* (London: Oxford University Press, 1958).

Carter, C. F., and Williams, B. R. (1959) *Science in Industry* (London: Oxford University Press, 1959).

Champernowne, D. G. (1958) " Capital Accumulation and the Maintenance of Full Employment," *EJ*, Vol. LXVIII, June 1958.

Champernowne, D. G. (1961) " A Dynamic Growth Model involving a Production Function," in *The Theory of Capital*, Proceedings of International Association Conference, edited by F. A. Lutz and D. C. Hague (London: Macmillan, 1961).

Champernowne, D. G. (1962) " Some Implications of Golden Age Conditions When Savings Equal Profits," *REStud*, Vol. XXIX, June 1962.

Champernowne, D. G., and Kahn, R. F. (1954) " The Value of Invested Capital. A Mathematical Addendum to Mrs. Robinson's Article," *REStud*, Vol. XXI, 1954.

Denison, E. F. (1962) *The Sources of Economic Growth in the United States and the Alternatives before Us* (New York: Committee for Economic Development, 1962.)

Desrousseaux, J. (1961). " Expansion stable et taux d'intérêt optimal," *Annales des Mines*, November 1961.

Domar, E. D. (1946) " Capital Expansion, Rate of Growth and Employment," *Em*, Vol. 14, April 1946.

Domar, E. D. (1947) " Expansion and Employment," *AER*, Vol. XXXVII, March 1947.

Domar, E. D. (1957) *Essays in the Theory of Growth* (London: Oxford University Press, 1957).

Dorfman, R., Samuelson, P. A., and Solow, R. M. (1958). *Linear Programming and Economic Analysis* (New York: McGraw-Hill, 1958).

Drandanakis, E. M. (1963) " Factor Substitution in the Two-sector Growth Model," *REStud*, Vol. XXX, October 1963.

Duesenberry, J. S. (1949) *Income, Saving and the Theory of Consumer Behaviour* (Cambridge, Mass.: Harvard University Press, 1949).

Duesenberry, J. S. (1958) *Business Cycles and Economic Growth* (New York: McGraw-Hill, 1958).

Eckstein, O. (1959) (Chief author) Staff Report on Employment, Growth, and Price Levels, prepared for consideration by the Joint Economic Committee, Congress of the United States, December 24, 1959.

Eisner, R. (1958) " On Growth Models and the Neo-Classical Resurgence," *EJ*, Vol. LXVIII, December 1958.

Fellner, W. J. (1956) *Trends and Cycles in Economic Activity* (New York: Holt and Co., 1956).

Fellner, W. J. (1958) " Automatic Market Clearance and Innovations in the Theory of Employment and Growth," *OEP*, Vol. 10, June 1958.

Fellner, W. J. (1961) " Appraisal of the Labour-saving and Capital-saving Character of Innovations," in *The Theory of Capital*, Proceedings of International Economic Association Conference, edited by F. A. Lutz and D. C. Hague (London: Macmillan, 1961).

Fellner, W. J. (1962) " Does the Market Direct the Relative Factor-saving Effects of Technological Progress," in Universities—National Bureau Committee for Economic Research, *The Rate and Directions of Inventive Activity* (Princeton: Princeton University Press, 1962).

Findlay, R. (1960) " Economic Growth and the Distributive Shares," *REStud*, Vol. XXVII, June 1960.

Findlay, R. (1963a) " The Robinsonian Model of Accumulation," *Ec*, Vol. XXX, February 1963.

Findlay, R. (1963b) "A Reply (to Robinson, J., 'Findlay's Robinsonian Model of Accumulation: A Comment ')," *Ec*, Vol. XXX, November 1963.

Fisher, F. M. (1963) " Decomposability, Near Decomposability and Balanced Price Change under Constant Returns to Scale," *Em*, Vol. 31, January–April 1963.

Fisher, F. M., and Ando, A. (1963) " Near-decomposability, Partition and Aggregation, and the Relevance of Stability Discussions," *IER*, Vol. IV, January 1963.

Fisher, F. M., Ando, A., and Simon, H. A. (1963) *Essays on the Structure of Social Science Models* (Cambridge, Mass.: M.I.T. Press, 1963).

Frankel, M. (1955) " Obsolescence and Technological Change in a Maturing Economy," *AER*, Vol. XLV, June 1955.

Furuya, H., and Inada, K. (1962) " Balanced Growth and Intertemporal Efficiency in Capital Accumulation," *IER*, Vol. 3, January 1962.

Gale, D. (1956) " The Closed Linear Model of Production," in *Linear Inequalities and Related Systems*, ed. H. W. Kuhn and A. W. Tucker (Princeton: Princeton University Press, 1956).

Gale, D. (1960) *The Theory of Linear Economic Models* (New York: McGraw-Hill, 1960).

Goodwin, R. M. (1953) " The Problem of Trend and Cycle," *YB*, Vol. 5, August 1953.

Goodwin, R. M. (1955) " A Model of Cyclical Growth," in *The Business Cycle in the Postwar World*, proceedings of International Economic Association Conference, edited by E. Lundberg (London: Macmillan, 1955).

Gordon, D. F. (1956) " Obsolescence and Technological Change: Comment," *AER*, Vol. XLVI, September 1956.

Gordon, R. A. (1961) " Price Changes: Consumers' and Capital Goods," *AER*, Vol. LI, December 1961.

Green, H. A. J. (1960) " Growth Models, Capital and Stability," *EJ*, Vol. LXX, March 1960.

Griliches, Z. (1963) " The Sources of Measured Productivity Growth: U.S. Agriculture 1940–60," *JPE*, Vol. LXXI, August 1963.

Guha, A. (1963) " Scarcity of Specific Resources as A Limit to Output," *REStud*, Vol. XXX, 1963).

Haavelmo, T. (1954) *A Study in the Theory of Economic Evolution* (Amsterdam: North-Holland Publishing Co., 1954).

Habakkuk, H. J. (1962) *American and British Technology in the Nineteenth Century* (London: Cambridge University Press, 1962).

Hahn, F. H. (1950) " The Share of Wages in the Trade Cycle," *EJ*, Vol. LX, September 1950.

Hahn, F. H. (1951) " The Share of Wages in The National Income," *OEP*, Vol. 3, June 1951.

Hahn, F. H. (1960) " The Stability of Growth Equilibrium," *QJE*, Vol. LXXIV, May 1960.

Hahn, F. H. (1961) " Money, Dynamic Stability and Growth," *Met*, Vol. XIII, 1961.

Hahn, F. H. (1963) " On the Disequilibrium Behaviour of a Multi-sectoral Growth Model," *EJ*, Vol. LXXIII, September 1963.

Harrod, R. F. (1936) *The Trade Cycle* (London: Oxford University Press, 1936).

Harrod, R. F. (1939) " An Essay in Dynamic Theory," *EJ* Vol. XLIX, March 1939.

Harrod, R. F. (1948) *Towards a Dynamic Economics* (London: Macmillan, 1948).

Harrod, R. F. (1957) " Professor Fellner on Growth and Unemployment," *Kyk*, Vol. 10, 1957.

Harrod, R. F. (1959) " Domar and Dynamic Economics," *EJ*, Vol. LXIX, September 1959.

Harrod, R. F. (1960) " Second Essay in Dynamic Theory," *EJ*, Vol. LXX, June 1960.

Harrod, R. F. (1963) " Themes in Dynamic Theory," *EJ*, Vol. LXXIII, September 1963.

Hart, A. G., Kaldor, N., and Tinbergen, J. (1964) " The Case for a Commodity Reserve Currency," memorandum submitted to the U.N. Conference on Trade and Development, 1964 (U.N. document E/Conf. 46/P/7).

Hawkins, D., and Simon, H. A. (1949) " Some Conditions of Macroeconomic Stability," *Em*, Vol. 17, October 1949.

Hicks, J. R. (1932, 1963) *The Theory of Wages* (London: Macmillan, 1st edition 1932, 2nd edition 1963).

Hicks, J. R. (1950) *A Contribution to the Theory of the Trade Cycle* (Oxford: Oxford University Press, 1950).

Hicks, J. R. (1959) " A Value and Capital Growth Model," *REStud*, Vol. XXVI, June 1959.

Hicks, J. R. (1960) " Thoughts on the Theory of Capital—The Corfu Conference," *OEP*, Vol. 12, June 1960.

Hicks, J. R. (1961) " Prices and the Turnpike—the Story of a Mare's Nest," *REStud*, Vol. XXVIII, February 1961.

Howe, C. W. (1960) " An Alternative Proof of the Existence of General Equilibrium in a Von Neumann Model," *Em*, Vol. 28, 1960.

Inada, K. (1961) " Balanced Growth and Intertemporal Efficiency in Capital Accumulation," 1961 (unpublished).

Inada, K. (1963) " On a Two-sector Model of Economic Growth: Comments and a Generalisation," *REStud*, Vol. XXX, June 1963.

Inada, K., and Furuya, H. (1962) " Balanced Growth and Intertemporal Efficiency in Capital Accumulation," *IER*, Vol. 3, January 1962.

Johansen, L. (1959) " Substitution versus Fixed Production Coefficients in The Theory of Economic Growth: A Synthesis," *Em*, Vol. 27, April 1959.

Johansen, L. (1961) " A Method of Separating the Effects of Capital Accumulation and Shifts in Production Functions upon Growth in Labour Productivity," *EJ*, Vol. LXXI, December 1961.

Jorgenson, D. W. (1960a) " On Stability in the Sense of Harrod," *Ec*, Vol. XXVII, August 1960.

Jorgenson, D. W. (1960b) " A Dual Stability Theorem," *Em*, Vol. XXVIII, October 1960.

Jorgenson, D. W. (1961a) " Stability of a Dynamic Input–Output System," *REStud*, Vol. XXVIII, February 1961.

Jorgenson, D. W. (1961b) " The Development of a Dual Economy," *EJ*, Vol. LXXI, June 1961.

Jorgenson, D. W. (1961c) " The Structure of Multi-sector Dynamic Models," *IER*, Vol. 2, September 1961.

Kahn, R. F. (1959) " Exercises in the Analysis of Growth," *OEP*, Vol. II, June 1959.

Kahn, R. F., and Champernowne, D. G. (1954) " The Value of Invested Capital. A Mathematical Addendum to Mrs. Robinson's Article," *REStud*, Vol. XXI, 1954.

Kaldor, N. (1954) " The Relation of Economic Growth and Cyclical Fluctuations," *EJ*, Vol. LXIV, March 1954.

Kaldor, N. (1956) " Alternative Theories of Distribution," *REStud*, Vol. XXIII, 1956.

Kaldor, N. (1957) " A Model of Economic Growth," *EJ*, Vol. LXVII, December 1957.

Kaldor, N. (1959) " Economic Growth and the Problem of Inflation," *Ec*, Vol. XXVI, August, November 1959.

Kaldor, N. (1960) " A Rejoinder to Mr. Atsumi and Professor Tobin," *REStud*, Vol. XXVII, February 1960.

Kaldor, N. (1961) " Capital Accumulation and Economic Growth," in *The Theory of Capital*, Proceedings of International Economic Association Conference, edited by F. A. Lutz and D. C. Hague (London: Macmillan, 1961).

Kaldor, N. (1962) Comment (in Symposium on Production Function and Economic Growth), *REStud*, Vol. XXIX, June 1962.

Kaldor, N., and Mirrlees, J. A. (1962) " A New Model of Economic Growth," *REStud*, Vol. XXIX, June 1962.

Kalecki, M. (1939) *Essays in the Theory of Economic Fluctuations* (London: Allen and Unwin, 1939).

Kalecki, M. (1943) *Studies in Economic Dynamics* (London: Allen and Unwin, 1943).

Kalecki, M. (1954) *Theory of Economic Dynamics* (London: Allen and Unwin, 1954).

Kaneko, Y., and Morishima, M. (1962) " On the Speed of Establishing Multi-Sectoral Equilibrium," *Em*, Vol. 30, October 1962.

Karlin, S. (1959) *Mathematical Methods and Theory in Games, Programming and Economics*, Vol. I (London: Pergamon Press, 1959).

Kemeny, J. G., Morgenstern, O., and Thompson, G. L. (1956) " A Generalisation of the Von Neumann Model of an Expanding Economy," *Em*, Vol. 24, April 1956.

Kendrick, J. W. (1961) *Productivity Trends in the United States*, National Bureau of Economic Research (Princeton: Princeton University Press, 1961).

Kennedy, C. (1961) " Technical Progress and Investment," *EJ*, Vol. LXXI, June 1961.

Kennedy, C. (1962) " The Character of Improvements and of Technical Progress," *EJ*, Vol. LXXII, December 1962.

Kennedy, C. (1964) " Induced Bias in Innovation and the Theory of Distribution," *EJ*, Vol. LXXIV, September, 1964.

Kindleberger, C. P. (1961) " Obsolescence and Technical Change," *O.I.S.*, Vol. 23, August 1961.

Koopmans, T. C. (1951) " Analysis of Production on an Efficient Combination of Activities," in *Activity Analysis of Production and Allocation*, ed. Koopmans, (New York: Wiley, 1951).

Koopmans, T. C. (1957) *Three Essays on the State of Economic Science* (1957).

Koopmans, T. C., and Beush, A. F. (1959) " Selected Topics in Economics involving Mathematical Reasoning," *SIAM Review*, Vol. 1, No. 2, July 1959.

Kurz, M. (1963a) " A Two-sector Extension of Swan's Model of Economic Growth: The Case of No Technical Change," *IER*, Vol. IV, January 1963.

Kurz, M. (1963b) " Substitution versus Fixed Production Coefficients: A Comment," *Em*, Vol. 31, January–April 1963.

Kuznets, S. (1959) *Six Lectures on Economic Growth* (New York: Glencoe, 1959).

Lamfalussy, A. (1963) *The United Kingdom and the Six* (London: Macmillan, 1963).

Leibenstein, H. (1957) *Economic Backwardness and Economic Growth* (New York, 1957).

Leontief, W. W. (1941, 1951) *The Structure of American Economy 1919–1939* (New York: Oxford University Press, 1941, 2nd edition, 1951).

Leontief, W. W. (1961) " Lags and the Stability of Dynamic Systems: a Rejoinder," *Em*, Vol. 29, October 1961.

Little, I. M. D. (1957) " Classical Growth," *OEP*, Vol. 9, June 1957.

Lundberg, E. (1961) *Produktivitet och räntabilitet* (Stockholm: Norstedt, 1961).

McFadden, D. M. (1963) " Further Results on C.E.S. Production Functions," *REStud*, Vol. XXX, June 1963.

McKenzie, L. W. (1957) " An elementary analysis of the Leontief system," *Em*, Vol. 25, 1957.

McKenzie, L. W. (1963a) " The Dorfman–Samuelson–Solow Turnpike Theorem," *IER*, Vol. IV, January 1963.

McKenzie, L. W. (1963b) " Turnpike Theorems for a Generalized Leontief Model," *Em*, Vol. 31, January–April 1963.

McManus, M. (1957) " Self-contradiction in Leontief's Dynamic Model," *YB*, Vol. 9, May 1957.

McManus, M. (1963) " Notes on Jorgenson's Model," *REStud*, Vol. XXX, June 1963.

Malinvaud, E. (1953) " Capital Accumulation and Efficient Allocation of Resources," *Em*, Vol. 21, April 1953.

Malinvaud, E. (1959) " Programmes d'expansion et taux d'intérêt," *Em*, Vol. 27, April 1959.

Malinvaud, E. (1961) " The Analogy between Atemporal and Intertemporal Theories of Resource Allocation," *REStud*, Vol. XXVIII, June 1961.

Malinvaud, E. (1962) " Efficient Capital Accumulation, a Corrigendum," *Em*, Vol. 30, July 1962.

Mansfield, E. (1961) " Technical Change and the Rate of Imitation," *Em*, Vol. 29, October 1961.

Matthews, R. C. O. (1955) " The Saving Function and The Problem of Trend and Cycle," *REStud*, Vol. XXII, 1955.

Matthews, R. C. O. (1959) " Duesenberry on Growth and Fluctuations," *EJ*, Vol. LXIX, December 1959.

Matthews, R. C. O. (1960) " The Rate of Interest in Growth Models," *OEP*, Vol. 12, October 1960.

Matthews, R. C. O. (1964) " The New View of Investment: A Comment," *QJE*, Vol. LXXVIII, February 1964.

Meade, J. E. (1961) *A Neo-Classical Theory of Economic Growth* (London: Allen and Unwin, 1961).

Meade, J. E. (1962) " The Effect of Saving on Consumption in a State of Steady Growth," *REStud*, Vol. XXIX, June 1962.

Meade, J. E. (1963) " The Rate of Profit in a Growing Economy," *EJ*, Vol. LXXIII, December 1963.

Mirrlees, J. A., and Kaldor, N. (1962) " A New Model of Economic Growth," *REStud*, Vol. XXIX, June 1962.

Morgenstern, O., Kemeny, J. G., and Thompson, G. L. (1956) " A Generalization of the Von Neumann Model of an Expanding Economy," *Em*, Vol. 24, April 1956.

Morishima, M. (1958) " Prices, Interest and Profits in a Dynamic Leontief System," *Em*, Vol. 26, July 1958.

Morishima, M. (1959) " Some Properties of a Dynamic Leontief System with a Spectrum of Techniques," *Em*, Vol. 27, October 1959.

Morishima, M. (1960) " Economic Expansion and the Interest Rate in Generalised Von Neumann Models," *Em*, Vol. 28, 1960.

Morishima, M. (1961) " Proof of a Turnpike Theorem: The ' No Joint Production Case,' " *REStud*, Vol. XXVIII, February 1961.

Morishima, M. (1964) *Equilibrium Stability and Growth* (London: Oxford University Press, 1964).

Morishima, M., and Seton, F. (1961) " Aggregation in Leontief Matrices and the Labour Theory of Value," *Em*, Vol. 29, April 1961.

Morishima, M., and Kaneko, Y. (1962) " On the Speed of Establishing Multisectoral Equilibrium," *Em*, Vol. 30, October 1962.

National Bureau of Economic Research (1962) *The Rate and Direction of Inventive Activity*, Universities-National Bureau Committee for Economic Research (Princeton: Princeton University Press, 1962).

Neild, R. R. (1963) *Pricing and Employment in the Trade Cycle* (London: Cambridge University Press, 1963).

Neisser, H. (1954) " Balanced Growth under Constant Returns to Scale: Some Comments," *Em*, Vol. 22, October 1954.

Nelson, R. R. (1959) " The Economics of Invention: A Survey of the Literature," *JB*, Vol. 32, April 1959.

von Neumann, J. (1938) " Uber ein ökononomisches Gleichungsystem und eine Verallgemeinerung des Brouwerschen Fixpunktsatzes," in *Ergebnisse eines Mathematischen Seminars* (Vienna, 1938). Translated by G. Morgenstern as " A Model of General Equilibrium," *REStud*, Vol. XIII, 1945–46.

Niehans, J. (1963) " Economic Growth and Two Endogenous Factors," *QJE*, Vol. LXXVII, August 1963.

Nikaido, H. (1962) " Some Dynamic Phenomena in the Leontief Model of Reversely Lagged Type," *REStud*, Vol XXIX, October 1962.

Nikaido, H. (1964) " Persistence of Continual Growth near the Von Neumann

Ray—A Strong Version of the Radner Turnpike Theorem," *Em*, Vol. 32, January–April 1964.

Paige, D. (1961) " Economic Growth: the Last Hundred Years," *National Institute Economic Review*, Number 16, July 1961.

Pasinetti, L. (1962) " Rate of Profit and Income Distribution in Relation to the Rate of Economic Growth," *REStud*, Vol. XXIX, October 1962.

Pearce, I. F. (1962) " The End of the Golden Age in Solovia: A Further Fable for Growthmen Hoping to be ' One Up ' on Oiko," *AER*, Vol. LII, December 1962.

Phelps, E. S. (1961) " The Golden Rule of Accumulation: A Fable for Growthmen," *AER*, Vol. LI, Spetember 1961.

Phelps, E. S. (1962) " The New View of Investment," *QJE*, Vol. LXXVI, November 1962.

Phelps, E. S. (1963) " Substitution, Fixed Proportions, Growth and Distribution," *IER*, Vol. 4, September 1963.

Phillips, A. W. (1954) " Stabilisation Policy in a Closed Economy," *EJ*, Vol. LXIV, June 1954.

Phillips, A. W. (1961) " A Simple Model of Employment, Money and Prices in a Growing Economy," *Ec*, Vol. XXVIII, November 1961.

Phillips, A. W. (1962) " Employment, Inflation and Growth," *Ec*, Vol. XXIX, February 1962.

Pitchford, J. D. (1960) " Growth and the Elasticity of Factor Substitution," *ER*, Vol. XXXVI, December 1960.

Radner, R. (1961) " Paths of Economic Growth that are Optimal with regard only to Final States, a Turnpike Theorem," *REStud*, Vol. XXVIII, February 1961.

Reddaway, W. B., and Smith, A. D. (1960) " Progress in British Manufacturing Industries in the Period 1948–54," *EJ*, Vol. LXX, March 1960.

Robinson, J. (1938) " The Classification of Inventions," *REStud*, Vol. V, February 1938.

Robinson, J. (1952) *The Rate of Interest and Other Essays* (London: Macmillan, 1952).

Robinson, J. (1956) *The Accumulation of Capital* (London: Macmillan, 1956).

Robinson, J. (1960a) *Collected Economic Papers*, Vol. Two (Oxford: Blackwell, 1960).

Robinson, J. (1960b) *Exercises in Economic Analysis* (London: Macmillan, 1960).

Robinson, J. (1962) *Essays in the Theory of Economic Growth* (London: Macmillan, 1962).

Robinson, J. (1963) " Findlay's Robinsonian Model of Accumulation: A Comment," *Ec*, Vol. XXX, November 1963.

Rose, H. (1959) " The Possibility of Warranted Growth," *EJ*, Vol. LXIX, June 1959.

Rose, H. (1963) " Expectations and Stability in Neo-Keynesian Growth Theory," *QJE*, Vol. LXXVII, February 1963.

Rosenberg, N., and Ames, E. (1963) " Changing Technological Leadership and Industrial Growth," *EJ*, Vol. LXXIII, March 1963.

Rothbarth, E. (1946) " Causes of the Superior Efficiency of U.S.A. Industry as Compared with British Industry," *EJ*, Vol. LVI, September 1946.

Salter, W. E. G. (1960) *Productivity and Technical Change* (London: Cambridge University Press, 1960).

Salter, W. E. G. (1962) " Productivity Growth and Accumulation as Historical Processes," paper presented to International Economic Association Congress on Problems in Economic Development, Vienna 1962 (publication forthcoming).

Samuelson, P. A. (1947) *Foundations of Economic Analysis* (Cambridge, Mass.: Harvard University Press, 1947).

Samuelson, P. A. (1951) " Abstract of A Model concerning Substitutability in Open Leontief Models," in *Activity Analysis of Production and Allocation*, edited by T. C. Koopmans (New York: Wiley, 1951).

Samuelson, P. A., and Solow, R. M. (1953) " Balanced Growth under Constant Returns to Scale," *Em*, Vol. 21, July 1953.

Samuelson, P. A. (1953) " Prices of Factors and Goods in General Equilibrium," *REStud*, Vol. 21, 1953.

Samuelson, P. A. (1958) " An Exact Consumption-loan Model of Interest with or without the Social Contrivance of Money," *JPE*, Vol. 66, December 1958.

Samuelson, P. A. (1959) " A Modern Treatment of the Ricardian Economy: I. The Pricing of Goods and of Labor and Land Services. II. Capital and Interest of the Pricing Process," *QJE*, Vol. LXXII, February–May 1959.

Samuelson, P. A. (1960) " Efficient Paths of Capital Accumulation in Terms of the Calculus of Variations," in *Mathematical Methods in the Social Sciences*, edited by K. J. Arrow, S. Karlin, and P. Suppes (Stanford: Stanford University Press, 1960).

Samuelson, P. A. (1962) " Parable and Realism in Capital Theory: The Surrogate Production Function," *REStud*, Vol. XXIX, June 1962.

Samuelson, P. A. and Solow, R. M. (1956) " A Complete Capital Model involving Heterogeneous Capital Goods," *QJE*, Vol. LXX, November 1956.

Sargan, J. D. (1958a) " Mrs. Robinson's Warranted Rate of Growth," *YB*, Vol. 10, June 1958.

Sargan, J. D. (1958b) " The Instability of the Leontief Dynamic Model," *Em*, Vol. 26, July 1958.

Sargent, J. R. (1962) " The Stability of Growth Equilibrium: Comment," *QJE*, Vol. LXXVI, August 1962.

Sato, R. (1963) " Fiscal Policy in a Neo-classical Growth Model: An Analysis of Time Required for Equilibrating Adjustment," *REStud*, Vol. XXX, February 1963.

Schneider, E. (1958) " Income and Income Distribution in Macro-Economic Theory," *International Economic Papers*, No. 8, 1958.

Schumpeter, J. A. (1939) *Business Cycles* (New York: McGraw Hill, 1939).

Seton, F., and Morishima, M. (1961) " Aggregation in Leontief Matrices and the Labour Theory of Value," *Em*, Vol. 29, April 1961.

Shove, G. F. (1942) " The Place of Marshall's *Principles* in the Development of Economic Theory," *EJ*, Vol. LII, December 1942.

Simon, H. A., and Ando, A. (1961) " Aggregation of Variables in Dynamic Systems," *Em*, Vol. 29, April 1961.

Smith, A. D., and Reddaway, W. B. (1960) " Progress on British Manufacturing Industries in the Period 1948–54," *EJ*, Vol. LXX, March 1960.

Smithies, A. (1957) " Economic Fluctuations and Growth," *Em*, Vol. 25, January 1957.

Solow, R. M. (1956) " A Contribution to The Theory of Economic Growth," *QJE*, Vol. 70, February 1956.

Solow, R. M. (1957) " Technical Change and The Aggregate Production Function," *REStat*, Vol. 39, August 1957.

Solow, R. M. (1959) " Competitive Valuation in a Dynamic Input–Output System," *Em*, Vol. 27, January 1959.

Solow, R. M. (1960) " Investment and Technical Progress," in *Mathematical Methods in the Social Sciences*, ed. by K. J. Arrow, S. Karlin and P. Suppes (Stanford: Stanford University Press, 1960).

Solow, R. M. (1961) " Note on Uzawa's Two Sector Model of Economic Growth," *REStud*, Vol. XXIX, October 1961.

Solow, R. M. (1962a) " Technical Progress, Capital Formation and Economic Growth," *AER Papers and Proceedings*, Vol. LII, May 1962.

Solow, R. M. (1962b) " Substitution and Fixed Proportions in The Theory of Capital," *REStud*, Vol. XXIX, June 1962.

Solow, R. M. (1963) *Capital Theory and the Rate of Return* (Amsterdam: North Holland Publishing Co., 1963).

Sraffa, P. (1960) *Production of Commodities by Means of Commodities* (London: Cambridge University Press, 1960).

Stone, J. R. N., and Brown, J. A. C. (1962) " Output and Investment for Exponential Growth in Consumption," *REStud*, Vol. XXIX, June 1962.

Streeten, P. (1959) " Unbalanced Growth," *OEP*, Vol. 11, June 1959.

Svennilson, I. (1963) " Economic Growth and Technical Progress—an Essay in Sequence Analysis," paper submitted to OECD conference on Residual Factor and Economic Growth, May 20–22, 1963 (unpublished).

Swan, T. W. (1956) " Economic Growth and Capital Accumulation," *ER*, Vol. XXXII, November 1956.

Swan, T. W. (1963) " Growth Models of Golden Ages and Production Functions," in *Economic Development with Special Reference to East Asia*, Proceedings of International Economic Conference, edited by K. E. Berrill (London: Macmillan, 1963).

Takayama, A. (1963) " On a Two-Sector Model of Economic Growth: A Comparative Statics Analysis," *REStud*, Vol. XXX, June 1963.

Tobin, J. (1955) " A Dynamic Aggregative Model," *JPR*, Vol. 63, April 1955.

Tobin, J. (1960) " Towards a General Kaldorian Theory of Distribution," *REStud*, Vol. XXVII, February 1960.

Tsukui, J. (1961) " On a Theorem of Relative Stability," *IER*, Vol. II, May 1961.

Uzawa, H. (1961a) "Neutral Inventions and the Stability of Growth Equilibrium," *REStud*, Vol. XXVIII, February 1961.

Uzawa, H. (1961b) " On a Two-sector Model of Economic Growth: I," *REStud*, Vol. XXIX, October 1961.

Uzawa, H. (1962) " Production Functions with Constant Elasticities of Substitution," *REStud*, Vol. XXIX, October 1962.

Uzawa, H. (1963) " On a Two-sector Model of Economic Growth: II," *REStud*, Vol. XXX, June 1963.

Uzawa, H., and Watanabe, T. (1960) " A Note on the Classification of Technical Inventions," Technical Report No. 85, Contract No. 225 (50), Applied Mathematics and Statistics Laboratories, Stanford University, 1960.

Verdoorn, P. J. (1947) " Fattori che regolano lo sviluppo della produttività del lavoro," *L'Industria*, 1947.

Verdoorn, P. J. (1956) " Complementarity and Long-range Projections," *Em*, Vol. 24, October 1956.

Walters, A. A. (1963) " Production and Cost Functions," *Em*, Vol. 31. January–April 1963.

Weintraub, S. (1958) *Approach to the Theory of Income Distribution* (Chilton, 1958).

Weizsäcker, C. C. von (1962) *Wachstum, Zins und Optimale Investitionsquote* (Basel: Kyklos Verlag, 1962).

Weizsäcker, C. C. von (1964) " Income Distribution and Technical Progress in Equilibrium Growth ", mimeographed.

Weldon, J. C., and Asimakopulos, A. (1963) " The Classification of Technical Progress in Models of Economic Growth," *Ec*, Vol. XXX, November 1963.

Winter, S. G., Jr. (1961) " A Boundedness Property of the Closed Linear Model of Production," Review P-2, 3, and 4, July 1961.

VI

COMPARATIVE ADVANTAGE AND DEVELOPMENT POLICY

By

HOLLIS B. CHENERY [1]

In the great revival of interest in economic development that has marked the past decade, attention has centered on two main questions: first, what determines the over-all rate of economic advance?; second, what is the optimal allocation of given resources to promote growth? Analysis of the growth rate has relied mainly on the Keynesian tools and has produced a multiplicity of aggregate growth models. The second question, however, reopens more ancient economic issues, and their analysis must start from the classical and neo-classical solutions. Only very recently have the two types of discussion tended to come together in the more comprehensive framework of general equilibrium analysis.

In the field of resource allocation, controversy centers around the implications of the classical principle of comparative advantage, according to which growth is promoted by specialization. The defenders of this principle draw their inspiration from David Ricardo, J. S. Mill, and Alfred Marshall, while the lines of attack stem from Friedrich List, J. A. Schumpeter, A. A. Young, and J. H. Williams. The chief criticism is that comparative advantage is essentially a static concept which ignores a variety of dynamic elements.

This issue is of great practical importance to the governments of underdeveloped countries, most of which take an active part in allocating investment funds and other scarce resources. The main purpose of the discussion has therefore been to discover workable principles for the formulation of development policy. The classical approach derives these principles from international trade theory, while its critics base their analysis on modern growth theory. Elements of a dynamic, general-equilibrium theory are needed to resolve the differences between the two approaches. The more general analysis is of very limited value, however, unless its empirical implications can be ascertained.

The present paper discusses the analysis of resource allocation in less-developed economies from three points of view. Section I tries to ascertain the extent to which the allocation principles derived from trade theory and

[1] The author is Professor at Harvard University. He is indebted to Moses Abramovitz, Bela Balassa, and Lawrence Krause for helpful comments. Research for this article was undertaken at the Cowles Foundation for Research in Economics under Task NR 047–006 Office of Naval Research.

from growth theory can be reconciled with each other without losing their operational significance. Section II compares various approaches to the measurement of optimal resource allocation in terms of their logical consistency and their applicability to different conditions. Section III examines some of the practical procedures followed in setting investment policy in underdeveloped countries in the light of the earlier discussion. Finally, some of the theoretical issues are re-examined to indicate their practical importance.

I. Conflicts Between Trade Theory and Growth Theory

The main contradictions between comparative advantage and other principles of resource allocation derive from their different orientation and assumptions. The classical analysis focuses on long-run tendencies and equilibrium conditions, while modern theories of growth are concerned with the interaction among producing and consuming units in a dynamic system. Since both approaches are familiar, I shall try to identify only the differences in assumptions and emphasis that lead to different policy conclusions.

A. *The Implications of Comparative Advantage for Resource Allocation*

The modern version of the comparative cost doctrine [20] is essentially a simplified form of static general equilibrium theory.[1] The optimum pattern of production and trade for a country is determined from a comparison of the opportunity cost of producing a given commodity with the price at which the commodity can be imported or exported. In equilibrium, no commodity is produced which could be imported at lower cost, and exports are expanded until marginal revenue equals marginal cost. Under the assumptions of full employment and perfect competition, the opportunity cost of a commodity, which is the value of the factors used to produce it in their best alternative employment, is equal to its market value. Market prices of factors and commodities can therefore be used to determine comparative advantage under competitive conditions. Long-term changes are not ignored, but they are assumed to be reflected in current market prices.

The Heckscher–Ohlin version of the comparative cost doctrine has been widely recommended as a basis for development policy because it provides a measure of comparative advantage that does not depend on the existence of perfect competition and initial equilibrium. This version states that a country will benefit from trade by producing commodities that use more of its relatively abundant factors of production. It will export these commodities and import commodities using more of its relatively scarce factors unless its pattern of domestic demand happens to be biased toward commodities using domestic factors. The critical assumptions in this analysis are that

---

[1] An excellent discussion and synthesis of the several versions of trade theory is given by Caves [7]. The terms " comparative advantage " and " comparative cost " are used interchangeably in most discussions.

factors of production are comparable among countries and that production functions are the same. These assumptions are not required by classical trade theory.

The applicability of the comparative cost doctrine to present-day conditions in underdeveloped countries has been re-examined by Viner and its validity has been reaffirmed with some modifications. Viner criticizes the Heckscher–Ohlin version because its assumption of comparable factors does allow for observable differences in their quality [63, p. 16]. In his recent answer to critics of the comparative cost approach [64], however, Viner admits the necessity of interpreting comparative advantage in a dynamic setting in which the efficiency of production may change over time, external economies may exist, and the market prices of commodities and factors may differ from their opportunity cost. As Nurkse points out [64, p. 76], these modifications rob the original doctrine of much of its practical value. It is now necessary to have an explicit analysis of the growth process itself before it is possible to determine, even theoretically, where comparative advantage lies; market prices and current opportunity costs are no longer sufficient.

B. *Implications of Growth Theory for Resource Allocation*

Modern growth theory is concerned with the interactions over time among producers, consumers, and investors in interrelated sectors of the economy. In the writings of such economists as Rosenstein-Rodan [43], Lewis [29], Nurkse [36], Myrdal [34], Rostow [44], Dobb [12], and Hirschman [23], there is much more emphasis on the sequence of expansion of production and factor use by sector than on the conditions of general equilibrium. Growth theory either ignores comparative advantage and the possibilities of trade completely, or it considers mainly the dynamic aspects, such as the stimulus that an increase in exports provides to the development of related sectors or the function of imports as a carrier of new products and advanced technology. With this different point of view, growth theorists often suggest investment criteria that are quite contradictory to those derived from considerations of comparative advantage.

The conflicts between these two approaches to resource allocation may be traced either to differences in assumptions or to the inclusion of factors in one theory that are omitted from the other. Growth theory contains at least four basic assumptions about underdeveloped economies that differ strongly from those underlying the comparative cost doctrine: (1) factor prices do not necessarily reflect opportunity costs with any accuracy; (2) the quantity and quality of factors of production may change substantially over time, in part as a result of the production process itself; (3) economies of scale relative to the size of existing markets are important in a number of sectors of production; (4) complementarity among commodities is dominant in both producer and consumer demand.

Some of the implications of these factors are developed by Rosenstein-Rodan [43] and Nurkse [36] as arguments for " balanced growth," by which is meant simultaneous expansion of a number of sectors of production.[1] Assuming an elastic supply of either capital or labor, these authors show that investment will be more profitable in related sectors, because of horizontal and vertical interdependence, than in the same sectors considered separately. Market forces will not necessarily lead to optimal investment decisions because present prices do not reflect the cost and demand conditions that will exist in the future. This effect of investment in one sector on the profitability of investment in another sector, via increased demand or reduced costs, has been called by Scitovsky [47] a " dynamic external economy." The imputation of these economies to the originating sectors may seriously affect the estimate of comparative advantage.

If we assume fixed investment resources instead of an elastic supply, the same set of factors provide an argument for concentrated or unbalanced growth [48] [50]. In order to achieve economies of scale in one sector, it may be necessary to devote a large fraction of the available investment funds to that sector and to supply increased requirements in other sectors from imports (or to curtail them temporarily). The optimal pattern of investment will then be one which concentrates first on one sector and then on another, with balance being approached only in the long run. Streeten [53] has developed further dynamic arguments for unbalanced growth from the fact that technological progress may be more rapid if increases in production are concentrated in a few sectors, while Hirschman [23] argues for imbalance to economize on entreprenurial ability.

The historical significance of the balanced growth argument has been examined by Gerschenkron [18], Rostow [44], and Ohlin [38], in the context of nineteenth-century industrial development in Europe. They show that vertical interdependence has been important in stimulating the growth of related industrial sectors, although the nature and origin of these complexes differ from country to country. In one case they may be related to exports, in another to expansion for the domestic market. The importance of interdependence among producers emerges fairly clearly from these historical studies.

The net effect of the discussion of dynamic interdependence and balanced *vs.* unbalanced growth is to destroy the presumption that perfect competition, even if it could be achieved, would lead to the optimum allocation of resources over time. Since the doctrine of comparative advantage in its conventional form is a corollary of general equilibrium theory, the theoretical qualifications that apply to the latter also apply to the former. If, then, the doctrine of comparative advantage is to be useful for development policy, the essential elements of the growth analysis must be combined with it.

[1] The term " balanced growth " has been given a variety of meanings, but the idea of simultaneous expansion on several fronts is common to all of them.

C. *Dynamic Modifications of Comparative Advantage*

Classical trade theory does not exclude changes in the supply of factors and other data over time, but it does insist that under perfect competition the effects of such changes will be reflected in the market mechanism. If, on the other hand, we take comparative advantage as a principle of planning rather than as a result of market forces, we can include any foreseeable exogenous changes in technology, tastes, or other data without going beyond the framework of comparative statics.

Some of the modifications suggested by growth theory are dynamic in a more essential way, in that a particular change depends not only on the passage of time but on other variables in the system. For example, the rate of increase in the productivity of labor in an industry may depend on an increasing level of production in that industry. Some of these dynamic elements can also be analyzed by methods of comparative statics if our purpose is only to choose among alternative courses of action.

The four assumptions of growth theory discussed above (Section B) lead to the following requirements for the analytical framework to be used in determining comparative advantage in a growing economy:[1] (1) recognition of the possibility of structural disequilibrium in factor markets; (2) the inclusion of indirect (market and nonmarket) effects of expanding a given type of production; (3) simultaneous determination of levels of consumption, imports, and production in interrelated sectors over time when decreasing costs result from the expansion of output; and (4) allowance for variation in the demand for exports and other data over time.

These changes destroy the simplicity of the classical system, in which allocation decisions can be based on a partial analysis because adjustments in the rest of the economy are reflected in equilibrium market prices. In the dynamic analysis, it may not be possible to state that a country has a comparative advantage in producing steel without specifying also the levels of production of iron ore, coal, and metal-working over time. In short, we are forced to compare alternative patterns of growth rather than separate sectors, and we cannot expect to find simple generalizations of the Heckscher-Ohlin type concerning the characteristics of individual lines of production.

Since there is no well-developed body of theory concerning the formal properties of the system just outlined,[2] I shall only try to indicate in a general way the modifications that some of these elements of growth theory will produce in the analysis of comparative advantage.

---

[1] Some of these criticisms of static analysis were made years ago by Williams [66], and a number of the elements were, of course, recognized by the classical economists themselves. I am not concerned with explicit criticism of the classical analysis, but with the possibility of reconciling it with growth theory.

[2] In his survey of modern trade theory, Caves [7] shows that attempts to introduce dynamic elements have been concerned mainly with particular aspects and have led not to new principles, but rather to extensions of static results.

Factor Costs. It is generally agreed that costs of labor and capital in underdeveloped countries do not reflect their opportunity costs with any accuracy because of market imperfections, but there is wide disagreement as to the extent of the typical discrepancies. Some types of labor may be overvalued while particular skills are undervalued. Factor costs may also change markedly over time as a result of economic development, so that an advantage based on cheap labor may prove quite limited in duration. As Lewis [29] and Hagen [21] show, the effects on comparative advantage of correcting for disequilibrium factor prices are often very substantial. (The effects of disequilibrium in factor markets are discussed further in Part II.)

Export Markets. Two of the main arguments against the trade pattern produced by market forces concern (1) the fluctuating nature and (2) the low income and price elasticities of the demand for primary products. The existence of cyclical fluctuation is well established, but the income and price elasticities vary considerably among primary commodities. Their net effect on the terms of trade of primary producers over time is a matter of dispute [64]. These characteristics are often used as an argument for reducing specialization in underdeveloped countries and for expanding industry for local consumption rather than expanding primary exports [41] [51].

These factors can be admitted without seriously modifying the principle of comparative advantage. The market value of the stream of export earnings should be reduced to reflect the drawbacks to the economy resulting from its variable characteristics, and this social value should be used in comparing investment in primary exports to other alternatives. When export demand has a low elasticity, marginal revenue should be used in place of average revenue. Since it is quite likely that the market evaluation of the attractiveness of an investment in exports will differ from this social evaluation, some form of government intervention may be warranted. It is wrong, however, to conclude from this analysis that continued specialization in primary exports may not be the best policy, because even the corrected return on exports may be greater than that on alternative investments. The supply of foreign investment may also be greater for export production.

Productivity Change. The possibility of rising efficiency as labor and management acquire increasing experience in actual production has long been recognized [66] and forms the basis for the infant industry argument. This argument has been generalized to include the effects of increasing production in any industry on the supply of skilled labor and management available to other industries. Since manufacturing is thought to have more important training effects than primary production [33] [41], the fact that improvements in factor supply are not reflected in the market mechanism may introduce a bias against manufacturing. The empirical basis for this argument has been questioned by several economists [46] [63], who assert that there is often as much scope for technological improvement in agriculture as in industry. Without trying to settle the empirical question that has been raised, it may be concluded that productivity change is an important factor and therefore that comparative advantage should be measured over time. It cannot be said, however, that allowance for this factor will always favor manufacturing.

Dynamic External Economies. As indicated above, dynamic external economies are received by an industry from cost reductions or demand increases in other sectors. Cost reductions may result from economies of scale, productivity increases, or new technology. The customary analysis of comparative advantage on a sector-by-sector basis would require that the cost reduction from simultaneously developing interrelated sectors be allocated separately to each. However, if a group of investments will only be profitable when they are undertaken together, comparative advantage can only be determined for alternative combinations of investments. As shown in [11], not only do market prices fail to produce the best investment allocation in this situation but any structure of equilibrium prices may also be an inadequate guide in the presence of economies of scale.

There is considerable evidence that external economies are more important in the industrial sectors than in primary production because of internal economies of scale, training effects, and high demand elasticities. Their omission from the market mechanism is therefore likely to bias resource allocation against manufacturing. The quantitative significance of this factor is very hard to determine, however, since it involves simultaneous changes in a number of sectors.

Uncertainty and Flexibility. The limited ability of policy-makers to foresee changes in demand and supply conditions puts a premium on flexibility in the choice of a development strategy. This factor not only argues against specialization in one or two export commodities but it also favors the development of a diversified economic structure which will enable the economy to shift to new types of exports or import substitutes when changing trade conditions may require them. Kindleberger [26] sees this factor as the main explanation for his finding that the terms of trade have favored developed countries although they have not favored countries exporting manufactured goods in general.[1] The argument is similar to that of Stigler [52] concerning the optimum choice of techniques in a manufacturing plant. The optimum design for a changing market is likely to differ from the optimum under static conditions because in the former case the proper criterion is lowest-cost production for varying operating levels and with changes in product design. Similarly, optimum development policy should result in a pattern of resource allocation that allows for unforeseen changes in supply and demand conditions even at the cost of some loss of short-term efficiency.

[1] This argument is also discussed by Caves [7, pp. 264–66].

II. The Measurement of Optimum Resource Allocation

The development of an adequate theory is only the first step in formulating economic policy. In order to reach practical conclusions, it is also necessary to specify the environment in which the policy-maker functions. Relevant aspects of a particular society include its general objectives, the policy instruments to be considered, and the information available. The theory must then be combined with these elements in such a way as to yield guides to action or " decision rules " for particular situations.

Although the growing science of operations research is concerned with the development of decision rules for business and military operations, less progress has been made in developing an operational approach to long-run economic policy. Tinbergen [55] and Frisch [15] have outlined a general framework for policy analysis, but it has had relatively little impact on the discussion of the development of underdeveloped countries. In this field the failure to specify adequately the decision-making environment and to distinguish between decision rules and the corollaries of pure theory has led to great confusion.

Since the information needed for overall economic analysis is available to a very limited extent in underdeveloped countries, there has been a considerable effort to derive decision rules or " investment criteria " that can be based on partial analysis. I shall group the various suggestions into three categories: (1) factor-intensity criteria; (2) productivity criteria; (3) programming criteria based on accounting prices. Although these various approaches often lead to contradictory results, each has some merit as a form of decision rule if properly qualified. In general, the theoretically more valid formulations require more information and must be replaced by cruder approximations when adequate data are not available. Since a major part of the literature in the development field has been devoted to the discussion of investment criteria, it is important to identify the sources of conflict among them and to specify the circumstances under which each may be approximately correct.

In economic theory, capital and labor are assumed to be separately allocated in single units to different uses. In national planning, however, it is more convenient to consider the decision to install a given productive process or plant, representing the allocation of a group of inputs in specified quantities, as the basic choice. Investment criteria are customarily formulated for " projects " of this sort, since they form the basis for the decisions of planning authorities. This procedure recognizes that very small productive units are uneconomical, and it permits a consideration of different scales of output. The choice of techniques can be considered as a choice among projects producing the same output from different input combinations. In this way the allocation procedure can be divided into two steps: the choice of the best technique for a given type of product, and the decision whether to produce the commodity at all. The principle of comparative advantage is more directly relevant to the second type of choice, but the two cannot be separated entirely.

A. *Factor-intensity Criteria*

The simplest approach to any allocation problem is to concentrate on the scarcest resource. Since this is often capital in underdeveloped countries, it seems reasonable to choose the technique that uses the least capital to produce a given output. The same logic is applied to the choice of sectors of production: an underdeveloped country is advised to produce and export commodities that use relatively less capital per unit of output and to import items requiring more capital. Statements of this type occur in many economic writings of the past fifteen years. Buchanan [5] was among the first to state this criterion for investment in underdeveloped countries and to base policy recommendations upon it.

The " minimum capital–output ratio " criterion is valid only under the following restrictive conditions:[1] (1) Either capital is the only scarce factor in the system, or other inputs are so abundant relative to capital that the latter is the dominant element in determining cost differences. (2) Either the same output is produced by each investment alternative, or the market values used to compare the different products coincide with their social values. (3) Production takes place under constant costs.

The use of the capital–output ratio theoretically requires a measurement of the total capital used in producing a given commodity, including the capital used in producing all materials and services purchased. Alternatively, the indirect use of capital can be allowed for by deducting the cost of purchased inputs from the value of output and expressing the criterion as the ratio of capital to value added. This procedure requires the further assumption that market prices correctly reflect the use of capital in the rest of the economy.

A closely related allocation criterion is the capital intensity: the ratio of capital to labor. This test is derived directly from the Heckscher–Ohlin version of the comparative cost doctrine. If the same production functions exist in all countries and if capital is scarce relative to labor in the underdeveloped countries, comparative advantage in the latter can be identified by low capital–labor ratios. This approach does not assume that labor has zero opportunity cost, as does use of the capital–output ratio, but only that the ratio of labor cost to capital cost is lower than in the country's trading partners. To allow for differences in the quality of labor among countries, it is sometimes suggested that the assessment of relative labor cost should be made for labor units of equal efficiency—*e.g.*, the labor required in each

---

[1] A rigorous analysis of the validity of marginal and average factor-output ratios as indicators of optimum allocation in a two-factor system is given by Bator [4].

country to perform a given type of operation with the same capital goods and organization.

A principal criticism of the use of both these ratios is that they ignore the existence of other factors of production, such as natural resources. If either labor or natural resources has a significant opportunity cost, the capital–output measure must be replaced by the more general marginal productivity of capital criterion, which is discussed in the next section.

To judge comparative advantage by the capital–labor ratio is to assume either that this ratio will be the same for the same industry in all countries, or that capital is equally substitutable for labor in producing all the commodities traded. Deviations from these assumptions, along with the omission of other inputs and variations in efficiency by sector, make the capital–labor criterion a very crude approximation indeed to a proper estimate of comparative advantage.

B. *Marginal Productivity Criteria* [1]

A more comprehensive allocation criterion is the social marginal product of a given unit of resources in a given use. Where the factor-intensity criteria are at best correlated only with the increase in national income produced by a project, the productivity criteria try to measure the increase. The marginal productivity test is in turn less general than the overall programming approach, because it is based on a partial equilibrium analysis that is valid only for relatively small changes in the economic structure.

The several forms of marginal productivity criterion that have been proposed differ in the assumptions made about the social welfare function and in the extent to which allowance is made for the indirect effects of a given allocation. All versions are alike in assuming that the government controls, directly or indirectly, a certain fraction of the investible resources of the country and wishes to allocate them in such a way as to maximize future welfare.

Since the productivity criteria are usually applied to investment projects rather than to single units of capital, they are " marginal " only in the sense that a project normally constitutes a small fraction of the total capital invested in a given year. For very large projects a breakdown into smaller units would be more appropriate.

The Static SMP Criterion. As proposed by Kahn [25], the social marginal product (SMP) is a general equilibrium concept which is conventionally defined as the net contribution of a marginal unit (project) to the national product.[2] The related decision rule is to rank investment projects by their SMP and to go down the list until the funds to be allocated are exhausted.

---

[1] Surveys of these and other investment criteria are given by Castellino [6], Vaidyanathan [62], and the United Nations [61].

[2] To be more accurate, cost and output streams should be discounted to the present, but I shall not be concerned with differences in the time pattern of output of different projects.

Alternatively, any project having an SMP above a given level can be approved.

Kahn uses the SMP criterion to show the fallacies in the factor-intensity measures that had been advocated by Buchanan [5], Polak [40], and other writers. He points out that: " The existence of a particular natural resource, specialized skills, particular climatic conditions, or the importance of a particular product or service may make the SMP of capital higher in a line which is more capital intensive than in another which is less so " [25, p. 40]. He also argues that even when there is substantial rural unemployment, a considerable amount of capital and other inputs are required to transport, train, and house the workers who are to be employed elsewhere. Kahn's arguments against the simple capital-intensity criteria appear to have been generally accepted, although he admits that a lower capital–output ratio may be a useful guide when other information is lacking.

Some modifications in the SMP criterion were suggested by the present author [8] to allow for artificial elements in the price system (tariffs, subsidies, etc.) and to provide for the evaluation of labor and foreign exchange at opportunity cost rather than at market value. Further allowances for the difference between market price and social value can be made by estimating the benefits to be provided to other sectors in the form of external economies, and by including overhead costs in the estimate of the cost of labor. All of these elements are included in Eckstein's synthesis and extension of the productivity approach [14].[1]

The SMP criterion is entirely consistent with the general programming approach discussed below, which derives opportunity costs from an explicit analysis of total factor use. In the absence of such an overall analysis, the corrections suggested for the calculation of the productivity of investment are likely to be quite approximate. There is no logical conflict between the results of the SMP analysis and the dictates of comparative advantage because each is a corollary of a general equilibrium solution over a given time period.

The Marginal Reinvestment Criterion. A sharp criticism of the SMP criterion was made by Galenson and Leibenstein [17], who challenge some of its basic premises. They would substitute a different social welfare function in which the aim is to maximize *per capita* income at some time in the distant future rather than to maximize a discounted stream of income over time. They also assume severe restrictions on the policy instruments available to the government, and in particular deny its ability to affect the rate of saving by fiscal measures. Under these assumptions, it is necessary to take account of the division of income resulting from a project between profits and wages, since savings from the former are higher.

---

[1] Eckstein points out that the assumption of capital rationing implies a social judgment as to both the amount of investment in the current period and the discount to be applied to future outputs, since the market rate of interest is rejected for both purposes.

To maximize the total output at some distant future time, Galenson and Leibenstein easily show that the most " productive " project is not necessarily the one which maximizes national income in the near future but the one which leads to the highest savings. Since it is assumed that neither voluntary saving nor taxes can be extracted from wages, the most productive project will be the one with the highest profit rate per unit of capital invested.[1] The assumption that profits are saved and reinvested leads to the " marginal reinvestment quotient " as a decision-rule to be applied in place of the SMP.

Galenson and Leibenstein push their argument one step further and identify the most profitable project as the one with the highest capital–labor ratio. This result leads them to the paradoxical conclusion that the factor-intensity rule should be reversed: countries should prefer the most capital-intensive rather than the least capital-intensive techniques in order to promote savings and future growth. This conclusion involves an implicit assumption about the nature of production functions: that increasing the capital intensity will necessarily raise the average return to capital in each sector of production. This is obviously not true in general and is not necessarily true of existing productive techniques. The savings effect of a given project should therefore be measured directly and not assumed to vary in proportion to the capital–labor ratio.

Galenson and Leibenstein have been widely criticized for their extreme assumptions [4] [14] [24] [35], in particular for the use of a social welfare function in which the starvation of half the population in the near future would appear to be a matter of indifference and for the assumption that limitations on fiscal policy make a lower income preferable to a much higher one if the former has a higher savings component. Their analysis has nevertheless been useful in emphasizing that other effects of an investment beside its immediate contribution to the national product should be included in the productivity criterion.[2]

The Marginal Growth Contribution. Eckstein [14] has successfully reconciled the conflict between the Kahn–Chenery SMP approach and the Galenson–Leibenstein reinvestment approach, and in so doing he has provided a considerable generalization of each. First, he assumes that the social objective is to maximize the present value of the future consumption stream. With a zero discount rate, this objective approximates the long-term income objective of Galenson and Leibenstein, while with a high discount of future consumption it leads to the maximization of income in the short term. Second, Eckstein assumes that there is a different savings (reinvestment) coefficient associated with each project, but he allows for any savings rate out of wages and profits. From these assumptions, he derives a measure of the " mar-

---

[1] I omit the possibility of an effect on population growth, which leads Galenson and Leibenstein to state the criterion on a *per capita* basis.

[2] In [28] Leibenstein restates in more restrained form his arguments for including labor training, savings, population growth, and other indirect effects in a comprehensive productivity measure.

ginal growth contribution " of a given project that consists of two parts:
(1) an *efficiency term*, consisting of the present value of the consumption stream;
and (2) a *growth term*, consisting of the additional consumption to be achieved
by reinvesting savings.

The relative importance of the two terms depends largely on the rate
of discount that is applied to future consumption. Even with a low rate
of discount, the significance of the second term depends on how much variation there is in the fraction of income saved among different projects. If
the savings ratio is not related to the form of income generated, then, as
Bator [4] shows, there is no conflict between maximizing income in the
short run and in the longer run. Eckstein's formula provides for all possible
intermediate assumptions between the two extreme views of the determinants
of savings.[1]

In principle, one might include other indirect dynamic effects, such as
the value of the labor training provided, in the measurement of the total
productivity of a given project. There is a danger of double counting if
partial-equilibrium analysis is extended too far, however, and most indirect
effects can be more readily evaluated in the more general programming
framework considered below.

C. *Programming Criteria and Accounting Prices*

The allocation rules discussed up to now are based on the existing economic structure and are strictly applicable only for relatively small changes in
it. Although it may in many instances be necessary to rely primarily on these
marginal criteria for lack of data on the rest of the economy, it is important
to have some way of testing larger changes and of evaluating the errors that
are introduced by the marginal procedure. Furthermore, without a more
comprehensive analysis it is impossible to reconcile fully the conflicting policy
implications of comparative advantage and growth theory.

The difficulties of partial analysis increase with the number of modifications that have to be applied to market prices in order to arive at social value.
Both the factor-intensity ratios and the partial productivity measures assume
that there is one principal restriction on the system, the scarcity of capital.
They do not allow for the fact that in allocating capital according to any
one of these rules some other restriction on the system, such as the supply of
foreign exchange, of skilled labor, or of a particular commodity, may be
exceeded.

The programming approach to resource allocation begins with the problem of balancing supply and demand for different commodities and factors
of production. Until quite recently, practical programming methods have
been more concerned with ensuring the consistency of a given allocation of
resources with certain targets than with testing the efficiency with which

[1] Sen [49] independently formulated a more general investment criterion that is very similar to
Eckstein's, in which the SMP and reinvestment criteria are shown to be limiting cases.

resources are used. Historically speaking, the programming approach is thus the operational counterpart of the theory of balanced growth, from which much of its conceptual framework is derived.

One of the earliest attempts at formulating a comprehensive development program for an underdeveloped area was Mandelbaum's illustrative model for Southeastern Europe, undertaken during the war [31]. He starts, as many subsequent programs have done, from an estimate of the increase in national income required to absorb a prospective increment in the labor force. The allocation of capital and labor is made initially from demand estimates and by analogy to the structure of more advanced countries. The principle of comparative advantage is introduced only intuitively in modifying the initial projection. The main test of resource allocation is the balance of demand and supply for each sector and factor of production.

The development of mathematical programming methods makes it possible to carry out this type of analysis in a much more precise way. In several countries, consistent development programs have been formulated by using input–output analysis, as in the studies of the Economic Commission for Latin America [58] [59] [60]. It is only with the development of linear programming, however, that it is possible to reconcile the consistency criteria and the productivity criteria in a systematic way.

A link between the test of consistency (feasibility) in resource allocation and the test of productivity (efficiency) is provided by a consideration of the price implications of a given allocation. Assume that a set of production levels has been worked out so as to be consistent with the available supplies of labor, capital, and natural resources, given the structure of consumer demand and the country's trading possibilities. These sector production and trade levels constitute a " feasible program." Any such program implies a unique set of commodity and factor prices if the economy is in equilibrium. If production activities are assumed to operate at constant costs, linear programming provides a method of calculating the " shadow prices " corresponding to the equilibrium conditions, in which the price of each commodity is equal to its cost of production.[1] Prices are determined by the solution to the following set of simultaneous equations, one for each production activity included in the program:

$$(1) \qquad a_{1j}P_1 + a_{2j}P_2 + \cdots + a_{nj}P_n = 0 \qquad (j = 1 \cdots n)$$

where a_{ij} is the input or output of commodity or factor i by activity j, and P_i is the shadow price of commodity or factor i. The input coefficients may be measured at existing prices or in other convenient units. In an open economy, activities of importing and exporting are also included in the system, and the price solution contains the equilibrium price of foreign

[1] The assumptions of linear programming and methods of finding solutions to programming models have been discussed in a number of recent publications, such as [13].

exchange. An example of this calculation is given in Table 1, which will be explained shortly.

The use of shadow or " accounting " prices in evaluating investment projects has been suggested by Tinbergen [54] [56], Frisch [15] [16], and Chenery [9] [10]. Although Tinbergen does not use a linear programming framework, his accounting prices for factors have the same meaning as shadow prices: the opportunity cost implied by a given resource allocation.[1] He suggests computing the costs associated with a project by using accounting prices; any project that shows a positive net return over cost (including capital cost) should be approved. This test is equivalent to the SMP criterion, as shown below.

The general linear programming problem is to maximize the value of a linear objective function subject to linear constraints. In development programs, the principle constraints are that the demand for commodities and factors should not exceed their supplies; the function to be maximized is usually taken as the national income. Alternatively, the objective may be the achievement of a given increase in output at minimum cost in investment (including foreign investment). Other social objectives, such as a minimum employment level or a specified degree of regional balance, can be included as additional restrictions on the program. The instrument variables can also be constrained to fall within specified limits, as in the models of Frisch.[2]

To illustrate the meaning and use of shadow prices in evaluating investment projects, I shall take up a very simplified programming model that is worked out in more detail elsewhere [11]. The truncated system given in Table 1 covers only a small part of the economy, but it will serve to illustrate the way in which interdependence influences investment decisions and the effect of having more than one scarce factor.

The model contains four production activities (X_1, X_2, X_3, X_4) and three import activities (M_1, M_2, M_3). Each activity is represented in Table 1 by a column of coefficients, a_{ij}, showing the amount of input $(-)$ or output $(+)$ of commodity i when the activity is operated at unit level. (These coefficients are the boldface figures in columns 1 to 7.) The net output is taken as unity in all cases. The production activity X_1, for example, represents the production of one unit of metal products from 0·22 units of iron and steel,

---

[1] Tinbergen [56, p. 39] defines accounting prices as those " that would prevail if (i) the investment pattern under discussion were actually carried out, and (ii) equilibrium existed on the markets just mentioned " [i.e., labor, capital, foreign exchange markets]. The relation between accounting and shadow prices is discussed in Chenery [10] and Qayum [42].

[2] Frisch is one of the strongest advocates of the use of linear programming for development planning, as indicated in the preface to a recent methodological study: " In the beginning of 1959, during my work as a United Nations expert in Cairo, I was confronted with the problem of working out a methodology for *optimal investment programming* in a rapidly expanding underdeveloped country. I have always believed—and my Cairo experiences have confirmed it—that such a method must be formulated in terms which ultimately make the problem amenable to linear programming. Otherwise one is practically certain to be taken by surprise afterwards in unexpected balance of payments difficulties and other troubles " [16, p. 1].

TABLE 1—EVALUATION OF PRODUCTION AND IMPORT ACTIVITIES BY ACCOUNTING PRICES [a]

Commodities and Factors	Production Activities				Import Activities			Accounting Prices				Restrictions (12)
	X_1 (1)	X_2 (2)	X_3 (3)	X_4 (4)	M_1 (5)	M_2 (6)	M_3 (7)	Trial a (8)	Trial b (9)	Trial c (10)	Trial d (11)	
1. Metal Products	1·00 (3·41)				1·00 (3·41)			2·55	3·42	3·41	2·26	1000
2. Iron and Steel	−0·22 (−0·89)	1·00 (4·03)				1·00 (4·03)		3·60	4·82	4·03	3·50	1000
3. Iron Ore		−0·08 (−0·25)	1·00 (3·12)				1·00 (3·12)	3·30	4·42	3·12	2·19	0
4. Foreign Exchange				1·00 (4·01)	−0·85 (−3·41)	−1·20 (−4·81)	−1·10 (−4·41)	3·00	4·02	4·01	2·92	0
5. Other Inputs	−0·20 (−0·62)	−0·25 (−0·78)	−0·70 (−2·17)	−0·10 (−0·31)				3·00	3·20	3·10	2·20	—
6. Labor	−0·70 (−1·05)	−0·20 (−0·30)	−0·30 (−0·45)	−1·00 (−1·50)				1·50	1·50	1·50	0·50	—
7. Capital	−0·70 (−0·70)	−2·70 (−2·70)	−0·50 (−0·50)	−2·20 (−2·20)				1·00	1·00	1·00	1·00	—
Social Profitability [b]												
Trial a	−0·59	−0·41	+0·25	−1·00	0	0	0					
Trial b	−0·30	+0·37	+1·23	0	0	0	0					
Trial c	+0·15	0	0	0	0	−0·78	−1·29					
Trial d	0	−0·03	0	0	−0·22	0	−1·02					
Production and Import Levels												
Trial a	0	0	0	2050	1000	1000	0					
Trial b	0	1000	80	850	1000	0	0					
Trial c	1000	1220	98	0	0	0	0					
Trial d	1000	0	0	1464	0	1220	0					

[a] Based on Chenery [11], Table 1. Prices satisfy equation (1) except for P_4 in trial 1. Figures in parentheses are $(a_{ij} P_i)$ for trial c.

[b] Calculated from equation (4).

0·20 units of " other inputs," 0·70 units of labor, and 0·70 units of capital. The import activity M_1 provides an alternative way of supplying a unit of metal products by an expenditure (input) of 0·85 units of foreign exchange. A similar choice is provided between X_2 and M_2 (iron and steel) and between X_3 and M_3 (iron ore). The fourth production activity shows the resources used in the marginal export sector to provide a unit of foreign exchange.

In a complete programming model, the amounts of all commodities required for final use at a given level of income would be entered as restrictions on the solution. Similarly, the amounts of available capital and labor of different types would be specified. In this limited illustration, the problem is to supply requirements of 1000 each for metal products and iron and steel at minimum cost. Iron ore and foreign exchange are therefore taken to be intermediate goods having no net outside demand. " Other inputs," labor and capital are supplied from outside the model at prices reflecting their opportunity costs in the rest of the economy. The main difference in principle between this submodel and a complete programming system is that the prices of only the first four commodities are determined in the model in the present case, while in general all prices are so determined.

The four restrictions in the model consist of equations stating that the supply of each of the first four inputs must be equal to the specified demand:[1]

$$(2) \quad \begin{aligned} X_1 + M_1 &= 1000 \\ -0\cdot22X_1 + X_2 + M_2 &= 1000 \\ -0\cdot08X_2 + X_3 + M_3 &= 0 \\ X_4 - 0\cdot85M_1 - 1\cdot20M_2 - 1\cdot10M_3 &= 0 \end{aligned}$$

The objective is to minimize the amount of capital required to supply the given final demands, with the use of labor and " other inputs " valued at their opportunity costs in terms of capital. This is the same as supplying each commodity at minimum unit cost, since the amount of each to be supplied is fixed.

A feasible solution to the model contains either a production or an import activity for each of the three commodities plus the export activity for foreign exchange. The corresponding activity levels can be determined from equations (2) and are shown at the bottom of Table 1. The amounts of the outside factors (F_i)—labor, capital, and " other inputs "—required by each solution can then be determined from the following equations:

$$(3) \quad \begin{aligned} \text{Other inputs:} \quad F_5 &= 0\cdot20X_1 + 0\cdot25X_2 + 0\cdot70X_3 + 0\cdot10X_4 \\ \text{Labor:} \quad F_6 &= 0\cdot70X_1 + 0\cdot20X_2 + 0\cdot30X_3 + 1\cdot00X_4 \\ \text{Capital:} \quad F_7 &= 0\cdot70X_1 + 2\cdot70X_2 + 0\cdot50X_3 + 2\cdot20X_4 \end{aligned}$$

---

[1] I omit the possibility of overfulfilling demands, since there are no joint products in the present case.

The programming model thus contains two types of equations: price equations of the type of (1), and equations for the supply and demand of commodities and outside factors, (2) and (3). As outlined in [10], the general procedure for solving a programming model of this type involves three steps: (a) finding a feasible program or set of activity levels that satisfies the supply–demand restrictions; (b) calculating the shadow prices associated with the given program; (c) using these prices to determine whether any improvement in the initial program is possible. This procedure is repeated as long as any further improvements can be made.

The programming criterion used to compare projects or activities is the social profitability of each as measured from the shadow prices. Any profitable activity should be included in the program. It is the recalculation of prices that distinguishes this procedure from the partial programming approach suggested by Tinbergen. In either case, however, the test of social profitability of activity j can be expressed as:

$$(4) \qquad\qquad \Pi_j = \sum a_{ij} P_i$$

By definition, the activities that were used in determining the shadow prices will have a profitability of zero. The optimum solution is identified by the condition that all other activities have zero or negative profitability.

Some idea of the type of adjustment that results from moving from partial toward general equilibrium analysis may be given by determining solutions to the model in Table 1 under four different procedures: (a) the use of market prices; (b) correcting for the overvaluation of foreign exchange; (c) finding the optimum solution for the submodel alone; (d) finding the optimum solution for the submodel with changes in the opportunity costs of labor and other inputs determined from a general programming model. The accounting prices corresponding to each assumption are shown in columns 8 to 11 of Table 1. The calculation of social profitability of each activity, given the accounting prices, is illustrated in the table for trial c by giving cost and revenue figures in parentheses in columns 1 to 7.

Trial a. Assume that market prices are based on the cost of importing and are determined by setting profits on the import activities equal to zero, with a given foreign exchange cost of 3·00. The exchange rate is assumed to be overvalued, so that the price of foreign exchange is less than the cost of securing it through expanded exports. At these market prices only activity X_3 (iron ore) is profitable, but there is no domestic demand for iron ore unless steel is also produced (the export price is lower than that of imports because of transport costs). The use of market prices therefore leads to imports of steel and metal products, since the opportunity cost of expanding exports is not taken into account. The corresponding activity levels are shown at the bottom of the table.

Trial b. Assume now that we correct for the existing structural disequilibrium by setting the price of foreign exchange equal to its opportunity cost of 4·02 as determined from the export activity X_4. Allowance is also made for a rise in the accounting price of " other inputs," some of which are imported. A new set of accounting prices for commodities 1–3 is determined from the cost of imports. Substituting these prices into equation (4) shows that X_2 and X_3 are both profitable ($\pi_2 = 0.37$, $\pi_3 = 1.23$). Investment should therefore take place in steel, iron ore, and exports on this test.

Trial c. To find the optimum solution to the submodel by linear programming, we can start from trial b and recalculate the shadow prices from the activities that are included: X_2, X_3, X_4, M_1. The four shadow prices P_1 to P_4 are determined by applying equation (1), taking the prices of the outside inputs (P_5, P_6, P_7) as given. The elimination of excess profits from the prices of iron ore and steel lowers the cost of producing metal products, providing an example of pecuniary external economies. Instead of a loss, activity Q_1 now shows a profit of 0·15 and should be substituted for the import activity M_1. With the original prices for labor and capital, the optimum solution to the submodel is therefore to produce all three commodities and import nothing, since all import activities are unprofitable.

Trial d. If a similar analysis is carried out for the economy as a whole, it is likely that the initial estimate of the opportunity cost of labor (equal to its market price) will be revised. Assume that the shadow price of labor (equal to its marginal product in the rest of the economy) is only a third of its market price, or 0·5 units of capital. This lower labor cost will reduce the costs of production in different activities in proportion to their use of labor. Since exports are cheapened more than steel production by this calculation, it now becomes socially profitable to import steel and produce metal products. The optimality of this solution is shown by the prices in trial d, in which there is a loss of -0.03 on X_3. The optimum quantity solution is shown at the bottom of the table. Valuing other inputs and labor at their accounting prices, it has a capital cost of 5760, compared to 8200, 7470, and 7290 in trials a, b, and c.

The programming approach of trials c and d adds two elements to the analysis of accounting prices. The first is the inclusion of repercussions on input prices from investment in supplying sectors. This is one of the main types of dynamic external economies which are omitted from partial analysis. It is much more significant when there are economies of scale. The second element is the revision of the initial estimate of the opportunity costs of labor, capital, and foreign exchange. This revision is determined by the relation between supply and demand for these factors and thus takes into account the requirements of feasibility.[1]

The profitability criterion (usually called the " simplex " criterion) that is used in linear programming is logically equivalent to the SMP test if the

---

[1] An example in which these successive adjustments are calculated in detail is given in [10]. Frisch has outlined a computational procedure for handling large numbers of investment projects without going beyond the capacity of simple calculating equipment [16].

same prices are used in both. The two can be put in a comparable form as follows:

(4a) Social profit on activity j: $$\Pi_j = \sum_i a_{ij}P_i - k_j$$

(5) SMP of investment in activity j: $$(\text{SMP})_j = \frac{\sum_i a_{ij}P_i}{k_j} = \frac{\Pi_j}{k_j} + 1$$

where $-k_j$ is used for the capital input coefficient instead of a_{7j}. An activity having a positive social profit in equation (4a) will have an SMP of greater than $1\cdot0$ in (5), and the same projects would be accepted by either test. If the prices used are not the equilibrium prices, however, the project rankings by the two formulae will not necessarily be the same.

Although the example given here contained only one technique of production for each commodity, linear programming methods readily encompass alternative techniques. In a trial application of linear programming to Indian planning, Sandee [45] includes three alternative ways of increasing agricultural output—increased use of fertilizer, irrigation, and extension services—which are substitutes over a limited range. The four alternative techniques for producing textiles cited by Galenson and Leibenstein [17] could also be more properly evaluated in a programming model in which the cost of variation associated with their different requirements for materials, maintenance, and skilled labor could be included. However, it is only necessary to include alternative techniques in a programming model when the choice between them depends on the outcome of the solution. Probably in most cases the range of shadow prices can be foreseen accurately enough to determine in advance which technique is more efficient for a given country. The initial assumption can always be verified after the analysis has been completed by using the resulting prices.

Linear programming can be extended to include many of the indirect effects of investment that are suggested by growth theory. The production of trained labor, the effect on savings, or other indirect benefits can be considered as joint outputs whose value can be specified in the objective function. Similarly, indirect costs of production, such as the provision of housing to urban workers, can be included as additional inputs. The shadow prices computed from such an expanded system will therefore reflect nonmarket as well as market interdependence to the extent that it can be specified in quantitative form.

In formal terms, it is also quite easy to extend the programming model in time and to compute future prices for commodities and factors. The measurement of social profitability could then be made against a pattern of changing future prices. Given the degree of uncertainty attached to all future economic magnitudes, however, this is not likely to be a very useful procedure beyond the customary five-year planning period except in the most general terms. It would, however, be desirable to estimate the change in the equilibrium prices of foreign exchange and labor over a longer period of time, since these are the most important variables in choosing among investment projects.

D. *Investment Criteria and Comparative Advantage*

The linear programming approach provides a convenient link to the principle of comparative advantage because the optimal pattern of trade is determined simultaneously with the optimum allocation of investment. The model is considerably more general than that of market equilibrium because it allows for different social objectives and takes account of costs and benefits other than those entering the market. The limitations to the programming model are of two sorts: the form of the restrictions that are specified, and the omission of relationships that cannot be expressed in quantitative form.

The introduction of inelastic demands or increasing costs does not create any more theoretical difficulty in a programming model than in the corresponding general equilibrium system, although the computational aspects of such models have not been widely explored. The accounting prices perform the same function as guides to proper allocation, but the test of social profitability must be applied in marginal rather than average terms. In development programs, this modification is particularly important in the case of exports, where the price elasticity of demand is often rather low.[1] As Nurkse [37] points out, marginal comparative advantage for the underdeveloped countries may for this reason be quite different from that inferred from the average costs and prices of primary exports.

The existence of increasing returns creates the same problem for the programming model as it does for equilibrium theory. Marginal-cost pricing is not sufficient to determine whether an investment should be undertaken, and the total cost of alternative solutions must also be considered. Although practical methods of solving programming models containing decreasing costs are now being developed, they do not give allocation criteria that rely only on accounting prices. It is approximately correct to say that beyond a certain output level country A has a comparative advantage in the production of steel, but the precise determination of the break-even point depends on the level of output in other sectors also.[2]

The most serious theoretical qualification to the principle of comparative advantage comes from the type of nonquantitative interdependence among sectors that is assumed by Hirschman [23]. If, as he supposes, one growth sequence is more effective than another because it economizes on decision-making ability or provides a greater incentive to political action, a set of

---

[1] A programming model including this feature is given in Chenery [9].

[2] The nature of solutions to this type of problem is considered in [11], from which the data in Table 1 were taken. In this situation of decreasing average cost, the programming model may provide a greater improvement over the solution using partial criteria.

criteria having little or nothing to do with comparative advantage is implied. The empirical significance of these psychological and sociological factors remains to be established, but they lead to a conflict that cannot be resolved in economic terms.

When the practical limitations on information and analysis are recognized, the possibilities of conflict between comparative advantage and growth theory are greatly increased, and Wiles [65] suggests that marginal efficiency calculations may be less important. An aversion to risk-taking may be a valid reason for limiting the extent of specialization in the export of primary products beyond the amount that would be optimum in the light of more accurate information. An inability to measure the extent of economies of scale, labor training, and other sources of external economies also makes possible a continuing disagreement as to their magnitude.

III. Comparative Advantage and Balance in Development Programs

The inconsistent procedures that governments employ in formulating development policies are probably the most important source of conflict between the dictates of comparative advantage and of growth theory. Official pronouncements on development policy usually allege that both types of criteria have been (or should be) utilized in drawing up the program that is put forward, but the procedure followed in reconciling conflicts between the two is rarely made explicit. Since the analytical basis of most development programs is quite limited, it is important to look into the procedure that is actually used in order to discover sources of bias.

Development programs must simultaneously confront two sets of problems. In the short run, progress is hampered by structural disequilibrium in factor markets and in the demand and supply of particular commodities. This disequilibrium is reflected in the balance-of-payments difficulties that beset most low-income countries as they try to accelerate the process of development. In the longer run, the choice among sectors becomes increasingly important because the pattern of growth in each period will depend on the choices made previously. Development programs that are influenced mainly by the existing structural disequilibrium therefore tend to stress the need for greater balance between domestic demand and supply, while those that take a longer view tend to pay more attention to comparative advantage.

Although the procedures actually followed cannot be ascertained with any accuracy by an outside observer, these two aspects can be identified from characteristic elements in the analysis. The balanced growth approach is generally associated with target-setting in key sectors, stress on the avoidance of bottlenecks, and attempts to equate the supply and demand of labor, capital, and the more important commodities. The extreme cases of this type of procedure are found in the communist countries. Less extreme examples, in which some attention is paid to comparative advantage, are the procedures of the Indian Planning Commission and the U.N. Economic Commission for Latin America.

Characteristic 'elements of the comparative advantage approach are attempts to measure the relative efficiency of different types of production, the weighing of balance-of-payments improvements against other benefits to the economy (by means of accounting prices or otherwise), and usually a greater emphasis on partial analysis than on overall projections. Examples that will be cited are Puerto Rico, the Philippines, and Israel.

A. *Procedures Emphasizing Domestic Balance*

The planning procedures developed in the USSR and applied with some modification in other communist countries represent in extreme form the use of balance as a criterion for resource allocation and the virtually complete omission of any test of comparative advantage. As revealed in recent studies by Montias [32] and Balassa [1], the main tool of Soviet-type planning is a very detailed system of material balances specified in quantitative terms. Policy objectives are translated into production targets in which priority is given to heavy industry and other sectors that are expected to contribute to further growth (" leading links "). Prices are used mainly as rationing devices and have no necessary connection with production costs. The cumbersome calculations involved in arriving at balance of supply and demand for a large number of commodities limit the alternatives that can be tried out, so the main effort is to find a feasible program [32].

The question of comparative advantage scarcely arises in the USSR because of its size and diversified resources, although similar problems arise in connection with the choice of production techniques. When the Soviet planning system was transplanted to the satellite countries, however, it ran into difficulties because of its inability to determine the advantages to be secured from trade. According to Balassa [1, p. 264], the idea of comparative advantage did not exist in Hungarian development policy (at least until very recently), although trade has a high ratio to GNP. Exports are determined by import " needs," and the institutional structure is such as to encourage exporters to meet targets for exports without regard to production costs. Since prices do not reflect resource use, it is impossible to determine where comparative advantage lies and to what extent the trade pattern deviates from the optimum.

Despite their violation of most short-term welfare considerations, the success of Soviet planning methods in producing a rapid rise in the national product makes them attractive to many underdeveloped countries. In India, for example, Mahalanobis' " plan-frame " for the second five-year plan [30] draws heavily on Soviet methodology. He starts from the assumption that the rate of investment is determined by the level of domestic production of capital goods: " As the capacity to manufacture both heavy and light machinery and other capital goods increases, the capacity to invest (by using home-produced capital goods) would also increase steadily, and India would become more and more independent of the import of foreign machinery and capital goods " [30, p. 18].   His analysis implies that export possibilities are so limited that they can be ignored, so that the composition of demand is limited by the composition of domestic output.   In order to raise the level of investment, Mahalanobis concludes that investment in industries producing capital goods should be increased from less than 10 per cent to 30–35 per cent of total investment in the second five-year plan.

As Komiya [27] has shown, Mahalanobis' approach to development ignores price and demand considerations completely.   The targets for the four sectors in his model appear to be based mainly on the goal of creating heavy industry, which is assumed to be the key to future growth.   Criteria of efficiency and comparative advantage are entirely omitted from his analysis.

Although there are traces of the Mahalanobis approach in the second and third five-year plans formulated by the Indian Planning Commission, the final results are much less extreme.   One basic problem is that exports are expected to rise only half as fast as national income between the first and third plan periods, while demand for the goods initially imported tends to rise much more rapidly.   The inelastic demand for traditional Indian exports means that a considerable proportion of investment must be devoted to commodities that are presently imported.   Within this category, the principles of comparative advantage should apply.   In actuality, the emphasis has shifted somewhat from heavy industry in the second plan to agriculture in the third.   In the latter document [19], increasing self-sufficiency in basic industrial commodities—steel, petroleum, machinery, etc.—is listed as a high-priority objective, but so is the maximum development of agriculture.   Whether the resulting targets are consistent with comparative advantage is not considered in the published analysis.[1]

The balance-of-payments difficulties of many Latin American countries have also been a major factor in shaping the programming procedure developed by the Economic Commission for Latin America [57].   This approach has been applied in considerable detail in studies of Colombia [58], Argentina [59], and Peru [60].   One basic conclusion of these studies is that the growth of exports will be much slower than the growth of demand for goods that are currently imported.   Investment therefore has to be heavily oriented toward import substitution, and the equality of supply and demand must be tested on a commodity basis to avoid balance-of-payments difficulties. In the three cases mentioned, this balancing process is carried out by means of

---

[1] On the basis of a simplified linear-programming model, Sandee [45, p. 25] finds that " up to 1970 more effective ways to employ capital for development exist than highly capital intensive steel-making," suggesting that an analysis of comparative advantage would indicate more reliance on imports.   The nonmarket benefits of production are omitted from his analysis, however.

an input–output analysis in which imported goods are distinguished from domestic products in each category.

In principle, comparative advantage can be used in the ECLA procedure as a basis for the choice of import substitutes, but this has apparently been done only to a limited degree. Since the main emphasis is on balance, there is a danger that the initial assumptions as to levels of exports will not be re-examined after the extent of import substitution required by a given program has been determined. The result may be a considerably lower productivity of investment in import substitutes than in exports if the two are not systematically compared. The drawbacks to this procedure are more serious in small countries like Colombia and Peru than in a large country like India, in which imports supply a smaller fraction of the total demand for commodities.

B. *Procedures Emphasizing Comparative Advantage*

Among countries having development programs, procedures that stress comparative advantage are less common than those emphasizing balance. Practically all policy statements list among their priority criteria factors presumably leading to comparative advantage, but there is little evidence as to how they are applied in drawing up programs.

The development procedures of the government of Puerto Rico come as close to being a pure application of comparative advantage as Soviet procedures are of principles of balanced growth. Unlike many low-income countries, Puerto Rico has an elastic demand for its exports to the U.S. market and can attract U.S. capital for profitable investments. The government's policy has been to give tax remission for ten years and to provide overhead facilities, labor training, and other inducements to industries that will benefit the island's economy. In deciding which industries to promote, the Economic Development Authority has studied the long-term comparative advantage of a large number of alternative projects, since comparative advantage will lead to both satisfactory profits and maximum income. Low-cost labor (even with allowance for differences in productivity) has been the main element in comparative advantage, since most industrial materials must be imported. Allowance is also made for external economies in industries that will supply inputs to other sectors.[1]

Under this policy, the growth of *per capita* income has been as rapid (nearly 5 per cent annually) and the development of industry as marked (from 19 per cent to 25 per cent of GNP) over the years 1948–58 as in any country following a deliberate policy of balanced growth. The planning procedure depends very largely on the particular relation of Puerto Rico to the United States and its small size. These factors make it unnecessary to worry about the elasticity of demand for exports or the dangers of dependence on foreign sources for essential imports, which so preoccupy the Indian and Latin

---

[1] The Puerto Rican experience is discussed by Baer [2]; the evaluation procedures are described in mimeographed reports of the Economic Development Authority.

American planners. With reliable export and import markets, domestic balance is not a problem.

Since the assumptions of the classical model are not approached so closely in most underdeveloped countries as in Puerto Rico, the calculation of comparative advantage usually departs further from the market evaluation. In a more typical case the Philippine National Economic Council has outlined a procedure for applying the SMP formula under Philippine conditions [39]. This analysis starts from the market evaluation of the profitability of an investment and adds corrections for the project's effect on the balance of payments, its use of domestic materials, and its use of domestic labor, each with a suitable weight. This procedure may be justified by comparison to the linear programming criterion of social profit. In principle the proper correction to private profit is obtained by giving each a value equal to the difference between its shadow price and its market price.[1] In the Philippines, this would mean a bonus for labor and a penalty for foreign exchange use (or a bonus for foreign exchange saving). Higgins [22, pp. 654–62] shows that the weights assigned in the Philippines tend to exaggerate these effects. The use of the same weight for all domestic materials may lead to serious error, since not all are overvalued by market prices.

The government of Israel has developed one of the most systematic procedures for measuring comparative advantage as a basis for allocating investment funds and foreign exchange. In effect, the Ministry of Finance evaluates projects on the basis of accounting prices for foreign exchange and capital, taking into account the indirect use of foreign exchange in sectors supplying inputs such as power or industrial materials. The calculation is summed up as the cost in domestic resources of a dollar earned or saved, and it is applied equally to exports and to import substitutes. The calculation of domestic value added is also made by exporters as a basis for export subsidies [3, p. 23]. In allocating the government's development budget, priority is given to projects whose domestic cost of earning or saving foreign exchange is less than the current estimate of its accounting price. This procedure can also be rationalized by means of the linear programming criterion of social profitability. Instead of measuring the value derived per unit of investment with accounting prices for foreign exchange and labor, as in the SMP formula, the cost per unit of foreign exchange acquired is computed using an accounting price for capital. When the same shadow prices are used, all three measures give the same result.

Although it is dangerous to generalize from the limited evidence on development policies that is available, there appears to be some relation

---

[1] The social profit, Π_j, may be expressed as:

$$(4b) \qquad\qquad \Pi_j = \bar{\Pi}_j + \Sigma\, a_{ij}\Delta P_i,$$

where $\bar{\Pi}_j$ is private profit per unit of output calculated at market prices and ΔP_i is the difference between the market price and shadow price of commodity i. The elements ΔP_i may be regarded as weights attached to each input or output coefficient.

between the type of procedure adopted and the characteristics of the economy in a number of the cases examined. Small countries are forced to pay more attention to comparative advantage because they cannot hope to produce the whole range of manufactures and primary products, while large countries may be tempted to follow more autarchic policies.[1] The importance given to balanced growth also depends to a large extent on the country's recent experience with its export markets and the state of its foreign exchange reserves and borrowing capacity. Puerto Rico and Israel can both count on substantial capital inflows which make it unnecessary for them to approach balanced trade in the near future, while India has much less leeway.

IV. Conclusions

This paper has considered development policy from the standpoint of economic theory, as a problem in operations research, and as it is actually carried on by governments. Much of the confusion in the field stems from a failure to distinguish these different levels of analysis. Theorists are prone to suggest decision rules that omit some of the relevant institutional limits, while economists who have been working in particular areas often arrive at conclusions that do not fit other cases. As in other fields of economics, most of the disagreement can be traced to implicit differences in assumptions.

There are a number of contradictions between the implications of trade theory and growth theory. To make the two theories consistent, it is necessary to discard the assumption of equilibrium in factor markets, to allow for changes in the quantity and quality of factors of production over time, and to take account of internal and external economies of scale. Although under these assumptions market forces do not necessarily lead to efficient resource allocation, a pattern of production and trade can be determined that maximizes income over time. The commodities to be produced and traded cannot be determined by a simple ranking procedure along the lines of classical comparative advantage because of the interdependence among sectors. At best, it may be possible to say, for example, that a country has a comparative advantage in steel production for a specified set of production levels in supplying and using sectors. In advanced countries, this qualification may be unimportant, but in the less developed ones it is crucial in a number of industries.

Much of the attack on the use of comparative advantage is based on its omission of various nonmarket elements. It is assumed that the inclusion of the latter favors the development of industry, and special benefits are often attributed to capital goods and heavy industry. The intangible benefits stemming from trade in the form of new products, improved technology, and technical assistance tend to be overlooked in this discussion. Although I

[1] Japan is one exception to this generalization, partly due to its dependence on imported raw materials.

support the critics who wish to include more of growth theory in determining the desirability of specialization, I doubt that this extension will favor balanced growth to the extent that they suppose.

The other main theoretical attack on comparative advantage is aimed at its supposed support for continued specialization in primary exports. Granting the low elasticity of demand for many primary products, it is wrong to conclude that comparative advantage is thereby superseded by principles of balanced growth. The increasing shortage of foreign exchange makes it even more important to economize on its use and to seek efficient ways for increasing its supply. The comparison of domestic to foreign sources of supply that is implied by comparative advantage is no less relevant to this situation than to the case in which investment is more evenly divided between exports and import substitutes.

The aspects of growth theory which do not seem to be reconcilable with the notion of comparative advantage are the sociological and political effects of choosing one production pattern instead of another. While the concept of opportunity cost can be extended to include a number of nonmarket phenomena, such as labor training and overhead facilities, it can hardly be stretched to cover differences in fertility rates or political attitudes. So far as I can see, in the present state of knowledge of social phenomena, considerations such as these may be used to modify the results of economic analysis but cannot be directly incorporated into it.

At the level of operations research, the search for simple decision rules for investment in low-income countries seems to have been useful mainly in exposing the fallacies in some of the common rules of thumb. One can specify conditions under which ratios such as the capital intensity or the effect on the balance of payments would be a valid indicator of the desirability of an investment, but the apparent gain in simplicity is offset by the danger of applying the test in inappropriate circumstances. A more fruitful approach to partial equilibrium analysis is provided by the use of accounting prices to compute the social profitability of a given use of resources. This method allows simultaneously for several overvalued or undervalued inputs, and it can include whatever elements of general equilibrium analysis are available.

Since market forces cannot be relied on to balance supply and demand under conditions of initial disequilibrium and accelerated growth, a principal concern of development policy is to ensure the inconsistency of production levels with commodity demands and factor supplies. The technique of linear programming is designed to combine the test of consistency with the test of the social profitability of a given resource use. Although it cannot be applied very extensively in underdeveloped countries as yet, the programming methodology serves as a guide to improved practical measures.

To most economists, a survey of the procedures actually followed in designing development policy would probably suggest that balance is overemphasized and that the potential gains from trade are often neglected. This emphasis may be partly justified by the greater uncertainties attached to trade and by an aversion to risk that is greater than seems warranted to the outside observer. Better understanding of the working of the underdeveloped economies and better information for planning are needed to redress the balance and enable countries to secure the potential gains from trade without conflict with measures for domestic development.

REFERENCES

1. B. A. BALASSA, *The Hungarian Experience in Economic Planning*. New Haven 1959.
2. W. BAER, " Puerto Rico: an Evaluation of a Successful Development Program," *Quart. Jour. Econ.*, Nov. 1959, **73**, 645–71.
3. BANK OF ISRAEL, *Annual Report, 1959*. Jerusalem 1960.
4. F. M. BATOR, " On Capital Productivity, Input Allocation, and Growth," *Quart. Jour. Econ.*, Feb. 1957, **71**, 86–106.
5. N. S. BUCHANAN, *International Investment and Domestic Welfare*. New York 1945.
6. O. CASTELLINO, " La Scelta degli Investimenti nei Programmi di Sviluppo Economico," *L'Industria*, 1959, No. 1, 60–76.
7. R. E. CAVES, *Trade and Economic Structure*. Cambridge 1960.
8. H. B. CHENERY, " The Application of Investment Criteria," *Quart. Jour. Econ.*, Feb. 1953, **67**, 76–96.
9. ——— " The Role of Industrialization in Development Programs," *Am. Econ. Rev., Proc.*, May 1955, **45**, 40–57.
10. ——— " Development Policies and Programmes "; *Econ. Bull. for Latin America*, Mar. 1958, **3**, 51–77.
11. ——— " The Interdependence of Investment Decisions," in Abramovitz *et al.*, *The Allocation of Economic Resources*. Stanford 1959.
12. M. DOBB, *An Essay on Economic Growth and Planning*. London 1960.
13. R. DORFMAN, P. A. SAMUELSON, AND R. M. SOLOW, *Linear Programming and Economic Analysis*. New York 1958.
14. O. ECKSTEIN, " Investment Criteria for Economic Development and the Theory of Intertemporal Welfare Economics," *Quart. Jour. Econ.*, Feb. 1957, **71**, 56–85.
15. R. FRISCH, *A Method of Working out a Macroeconomic Plan Frame with Particular Reference to the Evaluation of Development Projects, Foreign Trade and Employment*. Oslo 1958 (mimeo.).
16. ——— *A Powerful Method of Approximation in Optimum Investment Computations of the Normal Type*. Oslo 1959 (mimeo.).
17. W. GALENSON AND H. LEIBENSTEIN, " Investment Criteria, Productivity, and Economic Development," *Quart. Jour. Econ.*, Aug. 1955, **69**, 343–70.
18. A. GERSCHENKRON, " Economic Backwardness in Historical Perspective," in B. Hoselitz, ed., *The Progress of Underdeveloped Areas*, Chicago 1952.
19. GOVERNMENT OF INDIA PLANNING COMMISSION, *The Third Five Year Plan*. New Delhi 1960.
20. G. HABERLER, " Some Problems in the Pure Theory of International Trade," *Econ. Jour.*, June 1950, **60**, 223–40.
21. E. HAGEN, " An Economic Justification of Protectionism," *Quart. Jour. Econ.*, Nov. 1958, **72**, 496–514.
22. B. HIGGINS, *Economic Development*. New York 1958.
23. A. O. HIRSCHMAN, *The Strategy of Economic Development*. New Haven 1958.
24. ——— " Investment Criteria and Capital Intensity Once Again," *Quart. Jour. Econ.*, Aug. 1958, **72**, 469–71.

25. A. E. KAHN, "Investment Criteria in Development Programs," *Quart. Jour. Econ.*, Feb. 1951, **65**, 38–61.
26. C. P. KINDLEBERGER, *The Terms of Trade: A European Case Study.* New York 1956.
27. R. KOMIYA, "A Note on Professor Mahalonobis' Model of Indian Economic Planning," *Rev. Econ. Stat.*, Feb. 1959, **41**, 29–35.
28. H. LEIBENSTEIN, "Why Do We Disagree on Investment Policies for Development?" *Indian Econ. Jour.*, Apr. 1958, **5**, 369–86.
29. W. A. LEWIS, "Economic Development with Unlimited Supplies of Labor," *Manchester School*, May 1954.
30. P. C. MAHALANOBIS, "The Approach of Operational Research to Planning in India," *Sankhya*, Dec. 1955, **16**, 3–131.
31. K. MANDELBAUM, *The Industrialization of Backward Areas.* Oxford 1945.
32. J. M. MONTIAS, "Planning with Material Balances in Soviet-type Economies," *Am. Econ. Rev.*, Dec. 1959, **49**, 963–85.
33. H. MYINT, "The Classical Theory of International Trade and the Under-developed Countries." *Econ. Jour.*, June 1958, **68**, 317–37.
34. G. MYRDAL, *Economic Theory and Under-developed Regions.* London 1957.
35. H. NEISSER, "Investment Criteria, Productivity and Economic Development," *Quart. Jour. Econ.*, Nov. 1956, **70**, 644–47.
36. R. NURKSE, *Problems of Capital Formation in Underdeveloped Countries.* Oxford 1953.
37. —— *Patterns of Trade and Development.* Stockholm 1959.
38. P. G. OHLIN, "Balanced Economic Growth in History," *Am. Econ. Rev.*, Proc., May 1959, **49**, 338–53.
39. THE PHILIPPINES NATIONAL ECONOMIC COUNCIL, *The Five-Year Economic and Social Development Program for Fiscal Years 1957–1961.* Manila 1957.
40. J. J. POLAK, "Balance of Payments Problems of Countries Reconstructing with the help of Foreign Loans," *Quart. Jour. Econ.*, Feb. 1943, **57**, 208–40.
41. R. PREBISCH, "Commercial Policy in the Underdeveloped Countries," *Am. Econ. Rev.*, Proc., May 1959, **49**, 251–73.
42. A. QAYUM, *Theory and Policy of Accounting Prices.* Amsterdam 1959.
43. P. ROSENSTEIN-RODAN, "Problems of Industrialization of Eastern and South-Eastern Europe," *Econ. Jour.*, June–Sept. 1943, **53**, 205–16.
44. W. W. ROSTOW, "The Take-Off into Self-Sustained Growth," *Econ. Jour.*, Mar. 1956, **66**, 25–48.
45. J. SANDEE, *A Long-Term Planning Model for India.* United Nations pub. New York 1959.
46. T. W. SCHULTZ, "Latin American Economic Policy Lessons," *Am. Econ. Rev.*, Proc., May 1956, **46**, 425–32.
47. T. SCITOVSKY, "Two Concepts of External Economies," *Jour. Pol. Econ.*, April 1954, **62**, 143–51.
48. —— "Growth—Balanced or Unbalanced," in M. Abramovitz *et al.*, *The Allocation of Economic Resources*, Stanford 1959.
49. A. K. SEN, "Some Notes on the Choice of Capital Intensity in Development Planning," *Quart. Jour. Econ.*, Nov. 1957, **71**, 561–84.
50. J. SHEAHAN, "International Specialization and the Concept of Balanced Growth," *Quart. Jour. Econ.*, May 1958, **72**, 183–97.
51. H. W. SINGER, "The Distribution of Gains Between Investing and Borrowing Countries," *Amer. Econ. Rev.*, Proc., May 1950, **40**, 473–85.
52. G. STIGLER, "Production and Distribution in the Short Run," reprinted in Am Econ. Assoc., *Readings in the Theory of Income Distribution*, Philadelphia 1946.
53. P. STREETEN, "Unbalanced Growth," *Oxford Econ. Papers*, June 1959, **11**, 167–91.

54. J. Tinbergen, " The Relevance of Theoretical Criteria in the Selection of Investment Plans," in M. Millikan, ed., *Investment Criteria and Economic Growth*, Cambridge 1955.
55. —— *Economic Policy: Principles and Design.*   Amsterdam 1956.
56. —— *The Design of Development.*   Baltimore 1958.
57. United Nations, Department of Economic and Social Affairs, *Analyses and Projections of Economic Development.*   New York 1955.
58. —— *Analyses and Projections of Economic Development.* III. *The Economic Development of Columbia.*   Geneva 1957.
59. —— *Analyses and Projections of Economic Development.* V. *The Economic Development of Argentina.*   Mexico City 1960.
60. —— *Analyses and Projections of Economic Development.* VI. *The Industrial Development of Peru.*   Mexico City 1959.
61. United Nations, *Manual of Economic Development Projects.*   New York 1959.
62. A. Vaidyanathan, " A Survey of the Literature on Investment Criteria and Development of Underdeveloped Countries," *Ind. Econ. Jour.*, Oct. 1956, **4**, 122–44.
63. J. Viner, *International Trade and Economic Development.*   Oxford 1953.
64. —— " Stability and Progress: The Poorer Countries' Problem," in D. Hague, ed., *Stability and Progress in the World Economy*, London 1958 (with comment by R. Nurkse).
65. P. Wiles, " Growth versus Choice," *Econ. Jour.*, June 1956, **66**, 244–55.
66. J. H. Williams, " The Theory of International Trade Reconsidered," *Econ. Jour.*, June 1929, **39**, 195–209.   Reprinted in Am. Econ. Assoc., *Readings in the Theory of International Trade*, Philadelphia 1949.

VII

THE PURE THEORY OF INTERNATIONAL TRADE: A SURVEY

By

JAGDISH BHAGWATI [1]

THIS chapter surveys that branch of international trade theory which, following Marshall, is generally described as " pure." This epithet separates it from " monetary " theory. It is *not* to be taken to imply exceptional esotericism and abstraction from the problems of the real world. Indeed, I propose to give prominence to that part of the growing, new literature in pure theory which attempts explicitly to bring the theory on to the ground— through empirical verification of testable propositions, through measurement of the gains and losses from changes in trade policy and through the formulation of analytical and operational models to assist the developmental planning that is becoming a key characteristic of the developing nations.

The pure theory of international trade represents essentially the application of the theories of value and welfare to questions of international economics.[2] Although the distinction between them has not always been clear, it is none the less true that two different species of problems have been the subject of analysis in pure theory. There are questions of "positive" or "objective" analysis: for instance, what determines the composition of trade; how will tariffs affect factor prices; what is the effect of trade on the terms of trade? On the other hand, there are questions in " welfare " or " normative " economics: among them, does free trade maximise world real income; are tariffs superior to free trade from the viewpoint of national advantage; how do tariffs compare with subsidies as forms of State intervention? [3]

[1] The author is Professor in the Delhi School of Economics of Delhi University. This survey was partly written when I was with the Indian Statistical Institute. For correspondence and/or discussions, I am thankful to Professors H. G. Johnson, R. W. Jones, C. P. Kindleberger, B. S. Minhas, P. A. Samuelson and T. N. Srinivasan. V. Balasubramanian and R. Tagat have assisted with the computational work. [I have taken the opportunity provided by reprinting to add a few references to contributions that have appeared since 1964. These have been made in footnotes within square brackets; see *Addendum*, p. 239.]

[2] The pure theory of trade thus differs structurally from general theory in the kinds of questions asked, rather than in the kinds of assumptions made. This vexed question has been considered at length by Haberler [4, Chapter 1].

[3] The distinction between " positive " and " welfare " questions is recent in trade theory and appears to have been stated explicitly and emphatically only as late as 1933 by Ohlin [34]. Ohlin, who distinguished between these two aspects, criticised the classical economists for muddling them.

The range of questions that have been asked is impressive. The recent literature which is addressed to them runs into several dozen books and over two hundred papers. This makes a brief survey exceptionally difficult, even if confined to the developments in the past two or three decades.[1] This difficulty is compounded by the fact that the subject has already been extensively, frequently and recently surveyed. We currently have a cogent and lucid survey in a brief monograph by Haberler [4], revised only in 1961; a nearly exhaustive, full-length account in a 1960 volume by Caves [3]; an excellent, theoretical survey of some of the central analytical propositions of pure theory by Mundell [11] in 1960; and, most embarrassingly, a survey of some of the more impressive recent developments in pure theory by myself [1] as recently as 1961.[2]

To collapse the immense literature into a concise survey, to exercise the inevitable selectivity (with respect to both authors and problems of analysis) to maximum advantage, it is necessary to have a precise, logical frame. The structure of this paper is built squarely on the clear distinction between " positive " and " normative " pure theory.

Under positive theory, in turn, a distinction has been drawn between: (1) the propositions of " statics," which describe the properties of an equilibrium situation at *any given point* of time; (2) the propositions of " comparative statics," which concern the *differences* in the equilibrium values of variables between situations at *two different points of* (conceptual) time; and (3) the propositions of " dynamics," which involve time in an essential way.

The static propositions which have attracted the greatest analytical interest concern: (1) the pattern of trade: the determination of commodities as exports and imports; and (2) the configuration of factor prices. The analysis of the former question has further been enriched greatly by a recent, noticeable trend towards empirical verification. The propositions of comparative statics (which continue to be almost exclusively deductive) fall again into two classes: (1) those that concern the effect, on equilibrium prices and quantities, *under a pre-defined trade policy*, of an autonomous change

---

As Haberler [4, p. 3], however, has charmingly pointed out: " That his demand for not just a clear distinction between political evaluation and theoretical explanation, but for actual separation of these two areas by putting them into separate books or chapters, is easier postulated than accomplished is demonstrated by Ohlin himself. Thus, in an early passage of his celebrated treatise, in the midst of ' objective theory,' he proves in typical classical manner that interregional trade and division of labour result in an increased social product, without making it clear that this statement implies a value judgment on his part and is not merely ' objective analysis.' "

[1] Thus Lipsey's [7] concise and brilliant review of the theory of customs unions (part of the theory of discriminatory tariff changes) in this JOURNAL runs into several pages. And it deals with a comparatively recent field which forms only a small segment of the literature on pure theory.

[2] To these may be added Meade's celebrated works [8, 9, 10], which cover the entire field and the writings of Johnson [5, 6], which have done much to synthesise the literature on many aspects of trade theory. Mention may also be made of two papers: Lipsey's [7] 1960 survey of customs-union theory and the review in 1960 by myself and Johnson [2] of certain historical controversies in pure theory. [See also Kemp [143].]

in one of the following data: production functions, demand and factor supply; and (2) those that relate to the effect, on equilibrium prices and quantities, of a change in trade policy itself, while other data are constant. The development of pure theory has witnessed a synthesis and simplification of these propositions in comparative statics which elude the few, though diverse, attempts at dynamic analysis. This synthesis has also been accomplished in terms of an analytical framework characterised by primary factors of production and integrated processes of production. This constitutes a central limitation of the theory in a theoretical world where this conceptualisation has been replaced generally by the more general approach of process analysis and in a real world where a large portion of the world trade consists of intermediates and capital goods and an increasing number of developing nations' imports are coming to consist almost exclusively of these commodities.

The parts of this paper dealing with positive theory have therefore been divided into the following five groups:

1. Section I: *Theorems in Statics: The Pattern of Trade.*
2. Section II: *Theorems in Statics: Factor Price-Equalisation.*
3. Section III: *Theorems in Comparative Statics.*
4. Section IV: *Theorems in Dynamics.*
5. Section V: *Central Limitations of Pure Theory: Intermediates and Capital Goods.*

In the theory of welfare and trade the classification has been easier. There is, on the one hand, the " traditional " theory which is addressed to *qualitative* propositions that rank different trade policies (*e.g.*, free trade is superior to no trade) and can be classified according to whether they satisfy Samuelson's superior-for-all-income-distributions criterion. On the other hand, there is a growing, important segment of the literature which aims at *quantitative* measures of costs and benefits—prompted by the objective of making economic analysis policy-oriented. At the same time, the growth of centralised planning in many developing countries has raised the interesting questions of the *operational* use of trade theory's welfare insights and results as part of the complement of planning techniques; and some useful experience has been obtained.

The survey of welfare propositions in trade theory, therefore, has been divided into three major groups:

1. Section VI: *Welfare Propositions: Gains from Trade.*
2. Section VII: *Measurement of Welfare.*
3. Section VIII: *Trade Theory and Development Planning.*[1]

---

[1] Although the paper falls neatly into these eight sections, there are inevitably some overlaps. None the less, I would maintain that the proposed classification is the most advantageous from the viewpoint of assessing the current state, limitations and trends of the pure theory of trade.

I. Theorems in Statics: The Pattern of Trade

The theory of comparative advantage (or cost), which concerns the determination of the pattern of trade, constitutes perhaps the oldest set of analytical propositions in pure theory. It belongs to the realm of " statics " because traditionally it has been formulated as a theorem concerning the determination of (traded) commodities into exports and imports in a static, analytical framework. This is certainly true of the two major theories, Ricardian and Heckscher-Ohlin [1], that have dominated this field.

There are, no doubt, different possible ways in which an " international economy " may be simulated by a theorist. Each such " model " could be used to deduce analytical propositions. Indeed, the literature on pure theory contains a large number of such idealisations, among the most celebrated being those of Yntema, Mosak and Graham [3].[1]

From the viewpoint of propositions concerning the pattern of trade, the two models of significance are those of Ricardo and Heckscher–Ohlin [19, 34]. Not merely have these models been used to derive " logically true " theorems concerning the trade pattern.[2] These theorems have also now been adapted to formulate testable hypotheses (based on factors stressed in the respective models). And these hypotheses have been subjected to empirical verification in a series of excellent papers. In consequence, new theories have now been devised which provide *alternative* explanations of the pattern of trade. Prominent among these are the analyses of Kravis [22] and Linder [27]. These four theories concerning the pattern of international specialisation are discussed here, distinguishing clearly between the formulations as deductive, analytical propositions (which are logically true under a specified set of sufficient conditions) and formulations as testable hypotheses.

The Ricardian Theory

The Ricardian Theory can be construed in either of two ways: (1) as a highly simplified model which was intended to be, and served as, an eminently successful instrument for demonstrating the welfare proposition that trade is beneficial; or (2) as a serious attempt at isolating the crucial variables which can be used to " explain " the pattern of trade. There is little doubt that the former view is plausible. A careful study of the original texts yields supporting evidence; the most persuasive element is the fact that when both Ricardo and Mill discussed the " positive " (as opposed to " normative ") proposition relating to the effects of cheap corn *imports* from the colonies on profits, wages and rents, and thence on the approach of the stationary state, they were using the full-fledged classical model characterised by three

[1] For a summary statement of these and other models, Caves [3] is an excellent reference. A cataloguing of such models, however, is of limited interest, as any number of models can be put down as one wishes. Only those models which have been used to yield theorems are of significance; and then it is only in considering those theorems that they are best discussed.

[2] The phrase " logically true " is used there in the strict mathematical sense: a statement that is true in every logically possible case is said to be *logically true*.

factors and diminishing returns [1]. And yet the impact of the Ricardian
" constant cost " model in recent literature has been predominantly as an
idealisation which affords a significant clue to the structure of foreign trade.[1]

On the latter interpretation the Ricardian theory can be deduced directly
from the celebrated England–Portugal example in Ricardo's *Principles*. If
it is assumed that there are two commodities, a single factor (labour) and
constant returns to scale (in each activity),[2] the pre-trade commodity price
ratio will be a function exclusively of the (scale-free) output-factor ratios
contained in the production functions. The combination of a single factor
with constant returns to scale ensures that neither demand nor the level of
factor supply makes any difference to the equilibrium commodity price
ratio in a closed economy.[3] Since Ricardo assumes a similar model for each
country, it follows that the pre-trade commodity price ratio, and hence the
composition of trade, is exclusively determined by international differences
in relative output-factor ratios. If a_1 and a_2 are the output-factor ratios for
country I and b_1 and b_2 for country II in activities 1 and 2 respectively,
country I will export commodity 1 and import commodity 2 if $a_1/a_2 > b_1/b$,
(as this will imply that commodity 1 will be cheaper, and commodity 2
dearer, in country I than in country II *prior to trade*). The algebraic condition is frequently written as $a_1/b_1 > a_2/b_2$, which states the condition in
terms of " comparative factor productivities." If, however, the number of
commodities is increased beyond two, while maintaining the two-country
assumption, it is no longer possible to derive the " strong " Ricardian theorem
that the trade pattern is determined exclusively by international differences
in production functions (*i.e.*, by comparative factor productivities). The
model now implies a weaker proposition: there will be a chain in which all
commodities are ranked in terms of their comparative factor-productivity
ratios such that *it will always be true that each of a country's exports will have a
higher factor-productivity ratio than each of its imports*. The precise composition
of exports and imports (*i.e.*, where the chain will be cut, dividing the exports
and the imports) can be determined only by bringing demand into the
model [20]. This proposition will continue to hold also in the more general
framework of many countries and commodities, which represents a generalisation of Ricardo's two-country model by Graham. In an elegant generalisation

---

[1] This has been the result of two factors: (i) traditionally the question whether the Ricardian
theory should be construed as positive or normative has rarely been raised; it has always seemed
" natural " to construe Ricardo as though he were genuinely attempting to explain the pattern
of trade with his simple model; and (ii) the Ricardian " demonstration " of the benefits of trade,
long since challenged as inadequate by Barrett Whale, has now been superseded by the elegant
and more rigorous formulations of the new welfare economics and Samuelson's classic proof of
1939—so that it is no longer easy to see that the Ricardian preoccupation was predominantly with
normative aspects.

[2] The last assumption listed here need not be implicit in the preceding one, since fixed factors
like land may well be subsumed in the shape of the production function.

[3] The reason is that the resulting production possibility curve is non-strictly convex and
characterised by a constant rate of transformation.

of Ricardo's theory, drawing upon McKenzie's earlier work [78], Jones [69] has shown that, taking each pair of countries, comparing only the labour cost ratios of the commodities they are producing in specialisation, the Ricardian bilateral cost comparisons are necessarily satisfied. (These propositions relate, more generally, to the location of production in a free-trade world: their implications for the trade pattern are in conformity with the Ricardian theory.)

When international trade economists have attempted to formulate hypotheses based on the Ricardian theory, and test whether observable trade conforms to the postulated pattern, the real difficulty has been that of trying to adapt the one-factor Ricardian approach to the multi-factor real world. Two ways in which this adaptation may be made can be distinguished.

One way would be to focus on the fact that the Ricardian model empha-sises the crucial role of comparative differences in *production functions* so that the testable proposition should be developed in these terms. For instance, if the technology in activity i could be characterised by $Q_i = \lambda_i^{I} Q_i(K_i; L_i)$ for country I and by $Q_i = \lambda_i^{II} Q_i (K_i; L_i)$ for country II so that the *only* difference between the two countries' production functions for an identical activity is a multiplicative scalar ($\lambda_i^{II}/\lambda_i^{I}$ in this case), then the Ricardian testable hypothesis could be construed to mean that

$$\frac{\lambda_i^{II}}{\lambda_i^{I}} > \frac{\lambda_j^{II}}{\lambda_j^{I}}$$
$$i = 1, 2, \ldots m \qquad j = m+1, \ldots n$$

where commodities $i = 1, 2, \ldots m$ are country II's exports and commodities $i = m + 1, \ldots n$ are its imports. This would be a Ricardian hypothesis—as much as any other.[1] The possibility of testing such a hypothesis is not, by any means, remote. Minhas [33, p. 154] states, in a brilliant paper on the Heckscher–Ohlin theory, that "the isoquants in different countries, except for a pure scale change, look alike; and the marginal rates of substitu-tion are unchanged at given capital: labour ratios" when homohypallagic production functions are fitted to the data for certain comparable industries in Japan and the United States. This empirical evidence seems to provide the means to test the kind of Ricardian hypothesis formulated here.[2]

---

[1] The conditions under which this proposition is logically true could be established by an ex-tension of the theoretical work on the Heckscher–Ohlin theory and on the effects of neutral technical progress [5, Chapter I and III]. For instance, if all the assumptions which are shown to be sufficient for the logical validity of the Heckscher–Ohlin theorem are made with the *only* difference that the production functions are not identical, but differ between countries in the manner postulated in the text, it follows that the (Ricardian-type) hypothesis in the text concern-ing the pattern of trade will be logically true.

[2] Minhas comes close to doing this, but does not see the problem in this way because he is focusing on the implications of such "neutral" differences in production functions for the Heck-scher–Ohlin theorem. Credit must be given to him, however, for having seen the possibility of construing the Ricardian approach in the broader way (of differences in production functions) suggested here, as against the narrower approach of labour productivity ratios that is to be found in the literature.

The most frequent interpretation for the purpose of formulating a testable proposition, however, has been in terms of the factor productivities themselves. The comparative factor productivities, defined in terms of an arbitrarily chosen factor (almost always labour),[1] have been taken as providing the necessary clue to the trade pattern.

The intuitive and ultimate rationale behind this interpretation is easily stated (and, as will be evident later, has an important bearing on the procedure of testing). Since exports will take place only when domestic (pretrade) prices are lower than abroad, it follows that

$$\frac{P_i^{\mathrm{I}}}{P_i^{\mathrm{II}}} < 1$$
$$i = 1, 2, \ldots m$$

where $\frac{P_i^{\mathrm{I}}}{P_i^{\mathrm{II}}}$ refers to the price-ratio of commodity i, exported by country I, *prior to trade*.[2] Similarly,

$$\frac{P_j^{\mathrm{I}}}{P_j^{\mathrm{II}}} > 1$$
$$i = m + 1, \ldots n$$

where the commodity i is exported by country II. Hence

$$\frac{P_i^{\mathrm{I}}}{P_i^{\mathrm{II}}} < \frac{P_j^{\mathrm{I}}}{P_j^{\mathrm{II}}}$$
$$i = 1, \ldots m \quad i = m + 1, \ldots n$$

Now it is possible to write these prices (defined as equal to costs) in terms of three component factors:

$$P_i = a_i \cdot \frac{W_i}{L_i} \cdot \frac{TC_i}{W_i}$$

where a_i is the labour: output ratio, W_i is the wage bill (so that $\frac{W_i}{L_i} = w_i$ is the wage-rate) and TC_i the total cost (inclusive of profits, by definition) in activity i. If we now argue that it is, in practice, enough to focus attention on a_i and to ignore the other two factors (on the ground that either they are insignificant *or* they are identical between countries individually or as a

---

[1] There is nothing in the basic *structure* of the Ricardian model which requires that this single factor be labour. It could be anything else. However, it has mostly been taken to be labour. The reasons for this exclusive preference may be that: (i) the historical context of the labour theory of value, in terms of which Ricardo's comparative cost doctrine has usually been understood, makes it inevitable that the formal identity between labour and any other factor, as noted here, should have been missed, and (ii) there has been, until recently, also a widespread tendency, in economic literature generally, to take labour productivity as the index of " productivity " rather than, say, capital productivity.

[2] Where transport costs are present, lower pre-trade prices are only a *necessary* condition for exports; where transport costs (and similar cost-raising factors) are ignored, lower pre-trade prices also become a *sufficient* condition.

product), then we could substitute a_i for p_i in the above price-comparison. This would give us the condition

$$\frac{a_i^{\mathrm{I}}}{a_i^{\mathrm{II}}} < \frac{a_j^{\mathrm{I}}}{a_j^{\mathrm{II}}} \quad . \quad . \quad . \quad . \quad . \quad . \quad \text{(1)}$$
$$i = 1, 2, \ldots m \quad j = m+1, \ldots n$$

This is, in fact, the condition stated frequently as the Ricardian hypothesis.

This chain of reasoning also leads to a further formulation. It is possible to advance a variation of the hypothesis which brings into the picture the structure of the wage-rates as well. This can be done by rewriting the previous hypothesis thus:

$$\frac{a_i^{\mathrm{I}}}{a_i^{\mathrm{II}}} \cdot \frac{w_i^{\mathrm{I}}}{w_i^{\mathrm{II}}} < \frac{a_j^{\mathrm{I}}}{a_j^{\mathrm{II}}} \cdot \frac{w_j^{\mathrm{I}}}{w_j^{\mathrm{II}}} \quad . \quad . \quad . \quad . \quad \text{(2)}$$
$$i = 1, 2, \ldots m \quad j = m+1, \ldots n$$

This is, in fact, a statement of the Ricardian hypothesis which is in terms of comparative *unit labour costs* and not *labour productivity*. It is the hypothesis which is to be found in much of the empirical literature [1].

Although it appears relatively simple to go on from these formulations to their tests, there are some points of interest that need to be spelled out.

(1) To begin with, " indirect " tests of these hypotheses readily suggest themselves but can be treacherous. For instance, it has been customary to argue through an attempted demonstration of the international " similarity " of the inter-industrial wage-rate structure and the pattern of the total-cost/wages ratio. Caves [3, p. 272] has cited Kravis' [21, pp. 145–6] empirical results, which show that the ranking of industries by hourly earnings of workers is almost identical between Japan and the United States, to argue that these data lend force to the Ricardian hypothesis in terms of comparative labour productivity differences (as the determinants of relative price differences).[1] However, such a deduction leaves out of reckoning the possibility that the structure of the costs–wages ratio may be largely dissimilar between trading countries and makes implicitly an unverified assumption of " similarity " of this structure. This procedure, in any case, is unsound, since, although each of the two structures (costs–wages and wage-rates) may be internationally " dissimilar," their product may be similar as a result of these dissimilarities being offsetting. A method which proceeds in terms of investigating the similarities of individual structures will leave out this possibility and thereby constitute an unduly restrictive and false test for the empirical verification of the Ricardian hypothesis in question.

(2) But then, if a direct test of the Ricardian hypotheses were adopted, examining whether the labour productivity or unit wage–cost ratios for the exports and imports for two countries (taken bilaterally) conform to the postulated relationships, would that be enough? I do not think so. Let

---

[1] Similar data, showing similarity of industrial wage structures, have been produced for the United States, United Kingdom, Canada and (only a little less successfully) Sweden by Lebergott [23] None of this, however, adds up to anything impressive, since the coverage in terms of both activities and nations is severely limited.

me cast my argument in terms of hypothesis (1), which relates to labour productivity ratios—it is equally valid for hypothesis (2) relating to unit wage–cost ratios.

It will be recalled that hypothesis (1) is derived in two steps. (*a*) First, it is argued that the (pre-trade) prices are such that the relative price (defined as the domestic over the foreign price) of an exported good must be lower than the relative price of an imported good. This is a natural assumption to make; it merely reflects the assumption that the profit motive will direct the pattern of trade.[1] This, however, relates to the *pre-trade* prices. But the observed prices are inevitably *post-trade* prices. This should have posed an impossible difficulty in testing any proposition concerning the pattern of trade and prices. However, it is easy to get around the problem when one reckons with the fact of transport (and other) costs that lead to a difference in the post-trade f.o.b. and c.i.f. (landed) prices. This difference in f.o.b. and c.i.f. prices means that the price–trade proposition that the relative price of an exported good must be lower than that of an imported good will continue necessarily to hold (with the domestic price of a good defined f.o.b. and the foreign prices c.i.f. for exported goods). The proposition is necessarily valid empirically in a world which is characterised by natural and artificial cost-raising factors. It therefore calls for no conscious attempt at verification. This is indeed a great gain. It is, however, an advantage not shared by the other postulate that must be made before the Ricardian hypothesis can be derived. (*b*) This other assumption consists in arguing that prices can be approximated by labour productivities. This proposition takes generally the strong form that the linear regression equation fitted to observed labour productivity ratios (for each activity in both countries) and corresponding price ratios would yield a 45-degree line from the origin.[2] This strong assumption, which is equivalent to arguing that the inter-industry structure of the total cost per unit labour is identical between the trading countries, is only a sufficient condition for yielding, along with the price–trade assumption, the required Ricardian hypothesis. It is also the condition that is most frequently found in the literature on Ricardian theories [3, Chapter X]. A weaker, but still sufficient, assumption would be to make labour productivity ratios a monotonically increasing function of price ratios. But the weaker this assumption gets, the more difficult it becomes to interpret it in meaningful, economic terms.[3]

[1] Theoretically, of course, one can think of cases where the pattern of trade does not conform to this rule. For instance, the contrary possibility can arise if there are domestic distortions (*i.e.*, divergence of the domestic rate of transformation in production from the commodity price-ratios) [112]. In anticipation, I may point out that this qualification does not apply to the *post-trade*, relative price comparison for exportables and importables, to which I proceed immediately in the text.

[2] The labour productivity ratio here must be defined as the foreign labour productivity divided by the domestic; and the price ratio is defined as the domestic price divided by the foreign.

[3] In the tests of this assumption which I later attempt in this paper even the weaker hypothesis does not get through: the linear regressions yield very poor fits.

Since one does want to know why it is that the trade pattern is characterised, if at all, by the comparative labour productivity ranking postulated
by Ricardian hypothesis (1), I would argue that it is also necessary to supplement such a direct verification by a further verification of whether labour
productivity ratios exhibit the (underlying) hypothesised relationship with
price ratios.[1]   Unfortunately, neither the direct verification of the rankings
of exports and imports (for a pair of trading countries) in terms of their
comparative labour productivities or unit wage–cost ratios nor the necessary
supplementary test of the implied relationship between price ratios and
labour productivity or unit wage–cost ratios has yet been attempted.

The empirical literature that exists, in some abundance, concerns itself
with really different kinds of testable propositions concerning trade.   These
hypotheses do have some overlap with the Ricardian hypotheses (1) and (2),
with the unfortunate consequence that the surprisingly good results that
attempts at verifying them have turned up have been construed frequently
as validating the Ricardian approach [3, Chapter X].   The pioneering
study in this field is by MacDougall [28, 29], with follow-up by Balassa [13],
Stern [40] and MacDougall [30] himself.

Taking American and British exports of similar commodities to third
markets, MacDougall [28, 29] has conducted analysis which is tantamount
to investigating three hypotheses: $\dfrac{a_i^{\mathrm{II}}}{a_i^{\mathrm{I}}}$ is positively correlated with

$$\frac{E_i^{\mathrm{I}}}{E_i^{\mathrm{II}}}, \ (i = 1, \ldots k); \qquad \ldots \quad \ldots \quad \ldots \quad (3)$$

if

$$\frac{a_i^{\mathrm{II}}}{a_i^{\mathrm{I}}} \cdot \frac{w_i^{\mathrm{II}}}{w_i^{\mathrm{I}}} > 1,$$

then

$$\frac{E_i^{\mathrm{I}}}{E_i^{\mathrm{II}}} > 1, \ (i = 1, \ldots k): \qquad \ldots \quad \ldots \quad (4)$$

and $\dfrac{a_i^{\mathrm{II}}}{a_i^{\mathrm{I}}} \cdot \dfrac{w_i^{\mathrm{II}}}{w_i^{\mathrm{I}}}$ is positively correlated with

$$\frac{E_i^{\mathrm{I}}}{E_i^{\mathrm{II}}}, \ (i = 1, \ldots k) \qquad \ldots \quad \ldots \quad \ldots \quad (5)$$

[1] Concerning the derivation of the Ricardian hypothesis (1) in this two-step fashion, however,
there is just a little more that may be said.   It may be contended that labour productivities
approximate the *pre-trade* prices but that trade leads to boosted profits in the export industries with
no imputation to wages and no impact on labour productivities.   If so, one *could* find evidence for
the trade pattern exhibiting the Ricardian ranking in terms of comparative labour productivities
and/or unit wage–cost ratios, but *not* necessarily for the productivity or unit wage–cost ratios
being related in any way to the price ratios.   While, of course, this is theoretically possible (and
such a theory would have its own further implications which should then be tested), I do not find
it plausible.   Why should labour productivity ratios, for instance, be a good approximation to
relative prices before trade but cease to be so after trade?   This asymmetry seems to have no rationale.   In any case, the particular chain of reasoning used in the text, aside from being more
plausible, is also the one generally subscribed to; and hence its implications have been fully spelled
out.

where $E_i{}^I/E_i{}^{II}$ is the ratio of exports of commodity i by countries I and II respectively to third markets.[1] Stern has recently followed MacDougall's hypotheses and procedures closely, but introduced more recent data on productivity. MacDougall [30] has done the same. Balassa has tested hypothesis (3), using again the same new data on productivity, but does not consider hypothesis (4) and approaches hypothesis (5) differently, through multiple-correlation analysis.

Now, each of these three hypotheses has two main elements: (a) the adequacy of labour productivity (or unit labour-cost) ratios as an approximation to price ratios; and (b) the relation of price ratios (between prices of similar commodities exported to third markets by the United States and the United Kingdom) to quantity-ratios (of United States and United Kingdom exports of similar commodities).

It is easy to recognise the former as a proposition borrowed from the Ricardian analysis. The latter proposition, however, represents a departure from the Ricardian price–trade assumption. The assumption that the relative prices of exported goods will be lower than those of imported goods is now replaced by the postulation of some relationship between (United States–United Kingdom) price ratios of third-market exports and (United States–United Kingdom) shares in third markets. In hypotheses (3) and (5), for instance, the relationship takes the form of a negative correlation between the relative export prices; in hypothesis (4) the form is shifted: a country's exports are postulated to be greater when its price is relatively cheaper than its rival's, but nothing is stated about the effects of different degrees of relative price advantage on export shares.

Neither of the hypothesised price–trade relationships, however, seems to be plausible. It is difficult to see, for instance, the theoretical reason why the ratio of two rivals' third-market exports should, in a cross-section analysis, turn out to increase as the corresponding price ratio falls. The argument that relative prices of similar commodities and their relative sales can be correlated in *cross-section analysis* cannot be justified on the presumption that, for *any given industry*, a reduction in the relative price of a competitor will increase its relative sales. It is difficult to imagine that this presumption can be extended to cross-section data where different commodities will have varying " elasticities of substitution," depending on different degrees of product differentiation, quality differences, etc. as between different sources of origin (the United States and the United Kingdom in the present example).[2]

Despite these difficulties with the hypotheses (3), (4) and (5), the

---

[1] Hypothesis (3) is clearly inspired by Ricardian hypothesis (1) and hypotheses (4) and (5) by Ricardian hypothesis (2). It should be made clear here that MacDougall's papers contain much *other* analysis of considerable interest and that the papers are neither confined to testing the hypotheses listed here nor approach those questions in the same formal manner as set out here.

[2] This is perhaps what Caves [3, p. 269] also is hinting at in his critique of the MacDougall papers.

empirical verification is remarkably successful.[1] And yet, as already argued, this has little to do with the empirical verification of the Ricardian hypotheses (1) and (2). While this is true, the authors of these empirical exercises have turned up a great deal of data on export prices and on labour

[1] If one examines the evidence MacDougall [28, pp. 715–17] has produced one is astonished at the empirical support which is turned up for this hypothesis. For United States : United Kingdom export shares and price ratios, MacDougall produces supporting evidence, with twenty-three regressions and correlations, from 1913 to 1948; the lowest two correlation coefficients are −0·73. Fairly high correlation coefficients, with nicely negative regression slopes, are turned up, moreover, for United States : United Kingdom, United States : Japan, United States : Germany, United States : France, United Kingdom : France, France : Japan, France : Germany, United Kingdom : Japan and United Kingdom : Germany. As for the evidence on hypotheses (3), (4) and (5) themselves, the results can be systematised as follows:

I. *Hypothesis (3)*. The results of MacDougall, Stern and Balassa can be stated briefly:

Author.		Sample.	Year.	Regression equation.[a]	Correlation coefficient.
MacDougall	(1)	25 industries	1937	Regression slope = −4	−0·70
	(2)	39 ,,	1950	$x = -2·19 + 1·89y$	0·61
Stern	(3)	24 (= MacDougall 1937 sample)	1950	$x = 0·98 + 1·65y$ (0·57)	0·52
	(4)	39 industries	1950	$x = -0·68 + 1·27y$ (0·43)	0·44
	(5)	25	1950	$x = 0·91 + 1·49y$ (0·59)	0·46
Balassa [b]	(6)	28 ,,	1950 and	$x = -1·761 + 1·594y$ (0·181)	0·86
	(7)	28 ,,	1951	$x^* = -53·32 + 0·721y^*$ (0·103)	0·80

[a] x and y refer to the logarithms of the United States : United Kingdom export ratio and United States : United Kingdom labour productivity ratio respectively. x^* and y^* in the last regression refer to the ratios themselves. MacDougall does not state his 1937 regression equation.

[b] The productivity data refer to 1950 and the source is the same as that used by MacDougall and Stern. However, the export data refer to values instead of quantities and are for 1951 instead of 1950. For the latter, the reason is that 1950 was an " abnormal " year. For the former, the reason is that it is very tricky to separate export prices and quantities. Balassa prefers to work with values and justifies this choice on the ground that, with the estimates of elasticity of substitution being high in general, a positive correlation between productivity and export quantities will exist, so that the tests proposed are not vitiated. This argument, however, rests on the estimates of high elasticities of substitution—which, in turn, are based upon the very same separation of prices and quantities which Balassa is shying away from.

The results, on the whole, seem clearly to support the stated hypothesis mildly.

II. *Hypothesis (4)*. Here only MacDougall and Stern have produced evidence. Two different approaches can be distinguished. (1) One is to examine the industries directly and see how many conform to the pattern laid down by the hypothesis. (a) Using only the *average* wage levels for the United States and the United Kingdom (instead of individual industry wages), MacDougall found for 1937 that " where American output per worker was more than twice the British, the United States had in general the bulk of the export market, while for products where it was less than twice as high the bulk of the market was held by Britain " [28, p. 698], while the average American wage was twice as high as the British wage. Thus, out of 25 industries investigated, 20 conformed and 2 more would have if the measure of productivity were suitably adjusted. (b) Stern, with the average American wage 3·4 times the British wage in 1950, found that from 24 industries (comparable to MacDougall's 25), 20 conformed to the expected pattern. (c) For the larger sample of 39 industries, the exceptions were only 5. These three, strikingly favourable results were obtained when the *average* American and British wages were taken. Both MacDougall

productivities and unit wage-costs.   These data can be used to examine the proposition that relative prices can be approximated by comparative labour productivities and/or unit wage–cost ratios.   This can only result in the

---

and Stern, however, attempted to analyse the effect of taking individual wages for different products as well.   (d) Owing to data limitations, MacDougall could attempt this for only 13 industries.   His results showed a slight improvement: cigarettes became an exception, whereas pig-iron, glass containers and hosiery held the line.   (e) Stern, using the same sample, found a slight deterioration, although the expected pattern still continued.

(2) The other approach to examining hypothesis (4) is through statistical estimation procedures. Both MacDougall and Stern have estimated regression equations for logarithms of labour productivity ratios and export ratios, already listed earlier here.   These are used to estimate the validity of hypothesis (4).   (a) For instance, MacDougall found that his regression line, fitted to the 1937 data plotted on a double logarithmic scale, passed through the horizontal dividing line of 2 (i.e., American output per worker twice the British) at a point considerably to the left of a vertical dividing line at unity, marking the point of equality in the two countries' exports.   This implied that America tended to export only about *two-fifths* as much as Britain in 1937, when the American advantage in output per worker was exactly offset by the inferiority in advantage in average wage. (b) For the same sample of industries, Stern found in 1950 that America tended to export only about four-fifths as much as Britain when American output per worker and average wage-rates were 3·4 times higher.   This clearly came closer to hypothesis (4).   (c) For 39 industries, Stern's regression line passed almost exactly through the 3·4 point, appearing to verify hypothesis (4) totally.   All these estimates are for data using *average* wage-rates.   While this approach, on the whole and especially for 1950, appears to support hypothesis (4), it must be admitted that it represents an inadequate test from the viewpoint of hypothesis (4) itself: even though all observations conform to the postulated pattern, the estimated regression may register a deviation (from the point of intersection of the dividing lines); whereas the regression line may pass exactly through the point of intersection while the observed points deviate from the postulated pattern.

III. *Hypothesis* (*5*).   This hypothesis, relating unit labour cost ratios and export shares, has been tested directly only by Stern and, with a different formulation, by Balassa.   (a) For *average* wage data, of course, the regression and correlation coefficients for the estimated regression equations in the labour productivity hypothesis (3) should hold again, because all that happens is that the productivity ratios get each multiplied by a scalar (equal to the wage ratio).   The results derived earlier, therefore, hold.   (b) Stern, however, has produced the regression equation

$$x = 0·01 - 1·40y, r = -0·43$$
$$(0·38)$$

(where y is the logarithm of unit costs ratio), which lends some, though not very strong, support to the hypothesis being tested.   (c) Balassa approaches the problem in terms of the question whether the introduction of the wage ratios as an *additional* explanatory variable (in a multiple correlation analysis) improves the explanation of export shares.   Balassa's regression equation is

$$x^* = -181·2 + 0·691^* + 0·140\,z^*$$
$$(0·167)   (0·102)$$

where x^* is the export ratio, y^* the productivity ratio and z^* the wage ratio.   The multiple correlation coefficient is 0·81 (as against 0·80 in the simple correlation).   The partial coefficients are 0·77 (for x^* and y^*) and 0·24 (for x^* and z^*); the latter is not significant at the 5% level. For logarithms, Balassa's regression equation is:

$$x = -5·164 + 1·457y + 1·250z$$
$$(0·328)   (0·566)$$

The multiple correlation coefficient is 0·88 (as against the simple coefficient of 0·86).   The partials are 0·84 (x and y) and 0·11 (x and z); the latter is not significant at the 5% level.   The explanation which comparative labour productivities provide is not improved by adding wage ratios as an additional explanatory variable.   (It follows, therefore, that wage-structure differences between ratios do not have any systematic relationship with price differences.)

verification (or refutation, as it turns out) of the prop on which the Ricardian hypotheses (1) and (2) are generally rested. A full-blooded test of these hypotheses, directly examining the ranking of (bilateral) exports and imports by comparative labour productivities and/or unit wage–cost ratios, is impossible to carry out with this information and must await further research.

For the limited test outlined here, I have used two sets of data. For the MacDougall sample of 25 industries (reduced to 24 in Stern's calculations for 1950), the necessary data are available for 22 industries for 1937 and for 16 of these for 1950 (Table I). There is a slightly larger and different sample of 25 industries, used by Stern for 1950 (Table II). There are

TABLE I

Labour Productivity Ratios and Export Price Ratios (United States/United Kingdom) for 1937 and 1950

Industry.	1937.		1950.	
	Output per worker, U.S./U.K.	Price of exports, U.S./U.K.	Output per worker, U.S./U.K.	Price of exports, U.S./U.K.
1. Tin cans .	5·25	0·68	—	—
2. Pig-iron .	3·60	0·84	4·10	1·33
3. Wireless sets	3·50	0·64	4·00	0·95
4. Motor cars	3·10	0·91	2·40	2·63
5. Glass containers	2·40	0·69	—	—
6. Paper	2·20	0·72	3·40	0·90
7. Beer	2·00	1·30	3·00	1·00
8. Linoleum and oil cloth	1·90	1·04	2·60	1·11
9. Coke	1·90	1·08	1·90	1·36
10. Hosiery .	1·80	1·24	—	—
11. Cigarettes	1·70	1·08	2·50	1·08
12. Rayon weaving and making	1·50	1·19	—	—
13. Cotton spinning and weaving	1·50	1·03	—	—
14. Leather footwear	1·40	1·31	1·70	1·28
15. Woollen and worsted	1·35	1·42	1·80	1·44
16. Margarine	1·20	1·34	1·80	1·46
17. Cement .	1·10	2·12	1·20	1·33
18. Electric lamps .	5·40	0·51	3·60	0·92
19. Biscuits .	3·10	1·01	2·40	1·24
20. Matches .	3·10	0·86	—	—
21. Rubber tyres	2·70	1·12	2·40	1·42
22. Soap	2·70	1·24	2·50	1·10

Source: Stern [40, p. 278].

certainly many limitations to these data. The most serious ones, from the viewpoint of the current analysis, are three: (i) the f.o.b. price reflects gross value, whereas the labour productivity refers to the final, value-adding industry; the results would surely be more in conformity with the spirit of the Ricardian approach if the *indirect* labour productivities were also computed; (ii) the f.o.b. prices also include transport and other costs which add to the ex-factory price, whereas the labour productivity figures are not

TABLE II

*Labour Productivity Ratios, Export Price Ratios, Unit Labour Cost Ratios
and Wage Rates Ratios (United States/United Kingdom) for 1950*

	Export prices, U.S./U.K.	Output per worker, U.S./U.K.	Unit labour costs, U.S./U.K.	Wage-rates, U.S./U.K.
1. Cement	1·33	1·16	2·33	2·70
2. Sugar factories and refineries . .	1·32	1·48	1·89	2·79
3. Tanneries	1·01	1·68	1·92	3·23
4. Footwear (except rubber) . . .	1·28	1·71	1·68	2·88
5. Woollen and worsted . . .	1·33	1·85	1·96	3·63
6. Metal-working machinery . . .	2·64	2·21	1·79	3·96
7. Rayon, nylon and silk . . .	1·15	2·26	1·51	3·42
8. Generators, motors and transformers .	2·63	2·39	1·49	3·56
9. Tyres and tubes	1·23	2·41	1·50	3·62
10. Wirework	1·28	2·44	1·52	3·72
11. Soap, candles and glycerine . .	1·18	2·49	1·58	3·93
12. Rubber products (excluding tyres and footwear)	1·31	2·50	1·45	3·62
13. Tobacco manufactures . . .	1·08	2·51	1·02	2·56
14. Linoleum and leather cloth . .	1·11	2·56	1·27	3·25
15. Bolts, nuts, rivets and screws . .	2·06	2·56	1·71	4·31
16. Breweries and manufacturing of malt .	1·00	3·00	1·33	3·99
17. Pulp, paper and board . . .	0·90	3·38	1·08	3·65
18. Electronic tubes	0·68	3·55	1·10	3·91
19. Electric-light bulbs . . .	0·92	3·56	1·10	3·92
20. Paint and varnish . . .	0·90	3·63	0·96	3·50
21. Basic industrial chemicals . .	0·95	3·72	0·91	3·38
22. Radio	0·95	4·00	0·85	3·39
23. Blast furnaces	1·33	4·08	0·72	2·96
24. Electrical household equipment . .	1·70	4·12	0·96	3·95
25. Containers, paper and card . .	1·12	4·28	0·96	4·09

Source: Stern [40, p. 288].

adjusted for this when necessary; and (iii) in most exporting industries a differential is observable between the average domestic price and the average foreign price [3, p. 281], so that the approximation of labour productivity ratios to relative (export) prices may have to be adjusted analytically for this phenomenon. Notwithstanding these limitations, however, I have carried out the analysis in consonance with the tradition of economists to catalogue the difficulties and thereafter to ignore them. The results, as already hinted at, are seriously prejudicial to the usefulness of the Ricardian approach: though, it should be emphasised, the verdict cannot be final in the absence of better and fuller tests.[1]

The linear regressions of export price ratios on labour productivity ratios are almost entirely hopeless, whether we take logarithms or not. The six regressions, listed in Table III, uniformly fail to be significant except for the unlogged, MacDougall sample for 1937. The failures clearly overwhelm the sucess in verification.

Testing the relationship between comparative unit labour-costs and

[1] I am indebted to B. S. Minhas for assistance with the statistical analysis in this paper. The responsibility for any errors, however, is entirely mine.

TABLE III

Relationship between Labour Productivity Ratios and Export Price Ratios

Data.	Regression equation.*	Coefficients.
1937 (Table I)	$Y = 1{\cdot}72 \quad - \quad 0{\cdot}211X$ $(0{\cdot}2291) \quad\quad (0{\cdot}0450)$	$r^2 = \quad 0{\cdot}525$ $r = -0{\cdot}724$
1937 (Table I)	$\log Y = 0{\cdot}252 \quad - \quad 0{\cdot}525 \log X$ $(0{\cdot}1925) \quad\quad (0{\cdot}432)$	$r^2 = \quad 0{\cdot}0686$ $r = -0{\cdot}262$
1950 (Table I)	$Y = 1{\cdot}58 \quad - \quad 0{\cdot}169X$ $(0{\cdot}32605) \quad\quad (0{\cdot}1204)$	$r^2 = \quad 0{\cdot}129$ $r = -0{\cdot}359$
1950 (Table I)	$\log Y = 0{\cdot}264 \quad - \quad 0{\cdot}611 \log X$ $(0{\cdot}3769) \quad\quad (0{\cdot}5155)$	$r^2 = \quad 0{\cdot}0912$ $r = -0{\cdot}302$
1950 (Table II)	$Y = 1{\cdot}7044 \quad - \quad 0{\cdot}1470X$ $(0{\cdot}3291) \quad\quad (0{\cdot}1095)$	$r^2 = \quad 0{\cdot}0728$ $r = -0{\cdot}2698$
1950 (Table II)	$\log Y = 0{\cdot}2056 \quad - \quad 0{\cdot}2773 \log X$ $(0{\cdot}0816) \quad\quad (0{\cdot}1831)$	$r^2 = \quad 0{\cdot}0906$ $r = -0{\cdot}301$

* Y = Export price ratio, and X = Labour productivity ratio.

export price ratios, we find the results to be equally disappointing. Table IV lists the two linear regression equations for the 1950 data (Table II). Both relationships are insignificant (though they register a negligible improvement over the regressions for export price-ratios and labour productivity ratios alone).

TABLE IV

Relationship Between Unit Labour Cost Ratios and Export Price Ratios

Data.	Regression Equations.*	Coefficients.
1950 (Table II)	$Y = 0{\cdot}7227 \quad + \quad 0{\cdot}4141X$ $(0{\cdot}33194) \quad\quad (0{\cdot}23021)$	$r^2 = 0{\cdot}1233$ $r = 0{\cdot}3512$
1950 (Table II)	$\log Y = 0{\cdot}03785 + 0{\cdot}42113 \log X$ $(0{\cdot}0335) \quad\quad (0{\cdot}1997)$	$r^2 = 0{\cdot}162$ $r = 0{\cdot}40248$

* Y = export price ratio, and X = unit labour cost ratio.

Handling the influence of relative inter-country wage-rates alternatively through the introduction of wage ratios as an additional explanatory variable in a multiple correlation analysis, further, we find that the results for the available data are again poor (Table V). The correlations continue to be insignificant (though they register a slight improvement over the simple correlation, for the same data, between export price ratios and labour productivity ratios alone).

These results, limited as they are, cast sufficient doubt on the usefulness of the Ricardian approach (as generally understood). Contrary, therefore, to the general impression (based on the MacDougall, Balassa and Stern results), there is as yet no evidence in favour of the Ricardian hypotheses. This is perhaps not as unfortunate as it seems. For ultimately the practical utility of the Ricardian hypotheses is somewhat limited. Labour productivity, after all, is not a datum in the sense that production functions are.

TABLE V

Multiple Regressions between Export Price Ratios, Labour Productivity Ratios and Wage Ratios

Data.	Multiple regression equation.*		Coefficients.	
1950 (Table II)	$Y = 0.5572 - 0.2286\,X_1 + 0.3905\,X_2$ (7·8) (0·1140) (0·2182)		$r^2 =$ $r =$ Partial: $X_1 =$ $X_2 =$	0·191 0·437 −0·3931 0·3564
1950 (Table II)	$\log Y = 0.1646 - 0.4304 \log X_1 + 0.8011 \log X_2$ (0·0599) (0·2015) (0·5018)		$r^2 =$ $r =$ Partial: $X_1 =$ $X_2 =$	0·1850 0·4301 −0·4143 0·3220

* Y = export price ratio; X_1 = labour productivity ratio, and
X_2 = wage-rate ratio.

The reliance of the prediction on labour productivity unaccompanied by any explanation of why the labour productivity is what it is, and how therefore it may be expected to change, restricts the utility of the prediction. Moreover, even if we could forecast changes in labour productivity, we could not tell exclusively therefrom that the pattern of imports and exports would change in a specified manner; all we could say is that, if the pattern of exports and imports changes in any way, the new pattern will also be characterised by the postulated Ricardian ranking in terms of comparative labour productivities and/or unit wage ratios.[1]

The Heckscher–Ohlin Theory

An alternative approach to explaining the pattern of trade is attributed to the works of Heckscher [19] and Ohlin [34], but owes much to the work of Samuelson [38, 91]. Indeed, in its current form it has discarded so many of the variables which Ohlin explicitly listed as significant that it is almost certainly liable to be rejected by Ohlin as an adequate version of his original analysis! This approach breaks away from the Ricardian model and works in terms of an analytical framework which is in striking contrast to its predecessor. As we saw, the Ricardian model assumes one factor, and therewith (through the supporting assumption of constant returns to scale) makes the factor supply irrelevant in determining the trade pattern;[2] on the other

---

[1] I would not claim that *any* type of prediction concerning change in the pattern of trade is impossible. But even apparently simple predictions are not possible. For instance, if labour productivity increases in an export industry we *cannot* necessarily predict that the industry will continue to export its product (even if all other autonomous change in the trading countries is ruled out).

[2] This is, strictly speaking, not true in a model with more than two commodities. In this case demand must be brought in to " break the chain " of ranked commodities into exports and imports. But demand itself will be a function of the level of income, which will depend, among other things, on the factor supply.

hand, as we shall soon see, the Heckscher–Ohlin model assumes two factors and makes international differences in factor endowments the crucial and sole factor determining comparative advantage.[1] Moreover, whereas the former attributes to international differences in production functions the explanation of comparative advantage, the latter explicitly postulates the international identity of production functions.[2] The Heckscher–Ohlin theory is also different from the Ricardian analysis in having been presented *explicitly* as a contribution to the " positive " theory, as an attempt at explaining the structure of foreign trade, rather than with a view to establishing the welfare propositions of trade theory.

The Heckscher–Ohlin theorem states that *a country's exports use intensively the country's abundant factor*. This is an eminently " plausible-looking " proposition. One would expect that a country should be able to produce more cheaply those goods that are intensive in the use of a factor when that factor of production is (physically) abundant in the country relative to its trading partner. Of course one can think of some exceptions immediately. For instance, it is clear that this presumption rests on the similarity of production conditions between trading countries. There could obviously be a contradiction of the Heckscher–Ohlin proposition if *production functions* for individual industries were different between countries. Alternatively, the country may quite well have an offsetting preference for the *consumption* of these commodities—so that the pre-trade (relative) prices of commodities may turn out to be higher (rather than lower) abroad—thus refuting the Heckscher–Ohlin proposition. Some qualifications are less intuitively seen. One of the theoretically interesting qualifications [3] follows from the fact that, although, technologically, the production function for an activity may be identical between countries, the operative segments of it may be intensive in the use of a different factor in each country. Where such " reversals of factor-intensity " can occur the effect can be similar to that of differences in production functions and the Heckscher–Ohlin proposition need not hold.

Theorists have established a set of conditions which ensure the " logical truth " of the Heckscher–Ohlin theorem. These conditions differ, depend-

[1] Viner [44] has attempted to demonstrate that the factor endowment approach is to be found in classical writings. But his contention is not persuasive, based as it is on fragmentary remarks which do not add up to systematic analysis.

[2] It should be emphasised that these contrasts, which are based partly on the distinction between production functions and factors of production, raise the well-known question as to the proper definitions of these two concepts. It is interesting, in this connection, to recall that Ohlin appears to have taken it as apparent that production functions would be the same everywhere, because the same causes everywhere (and at any time) produce the same effects. However, as Haberler [4, p. 19] has pointed out, " if the concept of the production function is to be a useful tool of analysis, it cannot be identified with, or derived from, such unverifiable metaphysical propositions as ' the constancy of the laws of nature.' By hypothesising every conceivable circumstance which may affect output as a separate factor, the production function can, no doubt, be endowed with constancy, invariability, homogeneity, and what not, but at the price of emptying the theory of all empirical content and reducing it to a useless tautological system."

[3] It is also empirically possible, as Minhas' [33] study shows.

ing on the definition of "factor abundance." It is possible to choose between two definitions: the physical and the price definitions. Under the former, country I is abundant in factor x and country II in factor y when $(X/Y)^I > (X/Y)^{II}$, where X and Y refer to the quantities of factors x and y respectively and the superscripts to the countries.[1] Under the latter, the countries are similarly described when $(Rx/Ry)^I < (Rx/Ry)^{II}$ *prior to trade* where Rx and Ry refer to the rentals on factors x and y respectively.

When the physical definition is used the set of sufficient conditions for the logical truth of the Heckscher–Ohlin proposition is: (1) international identity of production functions; (2) non-reversibility of factor-intensities, such that a given commodity is factor x-intensive in relation to another at *all* relevant factor price-ratios; (3) constant returns to scale and diminishing returns (along isoquants) in each production function; and (4) identity of the consumption pattern between countries at each relevant commodity price ratio.[2] Samuelson [38, 39] has established that, under perfect competition and profit maximisation in perfect markets, condition (3) will suffice to generate a strictly convex production possibility curve, characterised by a unique relationship between factor and commodity price ratios (except at positions of complete specialisation in production). Using these propositions, it is possible to demonstrate in a two-commodity system that where two countries, with identical production functions for each activity (condition 1) and non-reversible factor intensities (condition 2) have different capital: labour ratios in the aggregate, the capital-abundant country will have a higher ratio of capital-intensive: labour-intensive outputs at *each* commodity price ratio. When condition (4) is added to this result it follows that the pre-trade commodity price ratios will be such that the capital-intensive commodity will be cheaper in the capital-abundant country. Hence the Heckscher–Ohlin theorem will be logically true. This result is valid for a multi-commodity model as well:[3] as Jones [20] has demonstrated, commodities can still be ranked, from technological and factor-supply data,

---

[1] The physical definition raises serious conceptual difficulties when applied to the factor "capital." As is obvious, it is impossible to collapse different varieties of capital equipment into a single index of "capital" in the same way as we reduce labour to man-hours. Of course, even with labour, the element of "human capital" raises equally knotty issues.

[2] Identity of tastes, *i.e.*, the aggregate preference map, is not adequate, since two countries may be at different levels of income and hence at different positions on their preference maps. Unless, therefore, the maps have homothetic isoquants, the result can be different consumption patterns at identical price ratios. For a disaggregated economy, with many individuals, the conditions which give rise to such aggregate identity of tastes are quite restrictive [66, 67]. It is also necessary, of course, that transport costs for individual commodities are not such as would shatter this chain of comparative advantage when the c.i.f. prices are considered (as they have to be from the viewpoint of the determination of the trade pattern). The trade theorists generally disregard transport costs; the omission of "distance" as a factor in most trade models represents a serious deficiency which vitiates the utility of many conclusions.

[3] The definitions of "factor abundance" and "factor-intensity" in a multi-factor model, however, are not so intuitive; but one can always adopt a convention [35, 53]. The results, however, are both more restrictive and less intuitive.

in terms of factor ratios, and are thereby uniquely ranked also in terms of comparative advantage, with demand being introduced (as in the Ricardian system) to " break the chain " into exports and imports.

When the price definition of factor abundance is chosen we can dispense with the condition of identity of consumption patterns.   This is because, when the other assumptions are made, a country which is capital-abundant will, by virtue of the unique Samuelsonian relationship between commodity and factor price ratios, necessarily have cheaper capital-intensive output. The use of the price definition, while it has this advantage over the physical definition, correspondingly leaves less scope for " explanation." [1]

Where the theory is deficient is in its not having been extended to a multi-country, multi-commodity framework.   The prediction holds when there are many commodities and two countries.   However, when there are many countries and commodities it is not clear, in the absence of theoretical analysis, what conditions will suffice to make the Heckscher–Ohlin hypothesis true—in any of the several alternative versions that are possible in a multi-country framework: (1) the comparison of factor endowments may be between country I and the sum of *all* the other countries of the world; or (2) it may be between country I and the *sum* of *all* the countries directly in trade with it; or (3) between country I and the sum of *all* the countries directly or indirectly in trade with it; or (4) between country I and *each* of the countries in direct trade with it, so that the Heckscher–Ohlin hypotheses would hold for *each* pair of countries (*bilaterally*).   There is little in the traditional analysis of the Heckscher–Ohlin hypotheses which affords a reliable clue to a meaningful choice among these different ways in which a Heckscher–Ohlin hypothesis can be interpreted in a multi-country framework.   Nor need we expect the conditions under which each of these hypotheses will be logically true to be identical either with each other *or* with those that have been spelled out for the restrictive traditional frameworks.[2]   This amounts to a deficiency in the literature (especially from the

---

[1] Lancaster has proposed inadvertently a third definition which states that a country is abundant in that factor which is used intensively in the exportable industry [14].   From the viewpoint of the Heckscher–Ohlin theory, this is totally tautologous and leaves *no* scope for " explanation."

[2] For instance, it is clear that if country I is K-abundant in relation to country II and L-abundant in relation to country III, and the Heckscher–Ohlin hypothesis holds for each pair of countries (say, I and II, II and III), then it is *impossible* that the export and import commodities of country I can be ranked in terms of K : L ratios such that all exports are K-intensive in relation to all imports.   The export and import commodities inevitably criss-cross, fouling up the strictly ordered chain on which the traditional Heckscher–Ohlin hypothesis and proof depend.   However, if this chain cannot criss-cross under the usual assumptions, as Jones has demonstrated, we have a contradiction *in terms of the traditional model* and apparently the pattern of international specialisation in production and in trade will necessarily have to turn out such that the bilateral formulation of the Heckscher–Ohlin hypothesis holds in a multi-country world.   Of course, what I have argued here is not intended to be a proof, in the strict sense, of an extension of the Heckscher–Ohlin hypothesis to the bilateral, multi-country formulation within the fold of traditional postulates concerning technology, etc.   The point I am making is really that the analysis of the Heckscher–Ohlin variety of hypotheses, in any or all of their possible versions in a multi-country framework, is not yet available and represents a serious lacuna in the literature.

viewpoint of empirical testing, since the real world unfortunately constitutes a multi-country, multi-commodity international economy).

Empirical testing of the Heckscher–Ohlin hypotheses has indeed been attempted in the literature, starting with Leontief's pioneer attempt at ascertaining the factor-intensities of the average exports and competitive imports in the United States [25]. It is typical of his and other contributions that, while factor-intensities are carefully ascertained, the factor-abundance of the country in question is usually left uninvestigated, except tangentially and vaguely. The result has been a failure to face up to the question raised by multi-country, multi-commodity analysis: how is factor-abundance to be interpreted? By *implication*, Leontief [25, pp. 386, 399] seems to favour the *bilateral* interpretation: "A comprehensive, two-sided explanation of our economic relationships with the rest-of-the-world will not, of course, be possible before the internal economic structure of at least one of the most important of our trading partners has been studied as fully as that of our own." Recent studies by Bharadwaj [16] for India, Tatemoto and Ichimura [42] for Japan and Wahl [45] for Canada have also implicitly adopted the bilateral interpretation by considering, in addition to the factor intensities of the average *aggregate* exports and competitive imports (which necessitates viewing the country's factor-abundance in a non-bilateral way), the factor-intensities of the average exports to and competitive imports from *specific* trading countries or regions.[1]

While Leontief [25], and nearly all of his many followers, have left this crucial aspect unsatisfactory, Leontief's attempted test has been of significance—for the perverse reason that it turned up the startling result that the United States exports are labour-intensive and its competitive imports capital-intensive.[2] Since the United States may be conceded to be capital abundant by any definition, this result did seem to contradict the Heckscher–Ohlin hypothesis—provided the statistical information and procedure could be accepted. There *were* objections on statistical grounds. For instance, the agricultural capital–output ratio was considered unreliable [18], but recomputation under different assumptions did not reverse the findings. Balogh [12] voiced compelling doubts concerning the implications of aggregation in the input–output matrix (used to compute indirect capital–labour ratios). Thus, the labour-intensity of the American export industries might be spurious and attributable to the aggregation of capital-intensive exportable products with " similar," non-export, labour-intensive activities. No evidence was produced to support this objection [1]: yet, it leaves a degree of doubt.

[1] In each of these instances, however, there is no discussion either of the alternative ways in which the Heckscher–Ohlin hypothesis can be interpreted or of the theoretical implication of the specific (bilateral) form of the hypothesis that is chosen or suggested.

[2] The tests have uniformly used the two factors, capital and labour. This choice, as also the definition of capital, are necessarily arbitrary. This arbitrariness is inevitable, and its justification lies in the argument that the theory being tested represents an abstraction.

While Leontief's exercise spurred the majority of the theorists on to a re-examination of the sufficient conditions for the Heckscher–Ohlin hypothesis [20, 36, 37], the plausibility of the Heckscher–Ohlin propositions is so powerful that some ingenuity was addressed to the task of rescuing it from the refutation that had emerged from Leontief's exercises (Leontief himself being one of this small group of analysts).[1]   This task is not entirely hopeless, since, although Leontief's results may be accepted, it is possible for the economist, *not* to change the form of the hypothesis, but to retain this form while redefining the concepts used.   This is a perfectly valid, scientific procedure: the hypothesis, with redefined concepts, can once again be subjected to empirical verification [1].   This is precisely what may be done with the Heckscher–Ohlin hypothesis, in the expectation that Leontief's United States results may be reversed.

There are many ways in which this can be done.   For instance, one could argue that the factor-abundance comparison should refer to the quantities of factors employed in the traded-goods sector, since the original formulation of the Heckscher–Ohlin theorem is logically deduced in a framework assuming no non-traded goods [1].   Or it could be argued that, since the traded-goods sector in some countries represents merely a geographical extension of a country's activities, these sectors being really foreign enclaves based on foreign capital and dominated by foreign economic considerations, it is sensible in such cases to merge these enclaves with the foreign country in question for obtaining the data for the Heckscher–Ohlin test [18].[2]   The most interesting attempts, however, have centred around

---

[1] Leontief also produced subsequently another paper [26] which reworked the calculations in the light of criticisms addressed to his original work.   For instance, instead of the inversion of only a 50-sector matrix earlier, he inverted a 192-sector matrix.   Adjustments were carried out concerning agricultural data.   None of this, however, reversed the findings concerning the refutation of the (unadjusted) Heckscher–Ohlin hypothesis.   Leontief also went into some theoretical issues, such as the examination of a linear, input–output model for international trade.   This has unfortunately been responsible for some confusion concerning the limitations of the empirical verification of the Heckscher–Ohlin hypothesis itself.   For instance, Valavanis-Vail [3, p. 279] has objected to Leontief's exercise on the ground that " input–output models (except with rare luck) are logically incompatible with international trade."   Whatever the analytical support for (any interpretation of) this statement, it is really irrelevant to the objective of Leontief's exercise and the methods used by him to achieve it.   The input–output table is used by Leontief (along with the labour and capital coefficients matrices) merely to *compute* the indirect capital and labour requirements for unit exports and imports.   The assumptions of input–output *analysis* are *not* necessary.   Although Leontief loosely talks of " reducing " exports by a million dollars and seeing what capital and labour are " released " thereby, this is *not* what is actually required.   All that is necessary, and this is really how Leontief's exercise should be construed, is to compute the total capital and labour requirements of the *current* (level and composition of) exports.   And this can be done by a purely " notional reduction " of (a representative bundle of) exports and the corresponding, computed, notional " release " of capital and labour.

[2] It is not necessarily correct to use such an adaptation of the Heckscher–Ohlin hypothesis. For the latter, what is relevant is the *availability* of factors of production *regardless of their ownership*. It is only in the extreme case where the investment is accompanied by full, complementary migration of other necessary factors to a piece of foreign territory (which itself does not serve as a factor

the fact that labour embodies (human) capital, and its implications for both factor-abundance and factor-intensity.

The easiest way of handling this has been to argue that the human capital element should be allowed for in the factor-intensity comparisons. For the United States, this seems to provide an important escape from the refutation of the Heckscher–Ohlin hypothesis. As many of the commentators have noted: (i) American export industries employ relatively more non-agricultural labour,[1] and agricultural labour is likely to be less educated and trained than non-agricultural labour [18]; and (ii) American export industries pay an average wage in excess of the national wage (suggesting that they intensively use skilled labour) [2] [21]. Thus, this computation of human capital (from an analysis of the labour inputs in the exporting and import-competing industries) added to the capital employed in measuring factor-intensities may quite possibly reverse the factor-intensity findings for the United States. However, we should also have to adjust correspondingly the measurement of factor endowments, adding the computed human capital to the measure of capital stock: a procedure which highlights the great conceptual difficulties that attend on both measuring capital meaningfully and comparing it between countries.

An alternative way in which the fact of labour efficiency differences between countries has been handled is by adjusting the labour supply itself by an efficiency factor.[3] Leontief [25, p. 26], in his original paper, argued that " labour " should be defined in " standard " units, after adjusting for varying degrees of efficiency. On this basis he asserted that the average American worker is three times as efficient as elsewhere and that " spread thrice as thinly as the unadjusted figures suggest the American capital supply per ' equivalent worker ' turns out to be comparatively smaller, rather than larger, than that of many other countries."[4] Hence, the Heckscher–Ohlin theory could be rescued from an apparent refutation (on the

---

of production) that it would be proper, from the Heckscher–Ohlin viewpoint, to adopt this approach. Not otherwise.

[1] The breakdown of labour (for a million dollars of exports and import replacements) between agricultural and non-agricultural labour was given by Leontief [25] as follows:

	Exports.	Import replacements.
Agricultural labour, man years	22·436	40·394
Non-agricultural labour, man years	159·872	127·069

[2] An alternative explanation, of course, is that they are the " dynamic," innovating industries, and hence pay higher wages.

[3] This method adjusts the measurement of the labour input, whereas the earlier method alters the measurement of the capital stock.

[4] In the original paper [25] Leontief argued for this threefold efficiency, but did not make any differential adjustment for the efficiency factor in export- and import-competing industries. This implicit assumption of an identical efficiency factor for labour in both these sectors was removed by Leontief in his later exercise [26] by an explicit weighting of labour in each sector by its average wage.

implicit assumption that this efficiency factor concerning labour is not neutralised by a similar efficiency factor attributable to the other factor of production).

Leontief's procedure, however, is not valid, although his suggestion is valuable. He does not state how the efficiency factor of three was arrived at. Leontief's argument in support of the assumed efficiency factor of three is that if it were not so it would be impossible to " explain the comparative surplus of labour which our figures unmistakably reveal " [25, p. 28]. This argument is unpersuasive because (as I have already argued elsewhere [1]) " it already assumes that the Heckscher–Ohlin theorem provides a valid explanation of the American pattern of trade when, in fact, the question being asked is precisely whether it does "; and (2) " it also assumes that only the hypothesis about threefold efficiency of American labour can reconcile the results with the Heckscher–Ohlin type hypothesis when, in fact, there *are* other ways in which such reconciliation could be attempted." The most interesting analysis, which has a bearing on this issue, is by Minhas [33]. As noted earlier, Arrow, Chenery, Solow and he continuously found that for individual industries in different countries the only significant difference between the estimated homohypallagic (CES) production functions consisted of an overall efficiency term, which meant that, whereas the isoquants continued to remain more or less the same, the scale factor changed. This means, as Minhas concluded [33, p. 159], that Leontief's requirement that the efficiency factor can be attributed to one factor *alone* is unsupported by his specific investigations.[1]

While these different ways in which the definitions of capital and labour have been adjusted, to explore the possibility of reconciling the United States pattern of trade with the Heckscher–Ohlin hypothesis, are of interest, perhaps the more significant innovations have emerged from the work of those who proceeded to apply Leontief's methods to the trade patterns of other countries. There have been four Leontief-type studies so far: Bharadwaj [15, 16] on India, Stolper and Roskamp [41] for East Germany, Tatemoto and Ichimura [42] for Japan and Wahl [45] for Canada. These

---

[1] Diab [18] also has attempted to test Leontief's conjecture, using Colin Clark's data. His results appear to sustain this conjecture. Diab's methods show that the United States has, in terms of " standard " labour, a lower capital : labour ratio than Canada, Great Britain, Netherlands, France and Norway. The procedure by which this conclusion is reached, however, is arbitrary. Diab assumes that: (1) labour is the factor which has to be reduced to " standard " units in each country; and (2) the Cobb–Douglas production function, identical for all countries studied, is known, for national output, in terms of capital and " standard " labour. With this production function, national output and capital known, it is then easy to determine the single unknown, " standard " labour, with the one equation [1]. Diab postulates a hypothetical production function (with " standard " labour), uses observed values of output and capital to deduce his " standard " labour and then attributes the discrepancy between the quantities of " standard " and observed labour to an " efficiency " factor. This is surely an arbitrary procedure, which can yield no acceptable results. For instance, one could well use the procedure, assuming that capital, and not labour, is the factor which should be reduced to " standard " units. Out of curiosity, I did this: the United States turned out to be overwhelmingly " capital "-intensive [1]!

have now given us a larger range of evidence with which to attempt an assessment of the Heckscher–Ohlin hypothesis. For Japan, exports are capital-intensive and imports are labour-intensive—on the surface again, a black mark against the tested hypothesis. For East Germany exports are capital-intensive and imports are labour-intensive—the authors find this consistent with the stated hypothesis, since the East German trade is three-quarters with the Communist block, where she is probably among the most industrialised of these nations. For Canada, exports are capital-intensive and imports are labour-intensive—presumably an unsuccessful verification, as Canadian trade is primarily United States-orientated.

Where many of these studies innovate is in departing from the Leontief method of taking the *aggregate* exports and competitive imports. They begin to explore the possibility of defining the Heckscher–Ohlin hypothesis in the *bilateral* form [1] (*i.e.*, for each pair of countries) rather than in terms of one country and (presumably) the rest of the world. Thus, Bharadwaj [16] goes on from the aggregative analysis to work out the factor-intensities of Indian trade with the United States, Wahl works with Canada–United States and Canada–United Kingdom trade, and the Tatemoto–Ichimura result is interpreted in terms of the geographic composition of Japanese trade. In the Indian case, when the Indo–United States trade is isolated for analysis, the factor-intensities are the *reverse* of those that obtain for total Indian trade. The Indian exports to the United States turn out to be capital-intensive and imports from the United States are labour-intensive, thus appearing to refute the Heckscher–Ohlin hypothesis. For Canada, the results again are identical with the aggregate results and refutation continues. For Japan, however, the result of disaggregation is beneficial. In the Japanese case the aggregative result is supposed to be attributable to the fact that 75% of Japanese exports go to the (presumably labour-abundant) under-developed areas and only 25% to the (presumably capital-abundant) advanced countries. It is widely accepted in Japan that the Japanese economy is somewhere in the middle of the advanced and under-developed countries and the " disaggregated " explanation is only a logical consequence. Tatemoto and Ichimura have computed the capital–labour ratios of Japanese exports to the United States and imports from the United States and find the latter higher than the former. Unlike the Indian case, therefore, a disaggregated approach *supports* the Heckscher–Ohlin approach in the Japanese study. The Japanese result thus demonstrates the possibility of profitably adapting the Heckscher–Ohlin hypothesis so as to state it in terms of *each pair of trading countries* (instead of in aggregate terms).

When these diverse bits of evidence and arguments are added up there is little doubt that an attitude of agnosticism is certain to be left in the reader's mind concerning Leontief's original refutation of the Heckscher–

---

[1] This bilateral formulation, it may be recalled, is only one of several formulations of the Heckscher–Ohlin hypothesis that we can have in a multi-country world.

Ohlin theorem.[1] Meanwhile, the empirical verification is progressing apace and evidence is accumulating on either side. The most interesting recent result has been Minhas' [33] demonstration that, far from being a theoretical curiosum (as Samuelson [38, 39] believed it to be), the reversal of factor-intensity is an empirical possibility of some significance. Since his data relate to the United States and Japan, the results appear to furnish additional ammunition to those who are sceptical of the utility of the Heckscher–Ohlin approach.[2]

The Kravis Theory

While the Ricardian and the Heckscher–Ohlin approaches have domi-nated the thinking on comparative advantage for many decades, recently some original theories have appeared in the field. Kravis [22], for instance, in the early period of gloom after Leontief's paper [25], argued that the commodity composition of trade is determined primarily by " availability." Trade tends to be confined to goods which are " not available at home " [22, p. 143]. By this phrase, Kravis intended to describe goods which are " unavailable in the absolute sense (for example, diamonds)," and goods where " an increase in output can be achieved only at much higher cost (that is, the domestic supply is inelastic)." The reason for trade to be restricted to items characterised by such unavailability is that tariff policies, transport costs, cartelisation, etc., tend to eliminate from trade those com-

---

[1] It is of interest to note that the Ricardian hypothesis (in terms of comparative labour produc-tivities) may be verified and yet the result may equally be in conformity with the Heckscher–Ohlin hypothesis. Thus, for instance, a capital-abundant country I may be exporting capital-intensive commodity x to country II in exchange for commodity y. Then, if transport costs are introduced and the necessary technological assumptions which underlie the Heckscher–Ohlin theorem are made, the capital–labour ratio in x will be higher in country I than in country II and therefore the output–labour ratio in x will also be higher in I than II. Similarly, the output–labour ratio n y will be lower in I than in II. Therefore, *both* the Ricardian and the Heckscher–Ohlin hypo-theses will be valid in this case. A similar example can also be produced for the more sophisti-cated Ricardian hypothesis stated in the text (involving comparisons of production functions). For instance, assume that the production function is identical for commodity y in both countries and that country I has " neutral " advantage in producing commodity x such that the same capital and labour produce λ times more of x in I than in II. Assume x to be capital-intensive at all factor price ratios and I to be capital abundant. Then if the Heckscher–Ohlin thesis holds, so does the sophisticated Ricardian hypothesis automatically. Further, it follows that in free trade equilibrium (with zero transport costs), the capital–labour ratios in I will be lower in each activity than in II. Since constant returns to scale are being assumed, the labour productivity in both x and y would be lower in I than in II, except that the efficiency factor λ in the produc-tion of x in I would offset the fall in labour productivity due to lower capital–labour ratio. As-suming that this offset leaves the labour productivity in x greater in I than in II, the comparative labour productivity ratio in x will be greater for I than in y. Hence the Ricardian hypothesis will be sustained in its comparative labour productivity form as well.

[2] Minhas' demonstration of the possibility of factor-intensity reversals is quite serious, since it contradicts one of the premises on which the Heckscher–Ohlin hypothesis is traditionally based. In fact, the damage it does is fatal because, if factor-intensities *are* reversed between two trading countries, for exports and imports, it is logically *impossible* for *both* countries' trading patterns to pass the Heckscher–Ohlin test (though, of course, one will).

modities which are available through domestic production, although at " slightly " higher cost. The reasons cited for unavailability, as defined, are: lack of natural resources (relative to demand) or technical change and product differentiation which confer temporary monopoly of production on the innovating country (until the trading partners have learnt to imitate).

The theory appears attractive. However, it is noticeable that Kravis does not get down to stating precise, testable hypotheses. While he fails to do so, one can still derive several from his suggestive ideas. (1) For instance, one could seize on his idea of the " inelasticity " of domestic supply and state the refutable proposition that *a country's imports will be characterised by domestic inelasticity of supply.* (Such an hypothesis would, naturally, have to be backed by an explicit definition of " inelasticity.") (2) Another hypothesis, based also on the concept of inelasticity, might be that *a country's imports will be characterised by the excess of foreign over domestic elasticity of supply.*[1] Both these hypotheses, and related formulations, however, neither get down below the surface *qua* explanations nor are capable of being tested without elaborate econometric estimates of supply elasticities. (3) A more interesting way of formulating Kravis-type hypotheses seems to be to go *directly* to the scarcities of natural resources and temporary scarcities through innovations. Kravis himself indicates that *a country's export-industries will show rates of technical progress higher than the national average.* (4) This could be turned into an alternative, plausible proposition, with traces of Ricardo [1]: *a country's export-industries will show higher rates of technical progress than the same industries in the trading partners.* (5) Perhaps the most promising approach would be to utilise Kravis' distinction between " unavailability " due to scarce natural resources and due to innovation. Thus, to the preceding two propositions, one could add a further clause: *or, will be intensive in the use, or consist, of raw materials which are relatively abundant in the country.*[2] Such Kravis-type hypotheses have, however, neither been clearly formulated and analysed so far nor tested systematically with empirical evidence.

The Linder Theory

Another novel and ingenious approach is attributable to a recent Swedish author, Linder [27]. He begins by attempting to explain the pattern of trade, but ends up by doing something quite different—and it is precisely in this way that Linder makes a contribution of some significance.

Linder starts with the distinction between trade in primary products and in manufactures. The former is natural resource-intensive, and Linder accepts the thesis that such trade must be explained in terms of " relative

[1] Cf. Kravis' remark: " it is the elasticity of supply abroad and its inelasticity at home that gives rise to [the United States imports]." [22, p. 150].

[2] This, of course, begs the question of defining relative abundance. Some working definition would have to be devised. In practice, of course, it is relatively easy to identify the industries whose advantage consists in access to raw materials; although, once again, the distinction between abundance in terms of price and physical units is relevant. For an interesting attempt at estimating the " resource-intensiveness " of activities entering trade in the United States see Vanek [43].

natural-resources endowments " [27, p. 92].[1]   Trade in manufactures, however, cannot be so explained.   Linder explicitly rejects the analogy.

He despairs, however, of being able to predict the *precise* composition of trade in manufactures.   This is a function of many factors: " technological superiority, managerial skills and economies of scale are perhaps the most important . . . " [27, p. 103].   The results cannot be congealed into a precise, predictable pattern.[2]   Economists, when confronted with questions that they could not answer, have usually changed the question.   Linder likewise virtually gives up the traditional inquiry and argues that, while the precise composition of trade in manufactures cannot be forecast, what one *can* have instead is a theory concerning the *volume* of trade (as proportion of national income) between different pairs of trading nations.

Linder's central thesis is that the *volume of trade in manufactures of a country with each of her trading partners, when taken as a proportion of the corresponding national incomes of these countries, will be higher, the greater the similarity in the demand patterns of the pair of trading countries.*   The " similarity of demand patterns " would be associated with the similarity of incomes *per capita*—although income distribution and similarity of taste patterns are additional variables.   However, tastes are internationally not very dissimilar according to recent evidence [27, p. 95].   Hence, provided income distribution is ignored, the last clause in the thesis can be rewritten to state: " *the closer the pair of trading countries in their incomes* per capita."

Although Linder has not rigorously formulated his analytical framework, the chain of reasoning which leads to this hypothesis is available.   (1) Firstly, the pre-condition for a non-primary commodity to emerge as an export is the presence of " home demand."   This is attributed to several reasons: foreign trade is only an extension of domestic trade; innovation centres on existing industries and gives them export possibility; etc.[3]   (2) Secondly, the existence of industry catering for internal demand implies that the internal demand pattern will determine the range of commodities that constitute potential exports.   (Linder tries here to introduce the concept of " representative demand "—to narrow down the range of potential exports.   The intention is to exclude those commodities for which the internal production is presumably not " large enough."   But Linder really leaves this idea

[1] Linder construes this as consistent with the Heckscher–Ohlin theory because he accepts the original Ohlin statement of his theory, which mentioned a whole host of factors of production, *inclusive* of natural resources.   Of course, to the extent that other factors of production are also brought in, the theory both becomes less impressive as an abstraction and is less successfully tractable analytically because of the consequence, for the definitions of " factor-abundance " and " factor-intensity," of more than two factors of production.

[2] Linder, while he admits this, does not quite reconcile himself to the conclusion.   He feels that *something* can still be said about the trade pattern.   But his observations (*e.g.*, that Sweden will export paper because of forest resources or that Eskimos are unlikely to export refrigerators) do *not* constitute a theory.

[3] One might add: the foreign market is risky (through Q.R.s and the possibility of entry which cannot be " controlled " with tariffs as in the domestic market) and the home market is not, so that producers generally do not wish to rely on the foreign market alone.

hanging in the air, without chiselling it down into clarity and precision.)
(3) Thirdly, where the overlap in the commodity-composition of the potential-export range of any pair of trading countries is *greater*, the possibility of a
larger volume of trade will obtain.   (4) Fourthly, the potential volume of
trade will be larger, the larger the income-level of either trading country
[27, p. 111].   (5) Fifthly, where the potential volume of trade is larger, the
actual volume of trade will also be larger (though tariffs, transport costs,
political connections which prompt discriminatory trade promotion, etc.,
may " distort " the relationship).   (6) Sixthly, a similar set of arguments
applies to imports.   Linder qualifies only to the extent of stating that his
" representative demand " concept is no longer necessary: this hardly
matters, however, in view of its imprecision.   (7) Hence the Linder thesis.

Many questions inevitably come to one's mind.   Aside from, and
related to, the looseness of concepts such as " representative demand," there
is lack of precision concerning the concept of the potential-export range.
Is it to be defined entirely in terms of the number of commodities with
domestic production, or is one to assign weights to commodities in terms of
their relative size in terms of some relevant index?   What are the conditions
under which the size of the trading countries can be expected to affect the
volume of trade?   And so on.[1]   But, despite these limitations (which
inevitably attend on pioneering analyses), Linder's work remains significant.

Our survey thus demonstrates that the theory of comparative advantage
has been greatly advanced recently.   New theories have emerged.   And it
has been the vehicle of the significant, recent trends towards empirical verification.   This trend has synchronised with a more general investigation
of the empirical validity of traditional theses about the structure of the
international economy: among the prominent contributions being Michaely's
[31] study of concentration in world trade and Coppock's [17] analysis of
the incidence of economic instability among the trading nations.

Meanwhile, analytical theory of the " traditionalist " persuasion, concerned with the statement of " logically true " theorems, has proliferated
at a great pace.   To this, we must now turn.

II. Theorems in Statics: Factor Price Equalisation [2]

The problem which has engaged the attention of many of the most
distinguished trade theorists concerns the relationship between factor

---

[1] Linder's brief attempt at empirical verification is also not fully satisfactory.   The trade
figures relate to aggregate imports, instead of imports of manufactured goods.   The relationship
investigated is with respect to *per capita* income, with no attempt at examining whether the explanation improves with additional variables like regional or fractile income inequality indices.
The statistical analysis is halted short of the estimation of regression equations.   Linder's hypothesis, while brilliantly suggestive, awaits both rigorous analytical formulation and empirical
verification.

[2] I have had the invaluable opportunity of corresponding with Professor P. A. Samuelson in
writing this Section.   Although I have drawn freely on this correspondence, especially for the
general case of many goods and many factors, the responsibility for any errors is entirely mine.

prices in different countries, under free trade in goods but factor immobility between countries.[1]   The question dates back to the writings of Heckscher [19] and Ohlin [34].   They considered trade to be an equalising factor with respect to factor returns in trading countries, though they cited several reasons why *full* factor price equalisation would not occur in practice.   In 1948 Samuelson [38] initiated the rigorous investigation of the conditions under which complete factor price equalisation would follow.

Samuelson [38, 39] stated everything that has ever been said subsequently as far as the restrictive case of two goods and two factors is concerned and, subject to certain sufficient assumptions to be noted shortly, managed to prove factor-price equalisation by establishing a *unique* relationship between (relative) factor and commodity prices.   In 1953 Samuelson [53], preceded by an investigation of Meade [50] into the two-factor, three-product case, offered the first serious analysis of the general case of many goods (n) and many factors (r), thereby extending the analysis to all the $n \geqslant 2 \leqslant r$ cases. In the process it turned out that the more general analysis was limited by the non-existence of the required mathematics, Samuelson having to content himself with the formulation of what were clearly overly-strong sufficiency conditions for uniqueness in the large (for $n = r > 2$).   Subsequent to Samuelson's 1953 analysis, progress has been registered in this area in the following respects: (1) Kuhn [47] has added an alternative sufficiency condition for uniqueness when $n = r \geqslant 2$;[2] (2) McKenzie [49] has provided a basic theorem which seems to overlap with Samuelson's 1953 sufficiency theorem, without either implying or being implied by it; (3) Nikaido and Gale are reported to have discovered a basic flaw in Samuelson's mathematical proof of the sufficiency condition for the uniqueness of equilibrium in the large; and (4) Samuelson [54] has extended the analysis to an investigation of the conditions under which free trade would equalise not merely rentals but also interest rates between countries.

In contrast to the difficulties of the general case, the case where $n = r = 2$ is strikingly simple and, since Samuelson's pioneering analysis, has been extensively surveyed [5, Chapter I; 3, Chapter III].   Samuelson used the

[1] I have referred only tangentially in Section I to one other problem, on which there is some, though scant, literature.   This is the question of the pattern of international specialisation in *production* (as distinct from *trade*).   The papers of McKenzie [78] and Jones [69] discuss this problem most elegantly in a Ricardo–Graham model with one primary factor of production and many countries.   While I am on the subject of omissions, I should also note that I have not dealt at any length with the question of the stability of trade equilibrium, although I might have included it in Section IV.   The interested reader will find useful and adequate discussion of the problem in the papers of Mundell [11] and myself and Johnson [2, Section IV] and in the volumes by Meade [9] and Vanek [93].

[2] Pearce [51], in an excellent paper which brings out the essence of the problem in an extremely simple fashion, has attempted to provide alternative sufficiency conditions.   But apparently Professor McKenzie has produced an example which contradicts Pearce's conjecture and the mathematical results of Nikaido and Gale also have had a similar effect.   Mention may also be made of Reiter's [52] contribution which demonstrates the intuitive, inverse theorem that identical production functions are implied by " universally observed factor price equalization."

following assumptions, which proved to be sufficient for the purpose: (1) linear, homogeneous production functions in each good; (2) diminishing returns along isoquants for each good; (3) non-reversible and different factor-intensities of the two goods at all (relevant) factor prices; (4) identity of production functions for each good between countries; (5) perfect competition and valuation of factors according to marginal value productivity; (6) incomplete specialisation in production in each country; and (7) absence of transport costs. The last assumption ensures commodity price equalisation, under free trade, between countries. The first five assumptions ensure a unique relationship between commodity and factor prices, under incomplete specialisation in production, which obtains identically between countries. With assumption (6), ruling out complete specialisation, therefore, commodity price equalisation necessarily entails factor price equalisation.[1]

When the general case, $n \geqslant 2 \leqslant r$, is considered the analysis is the simplest for the case $n = r > 2$. The kernel of the argument can be summarised easily.[2] If x_{ij} is the quantity of the ith factor used in the production of the jth good, ϕ_j the output of the jth good and q_j its selling price, constant returns to scale ensure that

$$\sum_{i=1}^{n} p_i x_{ij} = q_j \phi_j \ (j = 1, 2, \ldots n)$$

The quantities x_{ij} of factors used are determined by factor prices p_i and commodity prices q_j so that the n equations can be thought of as equations in $2n$ variables, p_i and q_j. For uniqueness, therefore, it is necessary that there be only one set of p_i corresponding to each set of q_j, and vice versa. It can then be shown that uniqueness follows if $|x_{ij}| \neq 0$, which consistutes a sufficient condition for factor-price equalisation in the small. It should be noted that, in the $n = r = 2$ case, $|x_{ij}| \neq 0$ turns into the familiar factor-intensity-difference condition, and uniqueness can be established *both* in the small and in the large because every element of the determinant is essentially one-signed. For the $n = r > 2$ case, however, Samuelson [53] argued that the condition that $|x_{ij}| \neq 0$ was not sufficient and an *additional* sufficiency condition would be that there should be *some* numbering of factors such that the leading principal minors of $|x_{ij}|$ of *every* order should be non-zero. It is this " strong factor-intensity " condition which has recently been reportedly re-examined by Nikaido and Gale and found to be inadequate. However, a further strengthening of the factor-intensity postulate, such that *every* principal minor is non-zero (for *all* naturally ordered sets, as distinct from only one, corresponding to *all*

[1] Of all these assumptions, the postulate concerning the non-reversal of factor-intensities has aroused the greatest analytical and econometric interest. The principal analyses in this direction were noted earlier, in Section I, when discussing the Heckscher–Ohlin theorem.

[2] Samuelson's [53] Appendix contains a lucid account of the argument concerning uniqueness. Pearce's [51] paper contains an easily comprehensible account, from which I have borrowed.

numberings of factors), appears to constitute a sufficient condition for uniqueness in the large (as per Samuelson's correspondence).

The cases where $n \neq r$ are more difficult and the results of the analysis more devastating to the prospects for factor price equalisation. Samuelson's results are most conveniently summarized as follows. Let the observed number of goods actually produced in both countries be $n^* < n$ and the factors actually used in production of these goods, and with positive prices, be r^*. Then, if $n^* \geqslant r^*$, and if for *some* subset of r^* goods of the n^* goods, the strong factor-intensity conditions of Samuelson-Nikaido-Gale (or alternatively Kuhn and McKenzie, not detailed here) are realised, then equalised goods prices imply equalised factor prices. If, however, $r^* > n^*$, factor price equalisation is generally not implied (though it may obtain under certain strong and bizarre assumptions).[1]

Although the bulk of the analysis has been centred on the question of the equalisation of the *rentals* earned by factors of production in a Walrasian general equilibrium system (with extension to intermediate products), the effect of free trade on *interest rate* equalisation has recently been subjected to analysis by Samuelson [54] in a hitherto unpublished paper. The analysis supports the inference that rental equalisation (except in certain limiting situations) will be accompanied by interest rate equalisation.[2] The possibility of introducing intermediate products without invalidating the factor price equalisation theorem, while demonstrated by Samuelson generally in his 1953 analysis, has further been recently demonstrated by Vanek [55], whose $n = r = 2$ analysis dovetails neatly into Samuelson's more powerful work.[3] Laing [48] has, on the other hand, opened up the investigation of the effects of increasing returns to scale; his results serve to underline the implication of Samuelson's analysis that constant returns to scale cannot be given up without invalidating the logical truth of the factor price equalisation theorem. Although the subject is, therefore, both of historic interest and still continues to attract fresh minds, one cannot help feeling that perhaps too great a proportion of the intellectual energy of trade theorists has been directed towards a question of limited utility. Of greater importance are the propositions in comparative statics which we must now discuss.

[1] Several illustrative examples could be produced. For instance, if $n = 1$ and $r = 2$, factor price equalisation will generally be forbidden.

[2] The inapplicability of the traditional models (used to examine factor prices equalisation) for the purpose of analysing the effect of trade on interest rates was suggested originally, by a reading of Harrod's [46] paper, to V. K. Ramaswami and myself at Oxford in 1958. We noticed Harrod's unwarranted transition from rental to interest-rate equalisation, while operating within the framework of Samuelson's 1948 and 1953 models. I wrote subsequently to Samuelson concerning this question, and he worked out the required analysis. Ramaswami also wrote independently a paper which is yet unpublished.

[3] Samuelson has drawn my attention to the fact that Vanek [55] has managed to prove the following intuitive theorem: that (where $n = r = 2$ and both goods also serve as intermediates) if the *direct* factor-intensities are in one direction, then the *total* factor-intensities (including indirect factor requirements as well) will always be in the same direction.

III. Theorems in Comparative Statics

The bulk of the analytical literature in pure theory is concerned with the implications of *differences* between two general equilibrium situations—or, putting it differently, with the effects of specific *changes* in a given general equilibrium situation.

Two classes of questions can be distinguished: (1) On the one hand, the effects of a change in *trade policy* are considered while assuming as given, for the trading country, the general equilibrium " data " (*i.e.*, tastes, the distribution of ownership or resources and transfer claims, factor supplies, production functions and general economic policy plus a specific trade policy from the outside world such that the precise offers of trade at varying terms of trade which the country has open to it are known and given): for instance, the effect of a change in a country's tariff rate on its terms of trade may be analysed. (2) On the other hand, the effects of a change in these " data " may be considered, while assuming the trade policy as given: for instance, the effect of capital accumulation on the terms of trade may be investigated.

Naturally it is not true, *strictly speaking*, that trade theorists have always considered the given " data " (trade policy), in the context of which the stipulated change in trade policy (data) takes place, as independent of the change itself. Thus, for instance, Myint [83] has argued that a change in trade policy from no trade to some trade will change the country's taste pattern itself—though no formal analysis is founded on this observation. An interesting illustration of the change in trade policy when the " data " shift is furnished by Kindleberger's [73] brilliant study of the trade policy reaction of different European governments to the influx of cheap American corn in the 1870's. The only other, and the most formal, example of such interaction is provided by the analysis of tariff retaliation. A change in trade policy prompts retaliation which alters the trade possibilities open to the country. A full, sequential analysis is usually presented, with the response mechanisms of each country specified, which properly belongs to the next section on dynamic analysis [5, Chapter II]. Aside from these instances, the last of which belongs elsewhere, while the others are not formalised into theorems, it does continue to be true that the interactions between changes in trade policy and in " data " have not been the object of serious analysis in the comparative statics of pure theory.

The effects of the shifts in trade policy and in data have been studied generally with reference to certain variables which recur with varying frequency in the numerous analyses. The terms of trade, the internal commodity price-ratios, the factor price ratio, output levels, the composition of trade and the levels of individual exports and imports are among those that turn up almost regularly. Yet, even among them, frequently important extensions of theory have by-passed the analysis of the impact on some variables, leaving many gaps in the literature (which merely need patient and much tiresome work to be filled out).

The models in terms of which the effects of the stipulated changes on these variables are studied vary as well.   And yet, it is true that, in the last three decades, an astonishing amount of synthesis has been effected and a large number of theorems worked out in terms of the model (already used in Section I) which, while inspired by the work of Ohlin and Heckscher, is very much the creation of Samuelson, springing directly out of his early work on the factor price equalisation theorem [38, 39] and, with Stolper, on the effect of protection on factor rewards [91].

This Heckscher–Ohlin–Samuelson (H.O.S.) model is characterised by two countries and (within each country) two commodities, two factors of production, production functions characterised in each activity by constant returns to scale and diminishing returns along isoquants, perfect competition and full employment of the given supply of the factors of production.[1]   The supply of each commodity, in this system, is exclusively a function of the terms of trade between the two commodities.   On the other hand, the demand for each commodity is taken to be determined by both the terms of trade and the level of domestic expenditure.   A detailed specification of an H.O.S. type model for the international economy (but omitting the specifications concerning the number of factors) has been provided recently by Mundell [11], who has also furnished therewith an excellent summary of many of the principal results (excluding those that depend upon the H.O.S. specification concerning the number of factors) in comparative statics of the pure theory of trade.   Meade's [9] work on trade and welfare contains many formal statements and applications of the H.O.S. model.[2]   Recently the H.O.S. model has been strikingly extended, with many of its " restrictive " characteristics removed.   Among the more significant of these extensions are: (1) the investigation of the *multiple country* (and multiple-commodity) case by Mundell [11, pp. 101–9] drawing upon Mosak's earlier work; (2) the analysis of demand explicitly in terms of the pattern of income distribution associated with an equilibrium situation, in contrast to the standard H.O.S. practice of assigning to aggregate, community demand the same properties as to individual demand—an extension introduced independently by Meade [9] and Johnson [66, 67]; and (3) the relaxation of the assumption of fixed factor supply to include the classical case of factors *in elastic supply* with respect to their rentals by several writers: Walsh [95], Vanek [92], Kemp and Jones [72], and myself and Johnson [60].

The theorems derived with the H.O.S. model (and its recent extensions)

[1] For certain limited purposes, the assumption of international identity of production functions for each activity is sometimes made.

[2] On the other hand, the *geometrical* applications of the H.O.S. model are innumerable.   Much ingenuity has also been expended on alternative geometrical depictions.   I am afraid this runs into rapidly diminishing returns, and I have deliberately refrained from entering into a survey of these geometrical techniques.

and others, can be surveyed under the two main heads:[1] (A) *shifts in data (other than trade policy)*; (B) *shifts in trade policy*. Under the former the analysis subdivides further into shifts in data internal and external to the trading country. Among the internal shifts are: (1) *changes in demand*; (2) *changes in factor supply*; (3) *technological change*; and (4) *changes in (non-trade) economic policy*. The external shift in data involves some shift in the foreign offers to trade and may be prompted by changes internal to foreign countries or by changes in trade policy abroad. Such external shifts are classified generally as (5) *changes in international demand*. Under shifts in trade policy, I shall consider mainly tariff policy, distinguishing between: (1) *non-discriminatory tariff change*, and (2) *discriminatory tariff change*. The literature on other forms of trade policy is either largely symmetrical with tariff analysis (as in respect of quotas and subsidies) or limited (as with state trading) so that it will be surveyed only tangentially in the course of the analysis of tariffs which dominate the analysis in the pure theory of commercial policy.

(A) *Shifts in Data (other than Trade Policy)*

(1) *Changes in Demand*

Problems relating to the changes in demand in trade theory have to be carefully defined, since demand is frequently understood by trade theorists as " international demand," which is different from demand *per se*. By international demand is meant the demand for imports (and supply of exports) at some given terms of trade.[2] This demand for imports represents the excess of domestic consumption over domestic production of *importables* corresponding to the defined terms of trade. A shift in international demand is therefore to be traced to a shift in domestic consumption and/or production (which, in turn, may be autonomous or induced by policy). International demand therefore reflects, and is to be distinguished from, internal (overall) demand. Internal demand in turn reflects individual tastes and the level and distribution of purchasing power. Shifts in internal demand therefore must be distinguished again from changes in individual tastes and in the level and distribution of (earned and unearned) income.

The propositions of pure theory have very nearly sidestepped the question of the effects of changes in *internal* demand. There is no formal analysis associated with the effects of changes in a country's tastes. The changes in the internal distribution of income have been brought into the fold of economic analysis only in so far as they *result* from changes in trade policy rather than as autonomous changes whose effects are spelled out.

---

[1] Since the literature using the H.O.S. model is admirably synthesised, I shall focus largely on this, while noting the main respects in which other types of models, which have been employed, differ in assumptions and/or conclusions. A fuller survey is ruled out by limitations of space.

[2] The locus of these international demands is nothing but the Marshallian " offer curve." International demand is also Mill's " reciprocal demand."

The only striking contrast is provided by the analysis of the effects of changes in the *level* of expenditure (and its accompanying effects on demand).   This is nothing but the celebrated " *transfer problem* " which concerns the analysis of the effects on the terms of trade of a transfer of expenditure from one country to another.   As for changes in "international" demand, trade theory is well endowed with controversies and literature concerning the effects on the terms of trade when the foreign reciprocal demand shifts while the country's own demand for the foreign products is unchanged. In the following summary I proceed to the transfer problem, leaving shifts in international demand (which relate to changes in the external data given to the country) to be treated in a later sub-section.

The effect of a transfer on the terms of trade has been of interest because a deterioration in these terms, from the viewpoint of the transferor country, would represent a "secondary burden" supplementary to the principal burden implicit in the transfer itself.   Ignoring transport costs and using the H.O.S. model (without the assumptions with respect to the factors of production and competition), the answer is immediately obvious: the terms of trade will deteriorate or improve according as $m_a + m_b \lessgtr 1$, where m_a is the marginal propensity to spend on importables in the transferor country A and m_b in the transferee country B [11, 88, 89].[1]   Since the propensity to spend on exportables, x_a and x_b, is here merely unity minus the propensity to spend on importables, the criterion can be rewritten in any number of alternative forms such as $m_a \lessgtr x_b$.   Where tariffs obtain, and it is assumed that the tariff proceeds are redistributed and spent by private consumers as part of their income, the proportion of the transfer eventually turning up as expenditure on imports will be naturally smaller than m_b, since there is a " leakage " each time the revenue is earned from expenditure directed at imports.   The criterion thus changes to whether the sum of the marginal propensities to spend on importables is greater or less than a value which is greater than unity [5, Chapter VII, p. 173].   Where transport costs are incurred, the formula must change again, except in the extreme case when the transport cost is incurred in the form of the exported good itself.   Where the transport cost is incurred, at least, partially, in the form of the imported good, it follows that the entire import expenditure does *not* accrue to the foreigner and, therefore, the criterion would again have to be that the sum of the marginal propensities to spend on importables be greater or less than a value greater than unity [89; 5, p. 174].[2]   Mundell [11,

[1] It need hardly be stressed that the full-blooded H.O.S. model is not necessary for the present analysis.   Only the stability conditions have to be assumed, to determine the direction of the terms of trade change purely in terms of the marginal propensities to spend on importables with respect to expenditure change.

[2] Economists have a propensity to answer impossible questions, and they have done so in the context of the transfer problem.   There has been a great deal of discussion as to whether, in the *real world*, the classical proposition that the terms of trade would turn against the transferor country still remains a " *presumption*."   Fundamentally, this seems to be the wrong question to pose *until* one has *first* investigated the empirical applicability of the analytical model used.   The failure to

p. 107] has extended the analysis to the multi-country case where a transfer from country i to country j will rearrange demand throughout the international economy—for commodities exported from countries other than i and j. The resulting formula does not admit of any *a priori* generalisation.[1]

While these criteria are devised in a full-employment framework Johnson [5, pp. 177–83], drawing upon earlier work by Meade, Harberger, Metzler, and others, has synthesised and extended the analysis for a Keynesian framework where output in each country is in perfectly elastic supply at a fixed domestic-currency price level, so that output, income and employment are determined by the aggregate demand for output. The resulting criterion involves, in the most general formulation, not merely the marginal propensities to spend on imports and exportables but also now the marginal propensities to save out of both pre-transfer and transfer income. As with the full-employment case, the criterion permits the transfer again to be under-effected or over-effected at constant terms of trade.[2]

(2) *Changes in Factor Supply*

There are three ways in which changes in factor supply enter the analysis in pure theory: (i) The effect of an *autonomous* change in factor supply has been analysed. We know now, for instance, how capital accumulation or population expansion will affect the terms and volume of trade. (ii) The effect of a *shift* in a factor of production from one country to its trading partner, on the terms and volume of trade, has also been investigated. (iii) Finally, changes in factor supply *resulting* from changes in trade policy, when the supply of factors is elastic with respect to their rentals, have also been considered. These, however, are properly treated with the analysis of the effects on changes in trade policy.

---

ask this key question seems to me to vitiate the utility of the entire discussion concerning what is " plausible " as a prediction. I also wonder whether it is useful to discuss what is generally " likely " when economic analysis and empirical work can enable us, subject to errors of interpretation and estimation, to make a precise prediction whenever necessary. [See also MacDougall [144].]

[1] Johnson [5, p. 176] anticipates this conclusion in a literary analysis. He also proceeds to introduce additional commodities differently—as non-traded goods in the two countries. However, the analysis is again not presented with full algebraic treatment and it is merely stated that: " The introduction of non-traded goods does alter the criteria, since changes in demand for such goods must be classed either as changes in (virtual) demand for exportables or as changes in (virtual) demand for imports, according to whether they are more substitutable in production and consumption for one or the other. In both these cases, however, the direction of change of the commodity terms of trade is not uniquely determined by whether the transfer is undereffected or overeffected at constant prices."

[2] The transfer will be undereffected or overeffected according as

$$\left(m_a' + m_b' - \frac{m_a}{s_a} \cdot s_a' - \frac{m_b}{s_b} \cdot s_b' - 1 \right) \lesseqgtr 0$$

where the transferor is country A and the transferee country B and $m_a' + m_b'$ is the sum of the proportions of the transfer by which expenditure on imports is altered by the financing and disposal of the transfer, m_a and m_b are the (non-transfer-income) marginal propensities to import in A and B respectively, s_a and s_b are the marginal propensities to save (from non-transfer incomes) in A and B and s_a' and s_b' are the proportions of the transfer by which savings are altered [5, p. 179].

(i). *Autonomous Changes in Factor Supply.* In surveying the literature on this problem, two central difficulties arise. Firstly, there is the difficulty of distinguishing models of growth into " static " and " dynamic "; only the former belong here. Sometimes a model is presented with factors increasing at a steady rate over time, and the resulting time-paths of several variables are worked out. And yet the analysis does not really involve time in any essential way except with respect to the " disturbance " itself. Basically, what is involved is working out, for each unit of time, the effects of the factor expansion and then repeating the analysis for each other period: time merely defines the nature of the " disturbance " (*i.e.*, the increase in the factor supply) which is itself independent of the equilibrium parametric values of the preceding periods. Surely it is sensible to treat such models as " static " in nature. The second difficulty consists in separating out models that refer to increase in factor supply and those that concern technical change. Frequently the same authors, for instance Johnson [5, Chapter III], analyse both questions in the same framework. Sometimes, however, the two are not even distinguished and merely " productivity increases " defined as increases in output (attributable naturally to either cause) are discussed, as by Mundell [11], or shifts in demand and supply schedules over time are defined without explicit distinction between different causes, as by Black [59]. Where these models are discussed is inevitably arbitary, and I have brought them in under the present sub-section.

The simplest and yet the most influential analysis of the effects of economic expansion accruing through increased factor supply is that of Johnson [5, Chapter III], who uses the H.O.S. model.[1] There is a great flood of subsequent contributions, among them by Corden [61], which explores the H.O.S. model further on this issue. The analysis of the effect on the terms of trade proceeds simply by noting that the excess demand for imports (dm) at unchanged terms of *trade* would equal the difference between the change in the demand for importables (dc) and in their supply (dp).[2] If this excess demand for imports is positive, then the terms of trade will shift against the growing country provided the stability condition is satisfied. And the precise change in the terms of trade can be obtained by equating the excess demand for imports due to growth with their excess supply due to adverse terms of trade [11, 111].

Since $dm = dc - dp$, the question of the properties of dc and dp has been

[1] Historically, the contributions occurred as a result of the interest in the causes of the dollar shortage in the post-war world. The explanation of the shortage, first propounded by Balogh [58], was in terms of the rapidly increasing productivity in the United States. Translated in terms of the H.O.S. model, with the adjustment mechanism defined in terms of the terms of trade, the explanation was inevitably formalised into a theory of the effect of growth (due to capital accumulation and technical change) on the terms of trade. The connecting link between Johnson's important contributions and the less formal writings of Balogh and others is a seminal paper of Hicks [3, p. 154] which reflects all the difficulties of a pioneering contribution.

[2] In the H.O.S. model the excess demand for imports implies an equivalent excess supply of exports, and the analysis can proceed in terms of *either* good.

raised. The former involves merely a weighted sum of the individual marginal propensities to consume importables. The latter, however, has prompted interesting analytical contributions. A proposition of Rybczynski [87] states that $dp \gtrless 0$ according as importables are factor K-intensive or factor L-intensive as the supply of K increases. Where the two commodities postulated have different factor-intensities, the output of the commodity intensive in the use of a factor will decrease absolutely as the supply of the other factor rises at unchanged terms of trade.[1] A taxonomic exercise, therefore, can be carried out, using such theorems to define the possible properties of dc and dp [5, Chapter III].

In an influential paper, written prior to the analysis discussed hitherto, Johnson [5, Chapter IV] used a model which assumed that each country consumed and exported one commodity and imported, but did not produce, the other.[2] In this model, which amounts to only a special case of the H.O.S. model, $dp = 0$, and it follows that dm must necessarily be positive unless the consumption of importables falls as output increases with factor expansion. Although it is tempting to say this is ruled out if there is no inferior good, it should be noted that, although the good is not inferior in any *individual's* consumption, it *may* be for the economy in the aggregate owing to changing income distribution (associated with a changed factor supply).[3]

Three other contributions are of interest—by Mundell [11], Ramaswami [86] and Black [59]. Mundell has extended Johnson's analysis to the multi-country case, noted earlier here. The same conclusions hold as in Johnson's [5, Chapter III] analysis, provided gross complementarity among the exports of different countries is ruled out.[4]

More novel is the analysis of Ramaswami [86], who has recently attempted

[1] This proposition follows immediately as follows $\frac{K}{L} \equiv \frac{Kx}{Lx} \cdot \frac{Lx}{L} + \frac{Ky}{Ly} \cdot \frac{Ly}{L}$, which states that the aggregate factor endowment ratio is a weighted sum of the factor ratios in the two activities X and Y. If the terms of trade are kept fixed so are the factor proportions in the model used. Therefore, $\frac{Kx}{Lx}$ and $\frac{Ky}{Ly}$ are fixed. So is L. Let K now increase. The resulting increase in $\frac{K}{L}$ can be accommodated then *only* by reducing Ly and increasing Lx if X is the K-intensive activity, such that $\frac{Kx}{Lx} > \frac{Ky}{Ly}$. Thus, the output of Y, the L-intensive activity, falls when K increases at unchanged terms of trade [61]. Since this argument is in terms of the relative factor endowments, it is easy to generalise the argument to the case where both factors increase in supply. Thus, for instance, if both factors increase at the same rate there will be a uniform expansion of the outputs of X and Y. If K increases more rapidly the analysis implies notionally a uniform expansion of X and Y (at the rate of growth of L) plus a *reduction* in the output of Y from this expanded level (resulting from the *excess* growth of K). And so on.

[2] Johnson [5, Chapter IV] formulated his analysis in terms of exchange-rate adjustment. In the model used by him, however, it is obvious that this is tantamount to terms-of-trade adjustment. An extension to the n-country case is also available.

[3] Mundell [11], in his otherwise excellent survey, does not make this point clear and relies on the " non-inferiority " of goods to give him necessarily positive terms.

[4] It is necessarily ruled out in the two-good model, for these two goods have to be substitutes. Gross substitutability among goods is shown by Mundell to guarantee the equivalence of the two-country and multi-country (-cum-multi-commodity) case.

to distinguish between the effects of " completed " accumulation and accumulation-in-progress on the terms of trade.   Characterising the analyses of Johnson and others as relating to the latter question, Ramaswami deploys altogether four models to explore the former problem.   These models reduce to two basic " types."   (1) One of the two goods in Johnson's model is assumed to play a dual role—as a consumer and also as a capital good, and accumulation is conceived as a demand shift, at constant prices, from consumption to investment goods.   The model is simple and can be easily put through the various paces.   For instance, any investment increase means increased demand for the dual-role good.   If the reduction in consumption exclusively falls on that good there is no reason to expect the terms of trade to shift.   If not, adjustment is clearly necessary.   (2) The other approach is to assume a *third* industry (" tools ") which serves as the capital good.   The analysis is a little more complex but still manageable.   The relative ranking of the factor ratios in the three industries adds to the scope for interesting taxonomic analysis.

While the analyses of Johnson, Mundell and Ramaswami are in the general equilibrium framework, Black [59] has produced a model which is strictly partial-equilibrium in its approach and correspondingly of little significance.[1]   Using the partial-equilibrium supply and demand schedules for commodities in a four-commodity (an export and domestic good for each country), two-country model, he introduces trend-shifts in these schedules to derive changes over time in the balance of payments and terms of trade. In contrast to the general equilibrium models, however, this approach leaves untouched the crucial question of how exactly these schedules may be expected to shift in response to accumulation (technical change, etc.).

(ii) *Transfers of Factors between Countries.*   Trade theory has also examined the impact of transfers of factors of production between trading countries. The analyses fall into two classes: (1) either the movement of a factor between countries is made contingent upon the presence of an international differential in its rental and the equilibrium condition postulates the elimination of international factor movements when international factor returns are equalised; or (2) an autonomous shift in a factor's location is analysed. The former is clearly more relevant when there is perfect freedom for factor mobility between countries; the latter is more appropriate to modern conditions where this freedom does not exist and the international migration of factors is subject to political decision-making.

Practically the only rigorous analysis in the former class is by Mundell [82], who uses the H.O.S. model.   Mundell postulates a tariff imposed on a situation characterised by international equality of factor rentals.   The

---

[1] Black describes his approach as Marshallian because his model essentially amounts to using the Marshall–Lerner devaluation analysis and introducing trend-shifts in the supply and demand schedules.   The Marshallian analysis can be interpreted, of course, in a partial sense or as an unhelpful general equilibrium approach (where the elasticites are *total* elasticities).   Black is interpreting the Marshallian approach in the former sense.

tariff raises the rental of the factor intensively used (in the strict Samuelson sense) and thereby precipitates a movement of that factor from the other into the tariff-imposing country.[1]   Ultimately, the factor prices are equalised, factor movement eliminated and commodity prices are also equalised.   The tariff is redundant and can be removed without affecting the new equilibrium reached.   Mundell has merely turned the factor price-equalisation theorem on its head and effectively proved a commodity price-equalisation theorem (when factor mobility is perfect but commodity mobility is not, thanks to the tariff).   The terms of trade and factor prices will be identical in the new equilibrium as prior to the tariff.[2]

Of greater interest than this variation on the factor price-equalisation theorem is the analysis by Johnson [5, Chapter III] of the effects of *given* transfers of productive factors between trading countries.   It represents essentially an extension of the analysis of the effect of growth on the volume and terms of trade: a transfer of factors can be analysed as a simultaneous (and equal) increase and decrease in the two countries' factor supply. Aside from the inevitable taxonomy, using propositions such as Rybczynski's, Johnson carefully argues that an income transfer may be associated with the factor shift.   Thus, for instance, profit remittances may follow upon capital transfer.   Or gifts may attend upon labour migration.   The " transfer problem " analysis may thus have to be superimposed upon the " growth- and trade " analysis to get a *total* picture.   Meade [9, Chapter XIX] has presented a more elaborate model, permitting international differences in production functions for each activity.[3]   However, his formal analysis excludes the " transfer problem " aspects of the question.[4]

(3) *Technological Change*

Although recent writings have underlined the desirability of treating technical change integrally with capital accumulation, trade theory is cast in the neo-classical tradition which separates them out.   The formal analyses of changes in technology again divide into those that treat such changes as autonomous and those which concern the transfer of technical knowledge from one trading country to another.

In the former category there are several contributions.   Using the

---

[1] It is equally possible to argue that the other factor may also move in the contrary direction. In fact, multiple (indeed, an infinite number of) solutions are possible, characterised by different international distributions of factors of production.

[2] This is easy enough to see when the factor-losing country has no monopoly power in trade. When the terms of trade can vary, the result still continues to hold.

[3] This extension is of considerable significance, since the formal H.O.S. model, with the assumption of internationally identical production functions, rules out one of the central reasons why international factor migration may be *desirable*.

[4] Caves [3, Chapter V] includes several Continental and other writings on capital movements in his survey. It is difficult, however, to extract anything formally rigorous from these writings.

H.O.S. model, on the technological side, Johnson [5, Chapter III] has formulated the proposition that " neutral " change in an activity will decrease the output level in the other activity, at constant commodity prices.[1] This proposition can be used to define the sign of dp and the taxonomic analysis thereon is similar to that for the change in factor supply, considered in the earlier sub-section. Findlay and Grubert [62] have extended the analysis of the effects of technical change, on output-composition at constant commodity prices, to the case of biased change. For two factors, say land and labour, they have shown that for labour-saving technical change in the labour-intensive activity there will be an absolute decrease in the output of the land-intensive activity. And that, for land-saving change in the labour-intensive activity, the fall in the output of the other activity does not necessarily follow. In general terms, there will be a fall in the output of an activity when there is technical progress in the other activity which saves on the factor used intensively in that activity.[2] Intuitively, these results are obvious. For instance, land-saving invention in the land-intensive activity has two effects: (1) the technical change, conceived *neutrally*, decreases the output of the other activity (Johnson proposition); and (2) the " notional " release of land reduces the output of the other, labour-intensive activity as well (Rybczynski proposition). The two effects thus reinforce the fall in the other activity's output. On the other hand, they oppose each other when the invention saves on the factor in which the activity is *not* intensive.[3]

Seton [90] has produced an alternative model to analyse the effects of technical change on the terms of trade. It has practically all the features of Johnson's [5, Chapter III] model, but Seton formulates his analysis in terms of concepts which underline the significance of the " weight " of the trading countries in international trade.[4] A distinguishing feature is his defining technical change exclusively as the " neutral " change discussed earlier, though Seton does not establish any propositions concerning its effect, at constant commodity prices, on the composition of output.

Kemp's [71] is practically the only other contribution of some interest in this field. He departs from the preceding analyses in introducing Keynesian unemployment. This renders the supply curves of exports and domestic goods perfectly elastic in his four-good model (with an export and a domestic

[1] Unlike with the Rybczynski proposition, the factor prices will change although the commodity prices are held constant.

[2] The definitions of " neutral," " labour-saving " and " land-saving " are in terms of technology alone. Neutral change merely amounts to multiplying the numbers on the isoquants by a scalar. Under " labour-saving " invention, at the *same* factor price-ratio, the land–labour ratio is increased; and for " land-saving " progress the land–labour ratio is decreased.

[3] Johnson [65] has ingeniously combined the analysis of technical change with a disaggregated-economy assumption to trace the effects of different types of technical change on the sign of dc.

[4] Seton's analysis is lucid, but the results are quite cumbersome, largely by virtue of the novel concepts used by him and his use of proportionate rather than absolute changes. I suspect, since his propositions are consistent with those deducible from Johnson's analysis, that Seton's formulae could be reduced to forms made familiar by the other models. [See also Sodersten [145].]

good in each of the two trading countries).[1]   The results of the analysis are
worked out for technological progress in both the domestic and export
industries.

(4) *Changes in Non-trade Policy*

A shift in " data " can also come from a change in the (non-trade)
economic policy pursued by the Government.   For instance, the Government may decide to impose a tax on *importables* (instead of on imports via a
tariff) in an open economy engaged in free trade.   How will this affect the
volume and terms of trade?   Such questions have rarely been posed directly
in trade theory.   They have, no doubt, been raised tangentially—mostly
in relation to *welfare* analysis.   For instance, Meade [9, Chapters V and VI]
has analysed the choice between an import duty and a consumption tax, and
between an export duty and a production tax, as a means of raising revenue,
the preference function being defined with respect to world advantage.
These analyses indirectly involve contributions to pure theory.

Practically the only *direct* analysis of such problems, however, is due to
Mundell [11], who has extended his survey of pure theory to include an
original contribution on the effect of consumption and production taxes on
the terms of trade (at market prices and factor cost).   For instance, a consumption tax on the imported good (with the revenue redistributed as
income subsidy to consumers) will always improve a country's terms of
trade because its net effect is to reduce the demand for imports by the
product of the compensated elasticity of demand for importables and the
tax change.   This proposition is intuitively obvious, since the tax can be
expected normally to reduce the world demand for importables.   Mundell
also notes the interesting fact that tariffs and (trade) subsidies can always be
simulated in their " real " effects by taxes and subsidies on commodities.
Thus, for instance, a tariff on Y (or an export duty on X) is equivalent, among
several other combinations, to a consumption tax on Y plus a production
tax on X or a consumption tax on Y plus a production subsidy on Y.

(5) *Changes in International Demand*

Until now, the autonomous shift has been located within the trading
country itself.   But the problem can also be posed in terms of an *external*
shift—*i.e.*, a shift in the *foreign offer curve* (which represents a schedule of trade
offers to the trading country at varying terms of trade).[2]   There is indeed a
considerable literature on the effect of such shifts on a trading country's
terms and volume of trade.   This literature was sparked off by an apparent

[1] In this respect Kemp's analysis comes close to that of Asimakopoulos [56], who has investigated the effect of a third non-traded good in a constant-cost model which is otherwise analogous
to the Johnson model.   Kemp's analysis, however, is rigorous, whereas that of Asimakopoulos
lacks in formal rigour in so far as the formal model is not fully specified.

[2] This shift will naturally be *internal* to the foreign country itself and will reflect any or more
of the four types of changes discussed earlier and/or a trade-policy change.   By the same token,
the analysis of this sub-section is of limited interest.

contradiction, in the results reached by Marshall and Graham, which has now been traced to different *definitions* of a shift in the offer curve.[1]

Naturally the results will vary with the definitions chosen; and, as Kemp [70] and Oliver [84] have demonstrated by analysing the effects of three different definitions, any number of definitions may be devised as one wishes. From the viewpoint of the usefulness of the economic analysis, however, the two definitions, adopted each by Marshall and Graham, appear to be the most meaningful and have their counterpart in the standard analysis of value. Marshall's analysis defines the change in international demand in terms of a change in the price at which the given quantity (of imports) is demanded; whereas Graham's definition is in terms of a change in the quantity demanded at given terms of trade. Johnson and myself [2] have argued that each of these approaches has utility in the analysis of trade problems, and hence merits retention in the repertoire of trade theorists.[2]

(B) *Shifts in Trade Policy*

So far I have surveyed much of the central analysis of pure theory which concerns the effects of shifts in " data " while the trade policy (usually free trade) is assumed unchanged between the two situations being compared. However, many of the principal questions in trade theory have related to the effects of a shift in the trade policy itself. This is quite natural in view of the traditional preoccupation with the choice of commercial policy. Moreover, the trade policy most frequently analysed is tariff policy.

(i) *Non-discriminatory tariff change.* Within tariff theory, further, the analysis of non-discriminatory tariff change has received a disproportionate attention. Indeed, from the viewpoint of *systematic* theoretical analysis in its positive aspects, non-discriminatory tariff change is practically the only type of tariff change to have been analysed. As with all other positive analyses of trade policy, the theory of non-discriminatory tariff changes has sprung directly out of concern with questions of trade and welfare.

The assertion of the vulgar protectionists that tariffs would increase the share of labour in the national income has, in fact, prompted a thorough analyses, in terms of the H.O.S. model,[3] of the entire question of the effects

[1] In their analysis, however, the shift was in the country's *own* offer curve, the *foreign* country's offer curve remaining unchanged.

[2] I may quote [2, pp. 78–9]: " Broadly speaking, Graham's approach is likely to be more convenient when . . . the direction of change of international equilibrium can be predicted from the effect of the change on quantity demanded at the initial price. Examples are the transfer problem and the effect of economic expansion on international trade equilibrium. Marshall's approach, on the other hand, is likely to be more convenient when the problem concerns the effects of a change in a country's commercial policy on its equilibrium prices and quantities, since the direction of change of this equilibrium can be predicted from the effect of the tariff on the quantity of imports demanded at the initial internal price, and of the corresponding reduction of the external price on the quantity of imports the foreigner would supply. Marshall himself used this technique for the analysis of tariffs and subsidies; . . ."

[3] The assumptions concerning the factors of production are, however, not necessary to the analysis.

of non-discriminatory tariffs on commodity prices, factor prices, and the absolute and relative shares of either factor in national income.   In a classic analysis Stolper and Samuelson [91] revived the controversy concerning the effect of protection on the real incomes of factors and focused on the issue which was baffling most discussants—namely, how anything definitive could be said concerning the question posed *unless* the consumption pattern of the factors was specified.   In an ingenious exercise, within the framework of the H.O.S. model, the authors successfully demonstrated that conditions *could* be specified under which the impact of protection on the absolute and relative shares of factors could be definitively predicted without reference to the consumption pattern of the factors.   This was accomplished via the analysis of the impact of tariffs on factor prices.   Since, in the H.O.S. model, a unique relationship exists between factor and commodity prices, Stolper and Samuelson opened up, in effect, the entire modern analysis of the effects of tariffs on commodity and factor prices and on absolute and relative shares of factors in national income.   Metzler [80, 81] has subsequently extended the analysis to the " paradoxical " case where a tariff *reduces* the (relative) price of the importable commodity in the tariff-imposing country.   The analysis has been further extended with respect to an elastic factor supply by Kemp and Jones [72] and myself and Johnson [60], the interdependence of public and private consumption by Baldwin [57] and myself and Johnson [60], changes in income distribution by Johnson [67, 60] and the multi-country case by Mundell [11].

In the analysis the distinction between a prohibitive (*i.e.*, trade-eliminating) and a non-prohibitive tariff is of crucial importance, for two reasons: (i) with a prohibitive tariff, starting from free trade, the price of importables cannot be lowered by the imposition of the tariff (in the specified H.O.S. model), whereas it can be when the tariff is non-prohibitive; and (ii) a prohibitive tariff generates no revenue, whereas a non-prohibitive tariff does, creating the necessity to make some assumption about the revenue disposal. The assumption about revenue disposal is, in turn, of significance, since the results of the analysis depend upon it.   The two common assumptions in tariff theory are that *either* the Government spends it directly *or* that the revenue is redistributed as an income-subsidy to the consumers, who then spend it like earned income.   (The results vary unless the Government spends the revenue at internal prices in the same way as consumers do and government consumption does not alter private consumption.)

Subject to these further specifications, the H.O.S. model can be readily employed to work out a large number of formulae concerning the impact of tariff change on domestic and international terms of trade (and hence also on the absolute and relative shares in national income of each of the two classes of factors) [11, 60].   It would be tedious to record the numerous results here; besides, a fairly exhaustive survey has been provided by me elsewhere [1].   I would merely note here that the results under the strict

H.O.S. model naturally get modified when any of the assumptions are changed. For instance, letting one of the factors vary in response to its rental complicates the analysis considerably [60, p. 245]. Thus, in this case, the proposition, that, when the tariff proceeds are spent by the private sector, the terms of trade will *necessarily* improve for the tariff-imposing country (which follows from the fact that, at constant terms of trade, there is an excess supply of importables measured by the product of the compensated elasticity of demand for imports and the tariff change), is no longer valid and the terms of trade can deteriorate, even though this condition is satisfied [60, p. 246].[1] Similarly, for the case of a disaggregated private sector where changes in income distribution are allowed to play a role in determining the pattern of demand, the net result of such disaggregation is to make the aggregate marginal propensity to spend on imports a weighted sum of these propensities for the different individuals constituting the economy [60, pp. 235–8]. The extension to the multi-country case by Mundell [11], however, does not destroy the simple elegance of the traditional conclusions, for instance, with respect to the effects on the external and internal terms of trade. Gross substitutability among the exports of different countries to the tariff-imposing country is sufficient to sustain the two-country result; further restrictions need not be imposed on the pattern of expenditure out of redistributed revenue [68]. Kemp has also re-examined the standard H.O.S. conclusions in the framework of Keynesian unemployment [3, p. 74], establishing the conditions under which Metzler's " paradoxical " result would continue to hold.[2] Of some interest also is the recent analysis by MacDougall [75,76], which utilises the flood of empirical studies on the international price mechanism to investigate the empirical " likelihood " of Metzler's results and deduce the conclusion that it is relatively small.

(ii) *Discriminatory Tariff Changes*. Discriminatory tariff changes can be distinguished according as the discrimination is between countries or between commodities. Any particular tariff may discriminate in both ways, of course, as when it is levied on a commodity which is imported only from a single foreign source.

In contrast to the analysis of non-discriminatory tariff changes, the theory

[1] Kemp and Jones [72] have examined additionally the question of the levels of importable production and the variable factor's supply.

[2] (1) Under competitive conditions quotas are identical with tariffs (with redistributed revenue) and the analysis in the text is valid for them as well. Each tariff implies an equivalent quota and the other way round. Where, however, the quota system confers a domestic monopoly, the results are different. (2) Subsidies are perfectly symmetrical with the case where tariff proceeds are redistributed to the private sector. However, there is no sensible counterpart to the case where the Government spends the tariff proceeds itself [11]. (3) State trading can be easily analysed as well, for it merely turns tariff analysis on its head. Where tariff theory analyses the effect of specific tariffs (and subsidies) on the volume and terms of trade, the theory of state trading is concerned with the investigation, in effect, of the tariffs (and subsidies) which must be imposed to make a particular volume and terms of trade feasible [9]. (It may be remembered that *trade* taxes and subsidies can be reduced invariably to equivalent *production* taxes and subsidies.)

of discriminatory tariff changes, in its positive aspects, is singularly lacking in formal propositions concerning the determinants of behaviour of equilibrium variables. This is to be accounted for partly by the analytical dominance of the two-good, two-country (H.O.S.) model, which rules out the possibility of discriminatory tariff changes. Partly it is also the result of the preoccupation of discriminatory tariff analysts with welfare analysis. For instance, the formal analysis of preferential tariff reduction, prompted by the post-war interest in customs unions and free-trade areas, has been almost exclusively oriented towards questions like: will a customs union increase world welfare? rather than towards problems like: how will the terms of trade of the non-member countries be affected? No doubt, welfare analysis must be founded on positive analysis. But it happens that the kind of positive analysis that is subsumed in these welfare exercises in tariff discrimination rarely has the formal neatness that is now associated with the theory of non-discriminatory tariff changes.[1]

The formal theory of customs union begins with Viner's [94] examination of the assertion that a customs union, by virtue of its being a move towards free trade, would *improve* welfare. The models employed were not fully stated, but the arguments have none the less proved seminal. Viner considered merely shifts in the given production (of a single commodity), in an essentially three-country model, from one country to another. (Where the union results in the shift of imports from the lower-cost outside country to the higher-cost partner country, he described the shift as trade-diversion. Where the preferential tariff reduction merely eliminates the inefficient, domestic industry and replaces it with imports from the member country, he named the change trade-creation.) Lipsey [121] and Meade [79] have subsequently elaborated upon these basic concepts, stating their models more fully and introducing both the possibility of an *increase* in the volume of imports (as distinct from a mere shift in their origin) due to their cheapening domestically, as also the existence of imperfectly elastic supply curves. This has been done in the context of both a simple formalisation of Viner's (implicit) model into a two-good, three-country model [121] and a more complex version with more than two goods which admits of complementarity between imports from different sources [7, 79].

Unfortunately, all these analyses are welfare-orientated and, for reasons outlined earlier, fail to contribute, in their extant form, anything systematic and substantive to positive theory. It is only recently that Vanek [93] has directly posed the questions of positive theory in an interesting extension of

---

[1] This is itself attributable frequently to the way in which welfare analysis has been pursued. For instance, Lipsey [121], in a brilliant paper on customs union theory, is content with demonstrating a *possibility* (that, despite " trade diversion," both national and international welfare may be improved by a customs union) and does not carry the analysis through to a formal algebraic statement of the conditions under which the possibility will occur. Further again, Meade's [79] analysis is more in the nature of the demonstration of a method than a fully taxonomic and formal exercise.

the standard, Marshallian offer-curve analysis to the case of preferential tariff reductions in a two-commodity, three-country model. However, he halts his analysis short of the derivation of the conditions under which the possibilities stated by him will occur.[1] In a real sense, therefore, the question of discriminatory tariff change invites systematic and fresh analysis—in its positive aspects.[2]

IV. Theorems in Dynamics

In contrast to the general richness and synthesised character of much of pure theory in its comparative statics, dynamic propositions in international trade are comparatively few and bear no trace of any uniform design, each having been developed in virtual isolation. Dynamic trade theory, where it exists, has grown up in an essentially *ad hoc* fashion and has witnessed none of the interaction of analysis which usually accompanies the development of an area of knowledge and produces a common design, a unifying frame.

At the same time there is no dearth of interest in the dynamic aspects of trade theory, and a vast amount of non-rigorous but suggestive literature is available [3, Chapter IX]. This is supplemented by the occasional attempts of growth theorists to include international trade in their models (" for completeness," and more frequently to " show that it does not affect the validity of the approach and/or conclusions ")—as, for instance, by Chakravarty [137]. I have kept away from either kind of literature—from the former because these unverified conjectures provide a fertile source for fresh theoretical analysis but themselves do not constitute it;[3] and from the

---

[1] A fuller analysis, I am informed, has since been completed by him. [See also Mundell [146].]

[2] Part of the difficulty in systematically analysing the customs-union problems consists in the vast number of possible cases which logically must be catalogued and analysed. For instance, even in the extremely simplified two-good, three-country model we have seven logically different possibilities (as distinct from four mentioned by Vanek [93]), catalogued in the following matrix, *presented in terms of a single commodity* which may be an export (X) or import (M) of, or not traded (O) by, a country and where the three countries are the home country (H) the partner country (P) and the non-member country (N). The categorisation is in terms of the pre-customs-union position.

	H.	P.	N.
(1)	X	M	M
(2)	M	X	X
(3)	M	M	X
(4)	X	X	M
(5)	O	O	O
(6)	M	O	X
(7)	X	M	O

From the viewpoint of economic analysis, cases (1) and (2) are identical in structure; so are cases (3) and (4), so that the number of distinct cases may be considered to reduce to five. For the three-commodity model the possibilities are greater in number, and depend further on relations of substitution and complementarity between different goods.

[3] There are a few exceptions that I have made, partly to illustrate the non-rigorous character of these analyses, but mostly because they come close enough to formal analysis to merit brief comment.

latter because the trade aspects of the models are frequently the least interesting, for they are also treated as the least important.

Broadly speaking, the scant formal literature on dynamic propositions divides itself into: (1) those analyses where the inquiry concerns the effects of an *initial* change in the *trade policy*, and (2) those where the effects of an *initial* change in other *data* are being considered.[1]

(1) *Change in Trade Policy*

Perhaps the neatest dynamic analysis of the effects of a change in trade policy concerns that involving adaptive, mutual and sequential changes in tariffs. Starting with the imposition of an optimum tariff, levied by a country in a two-country world, the Cournot-type adjustment mechanism where each country alternatively imposes an optimum tariff leads eventually to the two possibilities demonstrated by Johnson [5, Chapter II]: (i) an eventual equilibrium where the optimum tariff of each country is the existing tariff; or (ii) each country moves into a " tariff cycle " such that the two countries oscillate between a pair of own tariffs. While the possibility of generalising the theory by changing the postulated reaction mechanism has been recognised previously, Panchmukhi [124] has recently formulated the theory of tariff retaliation in explicitly game-theoretic terms. It is highly improbable, however, that tariff retaliation can be studied profitably on the assumption that tariffs are levied, autonomously or in retaliation, to maximise the tariff-imposing country's advantage. Surely, the tariff levels *and* structure are prompted by distributional considerations (operating through pressure groups) rather than by considerations of national advantage.[2]

By contrast, the literature on the effects of changes in trade policy in the absence of retaliation is characterised by less sophistication, though greater relevance. Practically all the analyses relate to the effect of trade on the rate of growth of income—but the mechanisms postulated vary considerably, and so do the clarity and rigour that attend these contributions.

The earliest of these, and analytically impressive for its time, is the classical analysis of the effect of cheap food imports from the colonies on the approach of the Stationary State. Among the clearest exponents of this theory was Mill [32], who attempted to demonstrate how, through the consequential increase in the rate of profit and hence in the accumulation of savings and capital, the approach of the Stationary State would be put off. What is not available, however, is the *precision* that we have now come to expect in theoretical writing; and unfortunately the recent mathematical formulations of the Ricardian systems (by Samuelson and Pasinetti) leave out international trade altogether, although Ricardo traced out the essence of the sequence that Mill elaborated. Other ways in which such a dynamic

---

[1] The initial change itself may be defined to be a *continuing* one: for instance, a change in the rate of saving may be *permanent*.

[2] The question of tariff retaliation is considered at greater length in Section VI. since it has important implications for welfare analysis.

link between trade and growth has been established are: (i) via the effect of trade on the marginal capital–output ratio by virtue of the proposition that (free) trade increases real income [27, 132]; (ii) via the effect of trade on the distribution of income and hence on the average savings ratio [97, 99, 100]; and (iii) via the effect of trade through factor price rigidity on the level of employment, hence on real income and savings [27].[1]   None of these analyses are fully rigorous.   For instance, the analysts who argue via the effects on the distribution of income and hence on the average savings ratio never specify a model.   And yet the sequence is clear and the models are easy to invent.[2]

(2) *Change in Data*

The most interesting (though insufficiently formal) model, designed to analyse the effects of continuous accumulation on the trade pattern, has been presented by Bensusan-Butt [96].   He operates in a two-country, multi-commodity framework, with a simplified production technology such that each commodity has two alternative processes, one with and the other without machinery, which are known in both countries.   Starting with a situation where no accumulation has previously taken place, and the cost and price structure is identical between countries, and trade is absent in consequence, Bensusan-Butt unfolds a sequence in which the steady accumulation of capital in one country leads to progressive mechanisation, and emergence as exports, of industries in the accumulating country.   The resulting improvement in the other country's real income (initially through the rise of trade and subsequently through the postulated improvement in the terms of trade as the accumulation proceeds) is linked with the emergence of savings there, and the effect of this on the pattern of trade is examined.

While Bensusan-Butt's analysis examines the structure of trade, as it *evolves* sequentially, the rest of the dynamic analyses in the literature are concerned instead with the equilibrium time-paths of variables such as output, real income and terms of trade in a growing economy engaged in a *pre-defined* pattern of trade.

Srinivasan [104] has constructed an interesting two-country, three-

[1] Linder [27] considers his model applicable to underdeveloped countries and uses it to turn up immiserating growth paths of output. The model is, in fact, quite symmetrical between movement from free trade to no trade and a reverse movement. For any change will bring about unemployment (due to factor-price rigidity) in the industry which should contract, and hence the contraction of real income and possible reduction in the rate of growth. The model, not being mathematically formulated, does not specify *where* the incremental output is allocated and whether the mechanism of factor allocation envisaged would be compatible with the factor-price rigidity assumption. Also, it would be pertinent to consider whether it is right to ignore the effects of change brought about by increased output: it may well be that the change implicit in trade may *offset* the change involved by growth. The analysis offered by Linder is thus not fully satisfactory.

[2] For example, a model where tractors produce tractors and corn, and corn is exchanged for toys when trade opens, could easily be used to demonstrate how the possibility of trade can reduce the marginal capital–output ratio and raise the rate of growth (with given average savings ratio). For a treatment of several types of causal links between trade and growth in a historical context, Kindleberger [101] is an excellent reference.

commodity model where one country produces two goods (a consumer good and a capital good which produces all goods in the system) and the other country produces the other (consumer) good. Assuming: (1) the Paretian allocation mechanism to allocate the fully employed factors, labour and capital (good); (2) a fixed trade pattern involving the exchange of the former country's capital good with the latter country's consumer good; and (3) international lending predetermined by a linear relationship between exports and import values, Srinivasan introduces growth into the system by letting labour grow exponentially, capital accumulate through savings and neutral technical progress characterise industries in both countries. The equilibrium time-paths of income, terms of trade and comparative factor rewards are analysed.

While in Srinivasan's model the import demand functions are ingeniously implicit in the production and trade patterns specified, Johnson [5, Chapter V] has used the more conventional approach of specifying marginal propensities to import (and spend on imports) and used them in the context of a Harrod–Domar type of flow-analysis extended to the international economy. Johnson explores, in effect, the behaviour of the equilibrium rate of growth of output and income of a country over time under the assumption of international lending and also under the more realistic postulate of exchange-rate adjustment (when the time profile of the terms of trade becomes relevant).[1]

Far more complex, and for the same reason ineffective as theory, is the analysis of Brems [98], who, using a 52-equations system (among whose novelties is trade in producers' goods), solves it to derive two L-order difference equations (where L is the durability, in years, of capital goods). These yield solutions which establish relations, over the time-path, between the equilibrium values of variables such as the growth rates of the two trading countries.

These analyses nearly exhaust the literature on dynamic theory—except for the " omissions " justified earlier.[2] There is little doubt that, in contrast to the comparative statics of pure theory, dynamic trade theory still calls for further, systematic analysis and synthesis.

V. CENTRAL LIMITATIONS: INTERMEDIATES AND CAPITAL GOODS

Of greater significance is the negligible dent made so far by intermediate and capital goods in the theoretical models employed by analysts of international trade. To state this is *not* to assert that the present stock of know-

[1] Verdoorn [105] has attempted a rigorous analysis, of similar intent, but under the restrictive assumptions of: (1) fixed coefficients of production, and (2) independence of the foreign rate of growth from the rate of growth of the economy under consideration. Johnson [5, Chapter V] eliminates the former type of question altogether (because he operates with the concept of the marginal propensity to import), while his analysis is fully general on the latter question.

[2] Perhaps the only omission that I regret is that of some Japanese analyses that seem extremely interesting, though the sources I have been able to consult in English [102, 103] do not give enough formal account of these theories. I refer to the analysis of the " Marxist " economists S. Tsuru and H. Kitamura which links cyclical fluctuations with the *pattern* of trade [102]. [See also Oniki and Uzawa [147].]

ledge will not survive the required change in the formulation of the models. In fact, we do know, from such little analysis as already obtains in this direction, that the survival rate tends to be quite high! More important, however, is the fact that a vast range of interesting problems, applicable to economies using intermediate and (produced) capital goods, cannot get within the range of analysis until the theorists get away from the traditional picture of primary factors and integrated processes of production (with the inevitable concomitant feature of trade in consumer goods).

The introduction of intermediates and (produced) capital goods can be accomplished in principle in either of the following alternative ways: either these enter only domestic processes but not trade or they enter trade as well. For instance, a sector producing capital goods may exist though capital goods do not enter trade. The existing theoretical analyses in trade theory exhibit the entire range of these possibilities. For example, Samuelson's [54] interest-rate equalisation model has produced but untraded capital goods. So has Ramaswami's [86] model, which analyses the effect of trade on growth. On the other hand, Srinivasan's [104] dynamic model has a capital good which is both produced and traded. As for intermediate goods, the models used by McKenzie [78, 108] and Jones [69], which explore the pattern of trade in a Ricardo–Graham framework, distinguish between the cases where intermediate goods are traded and where they are not. Vanek [55], on the other hand, uses a two-sector model where the intermediates are identical with the final goods which enter trade.

A large number of propositions continue to be valid despite the introduction of intermediates and/or capital goods in the analytical models. For instance, as Samuelson [125] and Kemp [120] have shown, the proposition that free trade is superior to no trade is valid even when intermediates exist and enter trade. Similarly, Jones [69] has shown that the pattern of efficient specialisation in the Ricardo–Graham model will continue to satisfy the bilateral comparative cost rankings postulated by Ricardo, even when intermediates enter trade. The factor price equalisation theorem again has been examined, in the light of traded intermediate goods, by Samuelson [53] and Vanek [55] without leading to any qualitative change in the traditional propositions. On the other hand, certain propositions *do* change. For instance, the *exact* pattern of specialisation in the Ricardo–Graham model naturally changes with the possibility of trade in intermediate goods [69, 78]. The effect of growth on the terms of trade again is shown by Ramaswami [86] to change qualitatively with the introduction of a (produced) capital-goods sector.[1]

---

[1] W. Travis has recently demonstrated the drawback of the usual conclusion that tariff reduction is best carried out gradually (*i.e.*, piecemeal) to soften the impact of adjustment. Using an input–output framework, Travis shows how the adjustments in different activities demanded by different tariff changes may actually be mutually offsetting so that it may be wiser to have a simultaneous tariff reduction on many fronts than to opt for piecemeal, sequential tariff cuts. Here we have another example of the utility of having processes using intermediates explicitly in the models employed for analysis.

Of far greater significance, however, is the fact that a whole range of interesting and important questions slip through the analyst's hands unless intermediates and (produced) capital goods are introduced into the formal models. For instance, the recent G.A.T.T. [107] discussions on the exports of " new manufactures " from the industrialising underdeveloped countries have drawn attention to the disparity between tariffs levied on unprocessed and semi-processed items (on which tariffs are relatively lower) and those on finished manufactures. It is surely interesting to examine the effects, in both positive and welfare terms, of such tariff discrimination. But the analysis just cannot get off the ground with the traditional types of analytical models! [1] Let me take another important illustration. The traditional multiplier analysis in trade theory (which has already been discussed earlier in relation to the Keynesian treatment of the transfer problem) postulates the impact of exports and/or autonomous investment on the balance of payments and the levels of domestic output and employment. But there is an extension to the concept of the *import multiplier* as well, when one considers the situation frequently experienced by economies importing raw materials, when excess capacity develops due to the shortage of foreign exchange. An extra unit of exchange (say, through foreign aid) will then increase the level of domestic output directly by a multiple which is the ratio of value added to imported inputs (the latter being the only constraint). If, however, this output enters as input into other processes lying idle for want of materials, one can easily work out (through the input–output mechanism) a whole chain of increased outputs which, on summation, yields a multiplier-measure of the increased output attributable to the incremental unit of imports. This idea has been independently formulated in various writings, by Stolper [109, 110], several Japanese economists such as Akamatsu [106] and Kojima [103], and writers on the Indian balance of payments in recent years. It demonstrates forcefully how the exclusion of intermediates from analysis would rule out from examination one of the most significant aspects of the international trade problems besetting many economies. Since imported intermediates may also lead to extra output of domestically produced capital goods which may help break other bottlenecks at a future date, or the incremental exchange may be used to import capital goods which create capacity to break bottlenecks to domestic utilisation of capacity in other sectors of use, this whole notion of the import multiplier has a further time dimension to it and equally illustrates the role of produced and traded capital goods in any realistic analysis of the trade phenomena in the real world.

[1] We may note the related point that an apparently non-discriminatory tariff adjustment on all imports (say, 10% reduction in the tariffs on both alumina and aluminium) would be *de facto* discriminatory in its effects when the imports consist of both the raw material and the finished product. The effective reduction in the protective effect would be greater on the raw material. Incidentally, an analysis of the problem discussed in the text would call for some method of demarcating intermediates in a world where circularities in the Leontief flow-matrix may prevent an easy solution.

VI. WELFARE PROPOSITIONS: GAINS FROM TRADE

Welfare propositions are among the oldest in pure theory. Trade theory developed in the effort to demonstrate the fallacy of the protectionist prescriptions of the Mercantilist School. Today the range of analytical questions has increased astonishingly beyond the early preoccupation with the comparison of free trade with protection. To seek design and order in this vast literature is no mean ambition.

It is useful to start with the basic proposition that the aim of policy-orientated welfare economics is to provide a *ranking of policies*. This ranking may relate to *trade* policies (while the general equilibrium parameters and relationships, such as the known technology, are given). For instance, is a zero tariff (*i.e.*, free trade) superior to no trade? Is a 15% (non-discriminatory) tariff superior to a 20% tariff? Would an increase in the tariff rate be beneficial? On the other hand, the ranking may refer to policies relating to the general equilibrium *parameters and relationships*, such as the factor supply level (given the trade policy). For instance, for an open economy engaged in free trade, is migration desirable? Should the increment in capital stock be absorbed as domestic or foreign investment? [1]

The ranking of policies in pure theory further divides into two classes of propositions: (1) those that relate to *national* advantage; and (2) those that concern *international* advantage. Thus, for instance, the proposition that free trade is superior to no trade is sought to be established from both national and international standpoints. On the other hand, the proposition that (for a variable tariff rate) the optimum tariff is superior to free trade concerns only national advantage.

These rankings can further be classified according to the *criterion of welfare* employed. The Samuelsonian superior-for-all-income-distributions criterion has been widely used in the early development of the theory subsequent to the new welfare economics. On the other hand, it has been replaced extensively in recent years bv criteria which handle the problem of income-distribution in a non-purist fashion. Among them, two approaches can be distinguished, which divide mainly on the issue of the measurability of utility.

The *ordinalist* method sets up a community welfare function which *assumes* that the State adopts a policy of lump-sum transfers to fix the income-

---

[1] Although I have not done so in the text, the ranking of policies could also be classified into the ranking of *specific measures* and of *general forms of policy intervention*. Under the former, a characteristic illustration would be the ranking of two rates of tariffs. For instance, would a 5% tariff be inferior to a 3% tariff? Would a marginal reduction in the tariff rate increase welfare? Under the latter, a typical example would be the ranking of a tariff policy (without specifying a specific tariff rate) and free-trade policy. For instance, the proposition that an optimum tariff is superior to free trade is not formulated in terms of a unique tariff-rate comparison, but is rather valid in the sense that, corresponding to any income distribution chosen, there will be an optimum tariff rate which will be superior to free trade so that the utility possibility curve for an optimum tariff situation, with variable tariff rates, will lie outside (though it may touch) that for the free-trade situation.

distribution at some " desired " level.   The properties of this welfare function are then assumed to be parallel to those which are taken normally (with
some " plausibility ") to characterise individual welfare functions.   It is
only recently that Samuelson [126] has established the exact conditions
under which " social indifference curves " will enjoy these properties—so
that, in effect, the trade theorist must assume, *ipso facto*, these conditions to
obtain if he uses a social-welfare function with those properties.[1]   The
ranking of trade policies can then be carried out in terms of such a community preference function, corresponding to any " desired " income
distribution.

The other, alternative method of handling the problem of income
distribution so as to achieve a unique ranking of policies has been that
extensively used by Meade [8, 9].   He explicitly combines equity and
efficiency in a single welfare function by assuming *cardinality* and the possibility of *interpersonal comparisons of welfare* (through assigned weights).   This
method enables the analyst to judge the change in welfare between two situations for the actual market income-distributions achieved and without having
to conjure up a state of lump-sum transfers (which itself may be construed to
be an advantage, from the ethical and practical viewpoints, over both the
Samuelson criterion and the ordinalist method sketched earlier).[2]

[1] Often trade theorists omit mentioning the problem of lump-sum transfers and use community
preference functions as if the community were an individual.   This procedure is clearly sloppy.
It is also not uncommon for some theorists to assume that the economy is composed of individuals
with identical tastes and income (kept equal presumably by lump-sum transfers).   This, however,
is tantamount to assuming a single individual and, only in a limited, formal sense can one concede
the " reduced restrictiveness " of such an assumption!   It is also sometimes stated that the State
" ignores the question of income distribution " and then the analyst proceeds to operate with the
community indifference curves [129, p. 329].   This, however, is open to objection because:
(1) the assumptions under which the community preference function would be characterised by
the required properties (*e.g.*, convexity) would still have to be specified; and (2) the position implied
by the statement is untenable.   In what sense can one be " indifferent " to income distribution?
The only meaning that can possibly be attributed is that the State attaches equal weight to the
marginal utility of each individual—in which case the analyst ceases to be an ordinalist!

[2] Caves' [3, pp. 233–4] neat summary of Meade's method is useful.   " Suppose that a change
is made somewhere in the economy, such as the elimination of a monopoly position.   There will
be a primary gain in economic efficiency, because consumers now receive extra units of this particular product which they value above the cost to the suppliers.   In addition, because of relations
of substitutability and complementarity between this and other products, both in consumption and
production, expenditure patterns will change throughout the economy.   Spending on products
with no cost-value divergence may rise; spending on other products with very large divergences
may fall.   Changes of this type represent secondary losses; their opposites would represent secondary gains.   The process of summing these changes over the whole economic system is shown by
the expression:

$$u = \sum_{i=1}^{n} \sum_{=1}^{n} \sum_{s=1} (U_{ij} D_{ijs} - 1)\mu_j R_{js}\lambda_{ijs}$$

where the net change in utility (u) represents a summation, over all sellers, buyers, and commodities, of the unit revenue from each commodity (R) times the change in the quantity of that
commodity exchanged (x), times the rate at which the marginal value to the purchaser exceeds
the marginal cost to the seller ($D - 1$).   Subscript s denotes a commodity, i a buyer, j a seller.
In addition, distributional weights appear as μ_j, the weight attached to marginal income for the
seller, and U_{ij}, which stands for the ratio μ_i/μ_j."

Aside from the possible preferences on ethical and practical grounds, however, the shift in favour of these less-restrictive criteria has been prompted essentially by a change in the kinds of questions that economists are willing to accept from policy makers. The traditional analysis concerned itself with the ranking of specific policy measures (themselves distortionary) under otherwise " first-best " assumptions or, in ranking forms of policy intervention, compared only policies achieving fully optimal situations with those resulting in sub-optimal ones. In the former category, for instance, is the proposition that a higher tariff is inferior to a lower tariff. In the latter class the most prominent proposition has always been that an optimum tariff (which attains the first best solution) is superior to free trade (which leads to a sub-optimal solution when the country can influence its terms of trade). These rankings satisfy the Samuelson welfare criterion. Now, however, the range of policy questions has increased enormously. The policy-makers wish to know the answers to questions which inevitably involve comparing sub-optimal situations. Problems are posed such that " second-best " assumptions as also sub-optimal comparisons have to be made.[1] For instance,

[1] Second-best assumptions imply that, from the entire set of assumptions that are made to demonstrate the Pareto optimality of the competitive solution, one (or more) does not obtain. Given this definition of second-best assumptions, it is useful to classify these constraints, the departures from first-best assumptions, into two categories: (1) *Behavioural* constraints; and (2) *Environmental* constraints. In the former class we can consider non-utility maximisation and non-profit maximisation by decision-making units. In the latter category we may further distinguish between (i) *State-imposed* constraints and (ii) *others*. Among the State-imposed constraints, we have the imposition of direct and indirect taxes, subsidies, tariffs, restrictions of output levels, etc. The other constraints divide broadly into " *market imperfections* " (for instance, the presence of monopoly, a distortionary wage differential between sectors, divergence of the shadow rental to a factor from its actual rental, and national monopoly power in trade), " *technological characteristics* " (for instance, increasing returns to scale, and non-convexity of isoquants) and " *interdependence* " (for instance, externalities in production and in consumption).

Corresponding to the notion of second-best *assumptions* is the concept of second-best *solutions*. The difference between first-best and second-best solutions is, I suggest, best comprehended if it is founded on a distinction between those second-best assumptions that are *meaningfully* looked upon as removable (*in principle*) by intervention and those that are not. For instance, one can look upon a tax as removable and a wage differential as capable of being offset by a tax-cum-subsidy-on-labour-use, etc., so that the *standard first-best solution* (with all the first-best assumptions holding) is restorable. On the other hand, interdependence of utilities of consumers or increasing returns to scale or monopoly power in trade are not second-best assumptions which can be looked upon as capable of " elimination " so as to restore the *standard* first-best situation. With this distinction, in principle, between the different types of second-best assumptions, we can define the respective first-best and second-best solutions.

In the *former* class, where the second-best constraint is removable, the first-best solution is that which would obtain if the constraint *were* removed, *i.e.* it is the standard first-best solution. The functional forms (of the optimising conditions), as also the values of the solution, will naturally be identical with those obtaining for the standard first-best solution. In the *latter* case, where the second-best assumption is irremovable, the *first-best solution is that obtained by maximisation subject to the second-best assumption.* This solution may have the same functional form (of the optimising conditions) as for the solution under standard first-best assumptions. In general, the functional forms *will*, however, differ from those of the conditions for the *standard first-best solution*. Thus, for instance, where consumption externality obtains, it would be necessary for a consumer to take into account the impact of his utility on the other consumers. Or there may be production externality, for instance, under which a producer's decision concerning the level of production may be a func-

some distortionary taxes may have to be admitted into the analysis when two
tariff rates are being compared.   The policy-maker is apt to say: " I cannot
take off certain taxes.   Given these taxes, will a reduction in the tariff rate
be desirable? "   Another familiar illustration is provided by the policy-
makers, who argue that they cannot have universal free trade, but that a

---

tion of another producer's level of production.   Here again, the optimising condition for producers
will differ from that when no such interdependence obtains (yet the utility level reached will be
identical under a policy where the State, by policy intervention, assures the fulfilment of this
optimising condition under interdependence, and under the standard first-best solution when no
such interdependence obtains).   The second-best solution can then be defined in terms of this
first-best solution not being available under the postulates made.

We thus have: (1) the *standard first-best solution* (which obtains under universally first-best
assumptions); (2) the first-best solution (equivalent to the standard first-best solution) when the
second-best assumption is removable in principle; (3) the second-best solution when the second-
best assumption, though removable in principle, is not removable and removed in practice; (4)
the first-best solution (which may differ from the standard first-best solution in both functional
forms of the optimising conditions and, where comparison is meaningful, in welfare level reached)
when the second-best assumptions are irremovable in principle; and (5) the second-best solution
when these second-best assumptions are irremovable in principle and the corresponding first-best
solution cannot be obtained.

This analytical classification can be supplemented with a further set of remarks concerning the
ways in which the effects of second-best assumptions are (and often, without clarity, have been)
analysed.

(1) To begin with, the precise way in which the second-best solution should be delimited has
to be clarified.   For instance, if a country has monopoly power in trade the first-best solution would
involve the imposition of an optimum tariff.   Suppose that this is ruled out; then, is the second-
best solution to be determined on the assumption that no tariff can be levied or on the assumption
that only the optimum tariff cannot be levied?   Similarly, if a wage differential cannot be eliminated entirely, are we to seek a second-best solution on the assumption that it cannot be offset in
any degree or that it cannot be offset fully?   There is no unique answer: it all depends on what
restraints the policy-maker wishes to impose on himself.   But the need for a clear definition of
the problem must be underlined.

(2) Secondly, one has to distinguish between the second-best solution, which may necessitate
intervention in a decentralised economy, and the *actual* solution that would prevail (under the
second-best assumptions made) in the absence of the intervention that is necessary to bring about
the second-best solution.   Thus, if a distortionary wage differential between sectors obtains, the
actual solution will be different from the second-best solution [112]; the latter will call for intervention.

(3) It also follows that, starting from any actual solution, under second-best assumptions one can
ask how any intervention (other than that which produces the second-best solution) will influence
the level of welfare.   Thus, rather than investigate what is the second-best solution, the theorist
may merely interest himself in *changes* in welfare resulting from the variation in the use of one or
more policy instruments when second-best assumptions obtain.   Or he may even, using this method,
engage in " partial optimisation " and attempt to seek the optimal level of a particular policy
(*e.g.*, the tariff rate) instead of seeking the optimal, second-best policy from the *entire* range of policy
instruments.   In trade theory it is *only* the latter two varieties of approach which have been used
extensively; the question of the second-best solutions has hardly ever been posed!

This long footnote, highlighting different aspects of second-best theory, has been inserted
primarily to gain a clearer grasp of the structure of many contributions to the theory of trade
and welfare.   I do not claim any special merits for the analytical classification proposed here over
those currently available, except that it appears consistent and illuminates the logic of second-best
analyses purposively.   I am indebted to T. N. Srinivasan for many helpful conversations and for
drawing my attention to, as also making available to me, an important unpublished paper by Otto
Davis and Andrew Whinston on " Welfare Economics and the Theory of Second Best " (*Cowle
Foundation Discussion Paper*, No. 146).

free-trade area with continuing tariffs on outside countries may be feasible. If so, would a move to a free-trade area be beneficial (to the member countries and/or the world)?   Trade theorists have found that, in general, answers to such questions cannot be given, *even for particular cases* (*i.e.*, for instance, the latter question being asked in relation to a *specific* group of countries joining or opting out of a free-trade area rather than being formulated more generally so that the answer must be valid for all possible free-trade areas), unless the income distribution is specified.   In general, *both* the particularising of a question (in the sense just outlined) and the choice of an income distribution are necessary to the ranking of two alternative policies. Since these questions are of interest to policy-makers, the trade theorist has naturally eschewed all Samuelsonian scruples and, in either of the two ways discussed earlier, decided to handle income distribution in a non-purist fashion so as to enable him to get along with the business of ranking the contrasted policies.

This shift towards policy-orientation of a more realistic variety has logically led to the emergence of a new trend towards the *measurement* of losses and gains from changes in policy.   Partly this is a result of the shift to the non-purist welfare criteria.   Meade's method, for instance, is candidly cardinal, and the sheer process of determining the direction of the welfare change from a shift in policy involves the evaluation of the magnitude of this welfare change.   The measurement of losses and gains in welfare, however, has also been given great currency by ordinalists such as Johnson [132, 133], and the principal reason for this has ultimately to be found in the general demand for such measurement by those who debate policies.   Policies are maintained or changed largely for non-economic reasons; and the (economic) "cost" involved is a magnitude that is commonly demanded and bandied about in discussions of public policy.   Whether we like it or not, this is what the policy-makers do want;   and the trade theorist, in consonance with the best traditions in the profession, has begun to meet this need in an attempt to bring economic analysis closer to fulfilling the objective that provides its ultimate *raison d'être*.[1]   The result has been a definite and significant trend, in the welfare analysis of pure theory, towards measurement of welfare change.   It is important enough to merit detailed analysis in Section VII.

In the present Section we will survey the qualitative propositions of welfare analysis in pure theory, utilising the analytical classifications developed so far.   A full survey of the entire range of propositions is not necessary;   there are endless ways in which the same theoretical principle may be applied so that a full mapping of these applications in the literature would be both tedious and exhausting.   The analytical skeleton of the contributions to the analysis of welfare and trade has already been laid bare.

[1] Other interesting and important uses of the measures of gains and losses in welfare will be discussed in Section VII.

All that needs to be done now is to survey the central analyses so that the skeleton acquires flesh.

Ranking of Policies by Samuelson Criterion: National Advantage

Among the simplest rankings by the Samuelson criterion, in relation to national advantage, is the proposition that a *higher tariff rate is inferior to a lower tariff rate*. This is valid under first-best assumptions (inclusive of the absence of national monopoly power in trade) [1]. There are clearly a very large number of such propositions that could be worked out: for instance, that a *lower trade subsidy is superior to a higher trade subsidy* (under first-best assumptions).[1]

The rankings which have traditionally held the stage in the welfare theory of trade are, however, the two celebrated propositions that: (1) *free trade is superior to no trade*; and (2) *an optimum tariff is superior to free trade* (when a country has monopoly power in trade). To these Kemp [120] has recently added the proposition that (3) *restricted trade is superior to no trade*, and Ramaswami and myself [112] have argued that (4) *an optimum subsidy is superior to a tariff policy* (when there are domestic distortions).

The proposition that free trade is superior to no trade was shown by Samuelson [125], in a classic paper, to hold with standard first-best assumptions. However, its validity has subsequently been extended to the case where a country can influence its terms of trade through the exercise of monopoly power [120]. Although there have always been those who erroneously believe, and have sometimes continued to assert despite proofs to the contrary, that the proposition rests on an assumed mobility of factors of production, the proposition rests on no such postulate. Samuelson's 1939 proof [125] is clear on this issue; and Haberler [117] has subsequently provided a supporting geometrical argument which must make the truth accessible to more numerous economists. It is also necessary to note that the proposition, valid for all income distributions, holds only in the situation sense—such that, the utility possibility curve corresponding to the free-trade policy will lie uniformly outside (though it may touch) the utility possibility curve corresponding to the no-trade policy [120].[2]

The proposition that restricted trade is superior to no trade, which is also valid in the situation sense, has been shown by Kemp [120] to hold under

---

[1] These listed propositions hold because, in each case, the superior policy represents a " weakening " of the sole second-best assumption (*i.e.*, a tariff or a subsidy) in an otherwise first-best situation. Throughout the following analysis the statement that a policy is " superior " to another is to be taken to include whenever necessary the borderline case where the two produce identical welfare.

[2] It is not possible to demonstrate that the actual bundle of goods obtained by adopting free trade can be redistributed so as to make at le st one person better off while leaving others as well off as with the *actual bundle* in the preceding no-trade condition. This has always been understood, although some confusion has cropped up in the literature occasionally. Johnson [66, p. 259] has produced a good example, illustrative of the proposition that the redistribution of the *actual* bundle of goods so as to demonstrate the superiority of free trade over no trade may be impossible.

the standard first-best assumptions (except that the country may have monopoly power in trade).   By restricted trade is meant essentially trade restricted
in a manner which merely brings about a divergence between foreign and
domestic commodity prices.   Thus, the trade may be restricted by tariffs,
quotas or exchange control.   It is *not* correct to infer from this proposition
that *any* manner of restricted trade will be beneficial in relation to no trade:
for it is easy to conceive of forms of trade where the volume and/or value of
trade is lower than under free trade and yet the net effect is to lower the
country's welfare below the no-trade level.   Nor should the proposition be
read to mean that any trade is superior to no trade.   In fact, it can be shown
that (subsidy-) expanded trade may, for some income distribution, be inferior
to no trade.   The proposition refers exclusively, therefore, to restricted trade
(of the form defined here).[1]

The third proposition in this class is the celebrated dictum that an
optimum tariff is superior to free trade when a country has monopoly power
in trade.   This proposition was formulated, though not with modern sophistication, as early as Mill's *Principles* [32].   When a country has the ability
to influence its terms of trade the marginal terms of trade diverge from the
average terms of trade and a discrepancy arises, under free trade, between
the domestic rate of transformation in production and the foreign rate of
transformation.   This divergence can be eliminated and the equality of
these with the domestic rate of substitution in consumption achieved, resulting in the first-best optimum solution, when a suitable tariff rate is levied
[5, Chapter II; 118].   This optimum tariff rate will naturally depend on
the income distribution chosen.   Hence, the proposition holds only for
variable tariff rates, and in the situation sense.   For the multi-commodity
case an optimum tariff *structure* will exist, which in turn will vary with the
income distribution [118].

The proposition concerning the superiority of the optimum tariff has
been sought to be extended to the case where the imposition of the tariff
results in retaliation.   An investigation of this question requires a behavioural assumption concerning the foreigner's response (mechanism) and
another with respect to the country's own method of accommodation to
such response.   The early assertions that, in the event of retaliation (insufficiently defined), a country could not gain from imposing an (initially, pre-
retaliation) optimum tariff have subsequently been rejected as a result of
the demonstration that, for any given income distribution, with a Cournot-
type adjustment mechanism such that each country imposes an optimum
tariff while assuming the other's tariff rate as fixed, it is *possible* (though *not*
necessary) that, if and when final equilibrium is achieved with no country
under incentive to change the tariff rate, the country imposing the initial

---

[1] The analysis in the text could be adapted to develop the proposition that welfare increases to
a maximum as restriction decreases to free trade, then falls as trade is increasingly subsidised until
welfare has fallen below the no-trade level.

optimum tariff may still be better off than under free trade.[1]   While this
proposition is valid, it should be noted that the result of a retaliatory system
depends naturally on the response mechanisms assumed.   Alternative
" rules of the game " can readily be imagined.   For instance, the retaliation
may plausibly be a function of the ability of the affected income group to
coalesce into an effective pressure group—as Kindleberger's [73] historical
study of the political sociology of the European tariff response to the influx of
cheap American corn underlines.   In this case, an integration of the protec-
tion-and-real-wages theory with the tariff-retaliation theory is called for.
The easiest way in which one can demonstrate the dependence of the
stated proposition on the response-mechanism assumed is to postulate a
retaliatory tariff that eliminates trade (for all income distributions).   Here the
reversion to no trade clearly leaves the country in a position inferior to free
trade, *ruling out the possibility* of an improvement over the free-trade situation.

While the preceding propositions rank *trade policies*, the final proposition
considered here involves a ranking of one trade policy and another *trade
policy in conjunction with a different form of policy intervention*.   This proposition
is that, when domestic distortions (*i.e.*, a divergence between domestic rates
of transformation and domestic price ratios) obtain, an optimum (production) subsidy (with free trade) is superior to any tariff intervention.   The
former policy equates the foreign rate of transformation (F.R.T.) with the
domestic rates of transformation in production (D.R.T.) and of substitution
in consumption (D.R.S.), and thus turns out to be superior to a tariff policy
which cannot ensure this [112].[2]

Ranking of Policies by Samuelson Criterion: International Advantage

From the viewpoint of international advantage, the proposition that *free
trade is superior to any trade policy* is held to be valid [126].   The proposition
holds when all the first-best assumptions obtain (though the possession of
national monopoly power in trade, as long as not exercised, is permissible).
The propositions that *free trade is superior to no trade, free trade is superior to
expanded trade and free trade is superior to restricted trade* are only special cases of
the preceding proposition.[3]

---

[1] Two other results are of interest: (1) the adjustment process may result in a " tariff cycle ":
countries may mill around the same set of tariff rates and not settle down to an equilibrium pair
of tariff rates [5, pp. 42-3]; and (2) the equilibrium pair of tariff rates, where existent, will
generally differ, depending on which country starts off the process.

[2] I have deliberately refrained from describing the optimum subsidy policy which equates
F.R.T., D.R.T. and D.R.S. as a policy which produces the first-best solution.   This is because,
whether it does or not, will depend on *which* second-best assumption causes this domestic distortion.
Where an external economy produces such a distortion, the optimum subsidy will produce the
standard first-best solution [112].   Where, however, it results from a wage differential, for instance,
the optimum subsidy *cannot* produce the standard first-best solution, although it will, of course, be
superior to any tariff intervention [112].   Incidentally, this also helps to illustrate the undesir-
ability of trying to develop the theory of the second-best in terms of the violations of optimum
conditions rather than in terms of the second-best assumptions themselves as proposed here.

[3] Several diagrammatic proofs of these propositions can be found in the literature.   Formal,
mathematical proofs, however, are not easy to come by, although they could easily be devised.

Ranking by Other Criteria: National Advantage

The bulk of the literature in the theory of trade and welfare, however, concerns the ranking of policies which yield sub-optimal results under second-best assumptions with the aid of non-purist criteria of welfare change. These analyses can be conveniently divided into those exercises that seek to evaluate the change in welfare when a trade policy is changed and those that concern the welfare change when (the trade policy remaining unchanged) some given parameter or functional relationship (*e.g.*, factor supply, known technology, etc.) shifts.

(A) *Trade Policies*

The most frequent way in which the problem is posed involves a primarily negative orientation. For instance, much of the analysis in this area concerns the demonstration that, even if the income distribution is fixed at an arbitrary level, the proposition that free trade is superior to no trade will *not necessarily* hold if there are, say, domestic distortions in the economy. Meade, using his cardinal method, extends his analysis, on the other hand, to deriving the precise conditions (*e.g.*, elasticity of transformation in domestic production, the degree of distortion, etc.) under which the trade policies being compared will rank one way or the other.[1] The analysis is sometimes extended also beyond the ranking of two trade policies. For instance, instead of merely ranking a 5% tariff and zero tariff, using either the cardinal or the ordinal method, the analyst proceeds to ask what tariff rates (constituting the policy instrument available to the policy-maker) will *maximise* welfare. The optimum level at which the available policy instrument should be used is thus the aim of this analysis, which goes beyond a mere ranking of two arbitrarily chosen levels at which the policy instrument may be used.[2] While such analysis represents a process of social-utility maximisation, it should be emphasised that, except in the highly restrictive case where *all* other forms of policy intervention are excluded from the range of available policy instruments, this optimum level of the assigned policy instrument will not generally represent the optimum, second-best solution under the stated, second-best assumptions (irrespective of what welfare criterion is being employed). This is really a point of some importance, since the bulk of the optimising welfare analysis in trade is constrained by the fact that it has been directed at finding the optimum level at which a *specific* trade policy instrument (*e.g.*, a tariff) should be used rather than the optimum level at which the optimum policy instrument (or combination of instruments) should be used to maximise social utility, subject to the stated assumptions, in an open economy.

[1] Of course, he is concerned with the effects of *marginal* changes in policies, so that his analysis amounts to ranking, say, a given tariff and a marginally increased tariff.

[2] Since Meade's analysis is usually directed at investigating the effect on welfare of a marginal change in some tariff rate (*i.e.*, $\frac{du}{dt}$ where u is the level of social welfare and t the tariff rate), the optimum tariff level can be discovered readily by putting $\frac{du}{dt}$ equal to zero.

The kinds of problems analysed can be divided broadly into two classes according as the second-best assumptions relate to the: (1) domestic, or the (2) foreign sector. In the former category a wide assortment of second-best assumptions has been considered: external economies; monopolies in commodity markets; infant industry arguments; factor-reward differentials between sectors of use; factor-price rigidity and increasing returns to scale. In the latter class the stage is held by the theory of discriminatory tariff reduction. These arguments are briefly discussed here, to illustrate the prefatory analysis.

(a) *External Economies.* Where the standard first-best assumptions obtain, with the exception of externalities in production, the actual market solution will be characterised by a domestic distortion (*i.e.*, a divergence between the commodity price-ratio and D.R.T.). The classic example of such externality is the dependence of honey production on the level of neighbouring apple output. The time-honoured infant-industry argument also involves externality [8].[1] Recently the theoretical interest in the co-ordination of investment decisions has also given us another impressive example of external economies under a régime of decentralised decision-making [97].

The resulting domestic distortions have been shown to invalidate, for instance, the proposition that free trade is (necessarily) superior to no trade [112, 117]. It is no longer possible to rank these two trade policies uniquely, either for all income distributions or (more importantly) even with any assigned income distribution for all possible cases.[2] Similarly, it can be shown that no tariff rate may exist, in any given empirical case, which will produce greater welfare than free trade [112]. The reason is obvious. Under free trade, domestic distortions imply that F.R.T.($=$F.P.) $=$

---

[1] Although the infant industry case has been classified here, it must be admitted that, formally, it has dimensions of dynamic analysis which go beyond the traditional range of external economies. Allowing for this fact, however, the case for assistance to infant industries *does* rest on an assumption of externality, as pointed out by Meade [8] and recently by Johnson [133]. For a different formal description and analysis of the infant-industry case, Haberler [117] may be consulted: his analysis, however, does not bring out the externality aspect as forcefully as it needs to be.

[2] As stated earlier, the ranking will depend on, among other things, the degree of divergence, the elasticity of transformation in production and so on. In this connection it is probably necessary to point out that, in the standard analysis of external economies, it is not made clear that the externality may disappear at certain levels of output of either activity. With apple blossoms and bees, where the former are already too large relative to the latter, any increase in blossoms output by diversion of resources from bees' production will not be subjected to externality effects. In terms of the standard geometry (ignored throughout the text of this paper), the production possibility curve, for certain ranges of output combinations, may thus be characterised by the equality of D.R.T. and D.P. (domestic prices). If, then, free trade carries the economy's production within this range, the domestic distortions will be inapplicable and the standard, first-best solution (*i.e.*, free trade is superior to no trade) will become applicable. Thus, strictly speaking, the analysis in the text requires that the domestic distortions should be within the relevant ranges of production. This, in turn, makes very clear the crucial nature of income distribution: for, with one income distribution, an $x\%$ tariff may bring the economy within the range of domestic distortions, whereas, for another, it may not, thereby influencing the ranking of policies.

D.R.S.($=$D.P.) $\neq$ D.R.T. (where D.P. and F.P. are the domestic and foreign price ratios respectively). On the other hand, a tariff may equate F.R.T. and D.R.T., but will disrupt the equality of F.R.T. with D.R.S. Since two sub-optimal positions are being compared, the conclusions already stated follow readily. The optimal solution for domestic distortions is clearly a production subsidy (or tax-cum-subsidy) which will equate F.R.T., D.R.T. and D.R.S., and thereby achieve the first-best solution.[1]

(b) *Monopoly in Product Markets.* The monopoly argument is frequently taken to collapse into a simple case of domestic distortion. Hence, it is regarded as formally equivalent to the external economy argument. It follows, then, that, once again, free trade cannot be shown to be (necessarily) superior to no trade; and also that no tariff may exist, in any given case, which may yield higher welfare than free trade.

Where, however, the monopoly argument differs from the external economy case is in the fact that the degree of monopoly itself may be a function of the rate of tariff [133]. Take, for instance, the extreme case where the introduction of free trade eliminates the monopoly power and turns the domestic monopolist into a perfect competitor. In this case the proposition that free trade is superior to no trade, for instance, will still be valid. The formal identity with the external economy case therefore breaks down.

(c) *Factor-reward Differentials between Sectors.* The presence of a wage differential between sectors (for remunerating the same factor) represents a market imperfection, constituting a departure from first-best assumptions under certain circumstances.[2] Where it is distortionary, there are two immediate consequences. The rate at which this factor and any other factor are being substituted in production in different sectors will no longer be equal. This will result in a reduction in the transformation possibilities. The production possibility curve will " shrink in." Further, at each point on the shrunk-in locus the domestic price ratio will diverge from the domestic rate of transformation (*along the shrunk-in locus*), so that we also are in a situation characterised by domestic distortions.

---

[1] In the light of this analysis it is possible to understand the significant qualification introduced by Haberler [4, p. 57] in his discussion of the correct prescription in the infant-industry case: " It should also be added that it is, *a priori*, probable that in many cases not a customs duty but an export bounty would be in order in as much as external economies may be realizable in the export rather than in import industries. . . . The fact that the infant industry argument is almost exclusively employed to recommend import restrictions and practically never to justify the opposite . . . shows clearly the bias of those who employ it." Of course, Haberler's case would require, as the optimal solution, an optimum (production) subsidy to the export industry. It cannot be argued, however, that if this is ruled out the trade-subsidy policy (believed guardedly by Haberler to be desirable) will necessarily produce, or will even be " likely " to produce, better results than any alternative form of trade or other intervention.

[2] A detailed discussion of the conditions under which a wage differential may be regarded as distortionary is contained in the paper by myself and V. K. Ramaswami [112]. The qualifications to which the present analysis is subject are also considered there. Further comments on the problem are found in Johnson [133]. Credit for pioneering the problem belongs to Hagen [118].

From these two effects, it is easy to see that: (1) free trade is not (necessarily) superior to no trade; (2) an optimum production subsidy (or tax-cum-subsidy) which equates D.R.S., F.R.T. and D.R.T. (along the shrunk-in transformation locus) is superior to any tariff; and (3) an optimum subsidy on labour-use, which directly offsets the wage differential, produces the standard first-best result.

(d) *Factor-price Rigidity*. Haberler [117] has sharply distinguished between factor immobility and factor-price rigidity, showing that the former leaves the welfare propositions valid under first-best conditions unaffected, whereas the latter manages to invalidate them. By arguing that factor-price rigidity in the face of commodity price-shift will lead to unemployment, Haberler has demonstrated the possibility that free trade, for any assigned income distribution and given empirical situation, may produce a deterioration in welfare in relation to no trade.[1] Haberler's analysis has recently been refined by Johnson [133], who has investigated alternative ways in which factor-price rigidity may be defined and, in turn, combined with assumptions concerning mobility of the factors of production, to produce a varying range of propositions which confirm Haberler's results.

(e) *Increasing Returns to Scale*. When an activity in the system is subject to increasing returns to scale the locus of transformation possibilities may lose its convexity. Matthews [123] has demonstrated how, in this case, a

---

[1] This is illustrated by Haberler [117], for a given income distribution, as follows. Taking factor immobility as well, he shows production and consumption under no trade at S, with S.R

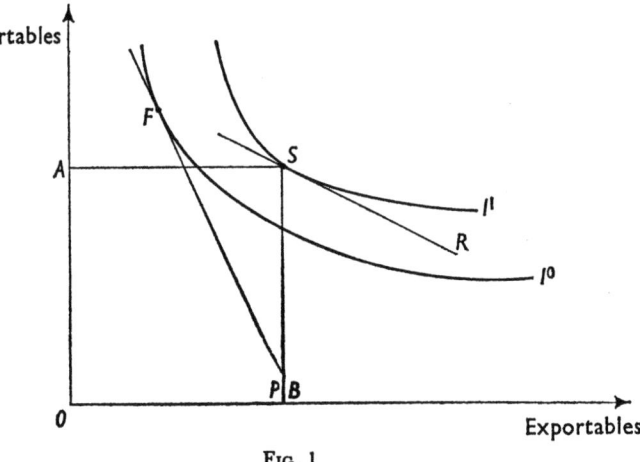

FIG. 1

as the price ratio between exportables and importables. With free trade at foreign price ratio F.P., the production in importables falls to P and consumption moves to F. The result is a deterioration in welfare. Free trade, for the given income distribution, is inferior to no trade. (It has to be assumed, of course, that the factor-price rigidity is due to institutional rather than voluntary reasons.) I might refer, incidentally, to the analysis of a similar problem [97], where the wage-rate in the agricultural sector is different from the marginal value product (whereas the industrial sector pays according to the marginal productivity principle), the wage-rate being "rigid" in the agricultural sector.

country may be worse off under free trade than under no trade. Thus, under this second-best assumption, it is not possible to maintain that free trade is (necessarily) superior to no trade.[1]

Concavity also underlines the fact that the optimising solutions (and corresponding conditions) strictly imply only local maximisation. It can be shown that the optimum optimorum may not be reached by free trade when there is concavity over some (though not the entire) range of the transformation locus, although free trade may continue to be superior to no trade.[2]

[1] However, questions of stability of equilibrium arise here which have to be carefully tackled. Tinbergen [127] has constructed an ingenious example which also illustrates the point in the text. In the accompanying illustration the production associated with free trade happens to be at P (which is a stable point) and the result is welfare deterioration in relation to no trade.

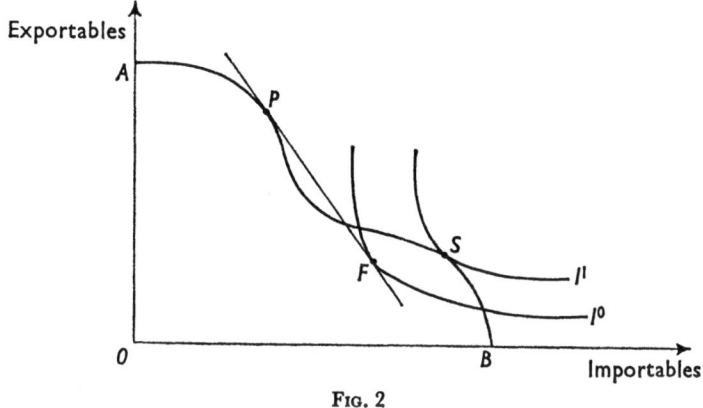

Fig. 2

[2] Thus, in the illustration, S represents the no-trade point, F and P the consumption and production points corresponding to free trade but representing only a local maximum, while F' and P' represent the equilibrium points corresponding to the optimum optimorum position under free trade.

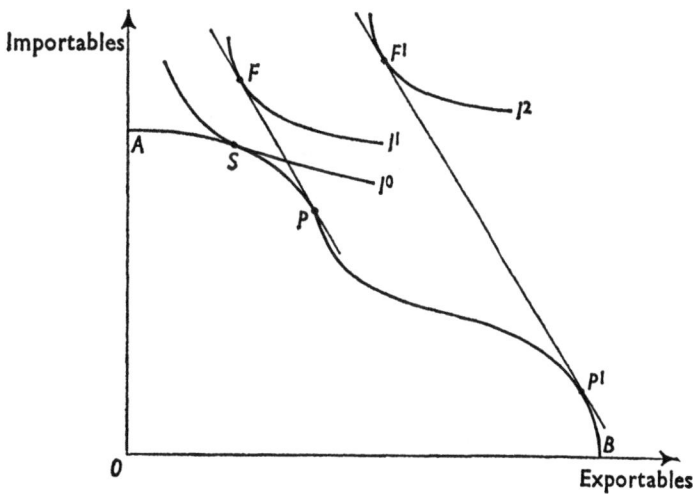

Fig. 3

(f) *Customs Unions.* So far we have been concerned with departures from first-best assumptions on the domestic side. The welfare problem has, however, also been posed in terms of distortions arising from the presence of tariffs, subsidies and other such policies in foreign trade. Thus, for instance, a typical question has been whether, with tariffs continuing on one country, if the tariffs on another are reduced the national welfare will be increased. For any two tariff rates compared in such a situation, the ranking is subject to the income distribution chosen. Even with the income distribution chosen, no unique ranking is generally possible on an *a priori* basis.

Take, for instance, the model where the home country A can import, without having the power to affect the terms at which it can import, a commodity from either of two countries B and C. For the levels of demands relevant to the defined situation, C supplies M cheaper than B, while A is the highest-cost producer. In the initial situation, assume a tariff rate t_o which permits C to compete successfully and secure A's market. Suppose, however, that A removes the tariff on imports from B but must continue to impose it on C's exports. If this makes B's export of M to A cheaper than C's, A is shifting its source of supply to a higher-cost producer. The former situation was characterised by D.R.T. = D.R.S. $\neq$ F.R.T.; the latter is as well (since the most favourable rate at which A can transform its exports into imports is that determined by C's c.i.f. price in A). The choice between them cannot be made on an *a priori* basis; the choice of income distribution will also influence the ranking [7, 121]. For any given income distribution, using the ordinalist method, the ranking can naturally be worked out for any *given* empirical situation. Meade's cardinalist method would also give a unique ranking for a specific *empirical* situation.

There are many other ways in which a similar problem can be set up. One may take a case where A specialises in X and exchanges it for both Y (from B) and Z (from C). There is a uniform tariff rate on the (perfectly elastic supply of) imports of both Y and Z into A. The actual situation, from the viewpoint of A's welfare, is characterised by

$$\left(\frac{P_y}{P_z}\right)_F = \left(\frac{P_y}{P_z}\right)_D \text{ but } \left(\frac{P_x}{P_y}\right)_F \neq \left(\frac{P_x}{P_y}\right)_D \text{ and } \left(\frac{P_x}{P_z}\right)_F \neq \left(\frac{P_x}{P_z}\right)_D$$

where the suffixes F and D refer to foreign and domestic price-ratios in A. Suppose now that the tariff on Z is abolished *while that on Y is continued.* Then the country moves into a situation where

$$\left(\frac{P_x}{P_z}\right)_F = \left(\frac{P_x}{P_z}\right)_D \text{ but } \left(\frac{P_y}{P_z}\right)_F \neq \left(\frac{P_y}{P_z}\right)_D \text{ and } \left(\frac{P_x}{P_y}\right)_F \neq \left(\frac{P_x}{P_y}\right)_D$$

The comparison is again between two sub-optimal situations in this case. No *a priori*, unique ranking is possible [7]; and the income distribution will in general influence the ranking even when a *specific* situation has been defined (with reference to the functional and parametric aspects).

(B) *Non-trade Policies*

So far only different trade policies have been compared. However, there is a considerable literature even on the effects of changes in the general equilibrium parameters and functional relationships on national welfare. Among the prominent contributions in this field are analyses of: (1) the effect of change in factor supply, and (2) the effect of technical change on welfare, when the economy is engaged in trade.

In the former category the analysis by Johnson [5, Chapter III] and myself [111] has shown how the effect of a change in factor supply on the growth of real income can be approximated, making allowance for the effect of the adjustment of the terms of trade *when the country has monopoly power in trade.*   The analysis has also been extended to establish the conditions under which the growth of factor supply may actually result in the deterioration of the country's welfare through the loss of real income from worsened terms of trade outweighing the direct gain from expansion—a possibility seen independently by Edgeworth, Johnson [5, Chapter V] and myself and now widely known as the case of "immiserising growth."   Basically the same analysis can be adapted to the investigation of the impact of transfers of factors of production from one country to another on each's welfare, since the only substantive difference is that the growth of factors of production is, in one case, net for the two countries, while in the latter case there is no addition to the factor supply of the two countries together but only its redistribution [5].

This analysis has also been turned around to examine the relative advantages of absorption of marginal increment in population or capital stock at home or abroad [119, 122].[1]   The analysis has further been reworked in relation to the effects of shifts in technology.   The results of Findlay and Grubert [62] have been used to examine the effect of different types of technical progress on national welfare, again under the second-best assumption of national monopoly power in trade [2].

Ranking by Less-restrictive Criteria: International Advantage

So far, the rankings have been concerned with national advantage. Largely owing to the nineteenth-century concern with international advan-

---

[1] This problem (unlike the others listed here) is of interest even under first-best assumptions for the economy.   For instance, if the rental on capital abroad is higher than at home, and reflects the marginal value product, it would appear to be to private and social advantage to invest abroad.   However, this is not correct, as what is socially relevant is the marginal return on the investments abroad.   If the country already has invested capital abroad a fall in its rate of return through further investment will reduce the previous return, and the net benefit to the country will be *less* than the average rate of return, as Jasay [119] has noted in a valuable contribution.   An important practical point may also be that the rate of return on foreign investment will always be less than the marginal-value product abroad because of corporation taxation [122].   And so on.   The possibility of affecting the terms of trade differently according as home or foreign investment is chosen, which arises only under the second-best assumption of national monopoly power in trade, introduces still further theoretical questions of interest.

tage, however, much interest still continues to be exhibited in questions of international advantage.

The great bulk of the questions have again related to the ranking of trade policies when some second-best assumption obtains. Meade [8, 9] has worked out numerous problems, investigating the optimum level of a specific trade policy under the stated second-best assumptions. There are other contributions, such as Viner's [9] and Lipsey's [121] analyses of customs unions and Ozga's [85] examination of unilateral tariff reduction by a country in a world with other tariffs. These reinforce the proposition that, in general, no *a priori* ranking of policies is possible and that the choice of income distribution can affect the ranking when second-best assumptions obtain and sub-optimal situations are being ranked.

Meade's exercises, for instance, range over many such comparisons: (1) A imports Y_1 and Y_2 from B; Y_1 and Y_2 are substitutable or complementary in A's consumption. A duty at $t_2\%$ is levied on the import of Y_2 and cannot be removed. Would a tariff on the import of Y_1 be then worthwhile and, if so, what is its optimum level? (2) A imports Y_1, which is complementary or substitutable in A's consumption with X_2, which A exports to B and on whose exports B levies an import duty. Should a tariff be imposed on the import of Y_1 into A, and, if so, what is the optimum level? (3) Or there might be second-best assumptions in the domestic economy of a country. For instance, if there is a divergence in the marginal cost and value of a commodity which competes with imports, would a tariff be worthwhile, and, if so, what is its optimum level?

Central Limitations of the Propositions

Regardless of the criterion of welfare change employed, the rankings considered hitherto are valid only in a static context. At least two serious limitations of these propositions spring from the admission of dynamic elements:

(1) The ranking of two tariff rates will be a function of how these two rates are reached. Starting from a current tariff rate of $\alpha\%$, moves to a tariff of $x\%$ and $y\%$ will, in general, rank x and y differently (for the same income distribution) than when the move takes place from an initial tariff rate of $\beta\%$. In fact, even the paths of adjustments from a single current position to each of the pairs of rates of tariffs ultimately reached may not be unique, so that, for different paths chosen, the ultimate ranking may be different. These possibilities, however, are ruled out, for instance, by the restrictive assumption of constant terms of trade (for all tariff rates) in Samuelson's 1939 proof [125] of the proposition that free trade is superior to no trade and, in Kemp's extension [120] of the proof to the case when the terms of trade will vary with the volume of trade, by the (implicit) assumption that the foreign countries' trade offers at different terms of trade are not a function of the trade policy of the country. This restrictiveness is serious

in a world where policy changes, especially in international trade, are inevitably accompanied by protracted negotiations concerning the reciprocity of " benefits," and the interdependence of countries' trade policies is an impressive and irrefutable fact [107].

(2) These propositions are further limited in their reliance on one-period, static criteria.   There are undoubtedly ways in which one can demonstrate that free trade is superior to no trade, for instance, in a multi-period, dynamic, welfare framework.   Thus, for instance, it can be established that, for the *same* initial conditions, time profile of consumption in each period, time-horizon and the structural composition of the terminal capital stocks (*e.g.*, the ratio in which they are to be held), free trade will lead to a *greater* quantity of terminal capital stocks than no trade [1].[1]   While, however, the conclusions of welfare statics can be sustained in welfare dynamics within certain frameworks, they are also refuted within others.   For instance, with a *terminal* preference function (*e.g.*, the income level in the terminal period), savings ratio a function of the income distribution, and the income distribution entirely a function of the market-imputed incomes, it is possible for free trade to be *inferior* to no trade.[2]

VII. Measurement of Gains and Losses

While, in these significant respects, the welfare propositions of pure theory have continued to be limited, the static methods of welfare analysis have been strikingly extended into the field of measurement of losses and gains (as between the welfare levels reached under the ranked policies). Some of the principal factors motivating this shift have already been analysed: the impact of the shift to less purist criteria of welfare and the general demand for such measurement.   To these we must add a third, interesting, factor: the analytical use of such measurement in determining a " scientific tariff " [132].   This itself has its origin in the practice of computing the economic cost of given policies.

Frequently policies are pursued for a specific non-economic objective. For instance, a tariff may be imposed to achieve an assigned level of domestic production of an importable commodity.   The cost of that tariff, then, is the cost of achieving this level of domestic production (which constitutes the non-economic objective).   This notion can be extended in two profitable ways:

(1) Suppose that a tariff is the only policy instrument available.   However, the non-economic objective, which consists of a *fixed-target* type of assignment (*e.g.*, achievement of a given level of import-competing produc-

---

[1] This model, from the seminal work of Dorfman, Solow and Samuelson [113], relies on two main assumptions: (1) perfect foresight; and (2) a centralised authority whose preference function specifies the time-profile of consumption, etc.

[2] I am afraid, therefore, that Caves [3, p. 265] is not correct in arguing that " static welfare economics is perfectly valid in a dynamic setting for the welfare problems discussed here if the assumption is made that factors of production and commodities are perfectly mobile, that is, can be re-allocated with infinite speed and zero cost."

tion or the reduction of imports to a specific value), can be fulfilled in numerous ways. For instance, if the objective is to achieve a given reduction in the value of imports this could be achieved by tariffs on *one* or *more* of the various imported commodities. We have here, then, a problem of choosing that tariff *structure* which *minimises* the cost of achieving the assigned non-economic objective. This is a familiar problem in economic analysis, with a standard solution.

Johnson [132], in a powerful and ingenious paper, has developed this analysis, christening the minimum-cost tariff structure as " scientific " [on the (*Oxford English Dictionary*) ground that it is evolved with the aid of expert knowledge]. He uses the notion of the scientific tariff to consider the kinds of tariff structure that would be called for under a wide range of non-economic objectives such as self-sufficiency, promotion of a " way of life," increased diversification, etc., each such general non-economic objective being reduced to a suitable, operational objective, such as reduction in the value of imports and increase in the value of import-competing production.[1]

(2) But this notion of the tariff structure that minimises the cost of a fixed-target type of non-economic objective is itself restrictive. For the analysis can be meaningfully extended to the case where the policy-maker is willing to consider a whole range of variables, representing *varying degrees of fulfilment of a non-economic objective*. For instance, a policy-maker interested in reducing the value of imports may not lay down a specific value of imports as the target, but would like to choose from varying values of imports *after* ascertaining the (*minimum*) costs attached to the tariff structures that lead to these targets. The choice made would then have the usual property (associated with maximising behaviour): any departure from the selected tariff structure would change the value of imports by an amount which, for the policy-maker, is not worth the change in cost involved. The scientific tariff structure associated with this choice thus exhibits the familiar optimality property from the viewpoint of the policy-maker.[2]

---

[1] There are two respects, however, in which the analysis, as presented by Johnson, may be misleading: (1) He equates the marginal benefit: marginal cost ratios for tariffs on different imports, as a condition for minimum-cost tariff structure. It should be emphasised that this is only a necessary condition (which would have to be rewritten for cases involving inequalities). (2) Secondly, he frequently talks of " measuring " a non-economic objective in terms of some observable variable: for instance, " the simplest possible measure of the benefit achieved by such a tariff [to provide national self-sufficiency and independence] in the value of imports excluded by it" [132, p. 342]. This gives the impression that Johnson is setting up an *independent* utility function to *measure* the welfare level reached (with respect to a non-economic objective) by a tariff structure: a procedure which may well be debated. What Johnson really is doing, however, is to translate vague objectives like " national self-sufficiency " into *precise* and usable objectives such as " reduction in the value of imports." And that is both necessary for the analysis to get off the ground and also a valid procedure.

[2] Johnson [132, p. 341] refers to this question of choice among scientific tariff structures in terms of choosing the tariff " level " (which is presumably to be obtained, in his formulation, by equating the marginal benefits and costs). This may be a little misleading because, in general, the scientific tariff structures for varying degrees of fulfilment of a non-economic objective may *not* be just scalar multiples of each other.

An important limitation of the foregoing analysis is that it specifies a non-economic objective and considers tariffs as the only available instrument variables. While, however, this approach does yield the scientific *tariff* structure, it is possible that the same non-economic objective could have been achieved at a *smaller* cost if the range of policy instruments had been wider. An interesting paper of Corden [128] illustrates this principle tangentially. Working with a two-good model (which eliminates the question of a tariff *structure*) and the fixed-target objective of attaining a *given level* of production of the importable good, Corden has shown that, for unchangeable terms of trade, a (production) subsidy is less expensive than a tariff, whereas, for variable terms of trade, a tariff-and-subsidy measure is superior to either a tariff or a subsidy. Johnson [133], drawing on Young's earlier work, has shown, on the other hand, that, for unchangeable terms of trade, a tariff is more efficient than a subsidy when the non-economic objective is an assigned reduction in the volume of *imports* (in a two-good model). These contributions already begin to pull away in the direction of a scientific *economic* policy, as distinct from a scientific tariff (or even trade) policy.[1]

While the measurement of gains and losses has been used *theoretically* to derive scientific tariffs, its *empirical* application has been for the more pedestrian but surer task of estimating the cost of changes in tariff policies. Among the most striking of these exercises must be reckoned Johnson's [131] attempt at measuring the gain to the United Kingdom from joining the European Common Market and Wemelsfelder's [135] study of the short-term effect of the lowering of import duties in West Germany.[2] These analyses carry the application of the welfare propositions of pure theory of trade very much further than the early, interesting, attempts, most prominently that of Marris [134], at estimating the foreign rate of transformation with a view to deriving directional policy conclusions concerning tariffs.[3]

Although these exercises represent a significant, new trend in the welfare analysis of pure theory, they none the less have limitations which reflect essentially the deficiencies of the conceptual framework underlying the measurements employed.

[1] Although the papers by Johnson [131, 132] and Corden [128] have been singled out in the text for their ingenious and path-breaking approach to the analysis of non-economic objectives, there are two other prior contributions which merit mention here. (1) Johnson's [129] analysis of the relationship between the tariff that would produce maximum revenue (a non-economic objective) and the optimum tariff (that equates F.R.T. with D.R.T. and D.R.S. under variable terms of trade) dates back to 1951–52. (2) Meade [9, Chapters V, VI] had also handled, in 1955, two problems which consist in the choice between a tariff and a domestic tax with a specific non-economic objective (of raising given revenue) from the viewpoint of minimising the loss in world welfare—thereby anticipating the approach in the contributions of Corden [128] and Johnson [133] towards the formulation of policy questions, not just in terms of trade policy, but in more general terms.

[2] There are other, less-impressive, estimates by Verdoorn and Scitovsky [7] of the gains from European integration.

[3] Marris' [134] study, while important as a pioneering empirical exercise in trade and welfare, is unpersuasive in interpretation and analysis of the statistical data.

Two different ways in which measurement has been attempted can be distinguished.   They reflect, in turn, the ordinalist and cardinalist methods of (non-Samuelsonian) welfare analysis discussed in the previous section.[1]

The former, ordinalist, procedure yields several alternative measures as in other applications of " surplus " theory.   The theorist can choose from a large number of possible measures, some of which have been analysed at length by Johnson and myself [2].   Johnson [132] happens to choose Hicks' compensating variation for his measurement.[2]   Meade's method, on the other hand, yields a unique measure of the cost of a change in policy.   This measure is tantamount to the Marshallian surplus measures, as is evident from the fact that his method estimates gains (losses) as the increase (decrease) in the volume of transactions in each commodity multiplied by the excess of utility derived by the buyer over the utility of that commodity to the seller, a divergence that is measured, for instance, in the case of a tax, by the rate of tax on the assumption that the price paid equals the marginal utility to the buyer and the price received the utility to the seller.   Both Johnson's and Meade's measures are identical except for the differences caused by: (1) Meade's assumption of small, and Johnson's of large, changes,[3] and (2) Meade's Marshallian measure and Johnson's use of the compensating variation.[4]

The identity, except for the differences noted, obtains despite the different views concerning utility measurement because of the fact that, from the present viewpoint, Johnson's assumption of a well-behaved community preference function (enjoying the properties of a *single* individual's preference function) converges on Meade's *de facto* assumption of equal weights for each buyer and seller.   In the two respects in which the measurements diverge, Johnson's analysis clearly is an improvement.   And yet, from the *operational* viewpoint, Johnson's ordinalist approach runs into an insuperable difficulty.   How is the analyst to estimate the contours (albeit at the relevant points) of the hypothesised social indifference map?   Meade's (theoretically less attractive) method runs into no such snags (though *other* difficulties of econometric measurement no doubt persist).   Since the aim of these exercises is to measure welfare changes *in practice*, operational methods may well be judged to be superior to analytically more impressive results.

---

[1] A partial-equilibrium approach to measurement has also been suggested by Corden and Johnson [130], but is subject to well-known drawbacks that are explicitly recognised by these authors.   [See also Wan [148].]

[2] Hence, the cost of protection, when a tariff is levied, is measured in terms of the compensation that would leave the country as well off, under the tariff, as previously under free trade.

[3] This introduces the fraction $\frac{1}{2}$ into Johnson's formulae, stemming from his having to integrate the area under the triangle for large changes.

[4] This leads Johnson to argue in terms of the " compensated " (*i.e.*, constant-utility) indifference curve and to use a pure substitution term for changed consumption, whereas Meade does not adjust for changed utility and takes the entire change in consumption in his measure of the gain in utility to buyers.   Johnson is equally more cautious in trying to adjust for rent in his measure of the production costs.

Either method, however, leaves out of reckoning, in consonance with the limitations of the conceptual static approach to welfare on which it is based, the dynamic elements in the absence of which the exercises are reduced in their usefulness.   For instance, in relation to the estimates of the gains from European integration, it has frequently been noted that these estimates ignore significant considerations like the effects of competition on efficiency, on innovation, etc.   They also omit the implications of improved bargaining power in negotiating tariff and other trade concessions.[1]

The most serious limitation springs from the conceptual difficulty of applying the surplus analysis when the economy is producing and/or absorbing commodities for purposes other than consumption.   How, for instance, is the " consumer's surplus " on the purchase of investment goods to be estimated?   To assert that this can be done as with consumer goods is to assume that the price paid for investment goods currently reflects the ultimate utility that will accrue from the production resulting from them.   This assumption, however, begs a whole lot of questions which are central to the issues of dynamic welfare economics.   For instance, the " correct " valuation of the investment goods will vary in general with the choice of the time-horizon.[2]   These issues cannot be conjured away.   They are compelling when welfare comparisons are being made.

While these limitations persist, welfare analysis in pure theory has clearly reached a degree of sophistication and feasibility of useful empirical application which is impressive.   These developments have brought within the fold of economic analysis many problems with direct policy relevance.

One of the major " casualties " of this progress has been the historic intellectual dominance of the " free trader."   The reorientation in the view concerning the role of the analyst—the acceptance of non-economic objectives, the willingness to consider sub-optimal situations instead of strictly utopian prescriptions—has overwhelmed the profession with a new mood of judging " each case on its merits " and tailoring policies to specific objectives and situations.   The few, surviving " free traders " have, in consequence, been in disarray.   At the turn of the century they readily admitted the solitary, twin examples of " good " tariffs: the optimum (under national monopoly power) and the infant industry tariffs.   They even proudly claimed that it was a " free trader," John Stuart Mill, who foresaw the formal arguments to support them.   With the breathtaking increase in the " deviations " from the free-trade case, however, this easy " theoretical " superiority over the pragmatic protectionists has disappeared.[3]   With it, the free traders,

---

[1] It should be noted, however, that the authors of the estimates are generally aware of most of these limitations.

[2] Moreover, the decentralisation of decision-making adds to the difficulties (*e.g.*, inconsistency and myopia in behaviour) created by imperfect foresight and necessitates a revised approach to the notions of " rational " decision making, and hence of welfare.

[3] I use the objective " pragmatic " with special emphasis.   The theological protectionist is as much at fault as the theological free trader.   But whereas the former has always been taken lightly, the latter has traditionally had an intellectual respectability which is now a rapidly wasting asset.

greatly reduced in number, have now taken to resting their case exclusively on " empirical," practical bases. Two varieties of arguments are frequent: (1) The unsophisticated argument is that, in practice, it is impossible to estimate the " distortions " and hence the tariff structure and level which they justify. Hence, faced with this ignorance, the economist should not advocate a move away from the free-trade situation. This contention must be rejected. Not merely does it ignore the growing trend towards estimation. It also attaches an unacceptable special weight to the situation of a zero-tariff. Indeed, even if the fact of ignorance were admitted, the most one could say was that no ranking of trade policies was possible in practice. Why should the free trader be at an advantage here? If it were contended that a departure from a given position would be incapable of positive justification, and hence free trade should be the policy, the free trader is surely worsted in the debate, since the given situation is almost always characterised by the absence of free trade. This entire approach to the validation of the prescription of free trade is thus unpersuasive. (2) A more sophisticated approach admits that distortions exist and welfare-increasing tariffs may be devised by economists. However, in practice, the way tariffs are politically engineered, they are almost always imposed so as to bring about a deterioration in welfare. This argument admits that the zero-tariff position may not be the optimal one. It merely asserts that the admissibility of tariffs will lead in practice to another sub-optimal position which is inferior. Hence the economist ought to support free trade as a political prescription.[1] It is surely difficult to accept this logic. Surely it is not demonstrable that tariffs will always be " perverse " or are " likely " to be perverse. It is equally unpersuasive to assume that politicians will readily accept the free-trade prescription when their revealed preference has continuously been for *some* tariffs (though not for no trade), but that they will reject the prescription concerning the " correct " tariffs and instead settle for perverse tariffs.[2]

[1] This argument has a long, historical tradition. It is worth quoting the famous passage of Edgeworth, arising out of Bickerdike's discussion of the case for optimum tariffs: " Thus the direct use of the theory is likely to be small. But it is to be feared that its abuse will be considerable. It affords to unscrupulous advocates of vulgar Protection a peculiarly specious pretext for introducing the thin end of the wedge. Mr. Bickerdike may be compared to a scientist who, by a new analysis, has discovered that strychnine may be administered in small doses with prospect of advantage in one or two more cases than was previously known; the result of this discovery may be to render the drug more easily procurable by those whose intention is not medicinal. . . . Let us admire the skill of the analyst, but label the subject of his investigation POISON " [4, p. 53].

[2] Ethical arguments are also current. For instance, some free traders claim to be " internationalists " and object to the optimum tariff argument as purely " nationalistic " and of the " beggar-my-neighbour " variety. At the purely ethical level, of course, no argument can be refuted. In this instance, however, one can point out that free trade is optimal internationally only in the situation sense, so that the problem of income distribution does remain with the " internationalists." Moreover, the free-trade case does not take cognisance of non-economic objectives *or* dynamic welfare complications.

VIII. Trade Theory and Developmental Planning

While any " orthodox " survey of international economics would undoubtedly have terminated with the preceding Section, it would be singularly unfortunate if I did not address a few closing remarks to the small but important and growing literature on developmental planning (*in practice*) in its trade aspects. Happily, the subject has been brilliantly analysed in a companion Survey paper by Chenery [139] so that I can confine myself to certain ideas which have value in supplementing Chenery's account.

Broadly speaking, the classes of models that have been used to guide the choice of trade (and production) policy divide conveniently into two sets: (1) the highly simplified, decision models which usually anchor on some striking characteristic of the planned economy; and (2) more elaborate, inter-industry models. The latter, in turn, classify into models that deal with mere consistency and those that also attempt partial or fuller optimisation.

Among the class of simple, decision models, several can naturally be identified. The two most interesting, however, appear to be those that are associated with the notions of a wage-goods bottleneck and a capital-goods bottleneck. For instance, a model that postulates the availability of wage-goods (say, food) as the constraint on increased investment and growth (in an overpopulated economy with surplus labour) has prompted in practice a trade policy characterised by imported foodgrains and focuses sharply on the role of PL480 variety of foreign aid to developing countries [136]. On the other hand, a two-sector model, with two different investment and consumption goods, helps to highlight the role of developing an adequate capital-goods production base in supporting the targeted rate of investment at some future date (if the economy is faced with a shortfall in exchange earnings currently and prospectively) and hence has resulted in the utilisation of exchange to build up capacity in heavy industries [141].[1]

The central limitation of these models, however, is that they can be treacherous in ignoring *other* equally important factors: as in most economic problems, planning is necessarily a complex process. Hence, more detailed, inter-industry models which *permit* the introduction of much other information, have come to be extensively employed in framing developmental plans. Among the operational models actually used, the formulations have generally been limited in being both static and centred on just consistency [140]. Using the Leontief, static-exercise approach, the analyst takes an autonomous

---

[1] While these simple models do often serve to make an important point clear, as for instance the necessity to have a capital-goods industry, they fail in giving a clear guide line on the *magnitudes* with which the planners should work. For the latter, more detailed work, involving also other constraints in the system, will be necessary. Reliance on the former alone, therefore, may do far more harm than good. For a discussion of some of the fallacies which have actually sprung from over-reliance on such simplified modes of reasoning, the reader may refer to my paper [97].

export vector and *either* uses the concept of an *import-structure* (involving an import-coefficients matrix analogous to the input-coefficients matrix [142]) to derive the import pattern and total corresponding to the assigned bill of goods *or* derives *imports as residuals* by taking an assigned set of production targets and setting them off against the requirements worked out from the assigned bill of goods. The former approach, using the notion of an import structure, is clearly inappropriate to a planning model which, in looking ahead, need not be tied down to an arbitrary, base-year import structure and, indeed, in doing so, rejects out of hand the important choice (available to the planner) between domestic production and imports. In this respect, the imports-as-residuals approach, used, for instance, in the Indian planning framework [140], is superior.[1]

It is possible, however, to introduce explicit optimisation into these procedures, at varying levels. The most interesting innovation, from the present viewpoint, is the operational determination of the *shadow* exchange rate, as outlined by Chenery [139] in his Survey and claimed to have been used to determine the choice between imports and domestic production of commodities for Israel by him and Bruno [138] in an excellent paper which develops a useful way of framing *alternative* programmes from which the planner may make his ultimate choice. While the objectives in these exercises are to achieve partial optimisation (in limited areas of the economy) and the frameworks are essentially static, the principle of optimisation used merely reflects the basic insights of the theory of trade and welfare, and there is every prospect that further work in this area will clear the way for an operational and empirically meaningful use of trade theory in developmental planning.[2]

IX. CONCLUDING REMARKS

The overwhelming impression that this survey leaves is one of an area of inquiry which has been unusually active and is witnessing the emergence of many new trends. A growing concern with empirical verification, an explicit introduction of dynamic modes of analysis, the recognition of the importance of intermediates and capital goods, a policy orientation in welfare economics leading to interest in measurement and the attempts at the operational use of trade theory in developmental planning represent, as of today, the gravitational centres towards which the analytical interests of the

[1] Of course, in choosing the assigned domestic production targets themselves, the planner may have *implicitly* made a choice on some sort of " optimising " lines. More usually, however, the domestic production targets are in varying degrees " arbitrary."

[2] For instance, if there are no distortions of any sort, either internally or externally, a static (traditionalist) optimisation procedure, in a programming framework, would yield the equality of F.P. and D.P., and of F.R.T. and D.R.T. In this sense, the programming approach merely reflects the insights of trade theory. This is, after all, what one would expect, since the proposition that free trade is superior to a tariff (under standard first-best assumptions) is a statement *merely* about the relationship between F.P. and D.P., and *not* about the institutions by which this equality is brought about. The unwary reader, therefore, should note that nothing of what may have been said in favour of *free trade*, for instance, is an argument in favour of *laissez-faire*.

profession are moving. In some of these respects trade theory is merely modernising itself, " catching up " with the advances in theory generally. But in others, as for instance in the measurement of welfare changes, trade theory is the innovator. Indeed, this is the way the subject has always grown: in a two-way flow of ideas with the general theory of value and welfare.

REFERENCES *

* The references have been classified into separate groups corresponding to the Sections in the text, while the numbering is consecutive for the groups together. The correspondence between the Sections and the groups is naturally not precise. The works listed do not constitute an exhaustive bibliography; the necessary and sufficient criterion for a work to be cited is that it should have been referred to in the text.

Introduction

1. J. Bhagwati, " Some Recent Trends in the Pure Theory of International Trade," Chapter 1 of *International Trade Theory in a Developing World* (Ed. R. F. Harrod and D. Hague; London: Macmillan, 1963).
2. J. Bhagwati and H. G. Johnson, " Notes on some Controversies in the theory of International Trade," ECONOMIC JOURNAL, Vol. 70 (March 1960).
3. R. E. Caves, *Trade and Economic Structure* (Cambridge, Mass.: Harvard University Press, 1960).
4. G. Haberler, *A Survey of International Trade Theory*, Special papers in International Economics, No. I (International Finance Section, Department of Economics, Princeton University, 1961).
5. H. G. Johnson, *International Trade and Economic Growth* (London: George Allen and Unwin Ltd., 1958).
6. H. G. Johnson, *Money, Trade and Growth* (London: George Allen and Unwin Ltd., 1962).
7. R. G. Lipsey, " The Theory of Customs Unions: A General Survey," ECONOMIC JOURNAL, Vol. 70 (September 1960).
8. J. E. Meade, *Trade and Welfare* (*The Theory of International Economic Policy*, Vol. II) (Oxford: Oxford University Press, 1955).
9. J. E. Meade, *Mathematical Supplement* (*Trade and Welfare*) (Oxford: Oxford University Press, 1955).
10. J. E. Meade, *A Geometry of International Trade* (London: George Allen and Unwin Ltd., 1952).
11. R. A. Mundell, " The Pure Theory of International Trade," *American Economic Review*, Vol. 50 (March 1960).

I

12. T. Balogh, " Factor Intensities of American Foreign Trade and Technical Progress," *Review of Economics and Statistics*, Vol. 37 (November 1955).
13. B. Balassa, " An Empirical Demonstration of Classical Comparative Cost Theory," *Review of Economics and Statistics*, Vol. 45 (August 1963).
14. J. Bhagwati, " Protection, Real Wages and Real Incomes," ECONOMIC JOURNAL, Vol. 69 (December 1959).

15. R. Bharadwaj, *Structural Basis of India's Foreign Trade* (Series in Monetary and International Economics, No. 6) (University of Bombay, 1962).
16. R. Bharadwaj, " Factor Proportions and the Structure of Indo-US Trade," *Indian Economic Journal*, Vol. 10 (October 1962).
17. J. Coppock, *International Economic Instability*, (Economic Handbook Series) (McGraw-Hill Book Company Inc., 1962).
18. M. Diab, *The United States Capital Position and the Structure of the Foreign Trade* (Amsterdam: North Holland, 1956).
19. E. Heckscher, " The Effect of Foreign Trade on the Distribution of Income," *Readings in the Theory of International Trade*, Edited by H. S. Ellis and L. A. Metzler for the American Economic Association (Philadelphia: Blakiston, 1949).
20. R. Jones, " Factor Proportions and the Heckscher–Ohlin Model," *Review of Economic Studies*, Vol. 24 (1956–57).
21. I. Kravis, " Wages and Foreign Trade," *Review of Economics and Statistics*, Vol. 38 (February 1956).
22. I. Kravis, " Availability and other Influences on the Commodity Composition of Trade," *Journal of Political Economy*, Vol. 64 (April 1956).
23. S. Lebergott, " Wage Structures," *Review of Economics and Statistics*, Vol. 29 (November 1947).
24. W. Leontief, " The Use of Indifference Curves in the Analysis of Foreign Trade," *Quarterly Journal of Economics*, Vol. 47 (May 1933).
25. W. Leontief, " Domestic Production and Foreign Trade: The American Capital Position Re-examined," *Economia Internazionale*, Vol. 7 (1954).
26. W. Leontief, " Factor Proportions and the Structure of American Trade: Further Theoretical and Empirical Analysis," *Review of Economics and Statistics*, Vol. 38 (November 1956).
27. S. Linder, *An Essay on Trade and Transformation* (New York: John Wiley and Sons, 1961).
28. G. D. A. MacDougall, " British and American Exports: A Study suggested by the Theory of Comparative Costs, Part I," ECONOMIC JOURNAL, Vol. 61 (December 1951).
29. G. D. A. MacDougall, " British and American Exports: A Study Suggested by the Theory of Comparative Costs, Part II," ECONOMIC JOURNAL, Vol. 62 (September 1952).
30. G. D. A. MacDougall, M. Dowley, P. Fox and S. Pugh, " British and American Productivity, Prices and Exports: An Addendum," *Oxford Economic Papers*, Vol. 14 (October 1962).
31. M. Michaely, *Concentration in World Trade* (Contributions to Economic Analysis) (Amsterdam: North Holland Publishing Co., 1962).
32. J. S. Mill, *Principles of Political Economy*, Edited by W. J. Ashley (London: Longmans, Green and Co., 1917).
33. B. S. Minhas, " The Homohypallagic Production Function, Factor Intensity Reversals, and the Heckscher–Ohlin Theorem," *Journal of Political Economy*, Vol. 70 (April 1962).
34. B. Ohlin, *Interregional and International Trade*, Harvard Economic Studies, Vol 39 (Cambridge, Mass.: Harvard University Press, 1933).
35. I. F. Pearce and S. F. James, " The Factor Price Equalisation Myth," *Review of Economic Studies*, Vol. 19 (1951–52).
36. R. Robinson, " Factor Proportions and Comparative Advantage: Part I," *Quarterly Journal of Economics*, Vol. 70 (May 1956).
37. R. Robinson, " Factor Proportions and Comparative Advantage: Part II," *Quarterly Journal of Economics*, Vol. 70 (August 1956).
38. P. A. Samuelson, " International Trade and Equalisation of Factor Prices," ECONOMIC JOURNAL, Vol. 58 (June 1948).

39. P. A. Samuelson, " International Factor Price Equalisation Once Again," ECONOMIC JOURNAL, Vol. 59 (June 1949).
40. R. Stern, " British and American Productivity and Comparative Costs in International Trade," *Oxford Economic Papers*, Vol. 14 (October 1962).
41. W. Stolper and K. Roskamp, " Input–Output Table for East Germany with Applications to Foreign Trade," *Bulletin of the Oxford University Institute of Statistics*, Vol. 23 (November 1961).
42. M. Tatemoto and S. Ichimura, " Factor Proportions and Foreign Trade: The Case of Japan," *Review of Economics and Statistics*, Vol. 41 (November 1959).
43. J. Vanek, " The Natural Resource Content of Foreign Trade, 1870–1955, and the Relative Abundance of Natural Resources in the United States," *Review of Economics and Statistics*, Vol. 41 (May 1959).
44. J. Viner, *Studies in the Theory of International Trade* (New York: Harper and Bros., 1937).
45. D. F. Wahl, " Capital and Labour Requirements for Canada's Foreign Trade," *Canadian Journal of Economics and Political Science*, Vol. 27 (August 1961).

II

46. R. F. Harrod, " Factor–Price Relations under Free Trade," ECONOMIC JOURNAL, Vol. 68 (June 1958).
47. H. W. Kuhn, " Factor Endowments and Factor Prices: Mathematical Appendix," *Economica*, N.S., Vol. 26 (May 1959).
48. N. Laing, " Factor Price Equalization in International Trade and Returns to Scale," *Economic Record*, Vol. 37 (September 1961).
49. L. McKenzie, " Equality of Factor Price in World Trade," *Econometrica*, Vol. 23 (July 1955).
50. J. E. Meade, " The Equalisation of Factor Prices: the Two-Good, Two-Country Three-product Case," *Metro-economica*, Vol. 2 (December 1950).
51. I. F. Pearce, " A Further Note on Factor–Commodity Price Relationships," ECONOMIC JOURNAL, Vol. 69 (December 1959).
52. S. Reiter, " Efficient International Trade and Equalisation of Prices," *International Economic Review*, Vol. 2 (January 1961).
53. P. A. Samuelson, " Prices of Factors and Goods in General Equilibrium," *Review of Economic Studies*, Vol. 21 (1953–54).
54. P. A. Samuelson, " Equalisation by Trade of the Interest Rate along with the Real Wage," *Mimeographed*, 1960.
55. J. Vanek, " Variable Factor Proportions and Inter-Industry Flows in the Theory of International Trade," *Quarterly Journal of Economics*, Vol. 77 (February 1963).

III

56. A. Asimakopulos, "A Note on Productivity Changes and the Terms of Trade," *Oxford Economic Papers*, N.S., Vol. 9 (June 1957).
57. R. E. Baldwin, " The Effects of Tariffs on International and Domestic Prices," *Quarterly Journal of Economics*, Vol. 74 (February 1960).
58. T. Balogh, " The Concept of a Dollar Shortage," *Manchester School*, Vol. 17 (May 1949).
59. J. Black, " Economic Expansion and International Trade: A Marshallian Approach," *Review of Economic Studies*, Vol. 23 (1955–56).

60. J. Bhagwati, and H. G. Johnson, " A Generalised Theory of the Effects of Tariffs on the Terms of Trade," *Oxford Economic Papers*, N.S. Vol. 13 (October 1961).
61. W. M. Corden, " Economic Expansion and International Trade: A Geometrical Approach," *Oxford Economic Papers*, N.S., Vol. 8 (June 1956).
62. R. Findlay and H. Grubert, " Factor Intensity, Technological Progress, and the Terms of Trade," *Oxford Economic Papers*, N.S. Vol. II (February 1959).
63. F. D. Graham, " The Theory of International Values," *Quarterly Journal of Economics*, Vol. 46 (August 1932).
64. H. G. Johnson, " Economic Development and International Trade," *National Konomick Tidsskript* (Arganj, 1959).
65. H. G. Johnson, " Effects of changes in Comparative Costs as Influenced by Technical Change," *Malayan Economic Review*, Vol. 6 (October 1961).
66. H. G. Johnson, " International Trade, Income Distribution and the Offer Curve," *Manchester School*, Vol. 27 (September 1959).
67. H. G. Johnson, " Income Distribution, the Offer Curve and the Effects of Tariffs," *Manchester School*, Vol. 28 (September 1960).
68. H. G. Johnson, " The Pure Theory of International Trade: Comment," *American Economic Review*, Vol. 50 (September 1960).
69. R. Jones, " Comparative Advantage and the Theory of Tariffs: A Multi-country, Multi-Commodity Model," *Review of Economic Studies*, Vol. 28 (June 1961).
70. M. C. Kemp, " The Relation between Changes in International Demand and the Terms of Trade," *Econometrica*, Vol. 24 (January 1956).
71. M. C. Kemp, " Technological Change, the Terms of Trade and Welfare," ECONOMIC JOURNAL, Vol. 65 (September 1955).
72. M. C. Kemp and R. Jones, " Variable Labour Supply and the Theory of International Trade," *Journal of Political Economy*, Vol. 70 (February 1962).
73. C. P. Kindleberger, " Group Behaviour and International Trade," *Journal of Political Economy*, Vol. 59 (February 1951).
74. A. P. Lerner, " The Symmetry between Import and Export Taxes," *Economica*, N.S. Vol. 3 (August 1936).
75. I. MacDougall, " Tariffs, Protection and the Terms of Trade," *Economic Record*, Vol. 37 (1961).
76. I. MacDougall, " A Note on Tariffs, the Terms of Trade, and the Distribution of the National Incomes," *Journal of Political Economy*, Vol. 70 (August 1962).
77. A. Marshall, *The Pure Theory of Foreign Trade* (Reprints of scarce Tracts on Political Economy) (London: London School of Economics, 1930).
78. L. McKenzie, " Specialization and Efficiency in World Production," *Review of Economic Studies*, Vol. 21 (1953–54).
79. J. E. Meade, *The Theory of Customs Unions* (Amsterdam: North Holland Publishing Co., 1955).
80. L. Metzler, " Tariffs, the Terms of Trade and the Distribution of National Income," *Journal of Political Economy*, Vol. 57 (February 1949).
81. L. Metzler, " Tariffs, International Demand and Domestic Prices," *Journal of Political Economy*, Vol. 57 (August 1949).
82. R. A. Mundell, " International Trade and Factor Mobility," *American Economic Review*, Vol. 47 (June 1957).
83. H. Myint, " The Classical Theory of International Trade and the Underdeveloped countries," ECONOMIC JOURNAL, Vol. 68 (June 1958).
84. F. R. Oliver, " Shifting Demand Schedules and the Terms and Volume of Trade," *Metroeconomica*, Vol. 12 (April 1960).
85. S. A. Ozga, " An Essay in the Theory of Tariffs," *Journal of Political Economy*, Vol. 63 (December 1955).

86. V. K. Ramaswami, " The Effects of Accumulation on the Terms of Trade," ECONOMIC JOURNAL, Vol. 70 (September 1960).

87. T. N. Rybczynski, " Factor Endowment and Relative Commodity Prices," *Economica*, N.S., Vol. 22 (November 1955).

88. P. A. Samuelson, " The Transfer Problem and Transport Costs," ECONOMIC JOURNAL, Vol. 62 (June 1952).

89. P. A. Samuelson, " The Transfer Problem and Transport Costs," ECONOMIC JOURNAL, Vol. 62 (June 1952).

90. F. Seton, " Productivity, Trade Balance and International Structure," ECONOMIC JOURNAL, Vol. 66 (December 1956).

91. W. Stolper and P. A. Samuelson, " Protection and Real Wages," *Review of Economic Studies*, Vol. 9 (November 1941).

92. J. Vanek, " An Afterthought on the Real Cost–Opportunity Cost Dispute and some Aspects of General Equilibrium under Conditions of Variable Factor Supplies," *Review of Economic Studies*, Vol. 26 (June 1959).

93. J. Vanek, *International Trade: Theory and Economic Policy* (Illinois: Richard D. Irwin Inc., 1962).

94. J. Viner, *The Customs Union Issue* (New York: Carnegie Endowment for International Peace, 1950).

95. V. C. Walsh, " Leisure and International Trade," *Economica*, N.S. Vol. 23 (August 1956).

IV

96. D. M. Bensusan-Butt, " A Model of Trade and Accumulation," *American Economic Review*, Vol. 44 (September 1954).

97. J. Bhagwati, " The Theory of Comparative Advantage in the Context of Underdevelopment and Growth," *Pakistan Development Review*, Vol. 2 (Autumn 1962).

98. H. Brems, " The Foreign Trade Accelerator and International Transmission of Growth," *Econometrica*, Vol. 24 (July 1956).

99. F. D. Graham, " Some Aspects of Protection Further Considered," *Quarterly Journal of Economics*, Vol. 37 (February 1923).

100. A. Johnson, " Protection and the Formation of Capital," *Political Science Quarterly*, Vol. 23 (June 1908).

101. C. P. Kindleberger, " Foreign Trade and Economic Growth: Lessons from Britain and France, 1850 to 1913," *Economic History Review*, Vol. 14 (1961).

102. H. Kitamura, *International Economics* (Tokyo), March 1951.

103. K. Kojima, " A Survey of the Theories on International Economics in Japan," *Japan Science Review (Economic Sciences, No. 1)*, Japan Union of Associations of Economic Sciences, 1953.

104. T. N. Srinivasan, " A Two-Country, Three-Commodity, Dynamic Model of International Trade," *Metroeconomica*, forthcoming.

105. P. J. Verdoorn, " Complementarity and Long-Range Projections," *Econometrica*, Vol. 24 (October 1956).

V

106. K. Akamatsu, " The Theory of Supply-Multiplier in Reference to the Post-War Economic Situation in Japan," *The Annals of the Hitotsubashi Academy* (October 1950).

107. G.A.T.T., *Basic Instruments and Selected Documents, Tenth Supplement* (Geneva, March 1962).

108. L. McKenzie, " On Equilibrium in Graham's Model of World Trade and Other Competitive Systems," *Econometrica*, Vol. 22 (April 1954).

109. W. Stolper, "Notes on the Dollar Shortage," *American Economic Review*, Vol. 40 (June 1950).

110. W. Stolper, "A Note on Multiplier, Flexible Exchanges and the Dollar Shortage," *Economica Internationale*, Vol. 11 (August 1950).

VI

111. J. Bhagwati, "Immiserizing Growth: A Geometrical Note," *Review of Economic Studies*, Vol. 25 (June 1958).

112. J. Bhagwati, and V. K. Ramaswami, "Domestic Distortions, Tariffs and the Theory of Optimum Subsidy," *Journal of Political Economy*, Vol. 71 (February 1963).

113. R. Dorfman, P. A. Samuelson and R. M. Solow, *Linear Programming and Economic Analysis* (New York: McGraw Hill, 1958).

114. M. Fleming, "The Optimal Tariff from an International Standpoint," *Review of Economics and Statistics*, Vol. 38 (February 1956).

115. W. M. Gorman, "Tariffs, Retaliation and the Elasticity of Demand for Imports," *Review of Economic Studies*, Vol. 25 (June 1958).

116. J. Graaff, "On Optimum Tariff Structures," *Review of Economic Studies*, Vol. 17 (1949–50).

117. G. Haberler, "Some Problems in the Pure Theory of International Trade," Economic Journal, Vol. 60 (June 1950).

118. E. Hagen, "An Economic Justification of Protectionism," *Quarterly Journal of Economics*, Vol. 72 (November 1958).

119. A. E. Jasay, "The Choice between Home and Foreign Investment," Economic Journal, Vol. 70 (March 1960).

120. M. C. Kemp, "The Gain from International Trade," Economic Journal, Vol. 72 (December 1962).

121. R. G. Lipsey, "The Theory of Customs Unions: Trade Diversion and Welfare," *Economica*, N.S., Vol. 24 (February 1957).

122. G. D. A. MacDougall, "The Benefits and Costs of Private Investment from Abroad: A Theoretical Approach," *Bulletin of the Oxford University Institute of Statistics*, Vol. 22 (August 1960).

123. R. C. O. Matthews, "Reciprocal Demand and Increasing Returns," *Review of Economic Studies*, Vol. 17 (1949–50).

124. V. Panchmukhi, "A Theory for Optimum Tariff Policy," *Indian Economic Journal*, Vol. 9 (October 1961).

125. P. A. Samuelson, "The Gains from International Trade," *Canadian Journal of Economics and Political Science*, Vol. 5 (May 1939).

126. P. A. Samuelson, "The Gain from International Trade Once Again," Economic Journal, Vol. 72 (December 1962).

127. J. Tinbergen, *International Economic Cooperation* (Amsterdam, 1946).

VII

128. W. M. Corden, "Tariffs, Subsidies and the Terms of Trade," *Economica*, N.S., Vol. 24 (August 1957).

129. H. G. Johnson, "Optimum Welfare and Maximum Revenue Tariffs," *Review of Economic Studies*, Vol. 19 (1951–52).

130. H. G. Johnson, "Discriminatory Tariff Reduction: A Marshallian Analysis," *Indian Journal of Economics*, Vol. 38 (July 1957).

131. H. G. Johnson, "The Gain from Freer Trade with Europe: An Estimate," *Manchester School*, Vol. 26 (September 1958).

132. H. G. Johnson, "The Cost of Protection and the Scientific Tariff," *Journal of Political Economy*, Vol. 42 (October 1960).

133. H. G. Johnson, " Optimal Trade Intervention in the Presence of Domestic Distortions," *Money, Trade and Economic Growth*: Essays in Honor of G. Haberler (Ed. by Caves, Johnson and Kenen; Rand–McNally 1965).
134. R. L. Marris, " The Purchasing Power of British Exports," *Economica*, N.S. Vol. 22 (February 1955).
135. J. Wemelsfelder, " The Short-term Effect of the Lowering of Import Duties in Germany," ECONOMIC JOURNAL, Vol. 70 (March 1960).

VIII

136. P. R. Brahmandand and C. N. Vakil, *Planning for an Expanding Economy* (Bombay: Vora & Co., 1956).
137. S. Chakravarty, *The Logic of Investment Planning* (North Holland Series) (Amsterdam: North Holland Publishing Co., 1957).
138. H. Chenery and M. Bruno, " Development Alternatives in an Open Economy: The Case of Israel," ECONOMIC JOURNAL, Vol. 72 (March 1962).
139. H. Chenery, " Comparative Advantage and Development Policy," *American Economic Review*, Vol. 51 (March 1961).
140. P. Desai, " The Development of the Indian Economy: An Exercise in Economic Planning," *Oxford Economic Papers*, Vol. 15 (October 1963).
141. P. C. Mahalanobis, " Science and National Planning," *Sankhya*, Vol. 20 (1958).
142. R. Wonnacott, *Canadian–American Dependence*, (Contributions to Economic Analysis) (Amsterdam: North Holland Publishing Co., 1961).

ADDENDUM

I have taken the opportunity provided by reprinting to add a strictly limited number of references to the most important contributions that have appeared during 1964–65.   For simplicity of record, these have been made in the text in footnotes within square brackets.

143. [An admirable new addition to the general literature is M. C. Kemp, *The Pure Theory of International Trade* (Prentice-Hall, New Jersey, 1964).]
144. [For a vigorous extension of the analysis of the transfer problem to the case of non-traded goods, see MacDougall, " Non-Traded Goods and the Transfer Problem," *Review of Economic Studies*, Vol. 32 (January 1965).]
145. [Mention may be made of a recent extended treatment of the theory of growth and trade, in the Johnson tradition, which has put this kind of theory through all possible paces: Sodersten, *A Study of Economic Growth and International Trade* (Almqvist and Wikseli, Stockholm, 1964).]
146. [A paper by Mundell, " Tariff Preferences and the Terms of Trade," *Manchester School*, Vol. 32 (January 1964), has now appeared.]
147. [A recent paper by Oniki and Uzawa, " Patterns of Trade and Investment in a Dynamic Model of International Trade," *Review of Economic Studies*, Vol 32 (January 1965), contributes a rigorous analysis of the interaction of capital accumulation and the trade pattern in a two-country world.]
148. [An important new contribution in this area is Wan, " Maximum Bonus— An Alternative Measure for Trading Gains," *Review of Economic Studies*, Vol. 32 (January 1965).]

VIII

REGIONAL ECONOMICS: A SURVEY

By

JOHN R. MEYER [1]

THE creation of a new area of specialization is always a matter of interest in any academic field and the phenomenal rise of what has come to be known as " regional analysis " in economics is no exception.

The manifestations of this emergence are many. Within the last decade both a new professional association and a journal dealing with problems of regional development have come into being. This new journal, published by the Regional Science Association, has, moreover, all the hallmarks of academic success; it has consistently grown in size, scope, number of contributors, and even in quality of typography. Also within the last decade, a full-edged and highly successful research institution, Resources for the Future, has been created which is greatly concerned with problems that conventionally are described as falling within the province of the new field. This organization reported in 1957 [102], furthermore, that no less than about 140 U.S. universities had serious research or education programs underway in regional studies and there are substantial reasons for believing that the extent of these activities has probably enlarged rather than contracted since that time. Similarly, conferences, almost innumerable, have been organized to discuss, evaluate, and promote regional science studies both here and abroad. Indeed, perhaps one of the most impressive testimonials to the appeal of the new field is that it has enlisted the official or semi-official interest of such diverse governments, among others, as those of Italy, France, Spain, Greece, Argentina, Turkey, Venezuela, India, Colombia, and Pakistan.

Economists and economics have long had, of course, special surges of interest or, less euphemistically, fads and fashions in their studies and research. Furthermore, if we construe economics as an applied science and argue, at least within limits, that most of the great steps forward in economic understanding and theory have come in response to specific policy challenges, this tendency toward temporarily pursuing certain lines of research with seemingly exaggerated zeal is not necessarily unfortunate. It may be, rather, the very substance and requisite accompaniment of intellectual progress in a field where progress often is concerned with generating principles or concepts for the understanding and solution of practical problems. Understanding

[1] The author is Professor of Economics at Harvard University. He wishes to thank the staff of the David Lubin Memorial Library at the United Nations Food and Agricultural Organization in Rome for their patient assistance with compiling and verifying the bibliography.

such research and its conceptual results or creations normally requires, in turn, an appreciation of the policy problems that have provided the stimuli.

It would be wrong, though, to infer that identification of these stimuli would fully explain the rise and recent popularity of regional economics. Nor would these alone provide an adequate basis for understanding recent developments in the field. Regional economics has very obvious and important intellectual forebears, and indeed it seems high probable that certain theoretical developments in general economics, particularly having to do with general interdependence systems, provided the conceptual basis without which regional economics could not have flourished. One very straight-forward explanation of the surge in regional economics, in fact, is to say that it resulted from a fortuitous blending of many economists' desires to apply certain recently honed conceptual tools and policy makers' desires to seek more adequate and analytical answers to complex problems related to regional and urban growth.

Sensible discussion of either the stimuli or the conceptual precursors of regional economics requires, moreover, a definition of just exactly what constitutes this new field. Special semantic problems, unique to the new field, are also quickly encountered, not the least of which is simply defining a region. The definitional problems will be considered, therefore, in Section I. As will become clear there, definitions of and in regional economics are not always easily come by, a difficulty probably shared in common with almost all new fields of specialization. Following these definitional exercises, a more thorough consideration of the policy-problem stimuli will be undertaken in Section II. Then in Section III, the theoretical foundations of regional economics, as borrowed from general economics, will be treated. This will be followed in Section IV by a discussion of the different approaches to regional economics that have emerged in actual regional studies. Finally, Section V attempts to summarize and provide some evaluation of all that precedes.

I. DEFINITIONAL PROBLEMS

An almost unavoidable temptation when first coming to grips with the problems of defining regional economics is to assert that it is simply *all* of economics scaled to whatever level is required to adequately measure or forecast economic activity for a specific geographic area. There would be considerable truth, moreover, in such a characterization, for regional economics has been, if anything, ambitious in its selection of objectives. Also implicit in such a definition is a strong urge to define regional economics in terms of particular study and policy objectives, thus emphasizing its pragmatic origins.

Difficulty in giving regional economics a distinct character in terms of conventional economic disciplines also partially explains and is explained by the tendency to place regional economic studies in a broader, interdisciplinary, framework. Almost from the beginning, the convention, at least in formal discourse, has been to speak of " regional analysis " and " regional science " rather than " regional economics." Included and welcomed have been such diverse fields as sociology, demography, geography, and history. Indeed, at times, *the* distinguishing characteristic of regional analysis has almost seemed to be its interdisciplinary aspect. This diversity combined with definitional uncertainty was very well expressed by Harvey Perloff in the introduction to the Resources of the Future survey already cited [102, p. v]:

> " No fully satisfactory way of classifying regional studies was found— not unexpectedly. Regional studies tend to deal with many features and often involve the use of several academic disciplines. Thus, no general system of classification can be expected to provide self-contained categories; there is inevitable spill-over. The subject classification employed in this report sets up categories whose cores, if not boundaries, are indentifiable and whose titles are widely used, with popular and technical meanings that are not too far apart. The topical categories employed are: (1) Physical elements and natural resources; (2) Population and human ecology; (3) Regional economic development; (4) Metropolitan studies and metropolitan planning, and (5) Regional history, literature, and sociocultural elements. Two other categories were found necessary: (6) Methods and techniques of regional analysis, and (7) Comprehensive regional studies."

A somewhat narrower (but still staggeringly broad!) definition of regional analysis specifically in terms of its objectives has been provided by Walter Isard [70, p. 413]:[1]

> " An analyst is perplexed with many problems when he looks at a region. One problem may be to identify specific industries which can individually or in groups operate efficiently and with profit in the region. Another related problem may be to improve the welfare of the people of the region, that is, to raise per capita incomes and perhaps achieve a more equitable distribution of income; the auxiliary problem of measurement of income and of the performance of a society is also present. Still another problem may be to avoid an industrial mix which is too sensitive to the ups and downs of national and world business, and which is composed too heavily of old, slow-growing, or declining industries; this is the problem of diversification. Finally, a fourth problem which can be mentioned is to plan industrial development for a region, as part of a system of regions, in an internally consistent manner. . . . [Another] pressing problem . . . and which for many regions is the most critical, is the problem of how to put to best use a limited, if not a niggardly, endowment of resources."

A distinctive aspect of Isard's definition is its exclusive emphasis on what economists would normally construe or recognize as economic problems.

---

[1] Isard's textbook [70], from which this quotation is taken, constitutes a good single-volume introduction to regional economics and contains excellent bibliographies arranged by subject.

This also gives it an immediate advantage as a definitional point of departure for organizing a survey article of this kind.

Still, it is much too broad—at least if the survey is to be short of monograph length and a complete tour of modern economics! Two simplifications, though, suggest themselves: these are to limit attention to (1) problems of regional analysis with unique conceptual characteristics, and (2) specific areas of particularly heavy interchange between conventional economic theory and regional economics.

The conceptually unique problems appear to be mainly empirical in character and center around the difficulties encountered in defining a " region." Traditionally three different approaches have been used in defining regions [21] [22] [34] [102] [119]. The first stresses *homogeneity* with respect to some one or combination of physical, economic, social, or other characteristics; the second emphasizes so-called *nodality* or *polarization*, usually around some central urban place; and the third is *programming-* or *policy-oriented*, concerned mainly with administrative coherence or identity between the area being studied and available political institutions for effectuating policy decisions. Naturally enough, regional definitions as established in practice often represent a compromise between these different pure types. In particular, availability and limitations of data can and do dictate departures from " ideal type " definitions in many situations.

Strictly speaking, moreover, the three traditional definitions of regional type are not mutually exclusive. In fact, all regional classification schemes are simply variations on the homogeneity criterion and it is somewhat misleading to suggest otherwise. The only real question is what kind of homogeneity is sought. Thus, a so-called program or policy region is essentially homogeneous in being entirely under the jurisdiction of some one or a few specific government or administrative agencies. A nodal region is homogeneous in that it combines areas dependent in some trade or functional sense on a specific center. Some so-called homogenous regions are homogenous with respect to physical characteristics, like geography or natural resource endowment, while others are defined to be similar in their economic or social characteristics. Finally, homogeneity with respect to statistical compilations, as noted before, may often be the real determinant of regional boundaries for practical purposes.

Some of the most interesting work in regional economics in a purely theoretical or conceptual sense has been concerned with the definition of indexes for measuring homogeneity when more than one dimension or measures of such qualities exist. M. J. Hagood [42] [43], for example, has performed some highly suggestive experiments with the use of statistical factor or component analyses as a means of defining homogeneous regional groupings for the United States in terms of agricultural and demographic variables. In the process, incidentally, she developed some interesting contributions to the clarification of factor analysis procedures and to the development of objective methods for stratifying a statistical sample [44]. Some interesting extensions of this work have also been made by V. V. Almendinger in connection with defining politically and socially homogeneous communities for the New York metropolitan region and Penn–Jersey transportation studies [1] [123].

As interesting as these statistical procedures might be to the applied statistician, econometrician, or psychometrician, however, it seems rather doubtful that they are of much tangible value to the regional analyst actually confronted with a problem of defining a geographic area for study. Given the pragmatic, problem-solving orientation of regional economics, it would seem that Joseph Fisher of Resources for the Future was probably understating the case when he said [34, p. W-6]:[1]

> " I should like to suggest that the most helpful region in many instances is what might be called the *economic development region* ... [where] ... the emphasis is on the development of policies, programs and actions to move the region from where it is economically toward predetermined economic objectives."

The same view is echoed at length in the writings of the most extensive contributor to the regional definition problem, Jacques R. Boudeville [21] [22], although Boudeville also seems to be arguing at times that only a nodal region is useful for policy purposes. Most major exceptions to a policy approach to the regional definition problem will occur, moreover, for the exclusively pragmatic reason of having to make adjustments to data availability.

The problem of regional definition becomes crucial whenever attempts are made to obtain estimates of regional income and product accounts.[2] Such estimates are often essential because policy objectives are commonly set in terms of achieving a stipulated *per capita* income or production level for a region. The income estimation problem at the regional level, unfortunately, clearly involves more than simply scaling down national income and product accounts. Indeed, many regional analysts would argue that the only way to properly estimate regional income categories would be to adopt a completely fresh approach, developed on the basis of entirely new regional or local sources of information [61] [103] [104]. Among other justifications, a fresh approach is urged on the grounds that the objectives of regional policy planning are so very different from those encountered at the national level that different concepts are immediately needed in the measurement of regional income and product. Some regional economists, moreover, would rather see national income accounts built up progressively from regional

---

[1] A very forceful endorsement of this pragmatic approach to regional definition can also be found in the writings of several others and particularly by E. M. Hoover [64].

[2] An excellent recent survey of the problems of regional social accounting can be found in R. N. Stone [112]. Somewhat earlier but still very useful discussions can be found in [130], particularly W. Hochwald's paper on conceptual issues [62]. For a discussion of some of the same issues but in a " dynamic context " see Isard and G. Freutel [72].

accounts than vice versa.   At the minimum a very compelling case can be made for keeping reasonably detailed and unaggregated records of local economic activity in order to create data at whatever level of aggregation is required for policy or research purposes [64].   In reality, though, practical considerations, such as limitations on available research resources, usually dictate that regional income estimates be derived from more readily available national income figures.

The special problems of regional income estimation mainly derive from the simple fact that regional economies are almost invariably more open, in the sense of being more reliant on external trade and institutions, than national economies.   The type of problem that bedevils the estimator of regional income is aptly illustrated by both the commuter who lives in one region and works in another and the large multiplant national corporation. Not only will large corporations typically have installations in different areas but ownership is likely to be dispersed in an unknown fashion over several regions.   Government activities, particularly at the federal level, are also difficult to distribute on a regional basis.   In general, regional income accounting is complicated by the fact that much needed data are often compiled only on a national basis, and by the conceptual problems associated with defining a resident, the commuter and large corporation being merely two of the more common examples of these difficulties.   These difficulties, though, are not insurmountable, since regional, state or other local income accounts suitable for many purposes have been or are in the process of being constructed [13] [14] [36] [46] [47] [60] [105] [107].

While regional definition problems do possess several reasonably unique elements not encountered in conventional economic analyses, they hardly would appear substantial enough to give regional economics a thoroughly distinct identity.   If the search for that identity is directed to locating points of particular conceptual emphasis within regional economics, without much question regional economics, especially as it has evolved and developed within the last decade, uses both location theory and international trade theory more than any of the other conventional economic disciplines.[1]   This is hardly surprising, of course, since both location theory and international trade theory emphasize economic relations between geographical areas.   It is significant, moreover, that Walter Isard, who has fathered much of modern regional economics, spent a great deal of his time in the late forties and early fifties, when the recent surge of interest in regional economic analysis first began, on the problem of integrating or synthesizing location theory and international trade theory [73] [68].   His particular objective was to correct what he considered to be an intrinsic failing in traditional international trade theory, its failure to pay attention to the cost of overcoming spatial separation.

[1] In the light of what has just been said about the difficulties of finding a unique identity for regional analysis, it is perhaps significant that international trade theory shares with regional economics a tendency to synthesize elements from almost all other phases of economic analysis.

One common alternative approach to defining regional economics is, in fact, to allude to it as the economics of spatial separation. This, however, would seem to be unduly confining, since the policy problems considered by regional economists have been considerably wider in scope than the location problems emphasized by such a definition. Indeed, in actual regional analyses spatial separation as such hasn't been so much the policy concern as the fact that resources, particularly labor, are not completely mobile between regions. The " economics of resource immobility " therefore might be a reasonably accurate, though still less than fully comprehensive, description of regional economics.

Before 1950, which would also be before the phrase " regional analysis " came into common professional usage, what generally was regarded as regional economics was heavily involved in business cycle theory and analysis. Indeed, in the forties studies relating to the interregional propagation and transfer of business cycles, those by R. Vining [116] [117] [118] and P. Neff [97] [98] being particularly important, were the dominant concern in regional economic studies. A discussion of this work will be omitted from this paper, however, on the simple grounds that this aspect of regional economics has been rather neglected in recent years.[1] The current emphasis, for better or worse, is on maximization under static conditions, a change almost inherent in the heavy introduction of international trade and location theory concepts into regional economics.[2]

II. Problems of Regional Economic Policy

Modern regional analysis, as reconstituted with a major emphasis on static maximization problems rather than the dynamics of the business cycle, has apparently met a number of desperately felt policy needs. Among other sources, the apparent success in the thirties and forties of the Tennessee Valley Authority has been a major encouragement and inspiration, both domestically and abroad, to those who would undertake to improve the status of economically backward or handicapped areas by government action, a task to which much of the recent applied work in regional economics has been devoted. In the United States a special interest in regional economics in the older South [63] and New England [53] [54] [89] [23] has been very much motivated by such considerations. To a lesser extent, and with a greater emphasis on growth possibilities not realized rather than on immediate economic difficulties as such, the same is true of some of the

---

[1] Symptomatic of the trend is the omission of cycle studies from Perloff's categorization scheme quoted above.

[2] Also eliminated from consideration here is the extensive work done in recent years on the development of benefit–cost ratios and similar measures of capital-investment effectiveness for water resource development. While this work has been of considerable interest to regional economists and closely related to certain aspects of their work, these contributions to capital budgeting procedures would appear to belong more to the realm of general capital theory since they possess no particularly unique regional characteristics.

interest in regional problems evidenced in the Rocky Mountain area [40]. Similarly, the Upper Midwest Economic Study, recently inaugurated at the University of Minnesota and already reporting research results [58] [77] [79] [110], has as one of its avowed aims formulating an " action program " to raise the region's rate of economic progress to at least parity with the rest of the country.

Interest in regional economic problems has long had a special source of stimulation in the United States because of the deliberately (and perhaps artificially) regionalized organization of the Federal Reserve System. Thus it is not surprising that much, perhaps even a preponderance, of the domestic empirical work in regional economics has been sponsored at least partially by Federal Reserve Banks. The already mentioned Upper Midwest Project and G. Freutel's work on interregional payment balances [36] are just two of the more important examples.

Much of the foreign interest in regional economic growth has had a similar source, but with a special emphasis on a variation of the balanced growth problem. In many countries experiencing rapid economic development a not uncommon circumstance is the existence of a sharp disparity of fortunes between newly industrialized urban areas and the rest of the country. An attempt is often made to ameliorate the political strains created by this so-called " economic dualism " by initiating special regional development programs. The efforts in Italy to expedite development of the Mezzogiorno, in Venezuela of the Guayana, in Brazil of the Amazonia North, in Argentina of Patagonia, in Chile of Aisen Province, are just a few examples of efforts to meet such political problems by either opening up new territory to settlement by economically oppressed groups or directly transferring more economic opportunity to such groups. Of course this same problem of balanced growth and attempts to effectuate income transfers to unfortunate areas are not unknown in the industrialized parts of the world either;[1] the U.S. government worries about West Virginia, the French about Brittany, and the English about Glasgow. In fact, one of the postwar period's earliest and most ambitious schemes to geographically redistribute economic opportunity was undertaken by the British with the " New Towns Plan," the evaluation of which provides some of the better reading on problems of economic policy formation in regional economics [108].

Actually, urban problems and analyses have assumed an increasingly dominant role in empirical research in regional analysis in the United States. To a certain degree this has been a function of simple financial support since the interstate highway program made substantial funds available for research activities associated with the highway construction. The nature of this support has had, moreover, some interesting effects on the direction of regional research efforts.

---

[1] A good summary of the sources of this problem and possibly policy solutions can be found in A. H. Conrad [31].

Many early research expenditures made under the interstate highway program were primarily concerned with making urban traffic forecasts and estimates. Two techniques usually were employed for this purpose. The first was the highly expensive one of making origination and destination counts by going to homes or stopping automobiles on the highways and performing interviews, and by making controlled cordon counts of the number of vehicles and persons passing certain points in the city. When interviews were performed, information was sought not only on origins and destinations but also on trip purpose (*e.g.*, whether for work, recreation, or shopping) and a record was kept of the mode of transportation employed. The main objective was to estimate the level of demand for highway capacity at different points within urban areas so as to determine the needs for new capacity and to locate the capacity with, it was hoped, maximum effectiveness.

Design of these origin and destination interviews obviously poses few conceptual or empirical problems of interest to economists, though many possibilities for improvement do lie in the province of statistical sampling procedures. Origin and destination studies by interview tend, however, to be highly expensive, and a full census of originations and destinations almost invariably was impossible. To fill the gaps a second estimation technique, known as gravity model analysis, normally was employed. Gravity models are based on simple sorts of analogues to physical models and they have had a long and controversial history in sociological analyses of regional characteristics [113] [124] [121] [26]. For gravity models in urban transportation analyses the traffic between two points is hypothesized to be positively related to the " mass " at each point and negatively to the " friction " operating on travel between the points. Friction can be measured in terms of distance, time, cost, and various other factors. Similarly, mass has been variously defined as population, the number of automobile owners and, in some more sophisticated models, as purchasing power or effective demand or even " potential " commercial or industrial " drawing power " (as reflected in retail and industrial employment or other measures of such activities).

When broadened in this fashion these models pose economic questions of some empirical interest and significance; without such broadening, of course, the models are rather puerile and mechanistic and devoid of behavioral content. It is not surprising, therefore, that much of the effort to broaden and improve gravity model applications to urban traffic analyses is traceable to the influence of economists who have worked on various urban transportation studies. Particularly pathbreaking in this respect were the transportation studies directed by J. D. Carroll for Detroit and Chicago and various papers that developed from those studies [125] [126] [24] [25]. An effort to incorporate economic and other behavioral information into the making of traffic projections also has been made as part of the Pittsburgh area transportation study [129] and the concurrent economic study of the

Pittsburgh region conducted by the Pittsburgh Regional Planning Association; particularly interesting in this regard is a paper by I. S. Lowry containing a number of suggestions for improving gravity models [87].

Considerably more revolutionary and experimental have been the efforts made in the Penn–Jersey transportation study to project future population distributions and thereby transportation demands by assuming that residential choices are made on the basis of certain rational economic considerations as embodied in a linear programming model [59] [48–52]. As will be explained in greater detail later, some critics would argue that with this linear programming model the pendulum has swung too far in the direction of letting economic considerations determine the projections. Be that as it may, it is clear that economists and regional economics are now thoroughly involved in urban transportation planning.

The interest of economists and regional analysts in urban problems has not been limited, of course, to transportation planning. The interdependence between urban transportation, land use, population growth patterns, and industrial development generally is considered to be so close that more purely economic studies of urban trends and patterns have become increasingly prevalent. Besides the already cited Pittsburgh Regional Planning Association effort, there was at an earlier date the New York metropolitan region study (which also included historical and political studies). Indeed, the reports growing out of this study form an excellent introduction to an understanding of urban economic problems [19] [28] [45] [55] [65] [81] [106] [109] [115] [123]. Similarly, the Upper Midwest study includes a special enquiry into the problems of the Twin Cities' metropolitan area. The new professional interest of economists in urban problems is, of course, symptomatic of a great expansion of concern about urban problems in general in U.S. society.

Transportation problems have also supplied a policy impetus to regional analysis in a larger geographic context than the urban area. Private intercity railroads, trucking lines, and local service airlines in the United States happen, for a number of historical and other reasons, to be regionally structured. To a lesser extent the same is true of the large commercial trunk airlines. Furthermore, recent " crises " in U.S. transportation have been positively correlated with railroad passenger volumes, short hauls (of both passengers and freight), and small volume shipments. These characteristics vary sharply from region to region, with New England clearly being the most disadvantaged.

In general, regional analysis apparently has filled a void by developing tools applicable to economic planning problems at a time when economic planning has been increasingly in favor in many circles and governments. Thus, the great strength or appeal of regional analysis would appear to be its essentially pragmatic character and, in particular, its willingness to integrate theory and data and to undertake empirically difficult analyses.

III. Theoretical Foundations

This emphasis on integration of theory and empiricism also shows itself in modern regional analysis' theoretical roots.   These, in large part, are " borrowings " of developments in general economics that occurred during the 1940's and can be listed under four headings: (1) a revitalization of location theory, particularly as contained in Losch's work, published in English in 1953 [83] but available in German in the forties; (2) international and interregional multiplier theory as illustrated by the work of Metzler [88], Goodwin [41], Chipman [30], and others: (3) Leontief interindustry input–output analysis [83] [84]; and (4) mathematical programming.[1]

1. *Location Theory*. With the possible exception of Löschian location theory, these theoretical developments all share the important quality of having obvious empirical possibilities. Indeed, one could say that they almost beg for empirical implementation. By contrast, Lösch's theory not only is highly idealized and stylized but has few immediate or obvious empirical possibilities and has thus far been devoid of any important empirical implementation. One plausible (but not necessarily correct!) explanation of its appeal in regional analysis is that it partially satisfies the search for an identity in the new field. Location theory had, and has, been generally overlooked in general economic studies and, by giving it special prominence, regional analysts partially distinguished their activities from the rest of economics. Furthermore, Lösch's theory still may prove to have empirical possibilities, as M. Beckman has forecast [16]. At present, however, the more eclectic and general, though less logically elegant, revisions of Weberian location theory developed by Isard [69] and largely anticipated by E. M. Hoover [64] would seem to have more practical utility.

2. *Multiplier Theory*. Interregional multiplier analysis, as an empirical device, is closely bound up in regional economics with the concept of an economic base. Furthermore, regional economists deserve at least some credit for pioneering the application of multiplier concepts. Homer Hoyt, a pioneer of urban economic studies, employed the concept of an economic base with its implicit multiplier concept as early as 1937 [127]. Revisions and improvements of the base concept have been stimulated, of course, by subsequent development of multiplier concepts in general business cycletheory.

The essential notions of the economic base-multiplier concept as applied in regional studies are the same as similar concepts used elsewhere in economics and are quite clear and simple, though subject to a number of modifications, qualifications or adjustments to provide greater meaningfulness or sophistication in actual application.[2]   The first step is to define certain activi-

---

[1] For bibliography and discussion of the literature on mathematical programming see [15] [32] [33].

[2] A comprehensive survey of the history, applications and concepts of economic base studies will be found in R. B. Andrews [3–12]. Other useful discussions of the base concept can be found in [66] [114].

ties as being exogenous or determined outside of the economy under analysis. Translating conventional international trade theory into regional terms, the " economic base " of a region is that group of industries primarily engaged in exporting from the region under analysis to other regions. An empirical multiplier is determined by observing the historical relationship between this export activity and total economic activity in the region. This empirical multiplier is then applied to estimates of economic base to forecast total economic activity.

A crucial aspect of the procedure is, of course, estimating the size of the economic base. In particular applications where the concern is so often with trying to improve the economic status of a specific region, attempts often are made to estimate the extent of new export activities that might have a chance of economic survival, thus creating a base for expansion in the general economy of the region under analysis. The usual procedure for defining new export possibilities is to make some sort of interregional production cost comparisons, and a common technique of doing this in regional analysis is to perform a so-called " comparative cost analysis " [70, pp. 233–44].

While based on ideas akin to those found in international trade theory, comparative cost analyses as applied in regional economics are different in that the cost comparisons usually are made directly and in absolute terms without reference to calculations of internal comparative advantage. Specifically, the comparisons normally are made strictly between regions on the apparent assumption of some sort of interregional market equilibrium existing in factor prices. Thus the procedure usually devolves to doing a set of cost comparisons for supplying certain products to specified markets from the given region as compared with alternative sources of supply for these same markets. The first step in the analysis is to look at factor or input costs that are particularly important or almost necessarily different between regions; thus transport costs are almost always analyzed and usually labor costs or costs of a peculiarly important input (e.g., power for aluminium, oil or gas for petrol-chemicals) are also analyzed.

The great virtue of comparative cost analysis is that of all partial analyses, empirical simplicity. It also suffers from the usual disabilities of partial analyses in that the needed preliminary simplifications may not be obvious or easily ascertainable in complex interdependent situations. Particularly likely to be ignored are such considerations as economies of scale, factor price changes induced by inelastic supply functions, and external economies attributable to urbanization or similar influences.

An attempt to correct many of these deficiencies in comparative cost analysis has been made by Isard, E. W. Schooler, and T. Victoriez with what they call " industrial complex analysis " [70, ch. 9] [74]. The basic innovation of industrial complex analysis is a somewhat more sophisticated attempt to define meaningful industrial groupings or complexes for cost comparison by using input–output matrices.   Also involved is a broadening of the considerations permitted to influence the cost comparisons, with particular emphasis on tests for the existence of scale economies.

The strongest objections usually made to economic base or multiplier analyses in regional economics are not concerned, however, with the legitimacy or illegitimacy of the cost comparisons by which the base is estimated. Some of the most vehement opposition to base analyses has been concerned with the question of simply finding a suitable definition of what is exogenous. Base analysis implies that a gap or discontinuity would be found if industries were arranged hierarchically according to the level of their export activity. However, in many cases where such an analysis has been undertaken, the ordering has been found to be essentially continuous.

Furthermore, even if a group of export industries can be identified readily, there are often reasons for denying that the multiplier coefficients will be stable over time.   In fact, a very common objection made to base analysis is that regional studies usually are concerned with economic development of an area and one of the main objectives of that development is to change the relationship between export and import activities.   It is quite obvious, moreover, that an economy can exist without exports and can grow without a growth of its exports, as must be true for the world economy taken as a whole.   Quibbles also have been entered, sometimes quite legitimately, about the reliability of multiplier coefficients estimated from historical data.

While the economic base concept is thus subject to many serious reservations and objections, it still has had a most remarkable vitality.   Indeed, some kind of economic base notion is to be found in almost all regional projection exercises, at least implicitly.[1]   The substantive issue is really not whether a base or exogeneity concept is to be employed but how much openness or interdependence will be tolerated.   Unquestionably, the remarkable durability of the underlying idea of exogeneity embodied in the base concept is simply that no other empirically implementable alternative now exists.

3. *Input–Output Analysis.*   This is even true of the second applied technique of great importance in regional economics, input–output analysis, and its closely associated matrix multiplier concepts.   Even in these more sophisticated and interdependent models some choice usually must be made of an exogenous bill of goods to be entered as " final demand."   In broad, idealized outline, the objective of an interregional interindustry input–output analysis is a matrix of input–output coefficients identified not only by industry but also by geographic areas or regions [70, ch. 8] [67] [92].   Thus, if there were 50 industries and 5 regions, the ideal matrix would contain 62,500 coefficients decomposable into 25 submatrices of 2500 (50 × 50) entries each;   for each region there would be 5 matrices, one of which defined

---

[1] A persuasive argument has been advanced by D. C. North [100], in fact, for defining regions, at least for purposes of historical analysis, so that they have homogeneous export bases.

its own interindustry relationships and 4 relating to trade relationships by industry with the other regions. Such an idealized table, however, is usually impossible to realize because of data insufficiencies. A central preoccupation of regional input–output analysis has therefore been the making of adaptations to overcome these data difficulties, and most of these adaptations involve aggregation aimed at eliminating some of the empirical detail needed to estimate the idealized table.

One obvious simplification is to treat each region as if it were an *almost* autonomous economic unit and proceed as with the estimation of an input–output table for a national economy by consolidating all inflows and outflows to other regions into an import–export sector. What this essentially amounts to is an aggregation over all rows and columns in the idealized matrix outside of the particular region of study, a record being retained mainly of the interindustry relationships within the region under study. This is probably the most common approach now taken to the estimation of regional input–output relations; two good illustrative examples of such tables can be found in the work of W. Z. Hirsch [60] and R. Artle [13].

A second approach, rather opposite in its aggregation procedure, is to completely forget about interindustry relations and concentrate on interregional trade patterns. This essentially amounts to aggregating over industries but not over regions. An illustrative example of such an approach is contained in the procedures proposed for the Upper Middle West study [58]. This procedure has the great advantage that interindustry coefficients for individual regions are usually very hard to come by, not uncommonly being estimated by simply assuming that the national coefficients apply within a region. Furthermore, an interregional trade-flow approach retains the emphasis where it usually is needed for policy purposes.

A third simplification is to define interregional trade coefficients for each commodity as an input, forgetting about interindustry differences in import patterns within each region. Thus, instead of having separate import input coefficients for each region and industry, a trade coefficient is constructed for each region by a particular type of input. This essentially reduces all the interindustry trade relationship submatrices between the specific region and regions other than itself in the idealized model to a single vector for each region. For example, if there were 50 industries in the model, instead of having 50 × 50 matrix of coefficients to define trade relationships between one region and another, there would be instead only a 50-element vector. The essential assumption lying behind this procedure is that if imports of a commodity are needed as inputs by industries of a given region, exactly the same relative imports of this commodity will be needed for all industries in the region. The aggregation is essentially over trade input coefficients, since industry destination of imported inputs is ignored. One great advantage of this scheme is that it is empirically implementable with available Interstate Commerce Commission data on commodity flows. Illustrative examples of this approach can be found in the work of H. Chenery [27] and L. Moses [93].

A fourth approach to data simplification for interregional input–output models is the balanced regional growth model developed by Leontief and Isard [84, ch. 4, 5]. It is based on the notion that a hierarchical arrangement or definition of industries is possible in which certain industries can be described as basically catering to national markets, and others to regional or local markets. The input–output analysis then proceeds according to this hierarchical ordering with activity levels for the national industries being estimated first. These national industry outputs are then allocated to the different regions according to regional participation coefficients to form part of the final demand for each region, the remainder being regionally produced commodities. Following this, the regional composition of interindustry activity can be estimated by conventional input–output methods; in fact, national interindustry relationships have usually been suggested for this exercise. The process can be carried down, of course, to as low a level of geographic disaggregation as data permit and objectives might require. As for applications, the New York metropolitan region study used a rather heuristic variation of this balanced growth approach in arriving at its projections [19] [115].

A fifth and most ingenious approach to data simplification in regional input–output analysis has very recently been advanced by Leontief and A. Strout [85]. The essence of the method is to use gravity-type structural equations to explain or estimate the magnitude of interregional flow. Specifically, the flow of a commodity from one region to another is assumed to be directly proportional to the product of its total output in a shipping region by its total input in a receiving region divided by the aggregate amount of the commodity produced and consumed in the entire economy, all multiplied by an empirical constant. (Leontief also permits every region to be both a shipper and receiver of a commodity which at the level of aggregation now employed in input–output he properly argues is a more realistic assumption than hypothesizing the economically rational solution of only one-way flows.) The constants can be statistically estimated by various methods or, what is most important from the standpoint of data conservation, by solving the equations of the regional input–output system, including the gravity-flow equations in the system. If this latter direct or " exact " solution, as Leontief calls it, is obtained, the existence of the balance equations inherent in input–output systems makes it possible to estimate the interregional flows without directly observing them; the only data needed are those on total outputs and inputs for all regions and the use made of each commodity as an input to internal production in each region. The crucial question, of course, is how well the flow estimates generated by use of the hypothesized gravity-flow structure approximate reality. In this regard initial experiments have been most encouraging. In fact, in tests on bituminous coal, cement, and steel shapes, the " exact solution " has performed about as well as least squares on projections and in some senses even better.

Input–output techniques are subject, of course, to a number of criticisms, since they embody so many important and controversial simplifying assumptions. These are so well known, to users of input–output as well as its critics, and so extensively catalogued elsewhere [91] [93] [128] that no repetition will be made here. Suffice it to say that regional input–output models tend to have all the problems of national models plus some additional ones of their own. In particular, there is at least some limited evidence that interregional trade coefficients may be even more unstable over time than interindustry coefficients [93]. Such instability almost surely applies as well to the regional participation coefficients used in the balanced regional growth model.

The fact still remains that with all its problems and difficulties input–output does have the great advantage of being an empirically workable model that provides an organizational framework and set of consistency checks that are difficult to achieve with less formal techniques. The danger does exist, though, that preoccupation with the empirical detail involved in establishing these models may lead to an oversight of importance, perhaps of such importance that it leads to grossly inaccurate estimates. Thus, it is often argued that an understanding of basic historical trends and forces is more essential to making good projections than accurate interindustry and interregional trade coefficients. Still this is not an intrinsic shortcoming of the model as such. Rather it is a question of what constitutes a proper allocation of research resources in regional analysis and, as will be observed in the next section, this is a question very much in dispute. Finally, it must be recognized that input–output and economic base analyses, with all their shortcomings and deficiencies, are the tools almost invariably relied upon at the present time when actual empirical work in regional economics must be performed.

4. *Mathematical Programming.* The fourth basic theoretical tool commonly employed in modern regional analysis, mathematical programming, is without question the best from a strictly conceptual point of view if one believes in a reasonably pervasive economic rationality.[1] It suffers, though, from two serious handicaps. The first is that of simple data availability; the data requirements for a good linear programming model are often staggeringly large and even further beyond what is currently available than the requirements for input–output. The second difficulty is that economic rationality is often either not obviously pervasive or, more accurately, is too complex to be readily incorporated into presently operational programming models.

---

[1] The conceptual aspects of applying mathematical programming to location and regional analysis problems are discussed by T. C. Koopmans and M. Beckman [78], Beckman and T. Marschak [16], L. Lefeber [80], B. H. Stevens [111], and L. N. Moses [94]. Actual applications of such techniques are reported by Henderson [56] [57], F. T. Moore [90], and K. A. Fox [35].

The most ambitious effort to date in the use of linear programming techniques in a regional project has been the Penn-Jersey study's household location model, and their experiences illustrate both basic difficulties [59] [48–52]. They started with the highly appealing and simple notion that different types of households have certain specific amounts that they can budget for " the bundle of services " associated with a particular type of house. Included in the definition of housing type was the amount of land consumed so that the selection of different housing types gives rise to different land-use patterns. Families differently located in the income scale and with different numbers of children or other characteristics are, moreover, hypothesized to have different willingness to pay for specific types of housing as expressed by the size of their budgets available for each housing type. Later the model was modified to make the budgets not only specific to housing types but also to areas on the grounds that it is more realistic to assume that families consider the residential location and its amenities as well as the structure and size of yard when deciding the amount that they are willing to pay for a particular house.

Still another modification, introduced in order to effect a considerable reduction in the computational burden, was simply to preselect the housing type in every geographic area that seemed most suitable for each family type in that area on the grounds that this selection was usually obvious without running the model. After the budgets had been estimated for each family type in each area and for every housing type, all costs for each housing type and location *not* associated with land acquisition were deducted from the budget estimate to determine the net rent-paying ability of each family for each housing type in a specific location. That is, transportation, structure, and amenity (schooling, public services, etc.) costs were subtracted from the total available budget to determine how much was left for land acquisition or rent. Households were then hypothesized to compete with one another for the available land, bidding rents up to a maximum (the objective function) subject to the constraints that all households get located and that total land-use does not exceed total land available. One immediate advantage of this research design is that it yields an estimate of the rent surface as an output rather than being required as an input, a considerable gain since urban land values or rents are difficult data to obtain.

The striking thing about this model is the degree to which the important behavioral considerations are built into the model prior to its actual running. This immediately raises at least a research resource allocation problem of whether it is wise to devote considerable effort to building such a model until the reliability of its inputs has been established. Particularly important among the prior questions are estimating the budgets by household type and location and choosing a particular housing type in each area for each family. Indeed, this choice of particular housing type in each locale is crucial in determining the actual land-use pattern. For example, if in the preselection process, housing types are chosen so as to yield the greatest per-acre rent-paying ability, a bias is built in toward finding high density land-use patterns. The converse is true if the housing yielding the greatest per-family rent-paying ability is preselected. In recognition of these difficulties, the Penn–Jersey group are now considering the preselection of housing types so as to provide the greatest per-family net rent-paying ability as determined by subtracting a prior estimate of the initial rent surface from the budget along with the other cost estimates. They would then proceed as before, maximizing rent-paying on a gross basis. This scheme, of course, immediately loses some of the advantages of not needing a prior rent surface, but this deficiency can be at least partially overcome by iterating the model a few times if the rents estimated by the model differ substantially from the rents assumed *a priori*.

Purists, of course, might still raise a number of quibbles about the behavioral assumptions incorporated in this model even as modified. It is, however, a highly imaginative and heroic attempt to apply the techniques of mathematical programming to an actual location problem, and by any standards it is the most ambitious effort of its kind yet undertaken in regional economics. As such, its trials and tribulations are surely suggestive, and it is difficult to escape the conclusion on the basis of that experience that programming may still be beyond available data and research resources, at least given the present paucity of prior or established knowledge about urban economics and location patterns. It is difficult, on the other hand, to conceive how the necessary knowledge and insights needed for adequately implementing these models will ever be acquired without such experimental undertakings.

IV. Types of Approach to Regional Studies

It is probably apparent by this point that if the important issues associated with data collection are put to one side, the basic disagreements arising in the application of regional analyses tend to be as much a matter of viewpoint or philosophical orientation as of technical detail. Specifically, two rather different approaches are discernible. In one the emphasis is on historical and behavioral characteristics; in the other the orientation is more toward quantification, forecasting, and the development of a logically rigorous framework for the analysis. To be sure, these distinctions are at least somewhat arbitrary, as most such classifications usually are. Thus, those with an historical–behavioral inclination also often try to make quantitative forecasts and those with an analytical–quantitative approach normally will try to develop an understanding of underlying behavioral patterns. Furthermore, one of the dominant concerns in the field at the moment is with finding means of fusing or synthesizing the best elements in different approaches into better, more comprehensive, procedures [70, ch. 12] [71].

Still, very important differences in emphasis do exist. For example, those with an historical–behavioral orientation tend to stress the analysis of trends and evolutionary patterns. They try to "dig beneath" the data to an understanding of motivations, particularly those leading to significant changes in structure and conduct. Thus their concern tends to be more with structural change than with its continuity. They are not too disturbed, moreover, if this structural change makes forecasting hazardous or uncertain or if their forecasts are not formally rigorous and consistent in all details. Their involvement tends to be more with whether what they have said and forecast is plausible in light of current or apparent trends in behavior. In keeping with this, they often will emphasize such considerations as entrepreneurship, market structure, and external economies that normally are not conveniently incorporated into the more formal analytical frameworks. [1] Finally, they are often quite willing to sacrifice a good static analysis even for an admittedly poor dynamic analysis, for as one proponent of this point of view, B. R. Berman, has so eloquently put it [18, p. 300]:

> "It may be argued that dynamic models are harder to construct than static, or that we cannot begin to fashion dynamic models until we have a static model of some believability. But for practical purposes . . . a crude dynamic model may be better than a highly tooled, multi-jeweled static creation."

Two leading prototypes of regional analyses with this emphasis on behavioral considerations are the New York metropolitan region study and, to a lesser extent, the Pittsburgh area economic study.

By contrast, those of the analytical-quantifier persuasion will emphasize formal structure and consistency. Far from being fascinated by structural discontinuities, they often will seek to establish empirically that behavioral instability, at least of sufficient impact to modify their structural parameters, is more the exception than the rule. They will be interested in developing relationships to explain structural change only if confronted with obvious necessity. Similarly, they are usually willing to sacrifice some dynamics to obtain better static models. They are also likely to be much more concerned with problems of regional income and social accounting. A good one-sentence summary of the beliefs held by those adopting this more formal approach was once rendered by Isard in defense of input–output procedures as follows [70, p. 341]: "When combined with intuition and hunch, input–output projections yield results at least as good as those based on intuition and hunch alone." Most of the work with regional analysis in Europe and in underdeveloped countries displays these more formalistic tendencies [82] [70], and the Penn–Jersey study with its emphasis on a linear programming approach is surely of this kind. The Upper Midwest study, on the other hand, represents a very interesting compromise or hybrid of the two different basic approaches.

---

[1] For a further expression of these views see B. Chinitz's Paper [29] on the implications of market structure and industry characteristics for regional development.

Some of these differences in approach are traceable to and explained by differences in policy orientations. The behaviorist seems to look to the making of piecemeal adjustments in existing institutions and public policy arrangements as the soundest procedure. He tends to formulate less ambitious goals and to think in terms of a series of short-run policy adjustments over time. This results in his emphasizing flexibility and adaptability. As R. Vernon stated when summing up the New York metropolitan study [115, p. 196]:

> "No projection of the economic and demographic characteristics of a metropolitan area can be free of the risk of error; no public or private planner can afford to assume that the potential error is small. From a policy viewpoint, this may suggest that planners and investors should regard the preservation of flexibility as a virtue in itself, a virtue worth paying for at the seeming sacrifice of other standards of performance."

By contrast, those with the more formal outlook are oriented more toward drawing up comprehensive development plans. This at least partially explains the popularity of this approach in underdeveloped countries confronted with long-range problems of considerable magnitude and often facing a requirement to justify loans for large-scale development investments before world banking and development authorities. Indeed, an emphasis on long-range, comprehensive planning apparently done to the best of current technical capabilities has an almost inherent and undeniable appeal, and perhaps the appearance of indispensability when undertaking capital budgeting decisions. Something of the ambition and confidence in policy matters of those advocating a more formal approach to regional analysis is connoted in the following statement by J. R. Boudeville [22, pp. 11–12]:

> "Regional Economy is a science of decision. It presupposes the determination of aims, the use of means and the choice of the most effective instruments to achieve those aims. ... The problem of bringing to light the interrelations of the economic trends and the coherence of the means and aims requires the presence of a regional command familiar with the new techniques. ... Admittedly, excellent regional schemes have been carried out without the aid of modern techniques. The Roman aqueducts and Gothic cathedrals did not wait for Strength of Materials calculations to be architectural feats. Similarly, we can admire the work of the pioneers of our time. Nevertheless, the role of the economist is to produce general rules superseding the old empirical approach and piecemeal work, which is always expensive."

The obvious, appropriately evasive, comment for any reviewer attempting to maintain at least an appearance of neutrality when confronted with such contrasting viewpoints is, simply, that each approach probably has a role.

In this case, moreover, such a statement is not only diplomatic but probably correct. Structural coefficients will be relatively stable in many circumstances while not in others. Even if not stable, moreover, structural estimates often will be required just simply to *begin* a rational analysis. However, if the initial analysis is not followed by studies aimed at understanding the patterns of change, the resulting forecasts and policy decisions are likely to be next to, but not quite, worthless. Furthermore, it does seem rational to build flexibility into the decision process, *but* in proportion to the degree of uncertainty attached to the crucial structural estimates used in making initial decisions. This degree of uncertainty also may very well vary for different aspects of the decision process and these differences too should be reflected in the degree of flexibility retained. In short, decision-making for economic policy is still a very crude science and it behooves the cautious man to be eclectic.

Whatever the orientation or preferences adopted on these issues, it seems rather difficult to deny that at the moment regional analysis tends to be somewhat stronger in the formulation of analytical frameworks than in fundamental understanding of any behavioral regularities at work shaping regional and metropolitan growth patterns. Particularly notable for their scarcity throughout the fifties were quantitative studies aimed at hypothesis-testing that were so common in most other fields of economics at that time. Indeed, ever since the interest in interregional analysis of business cycles diminished in the late forties, there has even been a relative lack of suggestions on hypotheses to be tested. Rather, the conceptual activity in regional analysis has been concerned mainly with the construction of logically consistent schemes for organizing and presenting data, particularly social accounts, with a secondary emphasis on normative policy prescriptions. Many of the hypotheses that have been developed from the theoretical work, moreover, have either been at a highly aggregative level, like those embodied in many economic base multiplier concepts, or have been such obvious abstractions as to not easily elicit serious statistical study, like Lösch's location theory. Accordingly, the work of those with an historical–behavioral bent at least serves the extremely useful purpose of beginning to fill this hypothesis void. Furthermore, this work illustrates the important point that bringing to bear certain aspects of conventional economic theory and thought now often ignored in regional economics can be highly productive of new insights and hypotheses in this field.

Further verification on this point has been provided recently by three excellent efforts [2] [96] [122] to develop formal models defining relationships between urban land-use patterns and explanatory economic factors. These models not only give an organization to the discussion that was badly needed but yield eminently testable hypotheses. Indeed, the only criticism that might be made is to regret that the authors haven't yet proceeded on to the testing, especially since the process probably would have sharpened the hypotheses. These theories all place almost exclusive emphasis on economic variables, like relevant prices and costs or proxies for costs such as " elapsed travel time " for access to places of work or other centers. It would seem highly probable that a number of sociological variables, like those commonly encountered in cross-section consumer budget studies, are required for a really adequate empirical explanation of locational choices. Of particular importance would appear to be variables defining family characteristics (e.g., number of children and employed individuals) when seeking explanations of residential choices.

The importance of these family-characteristic variables has been demonstrated, in fact, in results obtained by J. F. Kain [75] [76] in a study of Detroit residential location patterns based on data collected as part of the Detroit area transportation study. Kain, in collaboration with J. Niedercorn [99] and others, has also been testing other hypotheses about urban location patterns as part of the RAND study of urban transportation and land use. In this study the emphasis is on the relationship of urban transportation to metropolitan growth patterns, although other determinants of urban growth are also being investigated. The studies are, for the most part, formally econometric in character and based as much on intercity as intracity comparisons, thus taking advantage of the fact that the RAND project is liberated from the geographical and policy constraints that often have inhibited effective hypothesis-testing in specific regional studies. The plethora of available cross-section data based on intercity samples makes it possible to entertain a considerably widened range of hypotheses and tests with these data.

Of a somewhat similar character are a series of recent studies on urban transportation characteristics recently completed by the Northwestern University Traffic and Transportation Institute [95] [101] [120]. These studies, among other contributions, embody the first really substantial attempt to estimate demand and cross-elasticity parameters that are essential to intelligent formulation of urban transportation policies. The evidence produced is not, incidentally, comforting to those who believe that creation of more and better public transit, by government subsidy if necessary, will relieve automobile congestion in urban areas by attracting commuters away from their private automobiles. The cross-elasticity of demand between private auto and public transit commutation would appear to be so low that actual payments might have to be made to transit riders to induce any considerable shift in patronage.

That regional economics will benefit from the confrontation of hypotheses with actual data is also suggested by the results of those few quantitative studies that have been directed to the testing of hypotheses in regional economics. These tests, incidentally, need not be formidable or involve formal econometrics to have a high yield. For example, much of the New York metropolitan region study's activities involved the formulation, reformulation, and testing of hypotheses against available data, though only occasionally with formal statistical procedures. The tests were formal or consistent in an economic sense, however, since they were unified by continual reference to the basic hypothesis that underlaid the entire project, namely that New York is what it is because of its peculiar attraction for " external economy industries " that " have a compelling need to be close to other firms in order to make sales or hold down costs " [115, p. 6]. The model is " closed," moreover, by an ingenious historical explanation of why New York has developed a particularly advantageous position in these external or agglomeration economies [115, ch. 2].

These same traditions of combining historical and economic explanations and reformulating hypotheses as experience and data accumulate seem to have been perpetuated in the Pittsburgh area economic study, which has some of the same personnel and leadership as the New York study. In this study, though, the emphasis seems to be more on the special role played in regional growth by natural resource endowments; furthermore, the highly interesting hypothesis has been tentatively advanced that these resources, by inducing the growth of heavy, large-scale mass-production industries with a technological bias in their management requirements, have indirectly prevented Pittsburgh from realizing the same agglomeration economies for its size that other cities with more diversified, small-scale industries have experienced [29].

An orientation to hypothesis-testing is also evident in the background studies being prepared as part of the Upper Midwest study. These background studies, incidentally, are justified in the general research design of the main project both for their own sake and as a source of information on changes in coefficients needed to make desired long-range forecasts. The early focus in this study, for quite understandable reasons, has been on the recent technological revolution in agriculture and the implications of this revolution for labor-force migration. For example, L. A. Sjaastad, in a highly interesting study of migration patterns in the Upper Midwest, tests the hypothesis that since " a good part of what we consider human capital is an accumulation of skills and experience specific to an occupation ... income differentials could persist over long time periods even in a market system with no lags or imperfections save lack of perfect foresight " [110, p. 45]. His preliminary empirical evidence on migration patterns by age groups and geographic areas within the Upper Midwest lends, moreover, considerable support to the hypothesis.

This very basic question of resource mobility also has been studied empirically by W. H. Miernyck [89] and G. H. Borts [20]. Miernyck, in an interview study of displaced New England textile workers, also finds that the problems of adaptation to technological change tend to weigh most heavily on older workers and are far from being automatically self-correcting, at least in the short run. In fact, Miernyck finds that re-employment in the textile industry is about the only real hope for many older unemployed textile workers in New England because of their high degree of skill specialization; and such re-employment opportunities appear only slowly in a declining industry.

Borts considerably broadens the analysis, explaining the persistence of regional wage differences in terms of regional differences in capital movements, birth rates, the marginal efficiency of new investments, and export industry composition, as well as any residual labor immobility. Borts also presents a more refined analysis of the interrelationships between wage differences and labor and capital movements. He builds a strong case for the hypothesis that capital movements, exogenously induced by an expansion in demand for the particular industries or exports of certain regions, have been the principal factor sustaining interregional wage differences in the United States.

Support for at least part of this hypothesis is also provided by a study of changes since 1929 in the distribution of manufacturing activities in the United States by V. R. Fuchs [37] [38] [39]. A major conclusion is [38, p. 177]:

> " The most important redistributions occurred in labor-oriented industries such as textiles and apparel, or in industries oriented to natural resources such as chemicals, lumber and paper. The single most important locational development since 1929, the growth of the aircraft industry in the Southwest, is probably attributable more to climate than to any other factor."

Accordingly, Fuchs, like Borts, stresses the importance of exogenous factors in shaping regional growth characteristics. Indeed, a prime objective of Fuchs is to reject the hypothesis that locational changes in manufacturing can be explained endogenously by shifts in local market industries following demand into regions with newly expanded populations. In short, Fuchs tends to see changes in manufacturing locations much more as a cause than as an effect of population shifts.

A somewhat different view of these causal relationships is to be found in a study by H. S. Perloff, E. S. Dunn, E. E. Lampard, and R. E. Muth [105] on the relationships between regional growth, incomes, and resources. These authors, who have something to say (historically, conceptually, and empirically) on almost every aspect of the regional income differentiation question, guardedly adopt the view that for manufacturing " the tie to resources has not been dominant " while access to " terminal markets " deserves heavy emphasis as an explanation of locational shifts [105, p. 394]. The discrepancies between the findings of Perloff and associates and those of Fuchs are at least partly attributable to differences in definitions and choice of analytical procedures. Specifically, Fuchs chose to analyze the location of market-oriented industries directly while Perloff and colleagues put a major emphasis on the direct analysis of natural-resource-using industries;

furthermore, they define natural resources in the conventional fashion, thus excluding climate and low-cost labor, two factors which play a very prominent role in Fuchs's explanations.

Perloff, Dunn, Lampard, and Muth also argue that capital flows have not been and probably will not be in the future sufficient to quickly eliminate interregional differences in wages for similar skills. Outmigration of labor is therefore seen as required to achieve interregional equilibration of incomes, and this migration has occurred at such " painfully slow rates " that they favor positive governmental action to alleviate the difficulties. They clearly suggest (pp. 606–7), moreover, that this action should extend beyond policies aimed at improvement of the overall levels of national prosperity to specific regional aid programs. They grant, though, that general prosperity since 1940 has slowly but surely helped with alleviation of regional income imbalances. Furthermore, they associate the worst regional income imbalances with problems created by structural changes in agriculture, the major part of which may now be completed. The question therefore arises, but is left unanswered, of whether regional imbalances will be as serious a problem in the future as in the recent past.

No short summary can do justice, however, to this complex, thoughtful, and important study of regional problems. Among many virtues, it provides a wealth of data on regional changes and characteristics that have not been readily accessible previously. It will unquestionably be a standard reference for future empirical researchers in regional economics. Evaluated together with the other recent efforts to revive hypothesis-testing on regional problems, it leads to the almost incontestable conclusion that regional economics has both the data and hypotheses to become a behavioral as well as a normative science.

V. CONCLUSIONS

A basic theme of the preceding discussion is that regional economics has progressed significantly in the last decade and has been concerned, in a generally effective fashion, with contributing to the solution of a number of important policy questions. Some of this progress, however, has been achieved at the neglect of certain important questions and a diversion of effort from fruitful research channels. In short, regional economics is incomplete in a number of important respects, apart from the mere existence of a number of untouched research questions and problems. Specifically, the suggestion has been advanced that regional economics has reached a stage where it could benefit from some redirection of effort away from the design of broad conceptual frameworks and accumulation of regional income accounts toward the formulation and testing of behavioral hypotheses, with the initial emphasis being placed on hypotheses that could be quite readily developed from the application of general economic concepts already available.

Some redirection of effort along these lines seems justified if for no other reason than that many of the sophisticated research designs now being attempted in regional economics require a considerable input of " behavioral understanding " to be effective. The Penn–Jersey linear programming model, with its highly complicated structure of behavioral assumptions, is illustrative; in fact, the most immediate contribution of the Penn–Jersey study may be a better understanding of some behavioral characteristics because of research stimulated by the necessity to have reasonably realistic inputs in the model. Similarly, the validity and accuracy of many input–output applications obviously depend on a knowledge of the structural coefficients involved. These, in turn, are often undergoing continual change; and explaining these changes requires more knowledge of behavioral characteristics than is now normally available.

In a pragmatic, decision-oriented field like regional economics some attention also might be given to the highly practical question of when and whether more complex research designs yield sufficiently improved results to justify their costs. Particularly relevant would be some empirical tests of the effects of incorporating greater or less interdependence and aggregation into regional forecasting models. For instance, is a gain in accuracy always obtained from using a matrix multiplier in place of a highly aggregative composite coefficient of the type normally employed in so-called economic base analyses? If not, is there a pattern to the performance comparisons so that this information could be used to improve the allocation of research resources in future undertakings? In general, regional analysis might benefit from an incorporation of some of the ideas found in modern statistical decision theory and particularly the notion that the costs of obtaining better decisions should be compared with the obtainable yield.

The scarcity of hypothesis-testing in regional analysis is all the more regrettable when the availability of much excellent and highly relevant data is noted. Specifically, among other things, the nature of U.S. government census practices, the regionalization of the banking system, and the common requirement by the Bureau of Public Roads that a considerable proportion of any research funds made available under the interstate highway program be spent on local data-gathering and interview studies have resulted in a remarkable collection of cross-section data being available on regional, state, metropolitan, and even intracity characteristics. Indeed, it is hardly any exaggeration to say that regional economics is in many ways one of the most fortunately blessed fields in economics in terms of data availability.

Yet it gives an appearance, as noted previously, of being notably undernourished in data. The paradox is more apparent than real. The data problems in regional economics stem more from a choice of activities and interests by regional economists than from any other factor. With a few notable exceptions, regional economists have shown a great propensity for undertaking the difficult tasks first. For example, estimating input–output tables is difficult enough at the national level, even with all the statistics that are available only at that level of aggregation.   Mathematical programming often encounters serious data problems when confined to the analysis of a limited optimization problem within an individual firm.   Constructing good income accounts has proven a quite formidable task even for well-financed and -staffed national agencies.   In fact, it is still true in the United States, where national income accounting has been pioneered, that a number of notable deficiencies or guesses exist in the available social accounts.   It is at least relevant to ask, therefore, if constructing elaborate regional accounts, as advocated by many regional economists, is a justifiable expenditure of limited research resources until the more important limitations in the national accounts are removed.

Regional data problems are not, of course, unimportant or undeserving of attention.   Many of them must be solved, in fact, before certain important empirical investigations can be undertaken.   Furthermore, there is obviously a considerable demand in some quarters for better regional accounts as an aid to policy-making.   Nevertheless, a more nearly optimal allocation of research resources within regional economics would seem to involve less relative effort on income accounting and interregional trade-flow coefficient estimation and more attention to developing and testing hypotheses.   In the short run, moreover, a number of interesting and highly pertinent hypotheses could be subjected to at least preliminary testing with data that are already available and of quite respectable accuracy.

In sum, regional economics is very much what it is today because it has stood ready to attempt analytical solutions to difficult policy problems.   Its major contributions thus far have been to provide broad measures and frameworks needed to evaluate and organize these activities—and this is without question a considerable contribution.   Further implementation or realization on these efforts will require, however, greater knowledge of regional growth processes and related behavioral patterns than is now available.   To do this, regional economics almost certainly must become increasingly involved with hypotheses about the behaviour and role of financial organizations, market structures, entrepreneurship, private and public investment decisions, taxes, fiscal policies, and all the other subjects normally encompassed in economics but now encountered only occasionally in regional economics.   By contrast, relatively less effort is likely to be needed on studies concerned exclusively with constructing research frameworks and studying the effects of spatial separation for its own sake.   Since these two latter areas have tended to be the distinctive elements in regional economics in recent years, this suggests that regional economics may increasingly be indistinguishable from the rest of economics.   It is not clear, moreover, that such a development should be viewed with great alarm in a world made increasingly smaller and more homogeneous by political and institutional developments and by improvements in transportation, communications, and other technologies, with all that these imply for resource mobility.

REFERENCES

1. V. V. ALMENDINGER, *Topics in the Regional Growth Model: I*, Penn-Jersey Study Paper No. 4. Philadelphia 1961.
2. W. ALONSO, " A Theory of the Urban Land Market," *Papers and Proceedings Reg. Sci. Assoc.*, 1960, **6**, 149–57.
3. R. B. ANDREWS, " Mechanics of the Urban Economic Base: Historical Development of the Base Concept," *Land Economics*, May 1953, **29**, 161–67.
4. —— " Mechanics of the Urban Economic Base: The Problem of Terminology," *Land Economics*, Aug. 1953, **29**, 263–68.
5. —— " Mechanics of the Urban Economic Base: A Classification of Base Types," *Land Economics*, Nov. 1953, **29**, 343–50.
6. —— " Mechanics of the Urban Economic Base: The Problem of Base Measurement," *Land Economics*, Feb. 1954, **30**, 52–60.
7. —— " Mechanics of the Urban Economic Base: General Problems of Identification," *Land Economics*, May 1954, **30**, 164–72.
8. —— " Mechanics of the Urban Economic Base: Special Problems of Base Identification," *Land Economics*, Aug. 1954, **30**, 260–69.
9. —— " Mechanics of the Urban Economic Base: The Problem of Base Area Delimitation," *Land Economics*, Nov. 1954, **30**, 309–19.
10. —— " Mechanics of the Urban Economic Base: The Concept of Base Ratios," *Land Economics*, Feb. 1955, **31**, 47–53.
11. —— " Mechanics of the Urban Economic Base: Causes and Effects of Change in the Base Ratios and the Ratio Elements," *Land Economics*, May, Aug., Nov. 1955, **31**, 144–55, 245–56, 361–71.
12. —— " Mechanics of the Urban Economic Base: The Base Concept and the Planning Process," *Land Economics*, Feb. 1956, **32**, 69–84.
13. R. ARTLE, *Studies in the Structure of the Stockholm Economy: Towards a Framework For Projecting Metropolitan Community Development.* Stockholm 1959.
14. L. D. ASHBY AND E. P. TRUEX, *The Estimation of Income Payments to Individuals in North Carolina Counties.* Chapel Hill 1952.
15. W. J. BAUMOL, " Activity Analyses in One Lesson," *Am. Econ. Rev.*, Dec. 1958, **48**, 837–73.
16. M. BECKMAN, " Some Reflections on Lösch's Theory of Location," *Papers and Proceedings Reg. Sci. Assoc.*, 1955, **1**, N1–N9.
17. —— AND T. MARSCHAK, " An Activity Analysis Approach to Location Theory," *Kyklos*, 1955, **8**, 125–43.
18. B. BERMAN, " Analysis of Urban Problems-Discussion," *Am. Econ. Rev.*, May 1961, **51**, 299–300.
19. —— B. CHINITZ AND E. M. HOOVER, *Projection of a Metropolis.* Cambridge, Mass. 1961.
20. G. H. BORTS, " The Equalization of Returns and Regional Economic Growth," *Am. Econ. Rev.*, June 1960, **50**, 319–47.
21. J. R. BOUDEVILLE, " A Survey of Recent Techniques for Regional Economic Analysis," *Regional Economic Planning: Techniques of Analysis*, W. Isard and J. H. Cumberland, ed., Paris 1960, pp. 377–98.
22. —— " Frontiers and Interrelations of Regional Planning," paper given at *International Congress on Economic Development*, Vienna, Aug.–Sept. 1962.
23. A. BRIGHT AND G. ELLIS, ed., *The Economic State of New England.* New Haven 1954.
24. J. D. CARROLL, " Spatial Interaction and the Urban-Metropolitan Description," *Papers and Proceedings Reg. Sci. Assoc.*, 1955, **1**, D1–D14.
25. —— AND H. W. BEVIS, " Predicting Local Travel in Urban Regions," *Papers and Proceedings Reg. Sci. Assoc.*, 1957, **3**, 183–97.

26. G. A. P. Carrothers, " An Historical Review of the Gravity and Potential Concepts of Human Interaction," *Jour. Am. Instit. Planners*, Spring 1956, **22**, 94–102.
27. H. B. Chenery, P. G. Clark and V. Cao-Pinna, *The Structure and Growth of the Italian Economy*. Rome 1953.
28. B. Chinitz, *Freight and the Metropolis*. Cambridge, Mass. 1960.
29. ——— " Contrasts in Agglomeration: New York and Pittsburgh," *Am. Econ. Rev.*, May 1961, **51**, 279–89.
30. J. S. Chipman, *The Theory of Intersectoral Money Flows and Income Formation*. Baltimore 1950.
31. A. H. Conrad, " Unemployment in a Growing Economy: The U.S. Case and a Program for Balanced Regional Growth." Public lecture delivered at the University of Edinburgh April 19, 1962. Published by the Netherlands Econ. Inst. Div. of Balanced International Growth. Mimeographed.
32. R. Dorfman, " Mathematical or Linear Programming: A Non-Mathematical Exposition," *Am. Econ. Rev.*, Dec. 1953, **43**, 797–825.
33. ——— " Operations Research," *Am. Econ. Rev.*, Sept. 1960, **50**, 580–86.
34. J. L. Fisher, " Concepts in Regional Economic Development Programs," *Papers and Proceedings Reg. Sci. Assoc.*, 1955, **1**, W1–W20.
35. K. A. Fox, " A Spatial Equilibrium Model of the Livestock Feed Economy in the United States," *Econometrica*, Oct. 1953, **21**, 547–66.
36. G. Freutel, " The Eighth District Balance of Trade," *Monthly Review*, Federal Reserve Bank of St. Louis, June 1952, **34**, 69–78.
37. V. R. Fuchs, " Changes in the Location of U.S. Manufacturing Since 1929," *Jour. Reg. Sci.*, Spring 1959, **1**, 1–17.
38. ——— " The Determinants of the Redistribution of Manufacturing in the United States Since 1929," *Rev. Econ. Stat.*, May 1962, **44**, 167–77.
39. ——— *Changes in the Location of Manufacturing in the United States Since 1929*. New Haven 1962.
40. M. E. Garnsey, *America's New Frontier, The Mountain West*. New York 1950.
41. R. Goodwin, " The Multiplier as Matrix," *Econ. Jour.*, Dec. 1949, **59**, 537–55.
42. M. J. Hagood, N. Danilevsky, and C. O. Beum, " An Examination of the Use of Factor Analysis in the Problem of Subregional Delineation," *Rural Sociology*, Sept. 1941, **6**, 216–33.
43. ——— " Statistical Methods for Delineation of Regions Applied to Data on Agriculture and Population," *Social Forces*, March 1943, **21**, 287–97.
44. ——— and E. H. Bernert, " Component Indexes as a Basis for Stratification in Sampling," *Jour. Am. Stat. Assoc.*, Sept. 1945, **40**, 330–41.
45. O. Handlin, *The Newcomers*. Cambridge, Mass. 1959.
46. F. A. Hanna, " Cyclical and Secular Changes in State Per Capita Incomes, 1929–50," *Rev. Econ. Stat.*, Aug. 1954, **36**, 320–30.
47. ——— *State Income Differentials 1919–1954*. Durham 1959.
48. Britton Harris, " Plan or Projection: An Examination of the Use of Models in Planning," *Jour. Am. Inst. Planners*, Nov. 1960, **26**, 265–72.
49. ——— " Some Problems in the Theory of Intra-Urban Location," *Op. Res.*, Sept.–Oct. 1961, **9**, 695–721.
50. ——— *Regional Growth Model-activity Distribution Sub-model*, Penn-Jersey Study Paper No. 7. Philadelphia 1961.
51. ——— " Experiments in Projection of Transportation and Land Use," *Traffic Quarterly*, April 1962, **16** (2), 305–19.
52. ——— *PJ Area Systems*, Penn–Jersey Study Paper No. 14. Philadelphia 1962.
53. S. Harris, *The Economics of New England*. Cambridge, Mass. 1952.

54. —— AND OTHERS, *New England Textiles and the New England Economy: Report by the New England Governors' Textile Committee to the Conference of New England Governors*, 1958.

55. R. B. HELFGOTT, W. E. GUSTAFSON AND J. M. HUND, *Made in New York*. Cambridge, Mass. 1960.

56. J. M. HENDERSON, "The Utilization of Agricultural Land: A Regional Approach," *Papers and Proceedings Reg. Sci. Assoc.*, 1957, **3**, 99–114.

57. —— *The Efficiency of the Coal Industry: An Application of Linear Programming*. Cambridge, Mass. 1958.

58. —— "An Economic Analysis of the Upper Midwest Region," *Four Papers on Methodology*, Upper Midwest Economic Study Technical Paper No. 1, June 1961, pp. 1–22.

59. J. D. HERBERT AND B. H. STEVENS, "A Model for the Distribution of Residential Activity in Urban Areas," *Jour. Reg. Sci.*, Fall 1960, **2**, 21–36.

60. W. Z. HIRSCH, "Interindustry Relations of a Metropolitan Area," *Rev. Econ. Stat.*, August 1959, **41**, 360–9.

61. —— "Design and Use of Regional Accounts," *Am. Econ. Rev.*, May 1962, **52**, 365–73.

62. W. HOCHWALD, "Conceptual Issues of Regional Income Estimation," *Regional Income*, Nat. Bur. of Econ. Research Stud. in Income and Wealth, Vol. 21, Princeton 1957, pp. 9–26.

63. C. B. HOOVER AND B. U. RATCHFORD, *The Economic Resources and Policies of the South*. New York 1951.

64. E. M. HOOVER, *The Location of Economic Activity*. New York 1948.

65. —— AND R. VERNON, *Anatomy of a Metropolis*. Cambridge, Mass. 1959.

66. H. H. HOYT, "Economic Background of Cities," *Jour. Land and Pub. Util. Econ.*, May 1941, **17**, 188–95.

67. W. ISARD, "Interregional and Regional Input–Output Analysis: A Model of a Space-Economy," *Rev. Econ. Stat.*, Nov. 1951, **33**, 318–28.

68. —— "Location Theory and Trade Theory, Short Run Analysis," *Quart. Jour. Econ.*, May 1954, **68**, 305–20.

69. —— *Location and Space Economy*. New York 1956.

70. —— *Methods of Regional Analysis*. New York 1960.

71. —— AND J. H. CUMBERLAND, ed., *Regional Economic Planning: Techniques of Analysis for Less Developed Areas*, Papers and Proceedings of the First Study Conference on Problems of Economic Development Organized by the European Productivity Agency. Paris 1961.

72. W. ISARD AND G. FREUTEL, "Regional and National Product Projection and Their Inter-Relation," *Long Range Economic Projection*, Nat. Bur. of Econ. Research Stud. in Income and Wealth, Vol. 16, Princeton 1954. pp. 427–71.

73. —— AND M. J. PECK, "Location Theory and International and Interregional Trade Theory," *Quart. Jour. Econ.*, Feb. 1954, **68**, 97–114.

74. —— E. W. SCHOOLER AND T. VIETORISZ, *Industrial Complex Analysis and Regional Development*. New York 1959.

75. J. F. KAIN, "The Journey-to-Work as a Determinant of Residential Location," *Papers and Proceedings Reg. Sci. Assoc.*, 1962, 9 (forthcoming).

76. —— *A Multiple Equation Model of Household Locational and Trip-making Behavior*, The RAND Corp., April 1962.

77. A. KNUDTSON AND R. COX, *Upper Midwest Agriculture: Structure and Problems*, Upper Midwest Economic Study, Study Paper No. 3, Jan. 1962.

78. T. L. KOOPMANS AND M. BECKMAN, "Assignment Problems and the Location of Economic Activities," *Econometrica*, Jan. 1957, **25**, 53–76.

79. A. KRUEGER, "Interrelationships between Agricultural Income and Population," *Four Papers on Methodology*, Upper Midwest Economic Study Technical Paper No. 1, June 1961, 70–81.

80. L. Lefeber, *Allocation in Space*. Amsterdam 1959.
81. R. M. Lichtenberg et al., *One-Tenth of a Nation*. Cambridge, Mass. 1960.
82. E. A. Lisle, "Regional Planning and Urban Development." Paper given at International Congress on Economic Development, Vienna, Aug.–Sept. 1962.
83. W. W. Leontief, *The Structure of American Economy 1919–1939*. New York 1951.
84. —— et al., *Studies in the Structure of the American Economy*. New York 1953.
85. —— and A. Strout, "Multiregional Input–Output Analysis." Paper presented at International Conference on Input–Output Techniques, Geneva, Sept. 1961.
86. A. Lösch, *The Economics of Location*. New Haven 1953.
87. I. S. Lowry, *Design for an Intra-Regional Locational Model*, Pittsburgh Regional Planning Association Economic Study of the Pittsburgh Region, Working Paper No. 6, Sept. 1960.
88. L. A. Metzler, "A Multiple Region Theory of Income and Trade," *Econometrica*, Oct. 1950, **18**, 329–54.
89. W. H. Miernyk, *Inter-Industry Labor Mobility*. Boston 1955.
90. F. T. Moore, "Regional Economic Reaction Paths," *Am. Econ. Rev.*, May 1955, **45**, 133–48.
91. O. Morgenstern, ed., *Economic Activity Analysis*. New York 1954.
92. L. N. Moses, "Interregional Analysis," *Report on Research for 1954, Havard Economic Research Project*. Cambridge, Mass. 1955.
93. —— "The Stability of Interregional Trading Patterns and Input–Output Analysis," *Am. Econ. Rev.*, Dec. 1955, **45**, 803–32.
94. —— "An Input–Output, Linear Programming Approach to Interregional Analysis," *Report, 1956–57, Harvard Economic Research Project*. Cambridge, Mass. 1957.
95. —— and H. W. Williamson, "*Economics of Consumer Choice in* Urban Transportation." Paper presented at a Symposium on The Dynamics of Urban Transportation. Detroit, Oct. 1962.
96. R. F. Muth, "Economic Change and Rural–Urban Land Conversions," *Econometrica*, Jan. 1961, **29**, 1–23.
97. P. Neff, "Interregional Cyclical Differentials: Causes, Measurement, and Significance," *Am. Econ. Rev.*, May 1949, **39**, 105–19.
98. —— and A. Werfenbach, *Business Cycles in Selected Industrial Areas*. Berkeley 1949.
99. J. M. Niedercorn and J. F. Kain, "Changes in the Location of Food and General Merchandise Store Employment within Metropolitan Areas, 1948–1958." Paper presented at the Western Economics Association Meeting, Aug. 1962.
100. D. C. North, "Location and Regional Economic Growth," *Jour. Pol. Econ.*, June 1955, **43**, 243–58.
101. W. Y. Oi and P. W. Shuldener, *An Analysis of Urban Travel Demands*. Evanston 1962.
102. H. S. Perloff, *Regional Studies at U.S. Universities: A Survey of Regionally Oriented Research and Graduate Education Activities*. Washington, D.C. 1957.
103. —— "Problems of Assessing Regional Economic Progress," *Regional Income*, Nat. Bur. of Econ. Research Stud. in Income and Wealth, Vol. 21. Princeton 1957, pp. 35–62.
104. —— "A National System of Metropolitan Information and Analysis," *Am. Econ. Rev.*, May 1962, **52**, 356–64.
105. —— E. S. Dunn, E. E. Lampard and J. F. Muth, *Regions, Resources and Economic Growth*. Baltimore 1960.
106. S. M. Robbins and N. E. Terleckyj, *Money Metropolis*. Cambridge, Mass. 1960.

107. R. S. Rodd, " Information for an Economic Analysis of the Upper Midwest Region," *Four Papers on Methodology*, Upper Midwest Economic Study, Technical Paper No. 1, June 1961, 23–40.

108. L. Rodwin, " Planned Decentralization and Regional Development with Special Reference to the British New Towns," *Papers and Proceedings of the Regional Science Association*, 1954, **1**, A1–A8.

109. Martin Segal, *Wages in the Metropolis.* Cambridge, Mass. 1960.

110. L. A. Sjaastad, " Migration in the Upper Midwest," *Four Papers on Methodology*, Upper Midwest Economic Study, Technical Paper No. 1, June 1961, 41–69.

111. B. H. Stevens, " An Interregional Linear Programming Model," *Jour. Reg. Sci.*, Summer 1958, **1**, 60–98.

112. R. Stone, " Social Accounts at the Regional Level: A Survey," *Regional Economic Planning: Techniques of Analysis*, W. Isard and J. H. Cumberland, ed., Paris 1960, pp. 263–93.

113. S. A. Stouffer, " Intervening Opportunities: A Theory Relating Mobility and Distance," *Am. Soc. Rev.*, Dec. 1940, **5**, 845–67.

114. C. M. Tiebout, " The Urban Economic Base Reconsidered," *Land Economics*, Feb. 1956, **32**, 95–99.

115. R. Vernon, *Metropolis 1985.* Cambridge, Mass. 1960.

116. R. Vining, " Regional Variation in Cyclical Fluctuation Viewed as a Frequency Distribution," *Econometrica*, July 1945, **13**, 183–213.

117. ———— " The Region as a Concept in Business-cycle Analysis," *Econometrica*, July 1946, **14**, 201–18.

118. ———— " The Region as an Economic Entity and Certain Variations to be Observed in the Study of Systems of Regions," *Am. Econ. Rev.*, May 1949, **39**, 89–104.

119. ———— " Delimitation of Economic Areas: Statistical Conceptions in the Study of the Spatial Structure of an Economic System," *Jour. Am. Stat. Assoc.*, Jan. 1953, **48**, 44–64.

120. S. L. Warner, *Stochastic Choice of Mode in Urban Travel: A Study in Binary Choice.* Evanston 1962.

121. W. Warntz, *Geography of Prices: A Study in Geo-Econometrics.* Philadelphia 1959.

122. L. Wingo, Jr., *Transportation and Urban Land.* Washington 1961.

123. R. C. Wood with assistance of V. V. Almendinger, *1400 Governments.* Cambridge, Mass. 1961.

124. G. K. Zipf, *Human Behavior and the Principle of Least Effort.* Reading, Mass. 1954.

125. *Chicago Area Transportation Study, Final Report, Volume II, Data Projections.* Chicago 1960.

126. *Detroit Metropolitan Area Traffic Study, Part I, Data Summary and Interpretation.* Detroit 1955.

127. Federal Housing Administration, *Basic Data on Northern New Jersey Housing Market.* July 1937.

128. *Input–Output Analysis: An Appraisal*, Nat. Bur. of Econ. Research Stud. in Income and Wealth, Vol. 16. Princeton 1958.

129. *Pittsburgh Area Transportation Study, Vol. I, Study Findings.* Pittsburgh 1961.

130. *Regional Income*, Nat. Bur. of Econ. Research Stud. in Income and Wealth, Vol. 21. Princeton 1957.